Mycenaean Greece

J. T. Hooker

Department of Greek
University College, London

Routledge & Kegan Paul
London, Henley and Boston

First published in 1976
by Routledge & Kegan Paul Ltd
39 Store Street,
London WC1E 7DD,
Broadway House,
Newtown Road,
Henley-on-Thames,
Oxon RG9 1EN and
9 Park Street,
Boston, Mass. 02108, USA
Manuscript typed by the author
Printed in Great Britain by
Morrison & Gibb Ltd, London and Edinburgh
ISBN 0 7100 8379 3

IN MEMORIAM
T.B.L.W.

Contents

Contents

Illustrations

Mycenaean Greece

Preface

I wish to thank Professor R.F. Willetts for his invitation to contribute this book to the series of which he is general editor and for his constant encouragement. I am most grateful to Mr J.H. Betts and Mr J.S. Hutchinson, both of whom read the whole text and greatly improved it, to Professor O.J.L. Szemerényi (who read and criticized part of Chapter 2), and to Dr M.E.J. Richardson (who performed the same service for part of Chapter 6.) To Mrs B.M. Timmins and Miss B. Laverack I am indebted for the drawings.

My book, such as it is, I dedicate to the memory of the great teacher who introduced me to the study of the Bronze Age of Greece.

University College, London   J.T.H.
April 1976

1 The nature of the evidence

This book is not, and does not profess to be, a work of
archaeology.   Nor does it offer a comprehensive survey of
the Greek Bronze Age.   Readers who need such a survey will
go, as I have very often gone, to Mrs Vermeule's 'Greece in
the Bronze Age' (Vermeule, 1964).   With that masterly
achievement I cannot compete.   Again, I have not attempted
a short general treatment of the kind undertaken, with admirable results, by Taylour, 1964 and by Finley, 1970.   I
propose, rather, to discuss, from a historical point of
view, some of the crucial periods in the development of
Aegean lands during the Bronze Age.   The subject is often,
by its nature, controversial.   Fields in which historians
are in broad agreement with one another (and those fields
are still very wide) will be indicated comparatively
briefly, so as to concentrate on the investigation (and, it
is hoped, the elucidation) of the more controverted matters.
   My principal subject is the so-called 'Mycenaean' culture, which arose in Greece during the sixteenth century
BC, expanded in the next few generations, spread over the
Aegean and parts of the eastern Mediterranean during the
fourteenth and thirteenth centuries, and declined in the
twelfth century: a decline which was accompanied by widespread devastation.   Only Chapter 2 is concerned with a
topic which falls outside this period, but it is one to
which we are irresistibly led even by the most superficial
examination of the Mycenaean age: namely, the origin of
the 'Helladic' culture of mainland Greece.   The Mycenaean
civilization itself arose from the assimilation of this
Helladic culture with the 'Minoan' culture of Bronze Age
Crete.   It will therefore become necessary to consider
some problems which arise in the study of Minoan Crete;
for this cannot be dissociated from the Mycenaean world.
The outlines of Aegean prehistory in the Early and Middle

Bronze Age have been drawn with a firm hand by Branigan, 1970a and by Renfrew, 1972: books which enable me to take many things as read.

The epoch of human history known as the Bronze Age is, by definition, the period in which bronze came to be the predominant metal for the manufacture of weapons and of the more valuable domestic utensils. It used to be thought that the rise of bronze as a useful material was accompanied by the first appearance of many features which we loosely associate with 'civilization', especially urban civilization. But recent discoveries in Greece, the Near East, and Anatolia have shown that the main trends of development in the Bronze Age were already being followed by the close of the Late Stone Age ('Neolithic'). Towns of sizable proportions flourished long before the beginning of the Bronze Age, notably at Çatal Hüyük in central Turkey and at Jawa in Jordan. In Greece itself, domestication of animals, cultivation of crops, manufacture of pottery, and burial of the dead in graves with funerary offerings are all attested within the Neolithic period. What was once considered a unique mark of Bronze Age civilization, the use of writing, is known at a Neolithic settlement in Rumania (Hood, 1967). Finally, the diffusion of obsidian from the Cyclades shows the existence of means of transport and communication over a wide area, from Thessaly in the north to Crete in the south (Renfrew, 1972, 442-3).

The Bronze Age in Greece, no less than the Neolithic, is accurately called a 'prehistoric' period. In the Aegean area (unlike the situation in Mesopotamia, Anatolia, and Egypt) the peoples of the Bronze Age do not speak to us directly. No literary texts, no explicit statements of myth or of religious belief, no annals or historical records have come to light. Treaties and diplomatic letters, which testify to relations between states in other parts of the Mediterranean, are completely lacking here; in fact, we possess virtually no written document which looks forward or backward more than a year or so. In default of more permanent or informative documents, we have at our disposal five sources for the reconstruction of the course of events in our area: 1 the material remains ('monuments') of the Bronze Age civilization; 2 inventories and accounts kept by the Mycenaeans and Minoans in the Linear B script; 3 the Greek language, as recorded during the Bronze Age itself and again in the historical period (from about 700 BC); 4 references to and depictions of the Aegean peoples by contemporaries; 5 echoes of the Bronze Age in ancient Greek authors and Bronze Age survivals in the cults and legends of the classical Greeks.

It is the very profusion of types of evidence that often makes for difficulty.   Not only can evidence of one kind appear to contradict evidence of another, but two pieces of evidence may relate to different facets of the same problem: that is especially true of the change from the Early to the Middle Bronze Age in Greece (Chapter 2).   In any case, it would be wrong to think that all the types amount to evidence of equal value.

In the case of any conflict of evidence, the witness of archaeology ought always to prevail, because the whole concept of a Bronze Age is archaeological, not linguistic or legendary.   Without the evidence of the monuments, the Aegean Bronze Age as it is known to-day could never have been reconstructed.   It follows that, while an attempt may legitimately be made to reconcile the archaeological with other types of evidence, the monuments must never be accommodated within a spurious history cobbled together from fragments of legends and genealogies.   It is true that about both Mycenae and Troy (to say nothing of Crete, which was celebrated as the birth-place of Zeus himself) there accumulated not only separate episodes but whole cycles of legend which, fascinating in themselves, have been made immeasurably more so by the power of mighty poets.   But the legends have also passed through the distorting imagination of the most inventive of all ancient peoples: if the fictions of the poets had been less persuasive than in fact they are, Plato would not have thought it necessary to banish them from his ideal state.   It is, therefore, important not to be lured by the Greek story-tellers into a belief that what they narrate is to be equated with history.   And yet such equations are constantly drawn in works on the Aegean Bronze Age which give the appearance of being (and which, in other respects, may be) statements of fact.   In this connexion, I strongly agree with the remarks of Furumark, 1950, 182-3.

Beginning with the most important, I now discuss in greater detail the nature and value of the five types of evidence mentioned above.

1 The material remains of the Greek Bronze Age are known from surface finds and excavations in Greece and in other parts of the Mediterranean.   Systematic excavation began in the 1870s when Heinrich Schliemann uncovered parts of the Bronze Age sites of Mycenae, Orchomenos, Tiryns, and Troy.   Although his discoveries were soon followed by the excavation of many other settlements and tombs in Greece and peripheral lands, no clear chronological sequence either absolute or relative was established for the Aegean Bronze Age until Arthur Evans' excavations at Knossos, in northern Crete, early in the present century.   It is now

clear that Evans was too ready to fit the development of
other sites into a sequence he had worked out for Knossos;
and, even so far as Knossos is concerned, his chronology
is sometimes arbitrary (Levi, 1960 and 1962).   But, despite attempts which have been made to impugn it, Evans'
system has been found generally useful, so long as his
division into periods (made solely on the evidence of pottery) is not insisted on too stringently.   By subsequent
investigators, especially Blegen and Wace, who worked on
the Greek mainland, Evans' scheme has been modified and
extended so as to embrace the whole Aegean area.   Within
this area three separate, though often interacting, cultures can be distinguished: the Helladic in central and
southern Greece;   the Cycladic in the Archipelago;   and
the Minoan in Crete.   During the Bronze Age, each of
these three cultures is held to have passed through an
early, a middle, and a late phase;   and these phases are
susceptible of rough dating in absolute terms, because of
cross-references with other cultures, especially that of
Egypt (Warren and Hankey, 1974).   Some of these phases
are divided into three, which are further sub-divided.
Thus, it is customary to distinguish the Late Minoan Ia
(LM Ia) from the Late Minoan Ib (LM Ib) phase within the
Late Palace period at Knossos, and Late Helladic IIIb (LH
IIIb) from IIIc on the mainland.   The long LH IIIb period
itself can be divided (at least at Mycenae) into an earlier (IIIb1) and a later (IIIb2) phase (Chapter 5).
These distinctions are sometimes necessary, and even of
paramount importance, in establishing a sequence of
events;   but it should not be lost sight of that this sequence is in the last resort based on one type of arte-
fact, and one only: the pottery.   The divisions of the
Bronze Age which seem to rest on secure foundations are
set out in Table 1.

   Important changes on the mainland at c. 1900, 1600, and
1200 BC and in Crete during the fifteenth century will be
given detailed treatment in later chapters: meanwhile,
the principal features of the successive periods will be
reviewed very briefly.

   The civilization of the Middle Bronze Age in Crete
seems to have been considerably more advanced than that of
the Greek mainland.   Besides numerous smaller settlements, three 'palaces' of great size and importance reached their acme in the Cretan Early Palace period (nineteenth and eighteenth centuries BC):   at Knossos in the
north, at Mallia in the north-east, and at Phaistos in the
south.   Each of these sites, though participating in a
common Minoan culture, possessed an individual character
of its own: a fact made plain by the existence of local

pottery workshops and scribal schools which did not always
develop at the same pace or in the same direction as their
neighbours.   Rapid progress was made in a number of fine
arts, especially seal-engraving, fresco-painting, and pottery.   The use of writing for keeping accounts is well
attested at all three palaces and at some other sites as
well.   To all appearance, the Minoans at this brilliant
epoch had little to do with the Greek mainland.   They
established settlements at Melos and Kythera and took pottery to the island of Thera.   Egypt was a constant
trading-partner of Crete and the origin of several decorative motifs of Middle Minoan pottery, while the Minoans
maintained trading contacts (if they were no more than
that) with the sea-board of Syria and Palestine.

The palace of Knossos suffered a set-back toward the
end of the Middle Bronze Age, when large parts of it were
destroyed.   Recovery and rebuilding were swift: it was
this restored palace which Evans uncovered in his successive excavations.   The beginning of the Late Palace period
is well marked not only in the three palaces but also at
Ayia Triada in the south and at Zakro and Palaikastro in
the east.   The opening of the period was accompanied by
fresh Cretan expansion overseas.   While Cretan influence
remained paramount in those islands of the Cyclades which
had previously shown marked signs of an intrusive Minoan
culture, new Cretan settlements now began to appear farther afield, for example in Rhodes and on the Anatolian
coast.   Evidence from both the Cretan and the Egyptian
side suggests that connexions between these two areas remained close throughout the sixteenth and fifteenth centuries BC.   In Crete itself, Knossos seems to have established some kind of hegemony during the fifteenth century;
and, during this same century, most of the Cretan settlements apart from Knossos were destroyed, some of them
never being inhabited again.   The causes of their destruction and the character of Knossos in the Late Palace
period will be scrutinized in Chapter 4.

The destruction of Knossos is to be placed at the end
of the Late Palace period (c. 1375 BC).   It thus appears
that no Cretan site of any consequence, except Kydonia in
the west, escaped a major destruction in the fifteenth and
fourteenth centuries.   Subsequently, Knossos and some
other sites were re-occupied.   This 'period of re-occupation', as Evans regarded it, was basically Minoan so far
as its culture was concerned;   but the 'palatial' way of
life had come to an end, while there were fewer and less
extensive contacts with other parts of the Mediterranean
than had obtained in the palatial epochs.

On the mainland, signs of Minoan influence, more far-reaching than any previously attested, appear at Mycenae toward the end of the Middle Bronze Age and are accentuated in the first part of the Late Bronze Age.   In the second and third parts of that Age, fewer influences are felt directly from the Minoan culture of Crete; but many of the arts of the mainland (though not the monumental architecture of its great citadels) still descend, at however great a remove, from Minoan models.   Moreover, some of the religious practices of the mainlanders speak in favour of continuing contact with Crete (Chapter 8).   For the sake of convenience, these phases of the Mycenaean culture may be represented schematically:

First Phase of Minoan Influence (Middle Helladic and Late Helladic I pottery).   An imperfect fusion between Helladic and Minoan leads to the beginning of a distinctive Mycenaean culture, which is largely confined to the Peloponnese.   The most important evidence for this Phase comes from tombs in western Messenia and the two Grave Circles at Mycenae (and, more specifically, from funerary offerings buried with the dead)(Chapter 3).

Second Phase of Minoan Influence (Late Helladic II-IIIa1 pottery).   The almost complete fusion between Helladic and Minoan and the adoption on the mainland of Minoan art-forms and the external features of Minoan cult are accompanied by the penetration of Mycenaean culture to many parts of central and southern Greece and to Thessaly (Chapter 4).

Third Phase of Minoan Influence (Late Helladic IIIa2-IIIb pottery).   The Mycenaean culture, now developing (for the most part) independently of the Minoan, becomes dominant in the Aegean.   To this Phase belongs the Mycenaean expansion into the eastern Mediterranean and, on a much smaller scale, into Sicily and southern Italy (Chapters 5 and 6).   The closing stages of the Third Phase are marked by a series of destructions, after which many Mycenaean sites are re-occupied with movements of population (Chapter 7).

2 The deductions which can legitimately be made from the mass of archaeological material are limited.   It is especially hazardous to draw any conclusions of a political or social kind from archaeological evidence alone; while even the religious objects known from Bronze Age Greece show only the external manifestations of cult and do not always reveal what underlies them.   In this state of affairs, it is natural to turn to the documents written by the Minoans and Mycenaeans in the hope that, by fitting them into the archaeological framework, we shall be able to correlate the motives and the achievements of these peoples.   In the 1950s a nucleus of Greek words and forms

was identified and isolated in the Linear B tablets from
Knossos and the mainland.   The partial decipherment which
ensued has revealed something of the social, economic, and
political organization of some major Bronze Age settlements.   To that extent, we are much better informed than
before;   and yet, because the documents are of the most
austere and anonymous kind, amounting to little more than
lists and records of transactions, they also are relevant
only to the outward manifestations of the Aegean cultures:
they speak of methods, not of motives.

3 Not only the contents of the Linear B tablets but the
very dialect in which they are written can be pressed into
the service of historical reconstruction.   The dialectal
affinities of the Homeric poems (c. 700 BC) and the inscriptions of the classical period (sixth century and
later) throw light on the migrations of peoples and the
fragmentation of the Mycenaean world.

4 Contemporary references to Mycenaeans and Minoans
fall into three main classes: (i) paintings of Aegean
peoples in Egyptian tombs of the fifteenth century BC
(Chapter 4); (ii) allusions to Crete, and perhaps also to
the Greek mainland, in an Egyptian monumental inscription
of about 1400 BC (Chapter 4); (iii) allusions to a people
or country called 'Ahhiyawa' in Hittite documents of the
fourteenth and thirteenth centuries (Chapter 6).   As we
shall see, the utmost care must be exercised in assessing
these three classes.

5 The Bronze Age elements which survive in the legends
and literature of the Greeks from Homer downward call for
more extensive discussion, since the view taken of them
here needs some justification.

As is known, the ancient Greeks pondered deeply on
their own past; and their memory of places and customs,
and perhaps of persons also, was exceedingly long.   The
investigations of a long line of twentieth-century Homer-
ists, from Allen to Page and Hope Simpson, have shown that
the Catalogue of Ships in the second book of the 'Iliad'
preserves some accurate memories of Bronze Age sites in
Greece; and it is possible, though far from certain, that
the heroes and genealogies associated with those places
likewise have some basis in fact.   Mycenae especially
must have been well known to a narrative tradition which
culminated in the Homeric poems.   Nilsson, 1932 pressed
the evidence as far as possible in support of his contention that the main cycles of Greek legend and the Greek
epic tradition reach back into the Mycenaean period.
Even though his arguments do not convince me completely, I
think we would be indulging in the luxury of scepticism
too far if we were to deny the probability that other

sites than Mycenae (such as Pylos, Orchomenos, and Knossos) entered the epic tradition before the end of the Bronze Age.

But, while the events narrated in the Homeric epics must never form the basis of a historical reconstruction, the poems do describe, sometimes in surprisingly accurate detail, objects and practices which belong (and belong exclusively, so far as we know) to the Greek Bronze Age. Such are the silver-studded sword ('Iliad' 23. 807), the boar's tusk helmet (10. 261-5), and the body-shield of Ajax (7. 219-23).   These are, admittedly, isolated objects, whose presence in the 'Iliad' does not affect the structure of the poem as a whole.   It is otherwise with the pervasive use of bronze for weapons and utensils.   In this respect the epic has been shown, in recent years, to present a more faithful picture of the Mycenaean world than was formerly envisaged; for we now have slight, but unquestionable, evidence for the use in Mycenaean times of body-armour made of bronze as well as of bronze swords and spears.   When so much in the epic is indissolubly linked to the Bronze Age as it appears in the archaeological record, it does not seem right in principle to deny a Mycenaean origin to those references which could belong equally well to the Bronze or to the Iron Age.

Even so, the Homeric epics constitute a treacherous source of information, if we rely on them alone.   The great difficulty is that it is impossible to achieve a satisfactory separation of 'early' and 'late' elements in Homer (more precisely, features which entered the epic during the Bronze Age and during the subsequent Dark Ages respectively) by employing either linguistic or archaeological criteria.   For example, the Gorgon-charge on Agamemnon's shield ('Iliad' 11. 36) seems indubitably to have had its origin long after the end of the Bronze Age; and yet we find inextricably associated with it a reference to the typically Bronze Age technique of inlaying metal. Again, the duel in 'Iliad' 7 is fought between Ajax, with the cumbersome body-shield already mentioned, and Hector, who wears a shield of quite different type, lighter and of later origin (Chapter 5).   It is plain that such a combat could never have taken place in the real world.   The manner of disposing of the dead goes to the root of our problem here.   The people of the Aegean Bronze Age buried their dead: a practice attested by many hundreds, if not thousands, of tombs.   In stark contrast, the Homeric heroes are cremated, with funeral rites and offerings.   The practice of cremation is often described or alluded to by Homer; and the actual motive for cremation is more than once explained in the poems (e.g. 'Odyssey' 11. 218-22).

The evidence points to only one conclusion: namely, that the material culture reflected in the Homeric poems, no less than the language of Homer itself, is an artificial poetic creation formed from disparate and anachronistic elements, but the texture of the whole is so closely knit that the elements can rarely be separated from one another (Kirk, 1960; Snodgrass, 1974). It is for this reason that any history of the Bronze Age which begins with Homer is to be rejected: it is permissible to cite him as corroboration of the historical record, not as an independent witness in his own right (Jachmann, 1958, 13-6; Hampl, 1962).

No greater credence can be given to the two great historians of the fifth century BC, at least when they speak of the remote past. Herodotus took as his theme the great struggle between Greeks and Persians in the early part of that century. His quest for causes ('aitiai') leads him farther and farther back in time so that, in the matter preliminary to his main narrative, he draws on the longest memories of the Greeks about their past. Thucydides' history of the Peloponnesian War is based upon an examination of the motives, real or pretended, of contemporary statesmen. The fragments of prehistory contained in Thucydides' first book serve a purpose in the structure of the work as a whole. The maritime empire of Athens forms Thucydides' theme: it is, therefore, of interest to him to enquire into the nature and extent of two earlier thalassocracies which had held sway in the Aegean, that of Minos and that of Agamemnon which eventually superseded it (Romilly, 1956, 240-98; Parry, 1972, 55). When he travels back in time, Thucydides relies on no better sources than those used by Herodotus: basically Homer and the poets of the Epic Cycle, but at all events oral and literary traditions, not documentary evidence (Momigliano, 1958; Erbse, 1961, 25-6). Neither Herodotus nor Thucydides makes any original contribution to the study of the Greek Bronze Age; and, just as with Homer, their accounts carry weight only in so far as they are compatible with the archaeological evidence.

Even among writers as intelligent and imaginative as Herodotus, the intense curiosity felt by the Greeks about their past never rose above the level of antiquarianism. In the second century AD an extended guide-book to Greece and its antiquities was written by Pausanias, who, though admittedly no Herodotus, had his proper share of curiosity about the monuments he visited. The local cults in the places he saw held great fascination for him, and his accounts of them enshrine a good deal of material which goes back to the Bronze Age. But, although he describes

many monuments still visible in his own day, that is all he
does.   Like other Greek writers, he confines himself to a
description of visible relics and speculation about them,
and never envisages the possibility of excavation.   For
example, when he finds that the 'spear of Achilles' and
'Memnon's sword', which have been dedicated in temples, are
made of bronze, he quite correctly sees in this fact a confirmation of the Homeric picture that 'in the time of the
heroes' all weapons were made of bronze (3. 3. 8).   It
does not occur to him that a coherent series of objects
might be recovered from the heroic age.   Again, in his
description of Mycenae, he mentions that one tomb is
claimed for Atreus, another for Agamemnon, yet others for
Aegisthus and Clytemnestra, and so on (2. 16. 6-7), without
realizing that perhaps the claims could be investigated
further (cf. Wace, 1954b).

So much for the virtues and limitations of the five
types of evidence which are available to us.   Even such a
brief review makes it plain that no 'history' of the Aegean
Bronze Age can be written in the present state of our knowledge.   Such a history would need to be documented by religious, literary, and diplomatic texts of a kind common in
contemporary cultures but so far lacking in our area.   Nor
do the few allusions to the Aegean by Hittites and Egyptians help very much to fill the gap left by the Aegean peoples themselves.   Until that gap is filled, if it ever is,
we must first construct the archaeological framework and
then fit into it evidence from other sources.   Chapters 2
to 7 adopt a chronological treatment, investigating in succession the Middle Helladic period and then the principal
phases of Late Helladic.   In Chapter 8, an attempt is made
to describe the Mycenaean culture in general and to relate
it to the later civilization of Greece.

2   Before the Mycenaean Age

INTRODUCTION

Since the Mycenaean civilization cannot be fully understood
without a knowledge of its mainland ('Helladic') component,
we must first consider the origin and growth of Helladic
culture.   Our evidence will come from three sources: the
archaeological record;   the testimony of Greek and other
languages;   the statements of Herodotus and Thucydides.
Here, as always, the archaeological evidence will weigh the
most heavily;   but let us first take account of facts which
were known even before the rise of the modern science of
archaeology.

THE GREEK HISTORIANS

When the two great historians of the fifth century BC dwell
on the earliest records of their race, they give little
evidence of exact or certain knowledge.   That the inhabitants of Greece had not always spoken Greek is accepted by
both of them;   and this belief can be traced back to an
earlier representative of Ionian historiography than Herodotus.   Hecataeus the Milesian is credited by Strabo with
the statement that, before the coming of the Greeks, the
Peloponnese was inhabited by 'barbaroi', that is, by speakers of a non-Greek language (Jacoby, 1923, 23).
    So far as can be gathered from his confused and some-
times inconsistent remarks on the subject, Herodotus himself seems to think not of an invasion by Greek-speakers
but of the gradual Hellenization, both racially and linguistically, of a pre-Hellenic ('Pelasgian') stock.   From
his History (1. 56-8) I extract the following account,
omitting some sentences which are irrelevant to the present
purpose:

In earlier times [and it is clear that by these words
Herodotus means a period before, and perhaps long before, the Trojan War] there were two races living in
Greece: the Pelasgians, who never left their original
home, and the Hellenes, who frequently migrated.   During the reign of Deucalion, the Hellenes inhabited Phthiotis in Thessaly.   In the time of Doros, the son of
Hellen, they lived in Histiaia; later in Makednos,
later still in Dryopia; finally in the Peloponnese,
where they were called Dorians.   What language the
Pelasgians spoke I cannot say exactly.   If it is proper
to judge from those of the Pelasgians who still survive,
they spoke a non-Greek language.   If that was true of
the whole Pelasgic race, the Attic nation (being Pelasgic) must have learnt the Greek language at the same
time that they became Hellenized.   The Hellenic race,
on the other hand, have always spoken the same language:
they were weak so long as they remained separate from
the Pelasgians but, on being united with them, they have
grown to comprise a multitude of nations.
Unlike Herodotus, Thucydides does not say specifically that
the Pelasgian language was superseded by Greek; but perhaps the statement at 1. 3 of his History almost amounts to
that.   Thucydides believes that before the Trojan War the
Greeks engaged in no joint enterprises and were not even
called by the name 'Hellenes'.   According to him, the name
was used first in Phthiotis, at the time of Hellen and his
sons, and then spread very gradually among the originally
Pelasgic tribes.
    The belief that the earliest inhabitants of Greece, or
at least some of them, were 'barbaroi' became a common-
place;   and the recurrent statements to that effect in
ancient Greek authors add nothing by way of confirmation to
the accounts of Herodotus and Thucydides, while the ever-
increasing quantity of genealogical speculation tends to
obscure the one belief which is of crucial importance.
But this belief, that at some unspecified prehistoric epoch
a non-Greek language was superseded on Hellenic soil by
Greek, was so confidently and so persistently held that it
is worth submitting to the linguists for their judgment.

THE EVIDENCE OF LANGUAGE

The reconstruction of 'Indo-European', which nowhere sur-
vives but which is postulated as the ancestor of a widespread group of related languages stretching from Chinese
Turkestan to the Iberian peninsula, is rightly regarded as
the greatest single achievement of nineteenth-century lin-

guists.   It has been left to the scholars of the present
century to enquire more closely into the concept of Indo-
European itself and to wonder whether the peoples who spoke
Indo-European, as well as those who spoke the languages
which descended from it, can be identified from material
remains.   In other words, the methods and results of archaeology have been called upon to answer questions which
by their nature are, and ought perhaps to remain, strictly
linguistic.

Because of the wealth of literature which had survived
from classical and post-classical times, the Greek language
(together with Latin, Sanskrit, and Gothic) played a great
part in the first reconstruction of the parent-tongue.   As
the nineteenth century advanced, the knowledge of Greek,
especially in its dialectal forms, was filled out by the
discovery of inscriptions.   It became apparent very early
that, despite the overwhelmingly Indo-European character of
the Greek language as a whole, with respect to its vocabulary, morphology, phonology, and syntax, there remained a
large residue of words and forms which were loans from non-
Indo-European languages.   Among these were Semitic names
of commodities and materials such as 'chiton' (tunic),
'chrysos' (gold), and 'sesamon' (sesame).   Loan-words of
this sort are, of course, commonly exchanged between two
peoples who trade with each other but who speak different
languages.   Parallels in ancient and in modern times are
easily found.   But, embedded within a considerable number
of Greek words, especially names, there were seen to be
elements which did not belong to the Greek language as
otherwise attested, since they had not developed along the
usual lines of Greek sound-change.   There seemed, then,
good reason for supposing that such elements were the remnants of a pre-Greek, and pre-Indo-European, language upon
which Indo-European had been superimposed when speakers of
Greek first moved into the Balkans.   Toward the end of the
last century, it appeared possible to fix both in space and
in time this movement of Indo-European-speakers into
Greece: linguistic evidence was available in abundance,
and also the remains of many Bronze Age sites in Greece had
been uncovered.   The time seemed apt for a fruitful col-
laboration between archaeologist and linguist.

The basis for a study of the whole question, especially
from the linguistic point of view, was established by
Kretschmer, 1896.   When Kretschmer wrote, there was no
direct evidence of the languages spoken by the Bronze Age
inhabitants either of Greece or of Anatolia.   Nevertheless, it was plain that the Greek language, attested from
about 700 BC in literary sources, contained some Bronze
Age elements, which could be separated out more or less

certainly.   Inscriptions were known from south-west Anatolia written in local languages such as Lydian, Lycian,
and Carian.   The earliest of these dated from the seventh
century BC.   Kretschmer adopted a suggestion, which had
been made on phonetic grounds, that a series of Greek words
formed with the suffix -nth- were in origin not Greek but
had been borrowed from an unknown foreign language.   It
caused no surprise that these words were mostly the names
of towns (Korinthos), rivers (Koskynthos), mountains (Ara-
kynthos), and plants (hyakinthos):   words which tend to be
highly conservative in all languages.   Furthermore, it was
found that the Anatolian languages contained place-names
formed with -nd-, for example Lycian Thryanda, Carian Kary-
anda, and Lydian Kalanda.   A direct connexion was seen between Cretan Labyrinthos and Carian Labraundos.   Kretschmer supposed that both Anatolian -nd- and Greek -nth- reflected the same (non-Indo-European) suffix -nt-.   A second class of Anatolian names were formed with the suffix
-ss-/-s-/-z-, for instance Halikarnes(s)os, Panyas(s)is,
and Pttarazē.   To this class also there corresponded a
widespread Greek formation, namely that in -s(s)os: Knos-
(s)os in Crete, Korkessos in the Cyclades, Attic Kephisos,
Boeotian Keressos, and Mount Parnassos in Phocis.
    From the evidence of the Greek words containing -ss-
and -nth- Kretschmer drew the conclusion that in what he
called the 'prehistoric period', namely the period before
the arrival of Greek-speakers, a cultural and linguistic
continuum extended from southern Anatolia across the Aegean
to Greece and Crete.   No sharp dividing line ought, in his
opinion, to be drawn between this period and the succeeding
'Greek' epoch.   We should think, rather, in terms of a
gradual expansion of Indo-Europeans southward into Greece,
followed by amalgamation with the native populace, which
did not die out completely.   It was very unlikely, in any
case, that Indo-Europeans were not in Greece by the middle
of the second millennium BC.
    Kretschmer himself later modified his views in a number
of respects.   During the 1920s work was going forward on
the decipherment and elucidation of the cuneiform inscriptions found at Boghazköy in central Anatolia, which had
been the capital city of the Hittite empire in the Late
Bronze Age.   These documents proved to contain royal archives which dated, for the most part, from the fourteenth
and thirteenth centuries BC and were thus contemporaneous
with the heyday of the Mycenaean culture.   The documents
are written in several languages other than Hittite;   and
some of the languages represented, such as Hittite itself
and Luwian which is closely akin to Hittite, are clearly
Indo-European, though of a simpler and more archaic kind

than Greek or Sanskrit.   A peculiarity of Luwian, which it
does not share with Hittite, is that, instead of the genitive case to express the relationship between one noun and
another, it uses an adjective in -assis or -assas: for example Hullassassis, the god of the city Hullassa (Mittelberger, 1966;   Stefanini, 1969).   These Luwian formations
Kretschmer brought into connexion with the Aegean place-
names in -ssos and supposed that they were all part of the
same linguistic stratum, but a stratum which could no longer be regarded as pre-Indo-European, since Luwian was certainly an Indo-European language.   Kretschmer accordingly
modified his original theory so as to take account of the
new evidence from Anatolia.   He now reckoned with not one
but two incursions into Greece, the first by a people he
called 'proto-Indo-Europeans' speaking a language which
contained words with -ss- suffixes, the second by speakers
of Greek (Kretschmer, 1925).

THE EVIDENCE OF ARCHAEOLOGY

The results of philological research, therefore, enable us
to give an affirmative answer to the question, whether the
ancient Greek historians were correct in thinking that
Greek-speakers had intruded upon a territory previously inhabited by speakers of other languages.   We now have to
put to the archaeologist the consequent question: at what
time or times did this incursion of Greek-speakers take
place?
     Already by the early years of our century, the chrono-
logy of Bronze Age Greece had been established in broad
terms.   Within the Bronze Age three more or less distinct
breaks in the archaeological record were seen to stand out:
that is, epochs which witnessed the replacement of one type
of material culture by another.   These breaks occurred at
approximately the following points: (a) c. 1900 BC, marking the transition from Early to Middle Helladic;   (b) c.
1600 BC, marking the transition from Middle to Late Helladic;   (c) c. 1200 BC, marking the 'time of troubles' toward the end of Late Helladic.   Each of the breaks has
been thought, at one time or another, to represent the
point at which speakers of Greek first arrived.   They
must now be examined in turn, beginning with what seems to
me the least probable.
     (c) is plainly impossible to anyone who is persuaded
that Ventris successfully deciphered the Linear B script
and so established the presence of Greek in the Aegean by
the fifteenth century BC, at latest.   But, among those
who are not convinced that Ventris' decipherment is cor-

rect, it is sometimes supposed that the first speakers of
Greek entered Greece at the end of the Bronze Age and are,
in fact, to be identified with the destroyers of the Mycenaean civilization.   Above all Grumach, 1969 devoted an
eloquent monograph to the exposition of this thesis from
both the archaeological and the linguistic side.   But the
thesis is untenable.   Even if we grant, for the moment,
that there is no direct epigraphical evidence for the Greek
language in the Bronze Age, we have to reckon with other
facts which make it virtually certain that Greek was spoken
within the area of Mycenaean culture.   For example (as
was shown in the last Chapter) a great deal in the Homeric
poems reflects the material culture of the Mycenaean
period.   Grumach argues that the Greeks became acquainted
with this culture only after its decline, and subsequently
absorbed it into their own.   But such an explanation fails
to account for the nature of the Mycenaean elements in
Homer.   If we believe, with Grumach, that the Greeks were
at a low level of development and took over the high culture of the Mycenaeans, how are we to suppose that the
Bronze Age features first entered the Greek epic tradition
which culminated in the Homeric poems?   Was it by a wholesale translation of a corpus of poetry already in existence
or by a gradual assimilation of descriptions and narrative
themes?   The first assumption is not easy to reconcile
with the premise that the immigrant Greeks were at a low
cultural level;   the second is hardly conceivable, given
the sequence of events envisaged by Grumach, for he pos-
tulates the violent destruction of the Mycenaean settlements by Greeks, not the peaceful co-existence of Greeks
and Mycenaeans.

(b) can be discounted on purely archaeological grounds.
It is sometimes thought that an invasion of Greek-speakers
at the transition from Middle to Late Helladic followed an
earlier invasion at the beginning of Middle Helladic.
Palmer, 1965, 321-7 believes this earlier intrusion to
have been the work of Luwians;   while Best and Yadin, 1973
ascribe it to invaders from Thrace.   (Cf. Schachermeyr,
1968, 306-7.)   Even if these suggestions had the slightest plausibility in themselves, they fall to the ground
because no archaeological break is discernible at the end
of Middle Helladic: at least, no break so serious or so
widespread as to give any indication of the arrival of a
new people.   The facts were set out by Mylonas, 1962,
297-302;   and they constitute an insuperable objection to
the class of theory under discussion here.

(a) will be considered in greater detail, since it is
the only 'break' which can be associated, at all convin-
cingly, with the arrival of Greek-speakers.

It has been observed at many Bronze Age sites in Greece, especially in the eastward parts, that the replacement of the Early by the Middle Helladic culture was accompanied by violent destruction.   To mention only some of the sites where a violent change is attested in the archaeological record: Orchomenos and Eutresis in Boeotia;   Ayios Kosmas in Attica;   Korakou in Corinthia;   in the Argolid Asine and Tiryns;   Asea in Arcadia;   Malthi in Messenia.   How and for what reason was the Early Helladic culture superseded by the Middle Helladic?

Material remains give a reasonably consistent picture of the attainments of the Early Bronze Age population of Greece.   They were proficient in the use of metals, including gold and silver, and in the making of pottery by hand: their clay vessels were often glazed or decorated with patterns.   Their trading contacts with Anatolia to the northeast and with Crete and the Cyclades to the south, together with the fact that ships are sometimes depicted on their pottery, show that they were a maritime people.   Their way of life was urban and commercial rather than rural and agricultural;   and a number of places in central Greece, especially Prosymna, Tiryns, Athens, Lerna, and Corinth must have been considerable towns, some of which were fortified.   The dead were buried in built tombs or in graves cut out of the rock.

The Middle Helladic culture, which succeeded the Early Helladic between 2000 and 1900 BC, has been known in its principal manifestations since the last two decades of the nineteenth century;   but it was fully described and assessed for the first time by Blegen, 1921.   The Middle Helladic settlements on the Greek mainland were, in general, smaller and poorer than was the case either in the Early or in the Late Helladic period.   On the whole, the economy was based on agriculture rather than commerce.   The houses were of extreme simplicity with rectangular or, more usually, apsidal plans and contained, as a rule, no more than three rooms.   The dead were buried sometimes intramurally, sometimes in cemeteries outside the settlements: both pit-graves (simply dug out of the earth) and cists (shallow built tombs) were used as burial-chambers.

As usual, the most important body of evidence is provided by the pottery.   Two principal types were manufactured by the Middle Helladic people, and both differ from the Early Helladic styles.   The first is a matt-painted ware, whose affinities are unknown and are, in any case, not directly relevant to the present discussion.   The second type seemed, for a long time, to have no clear antecedents in Greece or in the Aegean area as a whole.   Examples of this distinctive pottery were discovered first at Orchome-

nos in Boeotia and were later called 'Minyan' in honour of
Homer's 'Orchomenos Minyeios'.   The purest form of Minyan
ware, found at Orchomenos and at other sites in Boeotia and
Phocis, is wheel-made, light grey in colour, and 'soapy'
to the touch.   Equally unmistakable is the sharp outline
of the classic Minyan pots (evidently modelled on metallic
prototypes) which are represented above all by goblets and
low cups with high-flung handles (Figure 3).   Grey Minyan
was exported to Melos, where it is found in association
with Cretan pottery, so suggesting that there might have
been direct contact between the Helladic and the Minoan
cultures in the Middle Bronze Age.   Later in the Middle
Helladic period the decline of Grey Minyan is accompanied
by the rise of a new type, yellow-buff in colour, which
forms a valuable link between Minyan wares and the 'Mycenaean' pottery of Late Helladic Greece.

In the course of his contribution Háley presented a map

Until a few years ago, it was thought possible to draw
three archaeological conclusions from the data given so
far: 1 the fact that many Early Helladic sites had been
burnt and also that the succeeding Middle Helladic civilization was fundamentally different appeared to rule out the
possibility of a continuous development and to point to a
violent disruption by alien invaders;   2 the pattern of
distribution of Middle Helladic sites and the varying types
of Minyan pottery found at different sites suggested that
the Middle Helladic people were sea-borne invaders who had
arrived from the east, established themselves in Boeotia,
and then fanned outward to other regions;   3 the Grey Minyan pottery was the ware brought with them into Greece by
these invaders.

It seemed possible to say, further, as the result of a
synthesis of the archaeological and the linguistic evidence, that the Middle Helladic invaders were the first
Greek-speakers to enter Greece.   This teaching is contained in two closely-linked papers which have become the
classic statement on the subject: Haley and Blegen, 1928.

In the course of his contribution Háley presented a map
on which he had placed the names in -ss- and in -nth-.
Blegen, for his part, showed that there was a close correlation between these place-names and the Early Bronze Age
sites, both in Greece and in Crete.   From this correlation
he drew the following inference: 'if we can identify the
pre-Greek layer, it naturally follows that we can also recognize as Hellenic the succeeding layer and we can thus
determine exactly where in the archaeological stratification the Hellenes first appear' (Haley and Blegen, 1928,
148.)   Blegen was thus able to conclude, with a high degree of confidence, that the destroyers of the Early Helladic settlements, the Middle Helladic invaders, and the

first Greek-speaking arrivals were one and the same people.
At this point, account must be taken of a site which is
closely associated with mainland Greece both archaeologi-
cally and in the cycles of legend.   Schliemann had no
doubt that the settlements he had uncovered at Hissarlik in
north-western Anatolia contained a city which could be
identified with the Troy of the 'Iliad'.   Together with
his collaborator Wilhelm Dörpfeld, who carried on the work
of excavation after his death, Schliemann reduced the succession of Trojan cities to a definitive order; and these
are now known, from the earliest to the latest, as Troy I,
II, III, and so on up to VIII.   The whole ground was gone
over again with meticulous care by the Cincinnati expedition: the results of these later excavations are contained
in the four volumes of 'Troy' (1950-8), edited by Blegen
and others.   Blegen, 1963 gives a broader and less technical account, rich in historical reconstruction.   It is
evident that a change of unusual magnitude occurred between
Troy V and Troy VI.   The citadel was enlarged and a
strongly fortified wall built.   In the stratum of Troy VI
were found, for the first time at this site, the bones of
horses and also a new kind of pottery, very close in shape
and technique to the Grey Minyan ware which Schliemann himself had found at Orchomenos.

The changes between Troy V and Troy VI, though great,
were not so violent and profound as in Greece.   Troy V
was not destroyed, but was adapted and enlarged.   Further,
the pottery of the earlier city persisted, though in small
quantities, alongside the new grey ware.   Nevertheless,
it is obvious that the occurrence of the two types of grey
ware, so similar to each other, at Troy and in Greece ur-
gently needs investigation; it is not, however, necessary
to introduce a gratuitous difficulty at the outset and
assert, as some writers have done, that the new ware made
its first appearance at exactly the same time on both sides
of the Aegean Sea, since no adequate chronological check
exists for this period.

The theoretical possibilities are four in number, and
each has had its adherents: either 1 Minyan ware began at
Troy and was introduced from there into Greece; or 2 it
was manufactured only in Greece and exported to Troy; or
3 the two types of ware were brought to Greece and to Troy
from some common source; or 4 the development in the two
areas was independent, though parallel.

An argument in favour of 1 was developed along the following lines by E.J. Forsdyke.   Although (he held) Grey
Minyan appears both in Greece and at Troy, it must have begun at Troy because the prototypes of some at least of the
shapes of Grey Minyan pottery are found at Troy but not in

Greece; furthermore, the Greek sites have yielded, side
by side with the perfected Minyan ware, vessels which are
only a faulty imitation of an alien forerunner.   It is
true that in theory Grey Minyan might have evolved both to
the east and to the west of the Aegean (as Childe was later
to suggest); but the fact that no earlier stages of Minyan
have been found in Greek lands tells against this possibility.   Commerce was hardly responsible for the importation
of Grey Minyan pottery to Greece: not only is there no
other evidence of trade from east to west, but the distribution of Minyan cups in Greece and their 'association with
domestic and sepulchral remains on many sites show that
they were brought and used by a foreign people' (Forsdyke,
1914, 153.)   This chain of reasoning led Forsdyke to the
conclusion that the cultural change on the Greek mainland
(what nowadays we call the change from Early to Middle
Helladic) was caused by the intrusion of hostile invaders
from the Troad.
      When Blegen accepted this conclusion, he set it along-
side his own inferences from the linguistic and archaeological evidence and arrived at the following synthesis:

      The two invading groups, one on the east, one on the
      west side of the Aegean, make their appearance at the
      same time.   They use the same technique in making pot-
      tery and they produce the same distinctive shapes of
      vessels in Grey Minyan Ware.   To each region they
      bring with them a great innovation, the horse as their
      beast of burden.   Through the whole ensuing period
      they keep up relations with one another.   Must we not,
      therefore, conclude that these two groups were kinsmen,
      branches of one and the same stock?   Many scholars now
      hold that the invaders who introduced Middle Helladic
      culture into Greece were actually the first Hellenic
      people to set foot in the peninsula.   If that view is
      correct - and it seems to me to rest on well-founded
      arguments - we shall have to accept the further con-
      clusion that the founders of Troy VI were also Greeks.
      (Blegen, 1963, 145-6.)

On the face of it, the case presented by Blegen is a compelling one;   but I believe that it is open to serious objections of a linguistic and of an archaeological nature;
and only after these have been considered can we hope to
arrive at a balanced view.

LINGUISTIC OBJECTIONS

It may be suggested, first, that the linguistic data have
often been misunderstood.   It is important to keep these

in mind when we turn to the evidence of the monuments, because archaeologists have usually assumed that they are
called upon to find a convincing archaeological answer to
the question posed by linguists: when did the Greeks arrive?   In consequence, the phrase 'the coming of the
Greeks' has long been in common use among prehistorians -
sometimes even as the title of articles and chapters of
books.   An expression like 'the coming of the Greeks' is
meaningless in itself, in that it purports to transfer to
a remote epoch a concept of ethnic or even linguistic
'Greekness' which properly belongs only to historical times
(McNeal, 1972).   Not only that, but the expression is
based on a misconception of the results of linguistic research.   Perhaps the misconception can be traced back to
Kretschmer, 1909.   In this well-known paper the dialect-
situation found in historical Greece was explained by postulating three separate waves of invaders moving into Greece
at widely different periods, each bringing with it a major
dialect of Greek.   This approach has left an indelible
mark on our thinking about the history of Greece in the
Bronze Age.   The theory of three invasions by Greek-
speakers is, indeed, often rejected to-day (in my opinion,
rightly so); but it has been found harder to escape from
the notion that there was at least one 'invasion'.

But an important point is often overlooked: namely,
that all the linguist, qua linguist, can hope to do is to
prove that the Greek language was not always spoken in
Greece but was preceded by another language; or, what is
more likely, by other languages, since nothing suggests
that the -ss- words belonged originally to the same language with the -nth- words.   The linguistic evidence does
not in itself impose, or even indicate, the conclusion
that Greek was brought to Greece by a certain group of
people at a certain time.   As we have seen, Kretschmer
himself had thought in terms of a gradual diffusion of
Greek-speakers into the peninsula.   In fact, it was never
necessary to speak of an 'invasion' at all, unless one took
the over-simple view that Indo-European formed a monolithic
entity, from which fragments were more or less violently
detached and flung across vast areas to form ultimately
the daughter-languages known for the first time in the
Bronze Age (so Schlerath, 1973.)

Attempts continue to be made to identify the Indo-
European people with this or that culture known from the
archaeological record.   Most recently, it has been claimed
that the monuments of the proto-Indo-European civilization
are to be found in the so-called 'Barrow' or 'Kurgan' culture which arose in southern Russia during the fifth millennium and subsequently, in the third millennium, spread

into the Near East and eastern Europe (Gimbutas, 1970;
Hammond, 1973, 26-35.)   Now it may seem unduly pessimistic
to deny that we shall ever attain certain knowledge of the
original homeland of the Indo-Europeans; and yet it is
hard not to take such a gloomy view (Pulgram, 1959.)   At
least three factors impede progress toward a convincing
solution:
1 Most serious of all, we can achieve no equation between
the archaeological and the linguistic character of the
Indo-Europeans, since direct evidence of their language is
entirely lacking.
2 Despite the assertion of Miss Gimbutas, the speakers of
proto-Indo-European can be assigned to more than one area
of origin.   The arguments of Bosch-Gimpera, 1961, 183-6
make it clear that there is little indication which, if
any, of these areas was their original home.   Even if we
could find a completely reliable method of discovering the
location of their homeland (for instance by a study of vocabulary), we should have established little of value for
the present purpose.   It is quite out of the question that
any migrants who entered Greece at the beginning of the
Middle Bronze Age, whether as invaders or as infiltrators,
came directly from the original Indo-European homeland:
in so far as it is legitimate to think of a homeland at all
in local terms, there can be doubt that in temporal terms
it must be placed at a period long before the beginning of
the Bronze Age (Krahe, 1957.)
3 The very notion of an Indo-European linguistic or cultural unity has been questioned, most recently by Pisani.   He
has brought arguments in favour of his contention that what
is called 'Indo-European' was never a discrete entity but a
loose conglomeration of languages, which were in origin
totally unrelated.   If that was so, the 'Indo-European'
period witnessed not so much the fragmentation of an
original unity as the coalescence, in varying degrees, of
smaller linguistic groups.
    Before returning to the detailed discussion of the Ae-
gean place-names, we must recognize that the task of establishing a synthesis between language and archaeology
over the whole Indo-European field, together with a convincing reconstruction of the movements of Indo-European
peoples, is at present impossible: Devoto, 1962 made a
strenuous attempt to arrive at such a synthesis, but (in
spite of the great merits of his book) he cannot be said
to have succeeded.   Yet, if the satisfactory correlation
of language and archaeology in the Indo-European domain
still eludes us, how can we have faith in theories which
profess to give answers in respect of one language only?

With regard to the -ss- and -nth- names, which bulk so
large in the linguistic discussion about early Greece, I
feel a certain amount of disquiet. Although Kretschmer
was unquestionably right to draw attention to the correspondence of the Aegean words in -ss- and -nth- with their
Anatolian counterparts, the far-reaching inferences often
drawn from this correspondence do not carry entire conviction. When Kretschmer wrote in 1896 he did not know from
epigraphical sources the name which a single place either
in the Aegean or in Anatolia bore in the Bronze Age. In
the 1950s, the direct knowledge of Anatolian place-names,
which had been available for some decades, was joined by
direct knowledge of Aegean place-names; but even now the
total number of toponyms in the Linear B tablets which are
closely similar to those of classical Greek is not more
than eight: a-mi-ni-so (Amnisos), e-ko-me-no (Erchomenos),
ko-no-so (Knossos), ko-ri-to (Korinthos), ku-pa-ri-si-jo
(an ethnic formed from a place-name ku-pa-ri-so, Kyparis-
sos), me-ra-to (Melanthos), o-ru-ma-to (Orymanthos), and
tu-ri-so (Tylissos.) Of these eight, only the three Cretan names (Amnisos, Knossos, Tylissos) can be associated
with known places. It is noteworthy that, in the maps
repeated without change by Schachermeyr in one publication
after another (in 1954, 1955, 1964, and 1967a), only three
out of the dense clusters of Greek place-names in -ss- and
-nth- are both attested in Bronze Age sources and refer-
able to actual places. It is inadmissible to use in evidence large numbers of names which are not certainly known
to have been attached to their respective sites in the
Bronze Age, since three implicit assumptions are thereby
made which everyone knows to be false: that a place never
changes its name through many centuries; that names are
never applied to new sites by analogy with place-names already in existence; and that migrating peoples never take
their place-names with them.
It is true that on the Anatolian side we are in better
case, since some eighty names in -s(s)a or -nda are mentioned in the Hittite documents; but here again it is hard
to place more than a few of them on the map - cf. Goetze,
1940 and Garstang and Gurney, 1959. I conclude that, although a body of evidence does exist which indicates a belt
of non-Greek place-names extending over the Aegean and Anatolian areas in the Early Bronze Age, it is smaller in extent than has often been supposed; and, in consequence,
it fails to confirm a correlation between Early Bronze Age
sites and non-Greek names on the scale suggested by Haley
and Blegen.

ARCHAEOLOGICAL OBJECTIONS

Quite apart from the objections which can be brought by the
linguist against a facile equation of Greek-speakers with
destroyers of the Early Helladic civilization, there are
serious archaeological difficulties as well.

It must be emphasized in the first place, at whatever
risk to Blegen's incisive argument which seemed to lead to
a solution of the problem, that he omits an all-important
step. Even if it were possible to prove the advent of the
speakers of a given language merely by pointing to a cultural change, there still resides a flaw in the reasoning.
It is, after all, incorrect to equate the 'destroyers of
the Early Helladic settlements' with the 'first Greek-
speakers'. That is to assume, as indeed Blegen and many
others have assumed without further argument, that the
'destroyers of Early Helladic' and the 'Middle Helladic
people' were one and the same. Such an equation is possible, of course. But quite a different explanation fits
the observed facts just as well. For example, the Early
Helladic sites might have been destroyed (not necessarily
all at the same time) by natural disasters, and the incursion of the Middle Helladic folk followed later. If that
was the course of events it would not be possible, as Blegen thought, 'to determine exactly where in the archaeological stratification the Hellenes first appear'. This
archaeological difficulty, like the linguistic difficulty
to which I have already referred, is overlooked by Blegen
and most of his followers (but not by Schachermeyr.)

Another objection concerns Blegen's method of argumentation. What is it that makes him think of two arms of a
common culture thrusting down to the west and to the east
of the Aegean, the first forcibly replacing Early Helladic
by Middle Helladic and the second initiating the culture of
Troy VI? One fact above all: the appearance in both
areas of similar types of grey ware.

Although it may be conceded that pottery is the one indispensable tool of the Bronze Age archaeologist, that is
not to say that pottery, by itself, can ever constitute an
adequate index to a whole civilization. Two civilizations
in different areas are not proved to be akin to each other
simply because they use the same type of pottery: especially when, as in the present case, the type of pottery in
question cannot be shown to have originated at even approximately the same time in the two areas.

When we look at the other material manifestations of
culture at Troy and in Greece, we find that they do not
notably confirm the view suggested by the pottery alone.
For example, Blegen, 1953, 10 makes much of the appearance

of the horse in Troy VI.   Until recently, horse-bones were
scarcely known in Middle Helladic Greece, but they are now
attested at Lerna (Gejvall, 1969, 37) and at Marathon
(Marinatos, 1970b, 13.)   Anyone who finds this fact of
great significance should bear in mind the high antiquity
of the occurrence of horse-bones in many other parts of
Europe (Hancar, 1955, 26-42) and the consequent possibility
that their rarity in Greece arises from lack of excavation.
With regard to building: in Troy VI 'far-reaching changes
manifest themselves in the field of architecture.   A
powerful fortification wall was built around a much enlarged citadel, characterized...by its more orderly style of
masonry' (Blegen, 1953, 5.)   It is doubtful whether such
citadels and such walls were in use at any Middle Helladic
site.   Massive works of this kind, built for defence or
prestige, appear first in Greece well into the Mycenaean
age, several centuries later than the beginning of Troy VI.
When we consider burial-customs, there is nothing at Troy
to set beside the well-attested monuments from Middle Helladic Greece.   The American excavators of Troy did indeed
find what they thought might be a 'crematory', but they
dated it to the last phases of the Sixth City; while for
earlier periods they came across no certain evidence at all
(Blegen, 1953, 393.)   In any case, there is no parallel at
Troy to inhumation in cist-graves, which forms the prevalent custom in contemporary Greece.

This lack of real harmony between the material culture
of Troy VI and that of Middle Helladic Greece ought to dis-
suade us from concluding, without serious reflexion, that
the two areas were settled by different branches of the
same intrusive people (cf. Bittel, 1956, 247-50.)   They
had, in fact, nothing significant in common, except that
they both used a grey pottery of similar type.   The possible origin of this pottery, and of the people who made
it, must now be investigated.

The results of excavation of three Greek sites during
the 1950s and 1960s modify very considerably the old picture of destructive invaders arriving in Greece at the end
of the Early Helladic period, invaders whose only known
affinities were with north-west Anatolia.   It was Lerna,
in the Argolid, which first gave cause to doubt the correctness of the traditional view.   The excavator of Lerna,
J.L. Caskey, observed that, although there was indeed a
serious destruction at this site, it fell at the transition between Settlement III and Settlement IV.   Now Settlement III contained pottery of a kind which at other sites
marked the Early Helladic II period, whereas Settlement IV
(with pottery typical of Early Helladic III) suffered no
destruction.

There is no break in the sequence between the settlements called Lerna IV and Lerna V, no general layer of
burnt debris, no sign of other catastrophe. The architectural succession continues with apsidal and oblong
buildings, and from the appearance of their plans and
masonry alone the excavator could not distinguish one
period from another. A change undoubtedly occurred,
however. It appears most obviously in certain classes
of pottery. (Caskey, 1960, 298.)
The new classes of pottery associated with Settlement V
(beginning of Middle Helladic) are precisely those matt-
painted and Grey Minyan wares whose first appearance formerly seemed always to be marked by destruction and the
arrival of intruders. But at Lerna there is nothing at
all to suggest that the new pottery-types were developed
by anyone other than the inhabitants who had been in possession since the beginning of Early Helladic II; in
other words, such a characteristic trait of the 'Middle
Helladic' culture as Grey Minyan ware need not be attributed to any invader.

Caskey's excavations at Lerna enabled him to give sharper definition than had been possible previously to the
successive phases of the Early Helladic period. By comparing his own observations with the excavation reports of
Ayios Kosmas, Zygouries, Asine, and Tiryns, he concluded
that the major destruction at all of these sites was contemporary with that at Lerna; the belt of destruction was
in consequence to be dated to the end of Early Helladic
II, not to the end of Early Helladic III. Eutresis alone
refused to conform to this pattern: there, the traditional date of the destruction at the very end of Early Helladic was confirmed by the comparative evidence from Lerna
(Caskey, 1960, 300-1.)

The evidence from two other sites may now be brought
into the framework of Early Helladic which Caskey established at Lerna. Excavations of Early Helladic settlements at Berbati (south-east of Mycenae) and at Lefkandi
on the west coast of Euboea have revealed how mistaken it
is to regard Grey Minyan pottery as a unified style which
always appears after a horizon of destruction. At Berbati, the Grey Minyan ware could be divided into an earlier group ('Grey Minyan I') associated with Early Helladic
pottery and a later ('Grey Minyan II'), which was contemporary with matt-painted ware. Although there was destruction by fire at Berbati, this occurred after the first
appearance of Grey Minyan I pottery and before the more
mature Grey Minyan II (Säflund, 1965, 158-9.) Lefkandi
also shows a development of Grey Minyan from a crude, for-
mative stage (contemporary with Caskey's Settlement IV at

Lerna), at which the pottery is often hand-made, to later
stages at which it is generally thrown on the wheel.   Lefkandi is unlike Berbati, however, in that it shows no sign
of destruction between the first and the later stages of
Grey Minyan (R.J. Howell in Popham and Sackett, 1968, 8-
11.)   (The horizons of destruction are shown in Table 2.)
    Some twenty years ago, in the course of his comprehen-
sive treatment of prehistoric Greece, F. Schachermeyr adduced an a priori argument in favour of his view that the
intruders (who, as he thought, arrived at the beginning of
Middle Helladic) did not bring the Grey Minyan ware with
them but developed it only after their arrival in Greece:
    It would be quite mistaken to connect the origin of Grey
    Minyan with the catastrophe and immigration at the be-
    ginning of the Middle Helladic period.   Pottery is very
    often not brought by migrants with them from their home-
    land but is borrowed locally.   And if, as happened at
    the end of Early Helladic III, the workshops were des-
    troyed and the typical Early Helladic ware was no longer
    manufactured, the ensuing transitional style owed no-
    thing to foreign influence but, rather, marked a hiatus
    between the old and the new.   (Schachermeyr, 1954,
    1468.)
This argument has always seemed to me very sane in itself,
and I cannot understand why adherents of the orthodox view
have so little time for it (e.g. Page, 1959, 88-90.)   Indeed, the essential correctness of this part of Schachermeyr's thesis has been confirmed by the discoveries at Lef
kandi, Berbati, and Lerna, which make it clear that in
some at least of the Greek sites the Grey Minyan style was
developed locally.
    What, then, of the grey ware at Troy?   In conformity
with his theory that Grey Minyan pottery was developed
locally by the Middle Helladic people, Schachermeyr considered that, once the new style had been perfected in
Greece, it was transplanted to north-western Anatolia by
way of Chalcidice and Thrace (ib., 1468-9.)   This suggestion, though perfectly reasonable at the time it was made,
can now be shown not to provide a complete answer to the
problem.   Nevertheless, I suspect that it contains at
least part of the truth, and I propose to bear it in mind
while examining the ceramic evidence from Troy and other
parts of Anatolia.
    The Anatolian pottery of the second millennium BC has
been deeply studied by J. Mellaart and D.H. French.   Mellaart, 1958 was a pioneering article which became very influential.   The author used archaeological evidence in a
very bold way to determine the movements of peoples west-
ward across Anatolia early in the millennium: movements

which he brought into connexion with the 'destruction-belt'
then thought universally to accompany the first appearance
of the Middle Helladic culture in Greece. Mellaart has
since retracted these far-reaching inferences from the evidence of the pottery, but that evidence retains its momentous importance. A later and more concise statement is to
be found at Mellaart, 1971, 700-2: detailed surveys of the
relevant ceramic remains are contributed by French, 1966;
1967; 1969.
    The thorough examination of the Anatolian pottery made
by Mellaart and French enables a great advance to be made
upon the rather crude historical reconstruction which was
in vogue for many years: according to this (as we have
seen), a grey type of pottery, closely resembling the Minyan ware of Middle Helladic Greece and, like it, lacking
local antecedents, was introduced at Troy at the same time
as its first appearance in Greece. This picture must now
be corrected in three crucial respects: 1 the so-called
'Grey Minyan' ware of Troy VI is not really intrusive but
represents a further development of the grey pottery already present in Troy V; 2 the evolution of a 'Minyan'
type of pottery is not, as was once thought, confined to
the Troad - on the contrary, it is attested as far south as
the island of Samos and, probably, even farther afield
(Buchholz, 1973); 3 the shapes of the grey ware at Troy,
with one exception, are not identical with those of Middle
Helladic Greece. These conclusions (unless they are upset
by subsequent discovery) allow no room for a theory which
brings the technique of Grey Minyan from Greece to Troy,
nor one which brings it from Troy to Greece (despite the
incomprehensible reference to a Grey Minyan 'offshoot in
Middle Helladic Greece' from Anatolia, Mellaart, 1971,
702.) Equally excluded is the hypothesis which traces
the grey ware in both areas back to a common source.
    The only explanation which fits the observed facts is
that two types of grey ware, similar but not identical to
each other, were evolved independently in Greece and in
Anatolia. It is possible (as French, 1973, 51 suggests)
that the Middle Helladic potters were inspired to develop
their ware in precisely this direction by the example of
their Anatolian colleagues. If such an inspiration could
ever be proved, it would point to much more than a passing
acquaintance between Middle Helladic Greece and the Anatolian coast. But, even as things are, some contact between Troy and Greece is strongly suggested by the exception mentioned under 3 in the preceding paragraph. The
large 'Lianokladi' type of goblet with wide ringed stem
(shape A 64, Blegen, 1953, 48; my Figure 3) is represented
by more than seventy-five fragments in the early phase of

Troy VI alone.   This shape is not, apparently, indigenous
in Anatolia; but it is well known at Middle Helladic sites
in southern Greece, and it intrudes even into Thessaly and
Macedonia.   For a long time, the occurrence at Troy of
this typical shape of Greek Grey Minyan constituted the
single link between the two areas so early in the Middle
Bronze Age; but it was a strong link, which left little
room for doubt that a line of communication had already
been opened up from Greece to north-west Anatolia.   This
hypothesis receives striking confirmation from the results
of Milojcić's excavations at Peukakia, near Volos, in Thessaly.   At the time of writing, only brief preliminary reports are available, but these speak of the discovery of
pottery of very varied provenience in a Middle Helladic
room: Minyan and matt-painted ware (some of it imported
from Boeotia) was found in association with Cycladic, Trojan, and Middle Minoan II pottery (JHS Archaeological Reports for 1970-71, 61; Miriam Caskey, 1971, 305; Milojcić, 1974, 45-51.)   Unless this deposit represents something altogether abnormal in contemporary Greece, it
proves the existence of a rather complex network of trading
relationships; even if (as is likely) the commerce with
Crete was by way of the Cyclades, direct contact with Troy
seems to be beyond question.   I believe that it was this
commercial intercourse between Greece and other regions
(beginning, perhaps, in a modest way in the Middle Bronze
Age) which paved the way for the greatly expanded commerce
of the Mycenaean period.

CONCLUSIONS

The conclusions which emerge from the foregoing discussion
are, on the whole, negative; but, such as they are, it
may be convenient to re-state them briefly.   Our linguistic evidence allows us to do no more than postulate the
arrival of Indo-European-speakers in Greece at some epoch
within the Bronze Age: it indicates neither the time nor
the manner of their incursion, and (save that the newcomers must have entered from the north or the east) it
says nothing about their immediate point of departure.
Even if the linguistic data did suggest an 'invasion' by
Greek-speakers, there would be no reason to identify these
with the makers of Minyan pottery; on the contrary, it is
now seen that the technique of manufacturing Grey Minyan
ware was developed locally in Gréece.   In any case, the
positive identification of the Early Helladic people with
a pre-Indo-European stock, on the one hand, and that of
the Middle Helladic people as Indo-Europeans, on the other,

cannot be sustained.   That being so, we must leave open
the possibility that speakers of Indo-European infiltrated
gradually into Greece, perhaps over a very long period; it
might be added that even the presence of Greek in the Linear B texts of the early fourteenth century BC does not
prove that the whole of southern Greece was already inhabited by Greek-speakers, but merely that Greek formed part of
the current administrative language (cf. Chapter 4.)

   If it is granted that the use of Grey Minyan ware and
the arrival of Greek-speakers are two separate events which
have no necessary or even probable connexion with each
other, are any purely archaeological conclusions possible?
Are the elements which have hitherto served, in broad
terms, to demarcate the Middle Helladic from the Early
Helladic culture sufficient to prove the superimposition of
a radically different population; and, if so, can this new
population be related to other peoples known in the record?
When it was thought that the decisively new element in the
Middle Helladic culture was Grey Minyan ware, hypotheses
which linked the Middle Helladic 'intruders' with Anatolia
were freely advanced.   Now we know that Grey Minyan pottery was already being developed in strata traditionally
associated with the Early Helladic people, we have to examine other manifestations of Middle Helladic culture, especially burial-habits and styles of building, in an attempt to connect them with other areas.

   It seems that Europe has replaced Anatolia as an area
whose relationship with Greece is seen to be of significant importance, both in the late stages of Early Helladic
and in Middle Helladic.   The regions to the north of
Greece are found to offer parallels to typical features of
the Middle Helladic culture while, on the other hand, imports from the north appear in Early Helladic strata: a
set of facts which is sometimes thought to attest a movement of peoples into Greece from the north at the end of
Early Helladic II.   This theory, in its broad outlines,
is not new (it was advanced, for example, by Kraiker,
1939, 210-1); but it is only in recent years that the
archaeological data from Yugoslavia and elsewhere have
been compared systematically with those of Helladic Greece.
Bouzek, 1972 favours the hypothesis that one, or perhaps
two, migrations took place from Europe into Greece in
Early Helladic.   Howell, 1973, 90-3 finds two parallels
between the 'Baden' culture of central Europe (the latest
phase of which is contemporary with Early Helladic II) and
Middle Helladic customs: 1 two houses with wooden framework, found near Belgrade, had apsidal ends, thereby dis-
playing a similarity to Middle Helladic practice both in
construction and in shape; 2 the same site gave evidence

of two customs typical of the Middle Helladic culture,
namely intramural burial and burial in pit-graves.   Hood,
1973b, 61-3 calls attention to two manifestations of the
'Kurgan' culture which appear in Greece: pottery with corded decoration from Thessaly and Macedonia (late Early Helladic?) and hammer-headed pins from Asea and Lerna (Middle
Helladic.)

None of these three scholars makes any far-reaching deductions from the facts presented: Hood, for his part, being content with the modest proposition that 'there seems
to be a certain amount of evidence for movements of people
from the north into Greece at the end of the Early Helladic
period' (Hood, 1973b, 59.)   Nevertheless, in case others
are inclined to regard a migration from the north as certainly established, some reservations ought to be expressed.   In the first place, the bulk of the evidential
material, both from Greece and from Yugoslavia, is exceedingly small.   It would be legitimate to regard the Baden
apsidal houses, for instance, as an aberration from the
norm rather than an expression of a practice typical of the
whole culture.   As for the minute quantity of corded ware
found in the north of Greece, and the hammer-headed pins in
the south, these merely attest sporadic contact between the
Helladic people and northern regions;   but contact so weak
and discontinuous as never to amount to full-scale migration.   Secondly, a methodological principle is involved.
In a short but penetrating paper, Milojcić, 1955a reviewed
the arguments which had been put forward on the basis of
the corded ware and other classes of evidence.   He was
unable to identify the shapes of the corded vessels represented in Greece with those from central Europe;   on
the contrary, the shapes appeared to develop organically in
Thessaly itself.   Having remarked on the absence of a
series of related and contemporaneous features which could
properly be ascribed to a group of invaders, he posed questions which are still unanswerable to-day: 'we may legitimately ask those who speak in favour of immigration to establish that the artefacts used by invaders appear at one
definite point in time and not at periods separated from
each other by many centuries and completely without any
interconnexion' (Milojcić, 1955a, 154.)

So the matter rests at present.   Many sites in central
and southern Greece witness a change (often a violent
change) at the end of Early Helladic II;   Eutresis undergoes the change at the end of Early Helladic III;   Lefkandi
sees a gradual evolution through the Early Helladic period,
and into Middle Helladic, without any sudden destruction.
These facts, when set together, point much more insistently
to a series of internal convulsions than to an incursion

from outside; and, despite the a priori likelihood that
cultural changes in Greece were closely connected with, or
influenced by, events in areas immediately to the north,
little is at present known which would substantiate such
connexion and such influence.

NOTES

The Greek historians

A different view of the legendary evidence is expressed by
Toynbee, 1969, 126-34.

The evidence of language

A modern survey of the Anatolian languages, from the Indo-
European stand-point, is given by Kammenhuber, 1968.
Even if Kretschmer's theory of an incursion by proto-
Indo-Europeans followed by Greeks is soundly based, it
needs modification in some important respects: Hester,
1957; Laroche, 1961; Lopez Eire, 1967 and 1970; Gil,
1968. It is, in any case, fallacious to suppose that this
proto-Indo-European ('Pelasgian') language can be reconstructed: cf. Hester, 1965 and 1968; Gindin, 1971; Fur-
neé, 1972, 30-96; Georgiev, 1973. Carnoy, 1960, follows
Kretschmer in thinking that Greek words in -ss- and -nth-
can be regarded as Indo-European.
On the Mediterranean 'substrate': Pisani, 1974.
On the Luwian evidence: Kronasser, 1960; Crossland,
1961; Wyatt, 1968; Kammenhuber, 1969b, 260-1.

The evidence of archaeology

Evidence of violent destruction at Early Helladic sites:
Bulle, 1907, 57 (Orchomenos); Goldman, 1931, 231 (Eutre-
sis); Mylonas, 1959, 162 (Ayios Kosmas); Blegen, 1921,
124 (Korakou); Frödin and Persson, 1938, 433 (Asine);
Müller, 1930, 203-4 (Tiryns); Holmberg, 1944, 180 (Asea);
Valmin, 1938, 52 (Malthi.)
Surveys of the Early Helladic culture: Schachermeyr,
1955, 182-96; Caskey, 1960 and 1971; Renfrew, 1972, 99-
120. The Early Helladic III period: Effenterre, 1975.
Surveys of the Middle Helladic culture: Schachermeyr,
1954, 1452-75; Buck, 1966; Howell, 1973; Caskey, 1973.
Middle Helladic pottery: Wace and Blegen, 1916; Buck,
1964.

Linguistic objections

Modern criticism of Kretschmer's theory of three invasions by Greek-speakers: Adrados, 1955; Chadwick, 1969a, 80-2; Wyatt, 1970b, 558.

Mallory, 1973 gives a survey of arguments for the location of the Indo-European homeland, with full bibliography. Palmer, 1972a, 361-5 offers acute criticism of the methods used to arrive at the location of the homeland.

Arguments in favour of 'convergence' as an explanation of Indo-European linguistic unity: Trubetzkoy, 1939; Pisani, 1959.   Arguments to the contrary: Thieme, 1953, 56-76; Nehring, 1961; Brandenstein, 1962 and 1965.   See on the whole question Scherer, 1972.

Further on the weakness of the evidence of names in -ss- and -nth-: Wyatt, 1970a, 94-5.   Some interesting parallels from medieval England are to be found in Wainwright, 1962.

Conclusions

The conflicting theories of linguists and archaeologists are conveniently summarized by Crossland, 1971.

3 The beginning of the Mycenaean Age (c. 1650–1525 BC)

THE EARLIEST CONTACTS WITH CRETE

The disturbances which affected the mainland of Greece during the latter part of the Early Bronze Age were not felt in the other major areas of Aegean civilization, namely Crete and the Cyclades. In both, the culture typical of each region followed an uninterrupted development, except that in Crete a series of earthquakes had a seriously retarding effect. But, in this epoch, the Minoan civilization of Crete possessed immense powers of self-renewal; and even the devastating earthquake which befell Knossos toward the end of the Middle Bronze Age only afforded an opportunity of re-building the palace in a still more ample manner than before. Prior to that, in the Early Palace period, the principal centres of Crete had witnessed a brilliant efflorescence of peaceful arts. Middle Minoan wares were carried from Crete not only to the Cyclades but as far as Egypt and the eastern Mediterranean.

Of greater significance even than the presence of Middle Minoan sherds at Abydos, in Upper Egypt, is the absorption of Egyptian motifs, especially that of the papyrus, on Middle Minoan palatial pottery. Cretan relations were particularly close with Phylakopi in the Cycladic island of Melos. Middle Minoan II ware was imported there early in the history of the Second City, while the decoration of native Melian pottery underwent a change as a result of Minoan influence. The wall-paintings of the Second City are so similar to Minoan frescoes in both style and content as to make it probable that they were produced by Cretan artists, or at the very least by native artists steeped in the Cretan art of naturalistic wall-painting. Commerce in the reverse direction is attested by the Cycladic vases which Evans found in the Temple Repositories at Knossos.

According to a commonly held view, the Greek mainland had little or no part in the commercial activity of the Middle Bronze Age. And it is true that in this period the mainland did not begin to rival the Minoans either in the originality and productiveness of their artists or in the volume of their overseas trade. Nevertheless, we shall fall into serious error if we deny to the mainland any interest at all in foreign commerce before the close of the Middle Bronze Age. It is precisely because of this erroneous thinking that the wealth of Mycenae in the 'Shaft Grave period' (which spans the transition from Middle to Late Helladic) has been found so difficult to account for. As I see it, the Shaft Graves take their natural place in the gradual increase in prosperity of mainland Greece, associated all the time with expansion overseas. Although this expansion was expecially marked at two epochs - the first in the Shaft Grave period and the second after the destruction of Knossos - there is some evidence of foreign contacts well back in the Middle Helladic period. In Chapter 2 I inferred from the discoveries at Peukakia and the occurrence of one type of grey ware in Troy VI that at least one important trade-route, between Greece and northwest Anatolia, had been opened up during the early part of the Middle Bronze Age; or perhaps it would be more accurate to say that the Early Bronze Age trade-route had never fallen into disuse. Commerce along this route was intensified later and continued throughout the greater part of the Late Bronze Age. At the same time, the presence of Minyan pottery at several sites in the Cyclades testifies to contacts between them and the mainland.

Signs of mainland influence in Crete are extremely sparse. Very little Minyan ware has been found there, while the style of Middle Minoan pottery owes nothing to Helladic prototypes. On the other hand, there are already signs within the Middle Helladic period of that Cretan influence on the mainland which was to become so potent at the beginning of Late Helladic. It is not possible to estimate the extent to which Crete and the mainland were in direct communication during the Middle Helladic period. We would judge from the juxtaposition of Minyan and Middle Minoan pottery at Phylakopi that at least some Cycladic sites might have acted as intermediaries. However that may be, some fragments of late Middle Helladic pottery from Korakou in Corinthia are decorated with patterns of Cretan origin, even though the vases themselves are not certainly imported from Crete (Blegen, 1921, 32.) Minoan decorative motifs occur also on sherds which have been recovered from Settlement V at Lerna, where Cycladic pottery was found as well (Caskey, 1956, 159;   1957, 152-4.)

There is one consideration, above all, which argues for
some degree of intimacy between Crete and the mainland as
early as Middle Helladic.   For a number of years, prehistorians have pondered the relationship of the vaulted type
of tomb found in Crete in the Early and Middle Bronze Ages
with the 'tholos', an underground built tomb of beehive
shape, which became prominent on the mainland after the
Shaft Grave era.   Persuasive arguments were put forward by
Wace, on the grounds both of construction and of chronology,
to show that there was no connexion between the Cretan
vaulted tomb and the mainland tholos (Wace, 1921, 394-6 and
in Persson, 1931, 144-5.)   Since Wace's investigations,
however, the gap in time between the latest known Cretan
vaulted tomb and the earliest example of a mainland tholos
has been reduced at both ends.   Blegen, 1954 has described
an early tholos in western Messenia, from which he concludes that the inhabitants of the mainland must have been
familiar with the principles of building underground tholoi
before the end of the Middle Bronze Age.   Although the
Cretan vaulted tomb was especially favoured in Early Minoan
times, many examples of the type were still being used in
the Middle Bronze Age;   and at least two appear, from the
pottery found in them, to have been built in the Middle
Minoan period itself.   No very long time can have elapsed
between the building of these tombs and the appearance of
the earliest tholoi on the mainland.   If the argument from
chronology is insubstantial, that from construction appears
equally so.   The alleged differences between the Helladic
and the Cretan type have been discussed recently and have
been shown not to be so serious as was once supposed.

THE SHAFT GRAVES

At the same time as the first large-scale appearance of
Minoan influences (c. 1650 BC), and for reasons which will
be discussed presently, Mycenae itself advances from the
status of a substantial but unremarkable Middle Helladic
site to that of the dominant city in the Argolid;   later
still, it becomes the major trading-centre of continental
Greece.   The assimilation of Helladic and Cretan elements
results in the rise of a new, well-defined culture known in
modern times as 'Mycenaean', after the centre where it
first appears and where its evolution can be traced in detail.   We may presume that Mycenae came to occupy an important place because its high citadel commanded a trade-
route to the Isthmus of Corinth.   It is not clear, however, why during the Bronze Age Mycenae became more important than, say, Tiryns (which also, at least in the four-

teenth and thirteenth centuries BC, possessed a strongly
fortified citadel) or Argos, which in the archaic and classical periods completely eclipsed the other Argolid cities.
The very circumstances which conferred so great a natural
advantage on Mycenae as a fortified place have meant that
we are not so well informed as we would like to be about
the settlements on top of the hill, since the steep slopes
have encouraged the collapse of the last palace built
there. Our information therefore comes mainly from the
contents of graves and, after the fifteenth century BC,
from walls, gates, and houses.

For the First Phase of Minoan Influence, the graves at
Mycenae offer testimony of unique value. Six Shaft Graves
(built tombs which had been sunk into the ground and arranged in a roughly circular area within the citadel) were excavated by Schliemann and Stamatakis, beginning in 1876.
A vivid account of the excavations and discoveries is given
by Schliemann, 1878. These graves, each of which is referred to by a Roman numeral, constitute what is now known
as Circle A. The graves and their contents were fully
described and illustrated in Karo, 1930a, which contains,
besides a full catalogue, a valuable assessment of the
historical background of the Shaft Graves.

During the 1950s a second grave circle (now known as B),
rather earlier than A but to some extent overlapping it
chronologically, was discovered outside the citadel and
excavated by the Greek Archaeological Service. The
graves of this circle are known by the letters of the Greek
alphabet. Their contents have been published by Mylonas,
1973: a publication which invalidates some historical. conclusions which were previously drawn in respect of Circle
A. The nature of the contents of the latest graves of
Circle B makes it clear that they were roughly contemporary
with the earliest graves in Circle A. This overlap mili-
tates against the theory, often voiced before the discovery
of Circle B and still heard even to-day, that the beginning
of Circle A marks the advent of a new people, or at least a
new dynasty, at Mycenae. It is not even legitimate to associate the intrusion of a new stock with the construction
of Circle B, since its excavator gave good reasons for believing that it incorporated parts of a still earlier grave
circle (Papadimitriou, 1954b, 263.)

The graves in Circle B are, in general, cruder and poorer in burial-offerings than those of A, but in details of
construction the graves of both circles are very similar.
At Mycenae, as at other mainland sites where the development can be studied over a long period, there is no real
break between Middle and Late Helladic: nothing which
points to any radical change in the underlying Helladic

culture.   Continuity is further attested by the practice,
in both grave circles, of placing 'stelae' (monumental
slabs of stone), sometimes decorated and sometimes not,
over some of the tombs: in particular, the stela set over
Grave Γ in Circle B has exactly the same decorative arrangement (upper register of spirals, lower register comprising a narrative scene) which is found on Stela V
(Grave V) in Circle A.   Finally, there is no essential
difference in character between the grave-gifts found in
Circle B from those of A (Table 3.)

Most of the pottery found in the graves of Circle B is
assigned to Middle Helladic, though in some cases to very
late Middle Helladic.   The typical ceramic shape is that
of the 'Minyan' stemmed goblet (Figure 3), which has nothing to do with Crete, while many decorative motifs of the
patterned ware are easily paralleled in the Middle Helladic
repertory.   Only a few pots from Circle B (for example nos
168, 169, and 170 in Grave N, with stylized vegetable decoration) give evidence of contact with Crete;   on the other
hand, the occurrence of birds on half a dozen jugs of Cycladic shape shows influence from the Cyclades, which is
continued in the pottery from Grave VI of Circle A.   (Mylonas, 1973, 270-310.)

A link with Crete is, however, provided by some of the
swords included in the burial-offerings of Circle B.   In
his examination of the swords in the later Grave Circle,
Karo found that they were divisible into two types, A (longer and narrower) and B (shorter and wider but with longer
tangs)(Figure 4.)   These two shapes are represented in
Circle B as well, both of them sometimes in the same tomb
(e.g. A, Γ, Δ.)   The latest discussions of the subject
leave little doubt that, of these two types, A at least
was present in Crete before its appearance in the Shaft
Graves (Sandars, 1961, 25;   Snodgrass, 1967, 15-6;   Branigan, 1968;   Mylonas, 1973, 314-7.)   In the light of this
distribution of sword-types, we can no longer assume, with
Persson and others (e.g. Persson, 1931, 61), that the
Aegean sword was 'invented' on the Greek mainland.   On
the contrary, it seems safe, in the present state of our
knowledge, to assign the origin at least of Type A to
Crete, even though the reasons for the presence of such
swords in mainland tombs continue to elude us.

The burial-gifts which Schliemann found in the graves of
Circle A are of such kind and number as to preclude any
single explanation of their occurrence.   Despite the Minoan traits displayed by many of them, these objects as a
whole are firmly rooted in a native Helladic tradition and
thereby disprove Evans' contention that at this time the
Argolid came under the cultural, or even the political,

domination of Crete.   The gifts do not form a homogeneous group of objects, comprising as they do everyday utensils of crude workmanship, trivial items of personal adornment, and unique masterpieces.   Some of the more important kinds of objects have to be considered in detail before the extent of Cretan influence in this phase can be assessed accurately.   It will be seen, finally, that we have to look even beyond Crete and the Cyclades in order to arrive at a full understanding.

Apart from swords of types A and B (which were found in considerable numbers in Graves IV and V), actual imports of objects from Crete are very rare in the tombs of Circle A. These include an egg-shaped pourer ('rhyton')(Karo's no 221 from Grave II) and a silver bull's head rhyton (no 384 from Grave IV.)   The bull's head rhyton is rightly regarded as a Cretan import, since it is so closely similar to rhyta from Knossos (Evans, 1928, 527-33) and from Zakro (Platon, 1963, pl 152α.)

Some of the offerings in Circle A are of purely Helladic type.   The gold death-masks, for example, which were found in Graves IV and V, have only remote parallels in Crete (Karo, 1930a, 180-1.)   A number of gold cups - certainly no 220 from Grave II and no 627 from V - are coarse local work of Minyan shape.   The discussions of Karo, 1930a, 77-8 and Snijder, 1936, 118 have shown that the great lion's head rhyton in gold plate from Grave IV (no 273) is very different in technique from the lions represented in Cretan art.   Lastly, in Graves I and VI we have some native Yellow Minyan and matt-painted pottery.   Despite the mainlanders' undoubted associations with Crete, it is noteworthy that pure Middle Helladic pottery remained in domestic use throughout the Shaft Grave era, being found in the latest grave as well as the earliest.

So far, we have considered the few purely Cretan and the many purely Helladic articles in the graves of Circle A. But it seems possible to identify two further classes: 1 objects made by Cretans to the order of mainlanders; and 2 objects made by mainland artists after Cretan prototypes. Naturally, the assignment of a given object to one class or the other involves the weighing of probabilities only; no final certainty is attainable.

1 The grave-goods of this class were, presumably, made by Cretan craftsmen of high skill to the order of mainland princes.   The expertise of the Minoans in depicting men and animals in movement, often violent movement, is exemplified by several artefacts.   The inlaid dagger-blades, especially, show a very high level of technical and artistic accomplishment.   According to Frankfort, 1936, 114, the technique of metal inlay is not of Cretan origin but

was learnt in Syria.   This possibility will have to be
reckoned with when we come to evaluate the historical
background of the Shaft Graves.   The artistry, on the
other hand, is purely Minoan.   The lion-hunt shown on
the dagger-blade no 394 in Grave IV is not only a very
convincing picture in its own right but is perfectly adapted to the special size and shape of the blade: the whole
reminds one of fresco technique (Figure 5.)   Lions are
also used very effectively for the design of another
dagger-blade, no 395;   but here no narrative is attempted
- three lions are shown running toward the point of the
blade, while the spaces between them are filled with jagged
projections which represent rocky scenery: a common convention of Minoan art.   On another richly decorated
blade, no 765 from Grave V, leopards are depicted stalking
their prey through an undergrowth of papyrus plants.   This
theme came to the mainland from Egypt by way of Minoan
fresco-painting (Evans, 1930, 115;   Smith, 1965, 76-7.)
     The most baffling object in Grave Circle A must be con-
sidered here.   This is a silver rhyton engraved with
scenes in relief: often, though for quite inadequate
reasons, referred to as the 'Siege Rhyton' (Karo's no 481
from Grave IV)(Figure 5.)   Only a few fragments are
extant.   On the largest of these, four olive-trees are
depicted to the left, while on the right towers rise on a
steep slope, with women gesticulating on the battlements.
The dress of some of the women and some details of the
towers look like Minoan features.   On the slope a battle
is in progress: in all, twelve defenders are shown -
their hair is dressed in a kind of 'crew-cut' and, with
the exception of two figures, they are all naked.   At
the lower edge of this fragment, the upper part of a man
is left: he wears a flowing plume and a tunic, and he
appears to be punting a boat.   Four boar's tusk helmets
belong, probably, to occupants of the boat.   A smaller
fragment of the rhyton is engraved with a pattern representing shallow water and a rocky sea-bed, very much in
the Minoan manner.   How are these fragmentary scenes to be
interpreted?   Many writers have thought that an actual
historical event is being commemorated; but I do not think
that this view can be seriously maintained, since it is impossible to relate the fortified town, the attackers, and
the defenders to any one region or any one period known to
us.   (Further details are given by Vermeule, 1964, 100-5;
Smith, 1965, 65-8;   Hooker, 1967a;   Sakellariou, 1975.)
     2 To this class belong some of the cups made of precious
metals.   They are of Helladic shape, but some of their
decorative details are derived from Minoan art.   I regard
the so-called Dove Cup, Karo's no 412 from Grave IV, as a

closer but inferior adaptation of a Cretan type by a mainland craftsman.   I cannot understand why a connexion
should ever have been made between this wretched object and
the 'drinking-cup of surpassing beauty' which Nestor is
said at 'Iliad' 11. 632-5 to have brought from Pylos to
Troy: that is the reminiscence of an altogether finer work
of art (Furumark, 1946.)
     The clay vessels of the Late Helladic I style (Furu-
mark's 'Mycenaean I') may also be assigned to the second
class.   This new style of pottery (already represented in
the latest graves of Circle B) was independently created on
the mainland in imitation of Minoan models.   Few examples
of the new style have been found outside the Argolid.   Most
Late Helladic I decorative motifs are borrowed from the
Minoan repertory;   but the Mycenaean pot-painter is content
to use only a small number of the wealth of motifs available to him, and he still has a predilection for abstract
patterns: an inheritance from Middle Helladic pottery.
Several Minyan shapes still persist, even when decorated
in the new style.   (Furumark, 1972a, 472-7.)
     The Late Helladic I clay vessels in the Shaft Graves
vary greatly in quality.   There is a wide gap between the
coarse work in Grave VI and such fine imitations of Minoan
ware as Karo's nos 856 in Grave V and 199 in Grave I.
Furumark, 1972a, 105 suggests that the finer ware is the
produce of actual Cretan 'factories' which had been established on the mainland by this time, and that the coarser
was made by native artists imitating Minoan imports.   I
have no better explanation to offer;   but I cannot quite
see why mainland potters should trouble themselves to produce coarse imitations of Minoan vases when all the time
Minyan ware of high technical excellence was being manufactured.   It is, however, possible that the cultural as-
cendancy of Crete was becoming so great and its artefacts
so highly prized that Mycenaean patrons insisted on having
Minoan objects;   or, failing them, imitations as close as
their own artists could make.   If the selection of vessels
preserved in the Shaft Graves accurately reflects the contemporary practice, we can say at least that Minoan vessel-
shapes were adopted in general for the finer ware, Helladic shapes being retained for articles of domestic use.
     In one of his resumptive chapters, Mylonas has achieved
some success in establishing a chronological and typologi-
cal sequence for the pottery found in Grave Circle B (Mylonas, 1973, 309-10.)   It is, in my opinion, equally necessary to work out a corresponding scheme for the pottery
from Circle A;   the results of this analysis will be seen
to have an important bearing on our historical enquiries
into the affinities of the Shaft Graves.   The scheme of

the pottery in Circle A (Table 4) assigns to their respective tombs three distinct types: 1 a solitary Cretan import; 2 vessels of purely Helladic antecedents; 3 Late
Helladic I ware.   Three vessels are of particular value in
establishing the chronology of the whole series: these are
no 956 from Grave VI, no 221 from II, and no 197 from I.
Karo, 1930a, 254 sees in no 956 the very beginning of Minoan influence; and this impression is confirmed by the
red-and-white decoration of the vessel, since only the
earliest pottery of the Late Minoan I style has details
painted in red (Evans, 1921, 611.)   Next in our scheme
must come no 221, the import from Crete, which also belongs
to a very early stage of Late Minoan Ia; Karo, however,
puts it later that no 956, presumably because two graves
cannot be contemporaneous and because, early as the decoration of no 221 shows it to be, it does not ante-date no
956.   Last in the datable series comes no 197, decorated
with floral and marine motifs, which Karo, 1930a, 256 holds
to be an imitation of a late stage of Late Minoan I.   These
observations enable us to say (assuming that the chronological sequence of Cretan pottery is soundly based) that
the graves of Circle A span the ceramic period lasting from
late Middle Minoan IIIb to early Late Minoan Ib, with the
massive deposits in Graves IV and V coming about mid-way
in the series.

The development of the engraved stelae, found over tombs
in both Grave Circles, shows some analogies with that of
the pottery.   Monumental work of this kind, decorated
(when it is decorated) in low relief or by incision, is
foreign to Crete, so far as we know.   Kantor, 1947, 40
has shown that there are no good grounds for postulating
an Egyptian origin.

The stelae of Grave Circle A were studied and classified
in exemplary fashion by Heurtley, 1921.   The two figured
stelae from Circle B may now be brought into his scheme.
Heurtley's Class I comprises the fragments of his Stelae
X and XI.   These are incised with crudely drawn scenes including warriors (?) and a chariot.   The scenes are drawn
within a frame.   To this class, so far as technique goes,
must belong Mylonas' no 490 from Grave A in Circle B; but
there the scene is not enclosed in a frame.   Two animals
confront a man who appears to be brandishing a spear.

The reliefs on stelae of Heurtley's Class II are arranged in panels.   The two best preserved examples, Stelae IV
and V (Grave V), are closely similar to each other and are
probably, as Heurtley thought, the products of the same
workshop.   On both, a panel filled with well drawn spirals
surmounts a panel containing a summarily rendered scene,
that of a charioteer driving to the right and confronted

by a warrior.   Mylonas is right to place in this class no 491 from Grave Γ (Circle B), so long as the syntax alone is taken into account: the centre of the stela has been cut away, but it is clear that the upper panel contains spirals drawn by an accomplished craftsman, while the lower has crude figures of beasts and men.   But one consideration suggests that this stela ought to be seen as representing a transitional type between Class II and Class III;   it is not simply a stereotyped rendering of chariot and warrior but a scene which incorporates some narrative elements.   To the right stands a burly figure wielding a club, and on the left a smaller human figure is depicted, apparently dead. Two confronted lions seem to have formed the centre-piece.

Only one stela, no I from Shaft Grave V, is contained in Heurtley's Class III, which he regards as the latest as well as the most ambitious of the series (Figure 5.)   A spiraliform framework is used to right and left, but the disposition into panels has been abandoned in favour of an animated rendering of two scenes: above, a chariot moving to the right and a fallen warrior (his body covered by a figure-of-eight shield) under the horses' hoofs;   below, a lion chasing a horned animal to the right.

In summarizing the characteristics of his Class II, Heurtley drew attention to the contrast between the finished work of the abstract motifs and the crude, stilted drawing of the figures.   The stelae of this Class, like the earliest Mycenaean pottery in the Shaft Graves, appear to be the work of mainland craftsmen who are just beginning to follow Cretan conventions of drawing.   This they are able to do quite successfully so long as they are dealing with abstract motifs such as rosettes and spirals; but, in the drawing of the chariot-scenes, there is little of the naturalism which the Minoans brought to the representation of similar subjects.   By arranging their designs in panels, the artists of the stelae are following a Helladic decorative principle, which is exemplified on matt-painted vases at Korakou (Blegen, 1921, 28.)   Three elements can therefore be discerned in stelae of the two Grave Circles: accomplished work in abstract motifs (Class II);   crude work in figures (also Class II);   more assured drawing of figures (Class III.)

I wish that conclusions of a more definite kind than in fact seem possible could be drawn from the miniature pictures on gems and gold rings.   Some connexion with Crete they must have: it is the precise nature of the relationship which is hard to assess.   Apart from the Lerna sealings published by Heath, 1958, no examples of glyptic art are known from the mainland until late in the Middle Bronze Age;   when they do appear, 'they illustrate in fact the fully developed Minoan glyptic style... As in all other branches of Art, the whole previous history of the seal-engravers' craft as known in Mycenaean Greece must be sought in its original Island home' (Evans, 1935, 549.) Lastly, some of the motifs have very close parallels on extant Cretan seals (Table 5.)

Given this similarity of subject-matter, together with the virtual absence of glyptic art on the mainland before the beginning of Minoan influence, we might suppose without more ado that the miniature pictures in the Shaft Graves were produced by Minoan artists. But, as well as the motifs, the structure of the drawings must be considered; in fact, to arrive at any worthwhile conclusion about the affinity of the Shaft Grave drawings, it is necessary to examine them in a wider context. Three scholars in particular have dealt with this problem of affinity: Agnes Sakellariou, 1966, 91-103 and 1974b; Kenna, 1960, 79-81; and Biesantz, 1954, 26-38. Despite many differences of detail and of terminology, they are in broad agreement that two contrasting styles are discernible in the glyptic art of the Aegean Bronze Age: one which tends to be free, dynamic, and naturalistic, and another which is statuesque and heraldic. They hold, further, that of these styles the first is typically Minoan and the second typically Helladic. Of the three writers named, however, only Biesantz has supported his claims by a rigorous analysis of the structure of selected drawings. For example, he compares a gold ring from Grave IV (Karo's no 241, my Figure 5) with sealings from Crete which also present two principal figures. He finds that, despite the similarity of motif, the drawings from the mainland and from Crete respectively are constructed on different principles, the Mycenae ring resembling the decorative technique of Helladic pottery, the Cretan sealings resembling the decoration of Minoan pottery. He concludes that, even though engraved seals and rings are not known on the mainland before the first appearance of Minoan influence, some at least of the Shaft Grave examples are the work of mainland artists; but mainland artists who had learnt their craft in Crete and, on their return to Greece, had treated Minoan motifs in a Helladic style.

If one looks at the whole range of glyptic art in Crete and on the mainland, one can easily find many examples of the two contrasting styles referred to; but, when it is remembered that Biesantz' researches have been conducted upon only a small proportion of the Cretan material, it is obvious that no final criterion has been established for the differentiation of a Minoan from a Helladic school of glyptic. Consequently, it does not seem possible to

classify the seals and rings from Circle A definitely as
Minoan or as mainland work.   It is easier to make positive
statements about the seals from Grave Circle B.   Of these,
nos 5 and 7 in CMS are undoubtedly Cretan; while the mixture of motifs seen on no 6 is paralleled in Minoan glyptic
art.

THE ORIGIN OF THE SHAFT GRAVES AND THEIR CONTENTS

No close or certain parallels to the Mycenae Grave Circles
have yet come to light.   The 'royal' graves at Alaca Hüyük
in central Anatolia have been tentatively brought into the
discussion (Mellink, 1956), but they disclose few of the
characteristic features of the Shaft Graves.   The group
of thirty-three graves, excavated at Nidri in the island
of Leucas (Dörpfeld, 1927, 217-50), resemble the Shaft
Graves in that they contain some burial-offerings in precious metals and that the precinct of the grave-area is
marked off by walls.   The paucity of ceramic remains in
the Leucas tombs makes dating difficult, but the earliest
of them seem to have been in use at least as early as the
first burials in Circle B at Mycenae.   It is possible,
therefore, that one and the same burial-practice is represented at Leucas and at Mycenae, even though this general
similarity does not extend to details(cf. Hammond, 1974.)
   N.G.L. Hammond has tried to trace the concept of a grave
circle back to the Middle Bronze Age tumulus-burials of
Albania and northern Epirus (Hammond, 1967 and 1973, 1-25).
He believes that during the Middle Bronze Age the practice
of tumulus-burial spread from north to south, since the
burials at Pazhok in central Albania ante-date the earliest graves of Circle B at Mycenae.   This argument contains two false inferences, which vitiate the whole case.
In the first place, we are not obliged to accept a date of
'1800-1700 BC' for the Pazhok graves, merely on the evidence of the weapons found in them.   Even if the date is
correct, we cannot be certain that the Pazhok burials are
earlier than the first construction of a grave circle at
Mycenae since, as was mentioned above, Circle B can be
shown to incorporate parts of an earlier grave circle.
Not even an approximate date can be given to this earlier
circle.   It is very hazardous to assert a diffusion from
north to south when neither at the northern nor at the
southern end can we be sure, within very wide limits, when
the practice in question first appeared.   In the second
place, Hammond has not succeeded in proving that the Grave
Circles at Mycenae were tumuli at all.   Wace, 1921, 124
argued against this assumption with respect to Circle A;

and the assumption does not hold good for Circle B either (Papadimitriou, 1952, 434; Mylonas, 1973, 249-54.)

In the absence of convincing antecedents or parallels for the Shaft Graves, I agree with Wace and Mylonas that most probably they represent a development peculiar to Mycenae itself.   Their increasing size and elaboration and the richness of the offerings in some of the later graves of Circle A cannot, however, be explained as purely local phenomena.   Their explanation calls for an enquiry into the oversea connexions of the early Mycenaean people.

Since the offerings in the graves of Circle A are so varied in character and are rich beyond parallel in Aegean lands, their origin has naturally been a matter of discussion since they were published by Schliemann.   Karo was easily able to refute Evans' opinion that the Minoan appearance of many objects in the graves proved the occupation of Mycenae by a conquering Cretan dynasty; and indeed the small number of Minoan imports in the Shaft Graves, together with the persistence of many Helladic traits, told heavily against Evans.   He had, however, found the strongest support for his theory of a Cretan conquest in the coincidence of the very rich offerings in the graves and the beginning of Cretan influence on the mainland.   The coincidence remained, and required an explanation of some kind.   Karo himself explained the apparently sudden accession of wealth, as well as the promiscuous character of the Shaft Grave treasures, by supposing that many of the objects found in the graves had been plundered from Crete by raiders from the mainland, who took advantage of the devastation in the island toward the end of the Middle Minoan period.   On Karo's view, many works of art in the Shaft Graves which are Minoan in style but Mycenaean in subject-matter were produced by Cretan craftsmen who had been captured during the raids and then set to work on the mainland as slaves (Karo, 1930a, 334-49.)   This theory appeared all the more plausible because, according to Karo, the mainlanders lacked natural resources of their own and so could not have acquired their wealth by means of commerce.

Later discoveries have made it necessary to modify Karo's conceptions about the rise of Cretan influence on the mainland.   Sufficient evidence has been presented above to show that the people of the later Middle Helladic period were not so isolated from the rest of the Mediterranean world as was once supposed.   It is now clear that there was some measure of intercourse between Crete and the mainland long before the mature Shaft Grave era: a fact which it is hard to reconcile with Karo's assumption that the growth of 'royal' power at Mycenae was connected

with the plunder of treasure from Crete.   The objects in
the graves of Circle A may represent, rather, an intensification of commerce with Crete and other places, of which
there is some evidence in the Middle Bronze Age.
The Cycladic connexions of the pottery in Grave Circle
B, already noted, are doubly important.   On the one hand,
they confirm the impression that mainlanders were in contact with Cretans in some parts of the Aegean at least,
since, by the time that Cycladic influences and imports
appear in Circle B, Cretan settlements were thriving on
the islands of Melos, Keos, and Kythera.   On the other
hand, the presence of Cycladic pottery in Grave VI shows
that links with the Cyclades are continued in Circle A
(Karo, 1930a, 254.)   To the extent that the pottery of
Circle A points to contacts with the Cyclades, these simply
carry on the intercourse of the previous period and do not
result from any sudden expansion of a warlike character.
Karo's theory of plunder must be re-examined, having regard to evidence which has come to light since 1930.   It
is perfectly possible that some (but only some) of the
precious objects in the Shaft Graves are the proceeds of
plundering expeditions, although it must be observed that
there is no trace in Crete of any incursion from the mainland.   It may be suggested, however, that Karo's theory
does not provide a complete explanation.   Above all, it
does not take sufficient account of the cosmopolitan nature
of the Shaft Grave offerings, which reflect intercourse
with areas far removed from Crete and the Cyclades.   The
connexions with central and northern Europe have been studied by Bouzek, 1965, 244-8 and by Piggott, 1965, 134-40.
These connexions, which cannot yet be worked out in detail,
are attested most vividly by the presence of amber in both
Grave Circles.   It has proved possible in recent years to
substantiate the view that this amber is of Baltic provenience (Beck, Southard, and Adams, 1972;   Renfrew, 1972,
467-8;   Mylonas, 1973, 350-2;   Harding and Hughes-Brock,
1974.)   Again, the gold diadems with seven circular
bosses found in Circle B as well as in A have a strikingly
close parallel in Grave 20 at Assur (1900-1500 BC)(Haller,
1954, 10 with pl 10a.)   The decoration of a somewhat different type of diadem, no 22 from Grave III, is very similar to that on a sixteenth-century Cassite ring from
Persia (Erlenmeyer, 1964 and 1965.)   Further, a miniature
stag cast in a silver-lead alloy (Karo's no 388 in Grave
IV) has long been recognized as belonging to an Anatolian
type represented at Kültepe (Bissing, 1923;   Akurgal,
1964, 75);   while the silver pin from Grave III, no 75,
was seen by Müller, 1918 as the interpretation of a motif
familiar in Hittite art.   Next, the gold ornaments in the

form of tight spirals (e.g. Mylonas' nos 413-25 in Circle B
and Karo's nos 56-9 and 63-8 in Circle A) resemble finds
from Mesopotamia (Higgins, 1961, 69.)   There is, finally,
the possibility (already noted) that the technique of inlaying metals originated in Syria.

So soon, therefore, as we look at the contents of the
Shaft Graves in the aggregate, we find a situation much
more easily compatible with trading relationships than with
casual plundering raids.   This impression is confirmed if
close attention is paid to certain details.

As I have shown in Table 4, it is possible to arrange
the pottery of Grave Circle A, heterogeneous though it is,
into broad chronological periods, with the Late Helladic I
vessels showing progressively greater influence from Minoan
prototypes.   It is this gradual development which provides
the strongest argument against the explanation of the Shaft
Grave treasures as the proceeds of plunder.   Examination
of the pottery leads to the conclusion that, while the native ceramic tradition retained its full vigour, some mainland craftsmen were beginning to imitate (not always with
great success) the decorative patterns of the Middle Minoan
III and Late Minoan I vase-painters.   The appearance of a
new style of pottery, arising from a fusion of Helladic and
Minoan elements, is not in harmony with the suggested presence of Cretan slaves on the mainland.   Why should these
not have continued to make pottery in the traditional
Minoan style rather than attempt the uneasy compromise represented by the Late Helladic I ware in the Shaft Graves?
On the other hand, if the 'slaves' had been set to work to
adapt Minoan decoration to Helladic shapes, workmanship of
a higher order would have been expected.   When all the obvious differences between pottery manufacture and the pro-
duction of other artefacts are allowed for, it remains true
that, in the one field where external tests can be applied,
both looting from Crete and manufacture by Cretan slaves
seem to be ruled out.   The most probable explanation of
the origin of the earliest Mycenaean pottery is that it was
made by mainlanders who had not yet mastered the techniques
of the new style.   These techniques they learnt, presumably, from Minoan craftsmen who, if they had been slaves,
would have been ordered to make the required pots themselves.   At least with regard to the manufacture of pottery, there must have been some degree of peaceful contact
between Cretans and mainlanders in the Shaft Grave era, although this may have amounted to no more than the migration
of guilds of Minoan artists to the mainland.

The theory of plunder may, perhaps, explain the abundance and variety of the Shaft Grave treasures: what it
cannot explain is the gradual development of mainland art

within Grave Circle A itself.   Another serious objection
to the theory becomes apparent as soon as the phenomena of
the Shaft Graves are compared with the history of the mainland in the succeeding period (my 'Second Phase of Minoan
Influence'.)

The evolution of the mainland in the Second Phase can be
understood only on the supposition of a long period of
peaceful intercourse between Mycenaeans and Cretans.   As
in the Shaft Grave era, there is no sign of an invasion of
Crete by mainlanders; while the circumstances in which
Minoan traits manifest themselves in Greece preclude any
theory of plunder.   At the same time, I know of no reason
to suppose that the Mycenaeans had at their disposal any
greater natural resources in the Second Phase than at the
time of the Shaft Graves.   Of the scholars who believe
that a theory of plunder explains the presence of the Shaft
Grave treasures, Miss H.L. Lorimer is the only one, so far
as I know, who has tried to resolve the difficulties which
become apparent when the Shaft Grave era is compared with
the following period.   She writes as follows:

Plausible, however, as the explanation is, [namely, that
the Shaft Grave treasures are the result of attacking
and despoiling Knossos at about 1570 BC] it does not
account for the spread of Minoan influence in Greece in
the period which immediately succeeds that of the Shaft-
graves, even allowing for the extraordinarily quick recovery achieved by Knossos.   It is conceivable that
large numbers of wealthy Knossians, warned perhaps by
preliminary earth tremors, escaped to Greece, taking as
much as possible of their portable property with them;
in such circumstances they might be able to purchase
permission to settle.   Artists and craftsmen might follow, bringing the implements of their callings.   (Lorimer, 1950, 19.)

Miss Lorimer was far too honest a scholar to minimize the
objectionable consequences of such a course of argument.
In the present case, we may object to her historical reconstruction on the ground that two hypotheses become necessary: one to explain the Cretan influences which appear in
the Shaft Graves (First Phase) and one to account for the
Cretan influences in the Second Phase;   the latter hypothesis is, moreover, rather involved.   I shall try to show
below that it is simpler to work with only one explanation,
whereby the Shaft Grave era and the periods immediately
preceding and following are seen as one historical unit,
throughout which trading relations with Crete, and with
other areas as well, were gradually extended.

Meanwhile, it is necessary to discuss an alternative explanation of the origin of the Shaft Grave treasures.   The

classic statement of this theory is found in Persson, 1942a, 178-96. Since then the theory has been adopted and extended by Marinatos; more qualified support has come from Schachermeyr. According to Persson's theory, princes from the Greek mainland led forces of mercenaries to assist the Egyptians in the expulsion of the Hyksos early in the sixteenth century BC. After the Hyksos had been driven out, the Egyptian king rewarded the Greeks with gifts of precious metals: these were taken back to Mycenae and used by Cretan and Helladic craftsmen to make the gold and silver objects which ultimately were placed in the Shaft Graves as burial-offerings. On their expedition to Egypt, it is said, the Mycenaeans saw for the first time horses and chariots, which on their return they depicted on the stelae of Grave V in Circle A.

The most serious objection to the 'Egyptian' theory, from the present point of view, is that it is vitiated by the same flaw which affects the theory of plunder: namely that, while it may provide an explanation of the presence of treasures at Mycenae, it utterly fails to account for the rise of Minoan influence and its continuation and intensification in the following period.

The evidence adduced in support of the Egyptian theory falls into three classes, each of which demands separate treatment.

1 The word 'hau-nebwet', referred to in Egyptian texts from the middle of the third millennium BC onward, is taken to mean 'inhabitants of the Greek mainland'. There is, however, no evidence that the Egyptians of the Dynastic period understood by this term anything else than the islands of the Mediterranean or the people living in them. The sole reason for identifying 'hau-nebwet' with mainland Greece is that it bears this meaning in administrative texts of the third century BC and later; but the writers of such texts were not always well acquainted with the meaning of ancient geographical terms. The word occurs more than a hundred times in Dynastic texts; but in none of them is there any indication that 'hau-nebwet' refers even to a well-defined place (Gardiner, 1947, 208.)

2 The Greek legend of Danaos is considered to enshrine a reminiscence of dynastic relationships between Egypt and Greece at the beginning of the Late Bronze Age. It is true that in the prevailing version of the legend Danaos comes from Egypt to the Argolid. From the account in Apollodorus 2. 1. 4-5 the stemma shown in Table 6 can be constructed. Agenor and Belos were twin sons of Poseidon by Libye: Agenor went to Phoenicia and his sons founded dynasties in Thebes, Phoenicia, and Cilicia. Belos remained in Egypt, where his sons Aigyptos and Danaos held

sway over different parts of the country;   after a quarrel
between the two brothers, Danaos fled to Argos, displaced
Gelanor, and named the inhabitants 'Danaoi' after himself.
According to a different version of the legend (preserved
by an ancient commentator on line 886 of Euripides'
'Hecuba'), Danaos is a Greek king, who expels his brother
Aigyptos from the Argolid.

A critical examination of the Danaos legend, considered
as evidence for events in the Bronze Age, must begin with a
negative statement.   The eponymous hero Danaos is completely unknown to Homer who, however, frequently uses the
name 'Danaoi' beside 'Argeioi' and 'Achaioi' as a generic
term for the Greeks.   Moreover, Homer never makes any connexion between the 'Danaoi' and Argolis;   and there is even
some reason to place the 'Danaoi' in the north of Greece
(Cauer, 1928, 282-3.)   On the other hand, the tradition
represented by the second version makes no mention of the
'Danaoi'.   It is evident that Danaos and the 'Danaoi' are
never brought into explicit connexion by any source with a
claim to be considered old.   That being so, it remains to
ask how the legend reached the form in which we find it in
Apollodorus.   The reason is that, in origin, the Danaos
legend was only a fairy-tale, bearing as it does several
characteristic marks of the genre, for example the themes
of flight and pursuit, the complementary distribution of
fifty daughters and fifty sons, and the formula 'all the
sons killed except one...' (Megas, 1933.)   Why, then, was
the legend of Danaos and Aigyptos ever superimposed on this
tale?   The answer is plain when we contemplate the family-
tree constructed on the basis of Apollodorus' account.   The
tree represents an attempt to bring into relationship the
great peoples of the eastern Mediterranean;   a connexion
is established not only between Greeks and Egyptians but
between both peoples on the one hand and Phoenicians on the
other;   and, as so often happens, a god is introduced as
grandfather of the principal heroes.   The whole structure
looks so much like an example of rationalization, the
aetiology typical of the Hellenistic mentality, that it is
devoid of value as historical evidence.

3 A number of actual objects from the Shaft Graves have
been thought to attest direct relations with Egypt.   The
difficulty is, as Furumark, 1950, 222 pointed out in words
which have been all too seldom heeded, that whenever Egyptian traits appear in the Shaft Graves they are accompanied
by Minoan features.   That is only to be expected, in view
of the powerful influence exerted by Egypt on Minoan art,
beginning with the Early Palace period.   If there appeared
in the Shaft Graves Minoan motifs rendered in an Egyptian
manner, it would be permissible to argue that the mainlan-

ders borrowed only their themes from Crete and then treated
them in a style which they themselves had acquired in Egypt.
But the opposite is true.   Some subjects of Shaft Grave
art are unquestionably derived from Egyptian originals;
but in every case we can say either that the Mycenaean ar-
tefact is rendered in a typically Minoan manner or that the
Egyptian type was known in Crete before its transplantation
to the mainland.   The first observation holds good for the
wooden box with ivory dogs attached (Karo's no 812/813 from
Grave V), the workmanship of the dogs being purely Minoan
(whatever the place of origin of the theme as a subject for
carved figures - Schweitzer, 1930.)   Again, it is certain
that some of the motifs on a dagger-blade from the same
grave (no 765) are borrowed from Egypt, notably the papyrus
reeds growing along a river-bank and the wild cats stalking
duck.   But we know that the motif of a cat stalking its
prey had been taken over by Cretan artists at least as
early as the Shaft Grave period, for it is seen on one of
the Knossos frescoes belonging to Evans' 'transitional
style' (Evans, 1921, 539-41);   and even before that the
papyrus motif had been assimilated into Minoan art (Furumark, 1972a, 138-9.)

As well as these objects, Grave V yielded a famous rhyton made in the shape of an ostrich-egg, with faience dolphins attached (Karo's no 828.)   No one doubts that the
ostrich-egg as a work of art came to the Aegean from
Egypt;   but, as Evans, 1928, 221-2 showed in a notably full
treatment, the ostrich-egg had been reproduced in ceramic
form in Crete by the Early Palace period (its reproduction
in the form of stone vases comes rather later and is contemporary with the Shaft Graves - Warren, 1969, 88-9);
while the use of faience is as much Cretan as Egyptian.

It can be seen that every one of the superficially Egyptian objects in Grave V either incorporates Minoan decorative features or represents a type known in Crete before
its appearance in the Shaft Graves.   Despite this, wooden
box, dagger-blade, and ostrich-egg are sometimes lumped together as intrusive artefacts which can have come only from
Egypt.   Mylonas, 1969b goes farther.   He deduces from the
presence of these Egyptian elements in Grave V that, of the
three persons buried there, the middle one is a woman: a
queen whom the king of Mycenae had brought back from Egypt.
The case would be much stronger if it could be shown conclusively that the 'queen's' corpse had been embalmed before burial.   Mylonas, of course, assumes that it had
been;   but I can discover in Schliemann, 1878, 342-3 no
actual evidence that this was so (though, indeed, he refers to the 'mummified corpse':   see Hood, 1960b, 62-3.)
Mylonas promises a closer investigation of a lump of earth

which may contain the remains of the 'mummy'; and it is to
be hoped that this enquiry will enable the question to be
settled.

It is claimed that Mycenaean mercenaries learnt the use
of horse and chariot in Egypt, where also they saw stelae
for the first time (e.g. Persson, 1942a, 187.)   As I have
already said, a place of origin cannot yet be assigned,
with any plausibility, to the Shaft Grave stelae; but the
presence of stelae in Circle B (to say nothing of those
found in Middle Helladic contexts at Eleusis and Lerna:
see respectively Mylonas and Travlos, 1952, 61-2; Caskey,
1954, 14) shows that the mainlanders used this kind of
grave-marker before the postulated expedition to Egypt,
for the earliest examples in Greece ante-date the expulsion
of the Hyksos.   It may well be idle to look outside Greece
itself for an origin of the stelae, since a people capable
of building and furnishing the Shaft Graves as we know
them would surely have had the ability of commemorating
the occupants of the tombs by the erection of rather crude
slabs of stone.   As we have seen, any foreign influence
which can be discerned in the conventions of drawing comes
from Crete or the Cyclades, not from Egypt.

There is no good reason to suppose that the Mycenaeans
learnt the use of the war-chariot in Egypt.   If, as Schachermeyr acknowledges in his detailed treatment of the
whole matter (Schachermeyr, 1951 and 1967a, 44-6), the
Minoans had already introduced a characteristic type of
flying gallop into Egypt (where it was subsequently absorbed into the main stream of Egyptian art), why should
they not have taken it direct to the Greek mainland as
well?   After all, the application of a Minoan convention
to a Helladic theme, even though the given subject was
not treated in the same way in Crete itself, finds many
parallels among the Shaft Grave offerings and is, indeed,
typical of the artistic relationship which existed between
Minoans and mainlanders at this period.   A final objection
to Schachermeyr's account is that, while claiming that
mainland Greeks must have seen chariot-scenes in Egypt at
the time of the campaign against the Hyksos, he can point
to no representation of the type in question from the
Hyksos period itself.

Nothing in the archaeological record either in Egypt or
on the Greek mainland is consistent with the belief that
the two areas enjoyed direct and intimate relations as
early as the Shaft Grave period.   In Greece, no certainly
Egyptian object has come to light in any Shaft Grave.   In
Egypt, there is a very small quantity of Late Helladic I-II
pottery (Wace and Blegen, 1939, 145); but exactly how much
of this is contemporary with the Shaft Graves has never

been established.   If we move from the domain of the practical to that of the theoretical, we shall find equally
little that speaks in favour of direct connexion.   It is
permissible to wonder whether the suggested intercourse is
a priori very likely, given the fact that between Egypt and
the mainland lay Crete, which at this very time was ap-
proaching the acme of its power and prosperity.   Schachermeyr, 1949, 341 dealt with this problem (which few besides him have even discerned) by a desperate expedient.
He suggested that the severe earthquake which devastated
the Knossian palace late in the Middle Bronze Age was accompanied by a flood: this caught the Minoan fleet in the
harbours along the northern coast of Crete and destroyed
it.   I hope that it will be possible to arrive at a more
convincing, if less spectacular, explanation of the course
of events.

CONCLUSIONS

The contents of the Shaft Graves themselves attest some degree of mainland trade with the Cyclades, with Crete, with
Anatolia, and with central and northern Europe.   Some of
the objects in the graves are of Baltic, Cretan, Syrian, or
Anatolian origin.   In quite another direction, the discovery of late Middle Helladic pottery in Sicily and the Aeolian Islands points to relations with the Greek mainland,
though not necessarily with Mycenae itself (Taylour, 1958,
182.)   The existence of a network of trade-routes, which
these facts compel us to assume, means that we have no
need of a hypothesis of plunder or warlike expansion in
order to explain the increasing wealth seen in the Shaft
Graves.   Such theories arose, partly, from the fact that
for many years the graves of Circle A were without contemporary parallels either in their manner of disposing of
the dead or in the precious objects they contain.   Now,
however, the same manner of disposition of the dead is
found in the earlier Grave Circle, whose discovery precludes any belief that the graves of Circle A contain the
members of a new and aggressive dynasty previously unrep-
resented on the mainland.   Despite the intrusion of many
Minoan features their culture was, in substance, the same
as that of their predecessors;   and there is no reason to
believe that the differences, such as they are, arose in
any other way than by peaceful and commercial relations
with foreign peoples.   For a long time, the discovery of
the treasures of Circle A did suggest the sudden accession
of wealth on a large scale.   It is, however, equally possible that the lords of Mycenae did not acquire their

wealth when Graves IV and V were constructed, but only then began to devote it to the manufacture of rich burial-gifts.

It would, naturally, be of great interest to discover the principal reasons for the rise of Mycenae at the time of the Shaft Graves.   Although, for the reasons given, I think we can safely exclude a sudden accession of wealth as the result of plunder or by way of reward from a grateful pharaoh, I do not find it possible to reach any positive conclusions.   All the time, we must remember that for the Shaft Grave period we possess only part of the evidence, namely the grave-furniture of a very small number of quite exceptional persons.   What were the circumstances of all the others?   Wace, 1921, 203 inferred the existence of a 'first palace' on the citadel, which would have been contemporary with the graves of Circle A; and more recently a small house has been excavated to the south of Grave Circle B which, like that Circle, spans the transition between Middle and Late Helladic (Orlandos, 1961c, 156-8.)   But neither within the citadel nor outside it has any discovery yet been made which would throw light on the way of life of the majority of inhabitants.   However, if speculation is permissible, the explanation advanced by Hawkes, 1940, 351-2 still seems to me the simplest and most plausible, namely that Mycenae grew to wealth and power mainly because of its strategic position, controlling as it did the trade-routes between the Isthmus and the Argive plain.   Now Dickinson, 1972a has suggested that there was some kind of special relationship between Mycenae and Crete, whereby Mycenae benefited from its control over the supply of some commodity which was of vital importance to the Minoans and for access to which they were prepared to pay heavily.   Although this suggestion may contain part of the truth, I cannot believe that it affords a completely satisfactory explanation for the rise of the wealth of Mycenae.   In my view, the wealth of the inhabitants of Mycenae in the Shaft Grave period should be dissociated from the appearance of Cretan influence; I hold that the mainlanders had long known the reputation of Cretan craftsmen but that they could not afford to patronize them extensively before the mature Shaft Grave era.

It is now much easier than it once was to believe that the display of precious objects in the Shaft Graves has no necessary connexion with the appearance of Minoan traits. This belief is confirmed by a comparison of two burial-sites in western Messenia, Peristeria and Kleidi, both of which are contemporary with the graves of Circle A at Mycenae.   Broadly speaking, we may say that Peristeria exhibits something of the wealth found at Mycenae but little sign of direct Minoan influence, whereas Kleidi yields

Late Helladic pottery of high quality (pottery which, by definition, owes much to Cretan inspiration) but no precious objects. These facts are not only relevant to our enquiry into the affinities of the Shaft Graves but raise larger questions about the nature of the mainland connexion with Crete in the Shaft Grave period.

At Peristeria, an elaborate and well-built complex of three tholoi has been excavated by Marinatos. The third tomb yielded an extraordinary deposit of precious burial-offerings which had been overlooked by robbers (Marinatos, 1966.) Neither the publication of these objects nor the manner of their display in the Chora Museum is worthy of their great importance; but enough is known about them to permit some tentative remarks. The objects of gold, striking enough in their own right, are doubly so when set side by side with the contents of the Mycenae Shaft Graves. The Peristeria offerings not only immediately recall the general character of the Shaft Grave treasures but even, in some cases, are apparently the products of the same school of craftsmen whose works are preserved in the Shaft Graves. The closest similarities are disclosed by miniature gold ornaments, a gold diadem decorated with nine bosses, and gold cups: details are given in my Table 3. Just as at Mycenae, so here the richness and exquisite workmanship of some of the offerings imply the existence of a wealthy settlement nearby. To that extent, I am in agreement with the observations of two contributors to 'The Minnesota Messenia Expedition':

> The rich grave goods from Peristeria now suggest that there was already notable royal wealth in Messenia in the sixteenth century, at about the same time that the burials were being made in the shaft graves of Mycenae. Royal wealth and monumental tomb architecture are fairly sure indicators of a flourishing economy and a broad base on which rulers could levy taxes, tribute, and forced labor... The record indicates that in Messenia (as elsewhere) there probably was a peaceful transition from Middle Helladic isolation to early Mycenaean dynamism. The grave goods from Peristeria suggest that innovative breezes were blowing in southwest as well as northeast Peloponnese as early as the sixteenth century BC. (McDonald and Hope Simpson, 1972, 138-41.)

I believe that more can be said about these 'innovative breezes', but only after taking account of the second relevant Messenian site, Kleidi.

The Bronze Age tumulus at Kleidi was found to contain very little except pottery, but that pottery (amounting to nearly 120 vessels) is of considerable importance in the present discussion. The excavator of the site provides a

detailed catalogue, with full comparative evidence from the
mainland and from Crete (Yalouris, 1965.)   He contributes
the following summary of the pottery-deposits:
> The co-existence within the tombs of pure Middle Hella-
> dic pottery, a fair number of vessels belonging to the
> Middle/Late Helladic transition, and Mycenaean pots
> which represent the survival or development of Middle
> Helladic types can be seen as an indication of the
> close connexion between Middle Helladic and Late Hella-
> dic, which has been emphasized in recent years, and also
> of the organic evolution from Middle Helladic to Late
> Helladic.   (Yalouris, 1965, 36.)

These are, of course, the same three pottery-types which
appear in the Mycenae Shaft Graves.   Not only that, but
it is possible to point to the close similarity between
individual pots from Kleidi and specific vessels in the
Shaft Graves (Table 4.)   Another group of tumulus-burials
in western Messenia, found near the site of the later palace of Pylos, was associated with a little pottery and
with some other objects, such as gold ornaments and bronze
cauldrons, of exactly the same type as examples from the
Shaft Graves (W.D. Taylour in Blegen, 1973, 156-76.)

I think it is certain that, whatever political conditions obtained later in the Mycenaean period, at the time
of the Shaft Graves Mycenae exercised no hegemony in a part
of the Peloponnese so remote as the coast of Messenia and
its hinterland.   That being so, we have to reckon with
the existence of local kingdoms (at least in the western
Peloponnese) which, so far as their material culture is
concerned, exhibit no significant differences from Mycenae
itself.   The results of excavation at Kleidi and Peristeria preclude us from thinking that the rise of a distinctive 'Mycenaean' culture took place first in the Argolid and then spread beyond that area only in the Second
Phase of Minoan Influence.   As happened in the palatial
periods in Minoan Crete, different parts of the mainland
evolved along parallel lines;   there is no question of the
sudden enrichment of one centre, its close association
with the activities of skilled Minoan craftsmen, and the
subsequent diffusion of the resulting culture to peripheral
parts of Greece.   We should rather say, in conformity
with the evidence from Messenia, that several areas of
Greece were being gradually enriched during the sixteenth
century BC: a process which in itself owed nothing to connexions with Crete but which did enable the wealthier centres of Greece to have their artefacts made by Cretan
craftsmen.   The evolution, in Messenia and in the Argolid,
of a homogeneous Mycenaean culture can have taken place
only in a context of trade-routes which linked different
parts of Greece with the outside world and with one another.

The origin of the precious metals used at Mycenae and at Peristeria is, at present, impossible to determine.   I used to believe that the inhabitants of the mainland in the Shaft Grave era had access to sources of gold in Greece and Thrace; but I no longer think that, even if these were in fact available, they could have accounted for more than a small part of the rich burial-offerings. Now that I have read Muhly, 1973 (where for the first time the Mediterranean trade in copper and tin is minutely analysed), I conclude that it is much more likely that the mainlanders acquired their precious metals, like their essential supplies of tin and copper, in the course of a varied and far-flung commerce, of exactly the kind which our discoveries in Greece would lead us to expect.

NOTES

The earliest contacts with Crete

Evidence for trade between Crete and other areas: Wace and Blegen, 1939, 141; Kantor, 1947, 18-20; Catling and Karageorghis, 1960; Smith, 1965, 130-7; Furumark, 1972a, 136-9.   General survey of tholoi by Rachet, 1971.   A derivation of the mainland tholoi from Cretan prototypes is regarded as likely by Hood, 1960a; Pini, 1968, 49; Branigan, 1970b, 152-8.   Pelon, 1974 argues for the independent development of tholoi in Messenia and their subsequent introduction into other parts of Mycenaean Greece.

The Shaft Graves

Middle Helladic graves in general: Blegen and Wace, 1930; Andronikos, 1961, 153-76; Vranopoulos, 1967.   Political independence of the mainland in the Shaft Grave period: Karo, 1930a, 342; Snijder, 1936, 116.   Egyptian influence in the Shaft Graves: Hooker, 1967a.   Art in the Shaft Graves: Vermeule, 1975.   The Late Helladic I pottery style: Dickinson, 1974.

4 The Cretan connexion
(c. 1525–1375 BC)

The Shaft Grave era on the mainland is followed by what I call the Second Phase of Minoan Influence, which extends over the fifteenth century BC.   Since the relationship with Crete is of decisive importance for an understanding of the material culture of the mainland, that subject will bulk very large in this chapter.   Three classes of evidence will be examined: first, the Mycenaean objects from the mainland itself (especially the pottery, seals, and artefacts in precious metals) and the deductions these allow us to make about the nature of the Cretan connexion; second, the Mycenaean and Minoan pottery which has been discovered outside the Aegean and its implications for the relationship between Cretans and mainlanders; last, events in Crete during the Late Palace period, with a discussion of Mycenaean elements which can be discerned at Knossos.

EVIDENCE FROM THE MAINLAND

In this period, the ceramic styles Late Helladic II and IIIa1 predominate on the mainland and Late Minoan Ib, II, and IIIa1 in Crete.   At Mycenae, the principal families were buried in tholos tombs: a type of interment which, as we have seen, had been in use earlier in other parts of Greece, especially Messenia.   Nine tholoi have been excavated at Mycenae, the earliest belonging to the start of our period and the latest, at the end of a long process of development, to the thirteenth century BC.   The three earliest are known respectively as Cyclopean, Epano Phournos, and Aegisthus.   Any precious offerings they once contained have almost completely disappeared, leaving, none the less, a quantity of pottery which testifies to the homogeneity of the early Late Helladic II ceramic style.   The families buried in the tholoi are sometimes referred to as the

Tholos Dynasty, in contrast to the preceding Shaft Grave
Dynasty; but there is nothing in the tombs themselves to
indicate a dynastic change.   At the same time as the appearance of the tholoi, or rather earlier, the first chamber tombs (vaults cut out of the rock of a hill-side and
approached by a dromos, or entrance-passage) were built at
Mycenae and in its neighbourhood: in time, they became the
standard mode of burial in Mycenaean Greece, continuing
well into the Late Helladic IIIc period.   The origin of
the chamber tomb, like that of the tholos, has been the
subject of debate.   In the case of the chamber tomb,
there is no reason to place its conception anywhere else
than the Greek mainland.   New chamber tombs continued to
be built at Mycenae in the thirteenth century BC, while
earlier ones were used for repeated burials.   The first
chamber tombs, as we might expect, contained a good deal
of domestic pottery, decorated for the most part with linear and geometric patterns and vegetable designs: few marine motifs appear.

As in the Shaft Grave era, so in this period little is
known of the palace of Mycenae.   It may be presumed that,
as with the other great Argolid settlement at Tiryns, some
thirteen miles to the south-east, traces of the earlier
structure were largely removed in the course of the extensive enlargement and re-building of the fourteenth century BC.   At both Mycenae and Tiryns, however, and also
at Thebes in Boeotia, there have survived fresco-fragments
from the earlier palaces; and these provide valuable evidence for the nature of the Cretan connexion.

As was seen in the last chapter, one or two sites in
Messenia shared to a remarkable degree the distinctive
Mycenaean culture of the later Shaft Graves.   Now, during
the fifteenth century BC, that culture became more widely
spread.   Settlements containing Late Helladic II pottery
are known in several parts of the Peloponnese.   As at Mycenae, the tholos tomb seems to have been used for the burial of local chieftains.   The few tholoi which have survived in an unplundered state show that very rich offerings
were sometimes buried with the dead.   Laconia, in particular, has been extensively explored (Waterhouse and Hope
Simpson, 1960 and 1961.)   Late Helladic I and II pottery
has been found at a dozen sites there, at four of which
(Analipsis, Kambos, Palaiochori, and Vaphio) tholos tombs
were built in Late Helladic II.   In Messenia, Kakovatos,
Routsi, and Tragana have yielded tholoi containing examples
of Late Helladic IIa pottery.   To the east, a tholos has
been discovered at Thorikos in Attica.   The importance of
Mycenae at this period should not be over-estimated.   It
was, undoubtedly, the most influential place in mainland

Greece; yet Mycenaean settlements were still rare outside
the Peloponnese.   The native Helladic culture was not entirely swamped by the Mycenaean which had grown out of it;
and in many places, including Mycenae itself, pottery of a
Middle Helladic type continued to be made throughout much
of the fifteenth century BC.

The Late Helladic II pottery style has been divided into
two successive phases, a and b (Furumark, 1972a, 477-97.)
The IIa style, like the Late Helladic I from which it evolved, was created independently on the mainland.   It discloses a much greater amount of Cretan influence than is
apparent in the pottery of Late Helladic I, and yet this
Cretan influence was never so great as altogether to sub-
merge the mainland elements: rather, the motifs borrowed
from Minoan pottery were transformed in characteristic
ways.   Considerably more IIa than Late Helladic I pottery
has survived; its execution is far more accomplished; and
it is much more widely dispersed.   The IIb style, on the
other hand, simply continues the tradition of IIa, with increasing stylization, diminution in the number of decorative motifs employed, and absence of new influences from
Crete.   It would hardly be legitimate to infer from this
difference between the two pottery styles alone that, in the
early part of the fifteenth century BC, relations between
Crete and the mainland were at first very close and then
fell off as the century advanced; but, as will be seen,
the accuracy of this picture, which may be tentatively
drawn from the evidence of pottery, is confirmed by the
nature of commercial relationships within the Mediterranean.

In the fifteenth century, as in the previous period,
actual imports of Cretan pottery are rarely found on the
mainland.   At the same time, a marked change is apparent
in the status of the potter's craft.   In the Shaft Graves
pottery plays only a humble part: it is simply accessory
to the rich offerings in metal.   But in the unplundered
tholoi, and even in some of the chamber tombs, clay vessels
are proportionately more numerous, and greater care has
been spent on their design and manufacture.   The most impressive type is the large 'Palace Style' pithoid jar (to
use Furumark's term), which usually has three vertical handles on its shoulder and is often richly decorated over its
entire surface (Figure 3.)   This type of vessel hardly
occurs in Cretan tombs until the Late Minoan II period
(late fifteenth century), but it takes a central place in
mainland tholoi from the beginning of that century.   The
finest series of entire jars comes from tholoi at Kakovatos
in Messenia.   Their decoration marks a great advance in
technique over the vases from the Mycenae Shaft Graves.

Vase 1 from Kakovatos, for example, reflects the resurgence
of the so-called Marine Style in contemporary Crete.   Argonauts are shown on the upper part, while on the lower
seaweed appears to grow from the rocks, very much in the
Minoan manner.   This imitation of the fully-developed Cretan Marine Style is very important in the present discussion;   not because it occurs often, but because the use of
the Marine Style at a site far removed from Crete indicates
the extent to which (at least in the domain of artistic
motifs) Cretan culture had penetrated the mainland at this
period.   In Late Helladic I, the mainland artist who was
copying the Cretan style used only a few conventional motifs from the Late Minoan Ia repertory;   while by Late Helladic IIb naturalistic decoration had begun to degenerate
into mere patterns.   But in the intervening period, short
as it was, a considerable number of motifs were assimilated, very little later than their appearance in Crete;   and
both marine and plant life was depicted with a greater fi-
delity to nature than at any other time, earlier or later,
on Mycenaean pottery.   The period of experiment seems to
be over: that of degeneration and petrifaction has not yet
set in.   We may infer from the first appearance of the
Marine Style, when it is set alongside other evidence, that
the early part of the fifteenth century marks the culmination of Minoan influence on the mainland.

A cemetery of chamber tombs at Prosymna, scarcely five
miles south-east of Mycenae, yielded artefacts belonging
to all three periods of the Mycenaean age.   Precious gold
objects and inlaid dagger-blades, which are most probably
of Late Helladic II date, continue the Shaft Grave traditions in style and technique (Blegen, 1937, 267-9 and 330-
2 with pl II.)   At Routsi, in Messenia, one of a pair of
tholoi was found in an unplundered state.   In the tomb
was the skeleton of a warrior together with burial-gifts
of swords, daggers, a spear-head, a gold seal, and gems.
Two very fine inlaid daggers are of Shaft Grave type.   The
first is an example of the Cretan Marine Style at its best,
while the second shows leopards stalking their prey (Marinatos, 1956, pl 101):   a similar subject to that of Karo's
no 765 from Shaft Grave V.   The vases, found at a lower
level, are mostly of fine Late Helladic IIa ware;   but one,
a squat 'stirrup-jar' (Figure 3), decorated with zig-zags
and double axes (Marinatos, 1956, pl 99β), looks like a
Cretan import: one of the few imports of Cretan pottery
in the whole Mycenaean age, and the earliest stirrup-jar
so far known on the mainland.

The development of minor arts in this period is represented by the seals and gold rings from Routsi and Vaphio.
The influence from Crete is seen to be even stronger than

in the Shaft Graves; and CMS no 261 at Vaphio, which presents a typically Minoan combination of talismanic motifs,
is regarded by Kenna, 1960, 52 as an import from Crete.
Many of the other Vaphio seals have a strong affinity with
Cretan glyptic; but, as with the Shaft Grave material, it
is not possible to say for certain whether they were produced on the mainland or in Crete.
  At Vaphio Tsountas found also two gold cups of very fine
workmanship, both of which are engraved with bull-scenes in
repoussé. The triple composition on each cup resembles a
frieze and, indeed, may be related to the art of the fresco, since scenes with bulls are attested on friezes at Knossos (e.g. Evans, 1930, 209-32.) In any case, the appearance of bulls as dominant features makes one look at once
to Crete, especially since scenes of bull-grappling are
known in Cretan art as early as the Middle Minoan age (cf.
Levi, 1925, 120, no 108; Popham, 1973, 58 with fig 38.)
The shape of the cups (often known, simply, as the 'Vaphio'
shape), though unquestionably Minoan in origin, was introduced into the mainland in Middle Helladic times, so that
its recurrence at Vaphio does not in itself prove a direct
borrowing from Crete. One consideration makes me hesitate
to assign a Minoan origin to the cups, namely the difference between the bulls and the type usually represented in
Cretan art: they are heavier, more formal and massive -
in fact, they bear much the same relationship to Cretan
bulls that the lion's head rhyton from Shaft Grave IV has
to Cretan lions. No certainty is possible about the origin of the Vaphio cups; but, having regard to the Helladic
appearance of the principal figures, I think it is likely
that they were made by Mycenaean craftsmen who had come
under strong Minoan influence (K. Müller, 1915, 325-31.)
A way out of the dilemma, but one which I shrink from following, has been shown by Davis, 1974, who suggests that
perhaps one of the cups is of mainland, the other of Cretan
fabrication.
  The extent to which Minoan motifs had penetrated the
mainland by the early fifteenth century BC is shown most
vividly by the objects of religious significance which now
make their first well-attested appearance in Greece. Among
this class, the Great Goddess Ring (Mycenae) and the Daemon
Ring (Tiryns) probably belong to our period. Detailed
discussion of these is deferred to Chapter 8; for the moment it may be remarked that, while the occurrence of cult-
scenes of Minoan type in itself proves little for the actual beliefs of the Mycenaeans, it constitutes good evidence for the mainlanders' interest in things Minoan and
the value they placed on them.

Fresco-painting, which formed such an impressive part of
the decoration of Minoan settlements not only in Crete but
also in Melos and Thera, was practised on the mainland at
least as early as the beginning of the fifteenth century
BC. As a result of his comparative study of mainland
frescoes Rodenwaldt, 1912b, 202 concluded that all the earliest paintings at Tiryns, Orchomenos, and Mycenae were
executed by Cretan artists. I think it safer to say that
the fragments of wall-paintings from the fifteenth-century
mainland palaces give the same impression that is suggested
by some of the Cretan monuments in the Shaft Graves: that
is, that they are thoroughly Minoan in style and technique,
but in subject-matter they answer more closely the demands
of mainland taste. Many fragments, for example, depict
scenes of warfare or hunting, which are rare, though not
unknown, in Crete. A frieze showing a warrior and his at-
tendants with chariots and horses was painted in the early
palace at Mycenae, while examples from Tiryns show chariots
and soldiers. On the other hand, one Tiryns fragment forms
part of a cult-scene, with a 'daemon' of Minoan type before
an altar. Wholly Minoan in spirit are the fragments depicting vegetable life. Two friezes of women belong to
this, the earliest phase of mainland fresco-painting. The
first, in the Kadmeion at Thebes, is dated by Reusch, 1956
to a period not later than 1500 BC. The fragments from
Mycenae of a frieze of women (perhaps carrying offerings)
are of the date and style of the Theban frieze. But, of
all the mainland frescoes of our period, the shield-frieze
at Tiryns most closely resembles an actual example from
Knossos. It is strikingly similar in its composition, use
of colour, and elaborate details, but it is on a much smaller scale than the Knossos frieze (Evans, 1930, 302-8.)
The evidence of the palace frescoes thus corroborates that
of the minor arts: even from the sparse remnants we can
detect a blending of mainland and Cretan styles, in which
neither is completely dominant.

While pottery of the Late Helladic IIa style was in
vogue, a veneer of Minoan culture was spread over many
parts of the mainland. But, when IIb pottery comes into
use, there are few signs of continuing contact with Crete.
The pottery of the new style has few affinities with the
contemporary Late Minoan II ware of Crete and has purely
mainland antecedents. Yet Mycenaean pottery, owing progressively less to direct inspiration from Crete, is more
widely diffused in Greece than before. It has been found
at many sites in central and southern areas, and even in
Thessaly, as well as in the Argolid. Two tholoi in Thessaly apparently belong to this period: one at Volos (the
ancient Iolkos), which contained a number of gold ornaments

and a little coarse IIb pottery, and the other at Yeoryikon, near the Pindus range.

In IIb pottery, the naturalistic Cretan motifs taken up
in the preceding period are stylized to the point at which
it is hard to believe that the artist is thinking in terms
of a real plant or a real creature. An entirely new class
of mainland pottery, 'Ephyraean ware', which descends immediately from Yellow Minyan, was created at this time
(Wace and Blegen, 1916, 182-3.) Only one shape and one
decorative scheme are found. The shape is that of the
Minyan deep two-handled goblet. A single motif is drawn
(in lustrous paint) in the field between the two handles.
This motif consists, most often, of a highly stylized
flower. In proportion and in technique the Ephyraean
goblets represent the highest achievement of Minyan ware,
and one with which Crete had nothing to do (Figure 3.)

Furumark, 1950, 264-5 was the first to draw attention to
the rich finds in a number of mainland tombs dating from c.
1400 BC and associated, in some cases, with Late Helladic
IIIa1 pottery. Since Furumark wrote, the IIIa1 style has
been studied afresh by Elizabeth French, 1964, on the basis
of a closed deposit at Mycenae. Renewed influences from
Crete are seen on pithoid jars from Berbati and Asine.
Some of the contents of the Dendra tholos also point to a
Cretan origin: for example the great gold cup, which is
decorated with octopods, dolphins, and argonauts and with
accessory details representing sea-anemones, coral, and a
rocky sea-bed. The whole bears indubitable marks of Cretan
workmanship and is dated by Persson, 1931, 43-6 to c. 1500
BC.   He thinks that the cup is part of loot plundered
from Crete in an expedition of about 1400.   The same date
and place of origin are suggested for the silver and gold
cup of 'Vaphio' shape with a bull-scene (Persson, 1931,
50-2.)   Some finely worked gems and gold rings come from
tombs dated to the end of the fifteenth century, and the
majority of them (e.g. CMS, nos 181-9) show purely animal
motifs.   Others suggest closer affinities with Crete:
such are a picture of bull-leaping on an Asine ring (CMS,
no 200) and a cult-scene of Minoan type on a worn ring
from Chamber Tomb 10 at Dendra (CMS, no 191.)   The bronze
corslet which Verdelis found in another chamber tomb at
Dendra was probably deposited there at a time not far dis-
tant from 1400 BC, to judge from its association with IIIa1
pottery and its resemblance to drawings of armour on the
nearly contemporary Linear B tablets at Knossos (Aström,
1967; Verdelis, 1967.)   Pottery closely similar to the
deposit in Dendra 10 was found in Tomb I on the Athenian
Agora.   This tomb is not only outstanding in size in the
Agora cemetery but rightly famous because of a masterpiece

of the ivory-carver's art which was discovered there.   The
larger of two ivory boxes ('pyxides') is carved with a
scene involving an attack on two deer by a winged griffin.
The wind-swept trees and rocky protrusions suggest Minoan
antecedents, but the formal style in which the figures are
rendered is more appropriate to a Mycenaean artist (Immerwahr, 1971, 166.)

The impact of Crete on the mainland at about 1400 BC is
quite different in character from the Cretan influences we
saw at work in the Shaft Graves.   There, the influence
from Crete became gradually stronger over a long period
and was, moreover, the prelude to the Second Phase, in
which intercourse between Crete and the mainland was particularly close.   By contrast, Cretan imports and signs of
Cretan influence appear quite suddenly in mainland tombs at
the end of the fifteenth century BC; and these Cretan
traits, so far from being developed in the Third Phase of
Minoan Influence, rapidly die out, leaving the arts of the
mainland to develop along largely independent lines.   Although, for reasons already given, the Shaft Grave treasures cannot be regarded as the result of plundering expeditions to Crete, such an explanation will account for
the nature and the date of the objects now under discussion.

So much for the Cretan connexion, as seen from the
mainland side.   The activities of Crete must now be considered, first in those oversea areas where Cretans and
Mycenaeans came into contact, then in the island itself.

EVIDENCE FROM OVERSEAS

A large number of sites in the Aegean, in the Levant, and
in Cyprus have yielded Minoan and Mycenaean pottery dated
to the sixteenth and fifteenth centuries BC.   But this
pottery, useful as it is in indicating the widespread
trade in which the Aegean lands participated during our
period, tells us little about the relative importance of
Crete and the mainland or about their interrelationships.
One or two sites, however, are more informative, either
because they have been excavated more thoroughly or because
they give evidence of actual settlement, not merely random
finds of Aegean pottery.   It is, unfortunately, upon the
basis of evidence from these few sites that our historical
conclusions have to be drawn.

There can be little doubt that, by the beginning of the
fifteenth century BC, Minoan colonies had been planted on
a number of islands in the Aegean.   Many years ago, clear
traces of a script derived from Cretan Linear A were discovered by the excavators of the Minoan settlement in Melos.

The picture thereby given of Minoan settlers and traders taking their script with them and using it for commercial purposes can be filled out considerably, now that Linear A signs have been found in Keos, Kythera, Naxos, and Thera as well.   At Thera, the last Cretan pottery is of the Late Minoan Ia style; but, at two other well-explored Cycladic islands, namely Melos and Kythera, we witness a development which may almost be taken as a model for what happened at Minoan settlements at Miletus and in Rhodes.   The last substantial deposits of Minoan pottery, or of local pottery made in imitation of it, belongs to Late Minoan Ib; thereafter, the imported pottery tends to be Mycenaean, in increasingly greater proportions.

A Minoan settlement was founded at Trianda, in the north of Rhodes, c. 1550 BC.   That the settlement was Minoan in origin is adequately proved by its pottery, buildings, and frescoes.   For more than a century Trianda was a flourishing Minoan site, producing local ware imitated from Minoan originals as well as importing pottery from Crete.   Small amounts of Mycenaean ware begin to appear in the second and third strata.   The Minoan settlement seems to have been abandoned a little before 1400 BC.   A good deal of Late Helladic IIIa2 pottery is found in Rhodes, especially at Ialysos, a Mycenaean settlement close to the already deserted site of Trianda.   Later in the fourteenth century BC, Mycenaean pottery penetrates the whole of the island.

That Cretan colonists went still farther afield is shown by the German excavations at Miletus, on the Anatolian coast.   The upper Bronze Age strata yielded rich quantities of Mycenaean pottery, beginning with Late Helladic I. But, in the deepest level, there were found remains of a building decorated with a fine fresco in the Minoan manner. A good deposit of Cretan pottery, of a transitional Middle-Late Minoan type, was discovered in this building, and in the same level some Late Helladic I pottery.   Above the burnt level, which belongs to the late fifteenth century, the pottery is exclusively Mycenaean.   Miletus thus provides evidence very similar to that from Rhodes.   A Minoan settlement is founded early in the Late Bronze Age; it maintains contact with Mycenaeans over a long period; and it is finally superseded by a Mycenaean colony at about 1400 BC.

The question of Egyptian relations with the Aegean in the sixteenth and fifteenth centuries BC is more complex and deserves special treatment.   After the expulsion of the Hyksos, the power of Egypt was on the increase during the Late Minoan period.   The early rulers of the New Kingdom pursued an aggressive policy abroad, especially in the Levant.   In the first half of the fifteenth century, Tuth-

mosis III made the Egyptian naval power paramount along the
Syrian coast, and Egypt seems to have exercised a general
suzerainty over the Syrian princes.   At the same time,
Egyptian sea-borne trade became increasingly important.   If
this resurgent Egyptian power is remembered, it will not
easily be assumed that either Mycenaeans or Cretans enjoyed
anything in the nature of a trading monopoly, at least in
the Levant.   Very few Aegean imports of the Late Minoan I-
II period have been found in Egypt.   The imported Aegean
pottery falls into the following categories:

Late Helladic I:	none	Late Minoan Ia:	one
Late Helladic IIa:	nine	Late Minoan Ib:	five
Late Helladic IIb:	six	Late Minoan II:	none

No far-reaching conclusions ought to be drawn from these
meagre quantities.   By themselves they cannot possibly
prove, as a number of writers have thought, that within our
period the mainland completely ousted Crete as the Aegean
trading-partner of the Egyptians (so, for example, Kantor,
1947, 37-8 and Merrillees, 1972a.)   When Merrillees makes
the end of the Late Minoan Ib ceramic style coincide with
the death of Tuthmosis II (c. 1500 BC) he is seriously in
error, since pottery of this type continued to be made far
into the fifteenth century.   Upon the basis of this error
Merrillees commits another.   He infers that Aegeans depicted in four fifteenth-century tomb-paintings at Egyptian
Thebes must be Mycenaeans, since by this time the Minoans
appear no longer to have had direct relations with Egypt.
The tombs are, in chronological order, those of Senmut,
Amenuser, Rekhmire, and Menkheperreseneb.   The paintings
show tributaries, or perhaps rather ambassadors, bearing
objects which are unquestionably of Aegean provenience
('Vaphio' cups, pithoid jars, bull-rhyta), but which could
have come equally well from Greece or from Crete.   Even if
Merrillees were correct in his deduction that, when the
Senmut paintings were executed (c. 1490 BC) Minoan pottery
was completely absent from Egypt, that fact must not be allowed to obscure another, which is far more significant:
namely, that figures in this earliest painting (and even
some of those in the later ones) resemble men depicted on
Knossian frescoes in pigmentation, in details of dress and
coiffure, and in beardlessness.   It is difficult to avoid
the conclusion that at least as late as 1490 Cretans were
to be seen about the Egyptian court.   It is true that the
'tributaries' on the Amenuser fresco look like mere copies
of the figures in Senmut's tomb, while on the Rekhmire
painting the artist began to represent Cretans but then
deleted the Minoan features and replaced them by non-Aegean
ones.   The latest of the series shows figures whose dress
and coiffure are only remotely descended from those of the

Senmut painting.   It has, accordingly, been argued that
first-hand acquaintance with Cretans (attested by the Senmut fresco) was gradually lost during the fifteenth century.
It may well be that the importance of Crete did diminish to
some extent in Egyptian eyes.   On the other hand, the
painters of the later frescoes do not betray an increasing
preoccupation with Mycenaeans.   Why should they, when they
are more interested in the Levantine peoples with whom
Egypt had progressively closer relations as the century advanced?

Whatever the state of affairs suggested by the distribu-
tion of Aegean pottery in Egypt and by the figures in the
Theban tombs, discoveries of a different character ought
to persuade us that some degree of direct contact between
Egypt and Crete, as well as that between Egypt and the
Greek mainland, persisted throughout the fifteenth century.

On the Egyptian side, account must be taken of a statue-
base inscribed with the names of peoples subject to Amenhopis III.   In the flamboyant manner of Eighteenth Dynasty
kings, the inscriptions assert Egyptian overlordship over
(among other places) Amnisos, Knossos, and Lyktos.   On the
Aegean side, both Crete and the mainland provide testimony
of contact with Egypt.   The mainland has produced a scarab probably dating from the reign of Hatshepsut (first
half of the fifteenth century) and a cartouche of Amenhopis
III (late fifteenth and early fourteenth century).   From
Crete the evidence is more telling still.   In the 'Royal
Tomb' at Isopata near Knossos (Late Minoan II-IIIa1) Evans
found alabaster vases of Egyptian origin.   More recently,
Alexiou has recovered further Egyptian vases from tombs at
Katsamba (also near Knossos and belonging to the same period as the Isopata tomb):   of great significance is an
alabaster vessel incised with a cartouche of Tuthmosis
III.   Alexiou rightly holds that this last vase points to
direct contact (perhaps even of a 'diplomatic' kind) between Knossos and the Egyptian court.

Egypt is shown to have had some degree of commerce with
both Crete and mainland Greece throughout our period.   Of
course there is no question of the colonization of any part
of Egypt by Aegeans.   Even the presence in Egypt of Cretan settlers, which some scholars have inferred from the
association of the word 'keftiu' with a list of names
(early Eighteenth Dynasty), cannot be regarded as certain,
since there is no cogent reason to accept the simple equation 'keftiu' = Crete.   'Keftiu' seems to be a term of
vaguer connotation, indicating foreign regions whose precise whereabouts were unknown to the scribes or of no consequence to them.

EVIDENCE FROM CRETE

During our period all the principal Cretan sites, Knossos
and Mallia in the north, Phaistos and Ayia Triada in the
south, and Gournia, Palaikastro, and Zakro in the east,
were brought to a violent end.   When Evans dealt with
these catastrophes in the fourth volume of his Palace of
Minos, he set in parallel two sets of facts: first, the
most advanced pottery burnt in the devastation of Cretan
sites outside Knossos belonged to the Late Minoan Ib ceramic phase, whereas the latest burnt pottery at Knossos itself (with which the Linear B tablets and sealings were associated) was of the succeeding Late Minoan II style;   second, the Late Minoan II period at Knossos had a militaris-
tic and bureaucratic colouring unprecedented in Minoan history and unparalleled at any other Cretan site.   Evans accounted for these phenomena in the simplest possible way.
He thought that the inhabitants of Knossos had destroyed
the other Cretan sites one by one and then, under the leadership of a new and aggressive dynasty, had assumed control of the whole island.   A different cause had obviously
to be found for the terrible fire which devastated the palace of Knossos itself c. 1400 BC;   and this Evans attributed tentatively to an earthquake (Evans, 1935, 885 and
942.)
     Evans' interpretation of the data available to him has
been contradicted by more recent writers.   Before considering their opinions, we must in fairness remark that investigations in more than one field have tended to confirm
Evans' position.   Students of Minoan pottery have added
sharper detail to the picture drawn by him, but they have
not altered it fundamentally.   After an examination of the
ceramic evidence from fifteenth century Crete, Furumark,
1972b, 82 concluded that Gournia, Pseira, Mochlos, and Palaikastro came to an end at some time before the close of
Late Minoan Ib.   The latest palace pottery from Ayia
Triada also, according to Furumark, belongs to Late Minoan
Ib.   Platon's excavations at Zakro show that there too
the palace was devastated in the same period (Platon, 1963,
187.)   The destruction of the Knossian palace must, without question, be placed at a later date than the end of
the other major sites.   Furumark, 1972b, 84 was able to
confirm the belief of other investigators (for instance
Evans, 1935, 357 and Schachermeyr, 1949, 347) that the
pottery actually in use when the palace fell belonged to
the very earliest phase of Late Minoan III: in Furumark's
nomenclature, Late Minoan IIIa1.   Now Popham, 1970, 79-88
reports the presence of Late Minoan IIIa2 pottery in burnt
material at Knossos: that would date the end of the palace
to about 1370 BC.

An alternative explanation of the destruction of Cretan
sites was first proposed by Marinatos, 1939 and has since
won many adherents. According to this theory, the eruption of the volcano on the island of Thera (about eighty
miles north of Crete), which buried the flourishing Minoan
settlement there c. 1500 BC, was responsible also for the
destruction of many sites in Crete itself. Despite the
weighty support which has been accorded this theory, I believe for the following reasons that it is less worthy of
credence than Evans' own explanation.

1 Although Thera undoubtedly witnessed two or even more
eruptions during the Late Bronze Age, including the explosion which destroyed a large part of the island, the only
eruption that can actually be dated took place in Late
Minoan Ia. That a later eruption, which is supposed to
have destroyed the Cretan sites, took place fifty years or
so after the first is a possibility merely, not a certainty.
After intensive search, particles from the eruption of
Thera have been found in Crete (cf. Hédévari, 1971; Cadogan, Harrison, and Strong, 1972; Vitaliano, 1974.) The
preliminary results 'seem to suggest that the eruption
could not have occurred much later than the end of Late
Minoan Ia' (Vitaliano, 19): a statement which ought to
disconcert those who seek to connect the eruption with
events in Crete in the Late Minoan Ib period.

2 The assertion that the Cretan sites were destroyed by
the effects of an eruption naturally implies that they were
destroyed simultaneously. Here is another fact which cannot be verified from the archaeological record. The excavation reports teach us merely that the horizon of destruction must be placed within the lifetime of a given
style of pottery; so far as that evidence goes, a generation or more could easily separate one destruction from
another.

3 It is hard to understand what is supposed to have been
the immediate cause of the destructions. A fall of pumice
and hot ash can hardly have put paid in such a wholesale
manner to the Cretan settlements, many of which were never
subsequently re-occupied. Tidal waves caused by the eruption must also be ruled out as an effective cause. They
are incompatible with the severe conflagration attested at
several sites, and they could not have affected an inland
and elevated site such as Phaistos (so Page, 1970, 38.)

4 The theory of volcanic destruction of Minoan sites
fails altogether to account for the sequence of events at
Knossos. At that site, no signs of a violent transition
from Late Minoan Ib to Late Minoan II have been discovered,
save for a few pieces of burnt pottery. So far from being
destroyed at the end of Ib, Knossos went on to witness the

brilliant epoch which corresponds to the ceramic periods of
Late Minoan II and Late Minoan IIIa1.   The survival and
indeed the aggrandizement of Knossos are impossible to reconcile with Marinatos' theory, while they are satisfactorily explained by Evans (Hood, 1971a and 1973c.)   The
building of numerous rich tombs in the neighbourhood, the
reconstruction of the palace itself, the genius of the potters, fresco-painters, and gem-engravers, and the vast resources and intricate organization reflected in the Linear
B archives prove that it was no period of decadence which
preceded the destruction of Knossos.   A fact may be added
which has become apparent only since the decipherment of
the Linear B script, but which makes it harder still to accept the theory of volcanic destruction.   The place-names
on the Linear B tablets show that at the very end of the
palatial period the Knossian bureaucrats had a close interest in many parts of the island, including some which, we
are told, had been blighted by the fall of volcanic ash and
so made uninhabitable.

When I turn to examine the last phase of palatial culture at Knossos, I find it hard to give a coherent account
or even to separate facts from theories.   But an attempt
must be made, since an accurate appraisal of this period is
essential to an understanding of the relations between the
mainland and Crete.

Before the last war, there was a prolonged debate between two opposed schools of thought about the main trend of
Aegean history in the sixteenth and fifteenth centuries BC.
The followers of Evans believed that the contents of the
Mycenae Shaft Graves put beyond question a Minoan dominion
in the Argolid.   In the next period, according to Evans'
school, there took place a considerable expansion of the
Minoan culture which, after the destruction of Knossos, was
transferred in its entirety to what Evans called its 'mainland branch'.   On the other side of the debate, Karo, Blegen, and Wace insisted that the culture of the mainland
continued to be basically Helladic and that the Minoan features seen there suggested artistic influence only, not political control.   Although Evans recognized that the closing stage of the palatial period at Knossos was different
in some important respects from the preceding phases of
Minoan history, he had no reason to suppose that it was
less deeply rooted in the native culture than any that had
gone before.   It is not surprising that the opponents of
Evans took quite a different view.   They wondered whether,
so far from there being a Knossian hegemony in the Aegean
in Late Minoan I and II, Knossos itself might have come
under powerful influence from the mainland, at least toward
the end of this period.

The demonstration by Ventris that the Linear B tablets
preserved by the fire at Knossos contain Greek words and
forms seemed to Wace and his school to provide a clinching
argument in favour not only of mainland influence in Late
Minoan II Knossos but of an actual invasion of Crete by
Greek-speaking dynasts from the mainland. It seemed inconceivable that, if the inscriptions recovered from the
ruins of the Knossian palace were written in Greek, the
palace had all the time been under the control of native
kings. It was thought, on the contrary, that the new warlike kings were Mycenaeans, who had seized Knossos at about
1450 BC and established themselves in the palace there,
building a throne room on the model of the mainland megara
and administering the whole island from this centre. After
quite a short tenure by Mycenaeans, the palace was destroyed either by a rival Greek power or by Cretan rebels.

The picture of Knossos under the sway of Mycenaeans was
vividly drawn by Wace, 1973. Although, in Wace's eyes,
the decipherment of the Linear B script afforded conclusive
proof of the Mycenaean character of Late Minoan II Knossos,
he was able to list a number of other features which pointed to the same conclusion. These alleged proofs of Mycenaean invasion and control must now be examined. If it is
found that a substantial number of them fulfil the stringent conditions needed to prove domination by a foreign
power, then we may conclude that the presence of the Greek
language in the Knossos tablets is satisfactorily explained in the way indicated by Wace. If, on the other
hand, those same features turn out to be inconclusive or
suggest that the palace at Knossos retained its essentially
Minoan character to the end of its existence, as Evans believed, we must not feel obliged to accept the new ortho-
doxy of Wace and his followers; for, of course, the presence of a foreign language may be due to many causes besides that of conquest. To begin with the pottery:

In 1920 it was observed that a class of vases similar to
the Ephyraean vases of the Mainland was found at Knossos
belonging to the same general date, the second phase of
the Late Bronze Age. The Knossian examples, however,
are less well made and less well designed... Further, it
became apparent that the type of vase called by Evans
an alabastron, which occurs throughout the Late Bronze
Age, is far more common on the Mainland of Greece than
in Crete... Vases of the Palace Style, large amphorae,
are on the Mainland a notable feature of the Late Helladic II period... Careful study of these three classes
of vases indicates that in all probability their occurrence in Crete is due to influence from the Mainland.
(Wace, 1973, xxvi-xxvii.)

In commenting on these remarks of Wace's, I observe that
it is now generally agreed that the reaction of Mycenaean
upon Knossian pottery is confined to two vessel-shapes, the
three-handled pithoid jar (Wace's Palace Style amphora) and
the Ephyraean goblet; for, since Alexiou's excavations at
Katsamba, there is no reason to see in the alabastron any
sign of foreign influence (Hutchinson, 1954.) Wace, who
is concerned to prove a Mycenaean domination of Knossos at
this time, concedes that Cretan imitations of Ephyraean
ware are markedly inferior to their mainland prototypes in
fabric and in design. How, then, can we reconcile the
suggestion of mainland domination with the fact that this
characteristic shape of Mycenaean pottery was being imitated, with no great success, by Cretan craftsmen? The invasion by aggressive mainlanders in which we are asked to
believe would, I suppose, have provoked the rise of a new
ceramic style, as it did in Rhodes. Failing the establishment of a new local style, the Mycenaeans would surely
have brought their own pottery with them; and yet only a
few pieces of mainland pottery have been found at Knossos -
meagre relics of two generations of Mycenaean overlords.

About the 'Palace Style' vases there is this to be said.
The large size of this ware, its relatively poor fabric and
florid decoration, and, above all, its appearance in graves
alongside weapons certainly suggest that its use was inspired by mainland habits.   There is, however, a fatal objection to the view that a conquest by mainlanders can be
deduced from the occurrence of Palace Style pottery at
Knossos.   This is that the Late Minoan II style grows organically out of Late Minoan Ib, which at Knossos overlaps
it chronologically.   Late Minoan II pottery, moreover,
uses a number of motifs which have clear antecedents in
Late Minoan Ib but in no phase of mainland ceramic.   All
this Furumark established in 1941 and corroborated in 1950,
with copious documentation.   More recently, Hood's discoveries of monumental Late Minoan Ib pottery to the north of
the 'Royal Road' at Knossos have enabled us to see more
clearly the true ancestry of the Late Minoan II Palace
Style (Hood, 1961, 294-5.)

Wace continues:
Other Mainland influences can be discerned.   The beehive tombs [tholoi] so characteristic of the Mainland,
especially in Late Helladic II, are represented by a
few examples at Knossos; and at Knossos alone in the
whole of Crete at this time, so far as our present knowledge goes.   On the other hand, on the Mainland between
forty and fifty beehive tombs are known: thus if number is the principal test beehive tombs seem to be a
feature of the Mainland, where their structural develop-

ment can be followed, rather than of Knossos.   (Wace,
1973, xxvii.)
This is a curiously self-defeating argument; as if one
could deduce the influence of one area on another, not from
the large number but from the small number of characteristic
remains.   In any case (as was seen in the last chapter),
the practice of building tholoi near Knossos probably was a
purely Cretan one, especially if Hutchinson, 1956 is right
in dating to Late Minoan Ia the construction of the tholos
on the Kephala ridge.
    Lastly, I refer to two features of the last palace at
Knossos which seemed to Wace, and have seemed to many
others, to confirm their belief that at this period Knossos
formed a Mycenaean enclave.   In Wace's own words: 'The
three palaces so far excavated on the Mainland at Tiryns,
Mycenae and Pylos have throne rooms.   Knossos has a throne
room which belongs to the latest part of the palace and
seems to be a later insertion into an earlier plan; the
other Cretan palaces have not so far revealed throne rooms'
(Wace, 1973, xxvii.)   The plain meaning of these words is
that all of the four palaces named contain rooms which are
so similar in character and intention that the same culture
must be held responsible for the creation of all of them.
It must, however, have been well known to Wace (for the
most cursory examination makes it clear) that there are
fundamental differences between the Knossos throne room on
the one hand and the mainland megara on the other. Neither
in shape nor in size nor, above all, in function does the
Knossos throne room bear the smallest resemblance to the
megara in the later mainland palaces (Figure 6.)   It is a
Minoan cult-place and, so far from pointing to any influence from outside, it actually constitutes one of the most
powerful proofs that the Knossian palace was still essentially Minoan.   That was put beyond all reasonable doubt
by Reusch, 1958, whose arguments have not yet been refuted,
or even challenged; they have simply been ignored, with
the result that public statements about the Knossos throne
room continue to echo, with increasing self-confidence, the
erroneous assumptions of Wace.
    With regard to the second feature, Wace writes: 'It has
been observed that the style of the frescoes of the last
palace at Knossos is much more akin to that of the frescoes
of Mycenae, Thebes, Tiryns and other Mainland sites than to
the style of the frescoes found at Phaestus and other Cretan sites.   The Cretan frescoes are naturalistic in character; those of Knossos and the Mainland are more interested in the human figure and in warlike scenes' (Wace,
1973, xxviii.)   The observation quoted by Wace is due to
Banti, 1953: a valuable paper on the styles of fresco-

painting in the Aegean.   Miss Banti believes that the
change of emphasis in the subject-matter of the Knossian
frescoes early in the fifteenth century BC is explained
best by postulating influence from the mainland, especially
since the movement toward the more pompous and ceremonial
style is not seen elsewhere in the island.   She points out
that in what we know of Mycenaean art man is the protago-
nist while nature is disregarded: it is this artistic
canon, she says, which has reacted upon Knossian wall-
painting to produce the frescoes of the developed Palace
Style.

Despite these arguments, I find it hard to believe that
the Knossian frescoes of any period show strong mainland
influence.   In order to show that the frescoes of Late
Minoan II Knossos point to Mycenaean supremacy there, it
would be necessary to prove that at the beginning of Late
Minoan II, for the first time, the Knossian frescoes display characteristics which may be derived with certainty
from the mainland.   No such proof can be forthcoming unless, first, a method for the precise dating of frescoes
can be worked out and, second, it is shown that some of
the traits shared by Knossos and the mainland came from the
mainland to Knossos and not in the opposite direction.   At
present, we are far from possessing any criteria by which
to date the terminus post quem of Aegean frescoes;   and it
is not surprising that the principal writers on the subject
differ widely in their chronology of Minoan fresco-painting.
It does seem to be true that the more ceremonial and formal style of the later frescoes at Knossos represents a
departure from the largely naturalistic school which flourished at the very beginning of the later palaces.   Marinatos' excavations at Thera, however, have revealed frescoes which cast doubt on the validity of an opposition between a mainland 'formal and human' style and a Minoan 'naturalistic' style.   At Thera, as early as the Late Minoan
Ia period, the fresco-painters were equally adept at rendering persons in formal poses, animals, and flowers (witness the so-called Ladies' Room, which is decorated on one
of its walls with large lilies and on others with exquisite
depictions of women - Marinatos, 1972, pl F);   and, so far
as I know, no one has taken those painters to be other than
Minoans.

So ends our brief investigation of the principal features of the last palatial phase at Knossos.   As a result
of the investigation, it seems necessary to contradict the
picture drawn by Wace and widely accepted to-day.   If my
arguments are firmly based, it must be conceded that there
is nothing in the archaeological material which points to
mainland control and, on the contrary, much that suggests a

continuation of native Minoan culture in its full vigour.
The same kind of reasoning which has led to a rejection of
Evans' theories about the Shaft Graves ought to prevail
when Late Minoan II Knossos is in question.   The Shaft
Graves, for their part, contain many artefacts inspired by
a Minoan tradition of craftsmanship;   and yet the evidence
of these objects is rightly thought not to outweigh that
of the underlying culture, which remains Helladic.   So,
vice versa, with Knossos in the later fifteenth century BC.
The alien elements, though undoubtedly present, are not so
numerous or so striking as even remotely to suggest that
there had ever been an invasion and a period of control by
a Greek-speaking people from the mainland.   They indicate
nothing more than a continuation of that symbiosis of the
Helladic and the Minoan which, beginning in the Shaft Grave
era, became still closer in the ensuing period.

   If the last palace at Knossos was still thoroughly
Minoan in character (a conclusion imposed by the archaeological evidence), how are we to explain the fact that its
archives are written in Greek?   To many scholars, the use
of Greek at Knossos in itself constitutes sufficient proof
of a Mycenaean conquest at the beginning of Late Minoan II.
Most of those, and they are few, who reject the idea of a
Mycenaean occupation reject also the validity of Ventris'
decipherment of the Linear B script.   Although I have no
doubt that his decipherment is essentially correct, I believe that it applies only to a part of our Linear B inscriptions, which are not written exclusively in Greek.
This is exactly the scribal situation which is encountered
when elements of one language are taken over into another.
It is a situation which occurs again and again in the diffusion of Akkadian in the second millennium BC over wide
areas of Anatolia and the Levant.   That diffusion was
brought about not by conquest but by commercial contact
and the need for a common trading language.   Much the
same kind of situation, it seems to me, called into being
the linguistic mixture which is seen on the Knossos Linear
B tablets.   The long intercourse between Cretans and
mainlanders, of which there is such abundant proof in the
sixteenth and fifteenth centuries, would have resulted in
the confection of some kind of lingua franca, or commercial 'jargon', which is seen first in the Knossian inscriptions and then (such was the conservatism of the
scribes) in the mainland texts of much later date.

CONCLUSIONS

The archaeological evidence from the mainland and from
other parts of the Mediterranean enables us to draw some
conclusions about the nature of their interrelationship.
At the beginning of the Late Bronze Age, both Crete and the
Mycenaeanized parts of the mainland show signs of immense
vigour, which manifested itself not only in a brilliant palatial culture and in the Shaft Graves respectively but
also in considerable activity far from the homeland.   In
Late Minoan I, the Cretan colonies in the Aegean enjoyed an
efflorescence corresponding to that of the palaces and
their dependencies in Crete itself.   New colonies were established in remote areas.   The Mycenaeans have left some,
but not many, traces of their involvement in those parts of
the Mediterranean (especially Egypt) with which the Minoans
maintained a commerce of long standing.   The same century
saw the gradual adoption on the mainland of Cretan arts
and, to some extent, of Cretan habits and beliefs.   The
exuberant flowering of the Minoan civilization in central
and eastern Crete and in some of the islands, together with
the complete absence of fortifications, points to a continuation of peaceful relations with neighbours and commercial partners.   The discovery of Mycenaean ware closely
associated with Minoan at Ialysos is in harmony with the
suggestion that mainlanders and Minoans were at most rivals
in trade, not overt enemies.   It is impossible now to assess the relative importance of Cretan and of mainland
commerce.   Our evidence (which may, however, be seriously
misleading because of the disappearance of perishable artefacts and commodities) suggests that, at any rate in Late
Minoan Ia, Crete had the major share of Aegean trade.   But
at this period, precisely when Cretan trade was prospering
in the Aegean, the mainland exported more than Crete to the
western Mediterranean.   Taylour, 1958, 182 has plausibly
suggested that it was just because of Cretan superiority in
the Aegean that the mainlanders sought a trade outlet to
the west.
     The period of closest intimacy between Crete and the
mainland, in which Crete decidedly took the cultural initiative, and which there is no reason to believe was other
than amicable, was succeeded c. 1450 BC by a phase of very
different character.   Not only does Cretan influence on
the mainland dwindle perceptibly, but Knossos itself takes
on a somewhat warlike aspect.   At about the same time,
other Minoan sites in Crete, and most of those elsewhere,
came to an end.   It is a matter of no great surprise that
we see some mainland features at Knossos in this phase:
those features (especially the use of the Greek language

and the construction of warrior-graves) are explicable as the result of prolonged intercourse between Crete and the mainland; and they afford no proof of a Mycenaean domination of Knossos, which remains strongly and even aggressively Minoan. How Knossos was destroyed we have no means of telling; but of one fact there can be no doubt, that the Mycenaeans were the beneficiaries of its destruction. It was only after the fall of Knossos, and the drastic curtailment (though not the extinction) of Cretan trade which ensued, that the great Mycenaean expansion described in the next two chapters came about.

NOTES

Evidence from the mainland

Mycenae. Tholoi: Wace, 1921, 283-402. Palace: Wace, 1921, 147-282. Chamber tombs: Tsountas, 1888; Wace, 1932.
    Late Helladic II pottery: Furumark, 1950, 156-62; Dickinson, 1972b.
    Frescoes. Relationship to Minoan frescoes: Platon, 1959, 332. Mycenae: Tsountas, 1887, 160-9 and 1891a, 1-11; Rodenwaldt, 1911b; Lamb, 1919 and 1921; Reusch, 1953a. Orchomenos: Bulle, 1907, 71-85. Thebes: Reusch, 1953b and 1956. Tiryns: Rodenwaldt, 1911a and 1912b.

Evidence from overseas

Linear A outside Crete. Keos: Caskey, 1970. Kythera: Coldstream and Huxley, 1972, 205-6. Melos: Edgar and Evans, 1904, 177-85. Naxos: Kontoleon, 1965. Thera: Marinatos, 1971, 43-5.
    Cypro-Minoan script. General: Daniel, 1941; Jacqueline Karageorghis, 1958 and 1961; Buchholz, 1969, 117-24. The earliest Cypro-Minoan inscription from Enkomi: Dikaios, 1963, 45-8 (archaeological context); Emilia Masson, 1969 (epigraphical commentary.)
    Foreign relations of Crete in Late Minoan I. General: Warren, 1967. Cyclades: Scholes, 1956, 39; Coldstream and Huxley, 1972, 291-303; Barber, 1974, 51. Rhodes: Furumark, 1950, 150-85; Hope Simpson and Lazenby, 1973, 135. Miletus: Weickert, 1959, 16-30, 43-52.
    Egypt. A sane and exhaustive monograph is presented by Vercoutter, 1956. Although he argues strongly for the 'keftiu'=Crete equation, the matter cannot be considered as proved, since persons labelled 'keftiu' in Egyptian pain-

tings as often have an eastern as an Aegean appearance:
Wainwright, 1956; Prignaud, 1964.   Aegean pottery in
Egypt: Stubbings, 1951a, 56-8 (Hankey and Tufnell, 1973
on the Late Helladic IIb jar at Maket.)   Aegeans in
Egyptian tomb-paintings: Smith, 1965, 69 with figs 90-2.
Statue-base of Amenhopis III: Edel, 1966 (cf. Buchholz,
1970.)   Egyptian scarab contemporary with Hatshepsut:
Blegen, 1937, 281.   Cartouche of Amenhopis III: Tsountas,
1888, 156.   Egyptian vases at Isopata: Evans, 1905,
555-6; at Katsamba: Alexiou, 1967, 46, 76-83.   List of
names containing 'keftiu': Peet, 1927.

Evidence from Crete

The Thera eruption: Marinatos, 1939; Nincovich and
Heezen, 1965; Page, 1970; Hédérvari, 1971; Hood, 1973c;
Vitaliano, 1974; Hiller, 1975; Luce, 1976.
The last Palatial phase at Knossos.   So far as I can
see, the suggestion that the Knossian palace was destroyed
at the end of the Late Minoan IIb period (e.g. Palmer,
1963 and 1969b) is not supported by discoveries in the
palace itself or in the rest of the Mediterranean: cf.
Boardman, 1963; Raison, 1963 and 1964; Aström, 1965b.
The archaeological background of the Knossos tablets:
Hooker, 1968; Popham, 1975.   Difficulty of dating
frescoes: Levi, 1962, 212; Cameron, 1968, 26.   Explanation of Greek elements in Linear B texts: Hooker, 1967b.
Diffusion of Akkadian: Labat, 1962.

5 The mature Mycenaean Age in Greece
(c. 1375-1200 BC)

The Mycenaean civilization reached its maturity and achieved its greatest expansion in the period after the fall of Knossos (Third Phase of Minoan Influence.) This epoch, marked by the ceramic styles of Late Helladic IIIa2 and Late Helladic IIIb, is the Mycenaean 'Palace Period' par excellence, in which a material culture of great uniformity was spread over central and southern Greece. This homogeneity, while embracing such features as weapons, cult-objects, frescoes, writing, tomb-types, megara, fortification walls, and, above all, pottery, does not entirely inhibit the creation of some local styles in imitation of the standard: this happens especially in Cyprus and Rhodes. Nor is the aggregate of these characteristics found at each and every Mycenaean site; perhaps only the two great Argolid settlements of Mycenae and Tiryns exhibit the Mycenaean culture in the whole range of its possible manifestations.

The present chapter will first describe, in fairly general terms, the chief marks of the material culture of the mainland at this period and will then examine in greater detail the peculiar features of the most important sites. In Chapter 6, the impact of the Mycenaeans on other peoples will be considered.

THE MATERIAL CULTURE OF THE MAINLAND

The building of megara and of powerful fortification walls in citadels, the deposition of terracotta figurines in tombs, and the application of the Linear B script to purposes of book-keeping comprise the striking innovations of our period. Other aspects of the material culture represent developments of mainland traditions which had grown up previously: above all, the pottery and the frescoes.

Much of the Mycenaean pottery of the period is a mass-produced ware which has survived in enormous quantities but is distinguished, nevertheless, by the fine quality of its paint and fabric. A few standard shapes are common, all of them continuing types which were evolved in the preceding ceramic periods: such are the three-handled jar, the alabastron, the stirrup-jar, the 'pilgrim flask', and the stemmed goblet or kylix. The need for very large numbers of vessels naturally led to the standardization of decorative motifs as well.

By Late Helladic IIb, as we saw in the last chapter, Mycenaean pottery had practically ceased to take up new Minoan motifs. After the fall of Knossos, the gap between mainland and Cretan pottery becomes still more marked. On the mainland, there sets in what Snijder, 1936, 123 calls a 'petrifaction'. All the life is drained out of the naturalistic motifs - as Snijder well shows by tracing the evolution of an octopus into a mere pattern which no one, who did not know that it came at the end of a long line of development, would take for an octopus (cf. Blegen, 1928, 146-7.) Very commonly, thick bands are drawn horizontally round the middle of the body; the zone below these lines is usually left blank, while the upper zone is filled with a row of ornamental motifs; for example, a series of scrolls, descended from the Cretan argonaut, is often found. This mainland style is different from the superficially similar linear decoration which was being developed on some types of contemporary Cretan pottery (Furumark, 1972a, 520-1.)

In a negative sense, the Mycenaean pottery of our period may be said to show a reaction against the Cretan, since it displays signs of the degeneration of Minoan motifs. In a positive way also the Mycenaean potters asserted their complete independence of Minoan taste. It is one of the inexplicable characteristics of both the Early and the Late Palace periods in Crete that, while marine and vegetable life is freely depicted on pottery, animals, birds, and human figures are not shown (Evans, 1921, 607-8); much less is there any attempt to paint a composition from the life. The absence of animal figures from Minoan pottery is the more surprising when it is remembered how often ceramic motifs were abstracted from frescoes, which often contained compositions with animals, women, and men. The restriction observed by Minoan potters is generally respected also in the mainland pottery of the earlier Mycenaean age (Late Helladic I-IIIa1.) Against this background the sudden appearance in Late Helladic IIIa2 of men, goats, bulls, and horses with chariots is all the more remarkable (Furumark, 1972a, 430-54.) It is true that, apart from

the early Laconian jug published by Demacopoulou, 1971,
such motifs appear first on Mycenaean pottery in Cyprus;
but, according to the analysis presented by Catling and
Millett, 1965b, this ware is more likely to have been made
in the Argolid than in Cyprus. Bulls and men recur on
mainland pottery throughout Late Helladic IIIb, but within
that period the chariot-motif becomes less common.

If we may judge from the similarity in subject-matter
between Mycenaean pottery and the latest palace frescoes,
and also from the presence in both media of the same stylistic traits, we might conclude (with Rodenwaldt, 1921,
25) that Mycenaean potters had taken over pictorial compositions from wall-painting and so had taken a step which
either had not occurred to the Cretans or (what is more
likely) had been rejected by them. But Furumark, 1972a,
452-3 shows that, while the Mycenaean pictorial compositions on pottery were based on concepts derived from frescoes, they were not copied from actual exemplars:

> What actually constitutes the difference between this
> ceramic style and other pictorial representations of
> Mycenaean art is the absence of anything Minoan. It
> seems evident that the vase-painters were inspired by
> frescoes in their choice of subjects and in certain com-
> positional features, but they represented the subjects
> as they actually appeared, not according to the conven-
> tions of the greater art. Thus we have here a rela-
> tively independent art, created by the vase-painters
> themselves.

This important observation would be quite consistent with
our picture of a self-confident and self-sufficient school
of potters and painters. I find difficulty mainly in
Furumark's phrase 'they represented the subjects as they
actually appeared'. I am not sure whether he means that
we have here a naturalistic school of vase-painters; if
so, it should be pointed out that scenes on typical chariot
craters are just as stylized in their way as the chariot-
scenes on the frescoes are in theirs; even more so, because of the necessity for the vase-painters to produce
large numbers of examples (Vermeule, 1964, 205 with pl
XXXII.)

The frescoes in the last palaces at Mycenae and Tiryns
emphasize the themes of warfare and the chase, with little
or no naturalistic decoration. They appear to be considerably more remote from the Cretan style of wall-painting
that was in vogue earlier in the Late Bronze Age, but we
cannot tell which of the later frescoes are the work of
mainlanders, which (if any) are the work of Cretan settlers. Many painted fragments at Tiryns represent hunts-
men, and from others the details of a boar-hunt can be re-

constructed (Rodenwaldt, 1912b, 123-7.)   The frieze of
women from Tiryns is similar to the earlier frescoes at Mycenae and Thebes, so far as its conception is concerned,
but it exhibits a notable coarsening.   Some features of
the Tiryns frescoes strike us as very un-Cretan when compared with the Minoan school.   Thus, in the boar-hunt
scene the bristles of the hunted animal are represented by
over-regular rows of short lines and markings on the hounds
by conventionalized blotches in unnatural colours (Snijder,
1936, 127.)   The chariot-frieze from Tiryns (Rodenwaldt,
1912b, 96-137) also looks un-Cretan (although, again, the
practice of depicting chariots itself is derived from Minoan art;   for the antecedents see Alexiou, 1964);   the
avenue of trees is too stylized to amount to anything more
than mere accessorial decoration, and the details of the
chariot are rendered with a pedantic care not typical of
Minoan fresco-painting (Figure 7.)   When all this is said,
the Tirynthian painters seem, in one or two respects, to
have followed the Cretan manner with an almost slavish fi-
delity.   A strict adherence to their tradition is seen
when the artist represents human figures, especially women.
The general deportment of the women is still Minoan;   their
hair-style, down to the latest frescoes, descends from Cretan painting, but Cretan painting of the Early rather than
of the Late Palace period (Reusch, 1956, 50);   and their
mode of dress shows no difference from that of the women
depicted on the earliest mainland frescoes (Rodenwaldt,
1912b, 76.)
     The small fresco-fragments from the megaron at Mycenae
belong to the same world as the chariot-frieze at Tiryns,
but with the interesting additional detail of a warrior
falling headlong beside a structure of Minoan appearance
(Rodenwaldt, 1921, 38-40.)   It is impossible now even to
guess at the precise interrelationship of the fragments;
but the connexion of warrior and monumental building of
Cretan type is well established in Mycenaean art and goes
back to the Shaft Graves (cf. Karo's no 481 from Grave IV.)
The theme of the 'falling warrior' itself is evidently Minoan, to judge from its appearance in a Theran fresco
(Marinatos, 1974, pl 93.)   Parts of other frescoes have
been recovered in recent excavations of houses lying to the
south-east of Grave Circle A.   Among these is a figure-of-
eight shield, recalling the earlier shield-friezes at Tiryns, Thebes, and also Knossos (Kritseli-Providi, 1973.)
More noteworthy still is a fresco with women which seems
to have religious affiliations (Taylour, 1969 and 1970)(my
Chapter 8.)
     Some of the frescoes from Pylos, now published by Lang,
1969, have close connexions with classes already known at

Mycenae and Tiryns; but others belong to an altogether different school which is closer to Minoan art (though, even so, not identical with it.)   In the first class we have a processional scene with ministrants of both sexes bringing offerings (Lang, pls 119-20); boars like the animals at Tiryns (Lang, pl 133); above all, a chariot with warriors (Lang, pl 123) and a battle-scene showing hand-to-hand fighting and the theme of the 'falling warrior' already seen at Mycenae (Lang, pl 124.)   But, besides these and in strong contrast to them, the painted scenes in the Pylian megaron are set in a fairyland of Minoan rather than Mycenaean affinities.   Four different compositions are involved, although, in the scheme presented by Lang, pl 125, they are taken to be parts of a larger whole.   The presence of the griffin and the lion is perhaps explicable as a very dim reminiscence of the decorative scheme of the Knossos throne room, and the bull also may have a remote Minoan ancestry.   But the remaining two scenes, the first with a lyre-player sitting on a rock and an unnaturally distended bird (both set starkly against a brick-red background) and the second apparently depicting men seated at tables, are quite without parallel in the art of Crete or of the mainland.   These pictures are, perhaps, the illustrations of myth; at the very least, they afford us a glimpse of an imaginary world, which is depicted without reference to the ruling conventions of Mycenaean painting.

A specialized school of art may be referred to here. During the last twenty years or so, there has come to light a group of painted larnakes (rectangular clay coffins, sometimes but not always provided with feet and lid.) They come from a Late Helladic IIIb cemetery at Tanagra in Boeotia, about eleven miles east of Thebes.   The examples which first became known had not issued from regular excavations.   They formed the subject of a detailed and important study: Vermeule, 1965.   Mrs Vermeule pointed to the unique and unexpected provenience of these larnakes, since up to that time the type had been associated exclusively with Crete, where it became a common method of burial in Late Minoan III.   Since the publication of Mrs Vermeule's paper, the site of Tanagra has been excavated and has yielded a further quantity of larnakes belonging to the same series.   Their great interest lies in the fact that, apart from the stelae of the Shaft Graves, they are almost the only examples of an explicitly funerary art to have come down to us from the Mycenaean age.   They are not directly dependent on Mycenaean vase-painting or fresco-technique for style or motifs, although the recurrent theme, a row of women, is similar to the subject of the processional frescoes.   On the larnakes, however, the

women hold their hands to their heads in a conventional attitude of mourning well discussed by Iakovidis, 1966a.   Besides the mourning women, some of the larnakes show scenes
which can be nothing else than representations of the dead
person's funeral, with its accompaniments.   On one speci-
men a mourning figure looks to the left and another to the
right, while between them two persons are laying the corpse
in the larnax.   Another larnax shows on one of its ends
the deposition of the corpse, and on the other end three
figures are seen mourning the body inside the larnax: one
of the long sides shows, to our astonishment, a picture of
three bulls with bull-leapers (Orlandos, 1969, 10, fig 6.)
This last feature, considered together with the absence of
larnakes from other Mycenaean sites and their use at Tanagra only after they were firmly established in Crete, suggests the direct indebtedness of this area to Minoan arts
and practices which never caught on in other parts of
Greece.   Only a close study of all the material, when it
is published in full, will show whether such a suggestion
can be verified or not.

But the larnakes represent a rare aberration, so far as
we can tell.   The standard modes of burial in Mycenaean
Greece continue to be those which were in use at the beginning of the Late Bronze Age, namely the tholos and the
chamber tomb.   (The emergence, or rather re-emergence, of
different tomb-types in Late Helladic IIIc will be discussed in Chapter 7.)   The two types are often thought to
have served different purposes: tholoi being intended for
'royal' burials, chamber tombs for the interment of humbler
families.   To judge from the elaborate and careful construction of the larger tholoi and from the comparatively
large number of simple chambers, there may be something to
be said for this distinction; but it should not be pressed
too far.   It does not seem right, for example, to insist
that each of the small tholoi found in Messenia is a king's
burial-place; nor, on the other hand, can we think that
the frescoed and benched chamber tomb near Thebes, approached by twin dromoi, was meant for any ordinary deposition
(Spyropoulos, 1971b.)

The existence of large cemeteries of chamber tombs is
well established.   Especially in the Argolid, these are
closely associated with important settlements known to us:
for example at Mycenae (Wace, 1932), at Tiryns (Rudolph,
1973), and at Prosymna (Blegen, 1937, 51-227.)   Elsewhere,
for instance at Volimidia in Messenia, although presumably
a settlement existed nearby, it has not yet come to light.
By contrast, the larger and more imposing tholoi tend to
occur singly (Menidi, Orchomenos, Pylos.)   Because most of
their contents have been removed, little remains whereby

they can be dated.   Only at Mycenae has it been possible
to work out a chronological scheme for the nine tholoi outside the citadel.   The last three, known respectively as
the Treasury of Atreus, the Tomb of Clytemnestra, and the
Tomb of the Genii, represent the culmination of the whole
type.   They received a very thorough treatment from Wace,
1921, 338-87, who places the construction of all of them
in the fourteenth century.   In the absence of adequate
amounts of pottery, his chronology cannot be regarded as
conclusive;   nor is the proposal of Mylonas, 1958, 194-200,
that the Mycenae tholoi are much later, supported by any
strong evidence - in any case, his dates of 1250 and 1220
for Atreus and Clytemnestra respectively seem impossibly
low (cf. French, 1963, 46, n. 29.)   Together with the
Lion Gate and the Cyclopean walls, whose construction may
be contemporaneous with it, the Treasury of Atreus well
expresses what is meant by Mycenaean 'monumentality' in
architecture.   As with the Tombs of Clytemnestra and the
Genii, both burial-chamber and dromos are built with carefully dressed blocks of stone.   The passage itself, some
forty yards long, is closed by a wall, while the massive
doorway leading to the tholos is surmounted by a lintel
and a relieving triangle and is itself decorated by a
façade (Wace, 1953b;   Higgins, Simpson, and Ellis, 1968.)
Both the Clytemnestra and the Genii tombs have a wall and
a façade, but they do not share with the Atreus tomb the
possession of a large side-chamber, roughly $19\frac{1}{2}$ feet
square, leading out of the tholos (Figure 9.)   This last
feature, which is sometimes found in chamber tombs at
Mycenae and Asine, recurs in only one mainland tholos, the
great structure at Orchomenos (perhaps designed by the
same hand), whose side-chamber moreover has a ceiling carved with rosettes and spirals (Bulle, 1907, 95-7.)   This
room can hardly, therefore, have had the function of a
charnel-house, suggested by Wace, 1921, 351 for the side-
chamber of the Treasury of Atreus.   On the contrary, it
is the most splendid part of the tomb-complex and so was
perhaps intended for the chief burial;   and the arrangement of the Treasury of Atreus was probably analogous.
   The major settlements of the Mycenaeans in the fourteenth and thirteenth centuries BC, no less than their
principal tombs, were of massive and monumental construction.   Long before the Mycenaean culture reached its acme
in this period, three hills dominating the Argive plain had
been chosen as citadels.   In time Tiryns, Argos, and Mycenae were fortified with immensely thick Cyclopean walls,
enclosing the chief administrative, ceremonial, residential, and perhaps religious centres of the communities.
Where necessary, for instance at the Boeotian sites of Gla

and Eutresis, the wall was extended to a great length so as
to protect the whole of the hill-top.   Thebes too was fortified with massive walls, which have left sparse remains.
At Pylos alone the existence of fortification walls, at
least in the mature Mycenaean period, cannot be established
with certainty.   Pylos does, however, resemble the palaces
at Mycenae and Tiryns in possessing a typical feature of
mainland culture: the megaron.   The term 'megaron' is applied to a large, almost square room which is often, though
not always, approached by way of a vestibule and a portico.
Megara are found already in mainland house-plans of the
Middle Helladic period.   But the megara of Pylos, Mycenae,
and Tiryns are of a special character; they are exceptionally large, their roof being supported by four columns,
and in the centre of the floor is set a great round hearth,
adorned with painted decoration.   It can hardly be doubted
that the megaron was the chief room of the palace, probably
possessing religious significance (Chapter 8.)
    Apart from the pottery, two classes of artefacts above
all exemplify the high degree of uniformity attained by the
Mycenaean culture of our period.   These are, first, small
clay figurines and, second, weapons.
    Figurines, most often in the shape of women but some-
times in animal-shapes, appear first at the very beginning
of Late Helladic III and, thereafter, they are found in
great numbers in the tombs and, to a smaller extent in the
settlements, of Late Helladic IIIb.   'Morphologically, the
female figurines may be classified into three categories,
which I signify by the symbols Φ, T, and Ψ, chosen by reason of the similarity between these letters and the main
types of figurines' (Furumark, 1972b, 86.)   These figurines occur not only in the mainland of Greece but in
Rhodes and in other areas of Mycenaean penetration such as
Cyprus and the Levant coast.   It is possible that in origin the Mycenaean type of figurine was inspired by Minoan
models (Laviosa, 1963 and 1968a); but, in their fully developed form, the Mycenaean figurines show a complete independence both from Crete and from the Near East.   By
reason of this independence, of their abundance, and of
their wide distribution, they constitute a typical mark of
Mycenaean culture, which makes its appearance just as that
culture is expanding and comes to an end with the fragmentation of the Mycenaean world.   The Mycenaean figurines
have been investigated in a very thorough manner by French,
1971.   Mrs French rightly rejects the fanciful speculations which have been made in the past about the function
of the figurines: speculations which were partly based on
the supposition, now shown to be erroneous, that figurines
occur only in tombs.   Since it is clear that they were

used in settlements as well, we would do better to see in their use some general religious significance (perhaps in some way the accompaniment of cult), without trying to be more specific (so French, 1971, 107-8.)

The Mycenaean weapons found in tombs in our period, both within and outside the mainland of Greece, are best considered in the context of Aegean warlike equipment as a whole.   Both actual artefacts and painted representations provide our evidence for weapons of defence and attack; but the depictions in art assume more importance than usual because the objects themselves are so liable to corrosion. The point may be illustrated by reference to the defensive equipment of the Shaft Grave period.   No example of the large body-shield has survived; but its existence and use in defence (long assumed from the descriptions of Ajax' shield in the 'Iliad') are confirmed by representations in the art of the Shaft Graves: for example Karo's no 241 (gold ring with battle-scene = CMS, no 16) and no 394 (lion-hunt on dagger-blade, my Figure 5.)   By the fourteenth century, however, the cumbersome body-shield (together with the figure-of-eight shield, also depicted in Shaft Grave art) had long given way to a smaller and lighter type, round in shape.   This development left the upper and lower parts of the body unprotected: a need which was met by the construction of body-armour and greaves, occasionally made of bronze.   The extreme rarity of armour and greaves in tombs must arise from the accident of preservation, since the style of fighting implied by the small round shield makes their use an imperative necessity.   The venerable boar's tusk helmet of the Shaft Grave period, though surviving sporadically to the end of the Mycenaean age (Yalouris, 1960, 44), was for the most part superseded by bronze and leather types.   The more mobile kind of warfare marked by the development of a lighter shield is reflected in the offensive weapons, especially the swords and spears, which were current in our period.   Within the fifteenth century, at the time of the closest intimacy between the mainland and Crete, two new sword-types, a 'horned' shape (Miss Sandars' Type C) and a 'cruciform' shape (Type D) were developed from Types A and B of the Shaft Graves (Figure 4.)   C is the more ceremonial type, rather better represented in the fifteenth century warrior-graves near Knossos than on the mainland.   It is of interest that the Mycenaean swords of Miss Sandars' Ci type, or swords betraying strong influence from that type, are distributed in Balkan countries as well as in the Aegean (Sandars, 1963, 145-6; Cowen, 1966, 311-2; Irimia, 1970.)   Derivatives of Type D in time become dominant in the Aegean, being comparatively short, strong, and serviceable (Sandars, 1963,

132.)   We might expect the evolution of the spear to resemble that of the sword;   and it is true that the swords
of Karo's Type A have an analogy in the massive spear-heads
found in some Shaft Graves (e.g. no 933 from Grave VI),
which must have formed part of heavy, thrusting weapons.
But the Shaft Graves contained also a much lighter type,
exemplified by no 448 from Grave IV, only about six inches
in length, which is more easily attributable to a throwing
spear.   The extreme scarcity of spear-heads in graves of
the fourteenth century and later does not allow us to follow in any detail the further evolution of this weapon;
but, if the palatial frescoes reflect actual combat, they
suggest that the two types, a heavy thrusting spear and a
lighter weapon for throwing, remained in use until the end
of the mainland palaces: the former type being depicted on
a Pylos fresco, Lang, 1969, pl M;   the latter in Lang, pls
121 and 122.   (It seems therefore that the use of both
types by the heroes of the 'Iliad' is an accurate reminiscence of the Bronze Age practice.)   The Pylos frescoes
show, with great vividness, the use of the short dagger in
hand-to-hand fighting (Lang, pls M, 123, 124):   a mode of
combat already practised in the Shaft Grave era, to judge
from a gold ring in Grave III (Karo's no 33 = CMS, no 9.)
Another ring from the Shaft Graves (Karo's no 240 = CMS,
no 15) depicts a hunting-scene: a chariot containing two
figures is drawn by a pair of horses at the gallop, and
one of the figures aims an arrow at a fleeing deer.   Horse-
drawn chariots in rapid motion are seen again on stelae in
Grave Circle A;   but it is more likely that they were taking part in races (or funeral-rides?) than in warfare or
the chase (Mylonas, 1951b.)   Later, in Late Helladic III,
the chariots on Cypriot craters and on the Tanagra larnax
already mentioned fit easily into the context of a funeral-
ride.   Not so the statuesque chariots on frescoes at Mycenae, Pylos, and Tiryns (e.g. Figure 7);   perhaps these
should be regarded as conventional representations of a
motif which had become standard in large compositions,
since it is not easy to imagine that in reality the terrain
of mainland Greece would ever have encouraged the development of such a method of warfare.
        The long-established arts of ivory-carving, jewellery,
and gem-engraving continue to be practised throughout our
period.   The development of all of these is analogous to
that of fresco-painting: that is to say, the introduction
of Cretan motifs into the mainland in the First Phase of
Minoan Influence is followed by the almost complete assimilation of Cretan and Helladic elements in the Second Phase;
later, in the classic Mycenaean age we are now considering,
the Helladic traits re-assert themselves, but never so far

that the artists lose their remembrance of, and to some extent their dependence on, Minoan originals.   In the field
of ivory-carving, the contrast between the dynamic schools
of the Second Phase and the more formal and heraldic style
of the Third may be observed by comparing the griffins on
the Athens pyxis (above, p. 66), which form part of a con-
fused but lively group of wild animals, with the statuesque
creature on an ivory plaque from Mycenae (Kantor, 1960,
figs 3 and 9B respectively.)   But, despite the predominance of this 'statuesque' style (well represented as it is
by numerous plaques from Greece and from Delos), the art of
ivory-carving on the mainland, at least in the hands of the
greatest masters, was capable of brilliant achievement
within the conventions of Minoan art.   The acme of this
'Minoanizing' style is represented for us by the group of
two women and a child, carved in the round, which Wace discovered at Mycenae (Kantor, 1960, fig 22.)   We have no
means of telling whether this is the work of a Minoan artist
or of a mainland school which followed Minoan tradition very
closely;   if the latter, the piece is no stereotyped expression of the tradition but a re-application of it to new
needs.   Apart from occasional masterpieces like the Mycenae
group, ivory was most frequently applied to the decoration
of furniture.   This fact might have been deduced simply
from the discovery of thrones in Cyprus dating from the
Archaic period, which were decorated with ivory and other
precious materials.   Ventris, 1956 saw that it is corroborated for the Mycenaean age by a group of Pylos Linear B
tablets, which record items of furniture equipped with
ivory plaques.   For example, Ta 707, 708, 721, and 722
mention thrones and foot-stools decorated with various
motifs, including figures of men, horses, lions, and (perhaps) pomegranates.   The practice of decorating wooden
structures with ivory plaques goes back to the Minoans.
Whether or not the box with ivory dogs in Shaft Grave V
(Karo's no 812/813) is pure Minoan work, we learn from
chariot-tablets at Knossos that chariots were sometimes
fitted with ivory (Lejeune, 1972, 304.)
    After the experimentation of the First and Second Phases
of Minoan Influence, Mycenaean jewellery conforms to a few
standard types in our period.   Beads, whether made of
gold, faience, lapis lazuli, rock-crystal, or glass, continue to appear in tombs, with gold tending to give way to
the other materials as the period advances.   Most often,
these beads take the form of stylized animal or vegetable
motifs rendered in shallow relief: for example rosettes,
volutes, and argonauts.
    The seals and rings of mainland Greece, which in the
Second Phase often depicted cults, now for the most part

bear animal-scenes.   Some of these continue types of very
long standing in Mycenaean miniature art.   For instance,
an amethyst from Grave Δ at Pylos (CMS, no 290) shows a man
plunging a short sword into a lion's mouth, just as on no
33 from Shaft Grave III.   Again, the originally Minoan
motif of an animal suckling its young, which goes back to
no 117 from the same grave, is seen on seals from Mycenae
(CMS, no 140) and Prosymna (Blegen, 1937, fig 582) and on a
sealing from Pylos (CMS, no 376.)   Other examples from
Pylos share their motifs with dagger-blades (lion-hunt -
CMS, no 331) or with pottery (octopus with very attenuated
tentacles - CMS, no 312.)   All six seals from the Menidi
tholos have traditional animal subjects (CMS, nos 384-9.)
A lentoid from Chamber Tomb 24 at Mycenae shows an ox standing in front of a highly stylized palm-tree (CMS, no 57.)
Griffins are outstanding among the animals, both because of
the fine workmanship devoted to the best of them and because of their close similarity to the 'statuesque' griffin
on the ivory plaque from Mycenae.   In earlier phases of
mainland glyptic, griffins had been portrayed in a more
realistic manner: witness the animal led by a robed figure
at Vaphio (CMS, no 223) and the walking griffin with distended udders at Routsi (CMS, no 271.)   But the griffin of
the mature Mycenaean period, crested, with outstretched
wings, lies tranquil in a heraldic pose: so especially on
the large gold plaque from Grave Δ at Pylos (CMS, no 293),
but also on a fine seal from Menidi (CMS, no 389.)   A similar conception of the griffin has inspired the antithetic group on a gold ring from Prosymna (CMS, no 218.)
     The system of writing called by Evans the Linear script
of Class B is attested first by the copious deposits of
inscribed tablets and sealings in the Later Palace at Knossos: deposits which belong in the main to a horizon of c.
1375 BC.   The use of the script did not die out in Crete
after the destruction of the Knossian palace, and a few
Linear B inscriptions are known from the fourteenth and
thirteenth centuries both at Knossos and at Kydonia.   In
my own belief, this script came into use at mainland sites
at least as early as its first appearance in Crete: its
rise in both areas is most plausibly ascribed to the Second
Phase of Minoan Influence.   But, while the reasons for
the first use of the script in Greece are of considerable
historical interest, they are not directly relevant to its
employment in the mature Mycenaean age.   The body of our
inscriptional material from that period falls into two main
classes: 1 clay vessels bearing painted inscriptions; 2
clay tablets, labels, and sealings incised with Linear B
signs while still soft and subsequently baked hard in
fires (Table 7.)   The inscribed stirrup-jars are of im-

portance in that they corroborate the inference, which may
be drawn from other classes of evidence, that commercial
relations between Crete and the mainland continued into the
Late Helladic IIIb period: the fabric of some of them is
Cretan, while their inscriptions contain place-names which
occur also on the Linear B tablets from Knossos. So far
as the mainland tablets are concerned, they offer little
direct evidence of contact with areas oversea, except in so
far as they record imported commodities. The tablets, indeed, seem to have served nothing but the immediate needs
of the bureaucratic apparatus of the palaces (for a different view, see Thomas, 1970a.) But, though the Linear B
script was of very limited application, it can be counted
as one of the identifying characteristics of the Mycenaean
civilization. With the exception of the few finds of
Linear B in Late Minoan IIIb Crete, the script is not
known to have been used anywhere in this period save on the
mainland of Greece; even in Cyprus, the writing-system in
use was not an adaptation from Linear B but (as was seen in
the last chapter) a descendant of the Cretan Linear A
script. The Linear B script, furthermore, is radically
different both in structure and in derivation from the
writing-systems in use at Amarna and Ugarit, centres with
which the Mycenaeans enjoyed commercial intercourse: a
difference which emphasizes the fundamental independence
of the Mycenaean culture from the contemporary civilizations of the Mediterranean.

THE MYCENAEAN SITES OF THE MAINLAND

The principal sites of the Mycenaean age are found in Argolis, Messenia, Attica, Boeotia, and Thessaly. It seems
right to look first at the Argolid and Messenia, since
these regions contain the three classic palatial sites of
Mycenae, Tiryns, and Pylos. The Mycenaean sites in Attica
and Boeotia will next be discussed, and finally the degree
of Mycenaean penetration into northern Greece.
   Moving inland from the Argolic Gulf, we find three considerable Mycenaean citadels guarding the routes across
the Argive Plain: first Tiryns, then Argos, and finally
Mycenae. Of these, Argos possesses the best natural position, set as it is on two easily defensible hills, the
loftier of these (Larissa) being exceptionally steep and
rocky. But, although the existence here of a powerful
Mycenaean citadel can hardly be doubted, in view of the
traces of Cyclopean walls (Vollgraff, 1928) found on Larissa and the large Mycenaean cemetery at Deiras (Deshayes,
1966), the Bronze Age buildings have been effaced by later

structures.   The virtual certainty that a Mycenaean citadel existed at Argos as well as at Tiryns and Mycenae, and
one perhaps comparable with them at least from a military
point of view, must be remembered when the political conditions of the Mycenaean world are assessed at the end of
the next chapter.

Some later buildings were erected at Mycenae and Tiryns
as well, especially in the Hellenistic age, but not to such
an extent as to obliterate the principal Mycenaean structures.   At both sites, it is relatively easy to trace at
least three broad phases of building within the fourteenth
and thirteenth centuries.   Absolute dating is rarely possible.

The first circuit-wall that can be distinguished at Mycenae was built, probably, early in the Late Helladic III
period: a fact which does not preclude the possibility
that the hill was equipped with a wall or walls in earlier
times.   From an entrance on the west side, a wall ran
eastward to a point at which there may have been another,
smaller gate; here, a retaining wall curved round south
and west, preventing the buildings within from toppling
into the ravine.   A further section of wall then completed
the circuit, leaving Grave Circle A immediately outside the
citadel to the south-west (Figure 10.)

At a later, but still unspecified, date important
changes were made in the arrangement of the walls.   To the
west, the old entrance was replaced by the so-called Lion
Gate.   Two antithetic creatures confront a column, in a
posture familiar from a long series of Minoan and Mycenaean seals (cf. CMS, no 46.)   (Despite the traditional name,
there is no compelling reason to regard the animals as
lions: contrast Aström and Blomé, 1965 with Protonariou-
Deilaki, 1965.)   They surmount a massive lintel, which is
itself supported by two monolithic gate-posts.   The gate
forms a rough square, measuring about ten feet along each
side.   The narrow road closed by the Lion Gate was fortified with a powerful bastion, so that the entrance-system
is designed not only to impress the visitor but to form an
important part of the defensive works of the whole site.
A large part of the wall leading south-east from the Lion
Gate was pulled down and re-built so as to take in a much
greater area of the hill-top, especially that occupied by
Grave Circle A.   In the north wall there was inserted a
so-called Postern Gate, smaller than the Lion Gate but,
like it, protected by powerful bastions.   At some time
after the building of the Lion Gate, a broad ramp was constructed, leading south from the Lion Gate to the east of
the Grave Circle.   The ramp was protected by a Cyclopean
wall, which ran from the east side of the Lion Gate.   To

the general period of the building of the Lion Gate and the
extension of the circuit-wall belongs the erection of several groups of structures within the citadel.   First comes
a building squeezed between the Lion Gate and Grave Circle
A, to which Wace, 1921, 38 gave the name 'Granary', a description which speaks for itself and which is applied to an
important class of Late Helladic IIIc pottery, first identified there.   South of the Grave Circle lies a complex of
five buildings, called respectively the House of the Warrior Vase (where Schliemann found the Late Helladic IIIc
crater of that name), the Ramp House, the South House, the
Citadel House, and Tsountas' House.   The recent discovery
of an altar and, in another room, of a bench with idols
shows that the area of the Citadel House and Tsountas'
House was a centre of cult (Chapter 8.)   To the south-east
a retaining wall was built to support the megaron of the
palace;   and it is the subsequent collapse of this wall
that led to the disappearance of the south-eastern corner
of the megaron.   The megaron was approached, by way of the
usual two small rooms, from an open courtyard, which gave
access to other rooms on its northern side.   Associated
with the palace-complex was Wace's Pillar Basement, which
was later filled in, apparently after a fire.   Later still
the 'Grand Staircase' was built to the south of the court,
providing a ceremonial access to the palace.   On the eastern slope of the citadel, Tsountas excavated a large,
multi-storeyed house, now known as the House of Columns because of the column-bases which were found in its courtyard (Wace, 1949, 91-7.)   Mylonas, 1966a, 73 has made the
attractive suggestion that the House of Columns is, in
fact, an eastward extension of the palace, containing store-
rooms and residential quarters.   Finally, toward the end
of Late Helladic IIIb, or perhaps within the IIIc period,
a small but vital extension was built at the north-east
corner of the circuit-walls, in order to provide a well-
protected means of access to an underground spring (Karo,
1934a.)
    It can be seen that the history of the citadel of Myce-
nae during our period is exceedingly complex;   and there is
little hope that it will be finally elucidated, unless many
more homogeneous deposits of pottery are isolated.   Such
deposits are at present known from only four areas of the
citadel: 1 thirteen superimposed strata (ranging from
Late Helladic IIIb to IIIc), found west of the Lion Gate
(Wace, 1921, 17-38);   2 'a large and compact homogeneous
group of vases' in the East Basement of the Granary (Wace,
1921, 51)(Late Helladic IIIc);   3 two well-defined layers
(the earlier Late Helladic IIIb1, the later IIIb2) at the
Citadel House (Wardle, 1969;   1973);   4 three IIIc strata

discovered by Mylonas in a westerly section of the outside
wall (Orlandos, 1968, 10-12.) The evidence of these deposits, taken together, suffices to establish the following sequence of events: a serious destruction, accompanied
by burning, overcame the Citadel House and the neighbouring houses at the end of Late Helladic IIIb (this was the
fire which preserved the Linear B tablets in the Citadel
House - W.D. Taylour in Chadwick, 1963, 34-46); a subsequent destruction affected the Granary early in IIIc; still
further horizons of destruction followed later in IIIc.
None of this evidence allows us to reach any firm conclusion about the destruction of buildings in the eastern part
of the citadel, namely the palace and the House of Columns.
We have already seen that a fire devastated the Pillar
Basement and that it was after this fire that a second
phase of building ensued in the palace area. This earlier
fire is vaguely dated to the middle of the IIIb period, but
without firm grounds. Whether the later fire, which destroyed the whole palace, was contemporaneous with the Late
Helladic IIIc destruction of the Granary (as Wace, 1956b
insisted) or with the IIIb2 destruction of the Citadel
House (Alin, 1962, 14) is impossible to determine. Alin
is quite justified in his criticism of Wace's deductions,
but his own date rests on the sole ground that no Granary
Style pottery has been found in the palace. Not only is
it inadmissible, in any case, to decide such an important
matter on purely negative evidence; it is doubly hazardous to do so here, because of the strong possibility that
valuable clues have been blurred or obliterated in the
course of excavations conducted over so many years. As
things are, it seems necessary to agree with Mylonas,
1966a, 77 that we simply do not possess sufficient facts
on which to base a sound judgment.

It is otherwise with the settlements outside the citadel. These were not excavated until the present century,
and a number of well-defined deposits of pottery enable a
sharper picture to be drawn than is possible in respect of
the citadel. These deposits have been studied during the
past decade by Mrs French; and it is largely due to her
researches that a comprehensible sequence of building-
phases can be established for these areas. The excavations by Wace in 1920 and again in the 1950s have uncovered a number of houses in various directions from the citadel. Despite the somewhat fanciful names given to these
houses (after a fashion started by Evans at Knossos), it
is hard not to see them as buildings in which the inhabitants of the town of Mycenae actually lived and worked in
the Late Bronze Age. To begin with the earliest known
group, lying north-west of the Lion Gate: the (second)

Cyclopean Terrace House with the adjoining Wine Merchant's
House, and a large structure known as Petsas' House which
is situated to the east of these.   Both the (second) Cyclopean Terrace House and Petsas' House rest on earlier
foundations.   These houses and also the Wine Merchant's
House were destroyed at the very beginning of Late Helladic
IIIb (Elizabeth French, 1965, 171-4.)   Upon the ruins of
the Cyclopean Terrace House was erected yet another (third)
building, which reached its end at some point within IIIb
(Alin, 1962, 17.)

Early in IIIb there ensues the most important building
phase of the town of Mycenae.   The construction of a group
of four houses south of the Tomb of Clytemnestra (the House
of Shields, the West House, the House of the Oil Merchant,
and the House of Sphinxes) is dated to this period by the
pottery found in the terrace beneath them: so with the
House of Lead, built on a terrace above the Treasury of
Atreus (Elizabeth French, 1963, 48.)   The Citadel House
was begun at about the same time (Wardle, 1969.)   It is a
natural supposition, but one unsupported by evidence, that
a major re-modelling of the palace was put in hand at about
this period.   However that may be, the whole group of four
houses south of the Clytemnestra tomb was violently destroyed at the end of Late Helladic IIIb1, apparently in a
simultaneous conflagration (Elizabeth French, 1967); again,
it is a possibility, but certainly no more, that the fire
reponsible for this destruction was associated with the
first of the fires which affected the palace itself in the
thirteenth century BC.   The Houses of Sphinxes, Oil Merchant, and Shields yielded (besides fine stone jars, ivory
artefacts, and fresco-fragments) about fifty Linear B tablets and sealings and an inscribed stirrup-jar (Bennett,
1958b.)   That the town suffered a final catastrophe is
suggested by a deposit of pottery, belonging to IIIb2,
which is associated with the destruction of the 'Great
Poros Wall' (running from north to south between the Tombs
of Clytemnestra and of Aegisthus.)   Mrs French identifies
this destruction with the one which overtook the Citadel
House (Elizabeth French, 1967, 72): according to her, the
ceramic evidence from within and outside the citadel 'seems
to mark a major sack of the city' (French, 1963, 51.)   The
destructions at Mycenae are set out in my Table 8.

The third major Argolid citadel, at Tiryns, offers a
number of similarities to that of Mycenae, both in its
over-all concept as a defensive position and in individual
architectural features (Wace, 1921, 12-13.)   The hill on
which it stands, however, is low-lying and gently sloping:
a circumstance which has imposed on its circuit-walls an
elongated shape, different from the arrangement at steeper,
rocky sites like Mycenae and Athens (Figure 11.)

Drawing on his profound knowledge of the lay-out of the citadel, K. Müller discerned three phases of building at Tiryns; but these are not directly comparable with the three phases at Mycenae, since the needs of the two sites were so different. It was not necessary, for example, to shore up part of the palace to prevent its falling into a precipitous ravine; nor, so far as we know, was there a grave circle whose inclusion within the ambit of the walls was thought, in time, to be an imperative necessity. The different phases of the Tiryns citadel simply mark the progressive enlargement of the space available for buildings and provision of walls of increasing thickness so as to protect the most vulnerable sections of the circuit.

The first building phase comprises the strengthening of the small area on the very summit of the hill (the 'Upper Citadel'), probably following the plan of an earlier citadel: the beginning of the palace is dated to the beginning of the Late Helladic IIIa ceramic period (Müller, 1930, 15-21.) During the second phase, which succeeded the first at some undetermined time, an area to the north of the Upper Citadel (the 'Middle Citadel') was secured by powerful walls on the outside. A double wooden doorway was set at the south-east and, after it had been affected by burning, it was replaced by a narrow passage leading to a stone gateway and protected by a strong bastion: a very similar arrangement to that of the Lion Gate at Mycenae (Müller, 1930, 70-3, with hypothetical reconstruction at fig 47.)

The third phase includes the addition of three monumental features: the great extension of the circuit-walls to the north, forming the Lower Citadel; the erection of a curved section of wall on the west side, which is of exceptional thickness even for Tiryns, to protect the narrow staircase giving access on that side; and the construction of 'galleries' in the south and east walls (Müller, 1930, 57-61.) The palace of Tiryns occupies the central part of the Upper Citadel: just as at Mycenae, it contains a large megaron with central hearth, approached from a court by way of two rooms. Unlike Mycenae, Tiryns possesses also a smaller (and perhaps older) megaron. It is natural to place the construction of the small megaron in the second building phase and that of the large megaron in the third; but there is no good ceramic evidence for dating any part of the palace, and we are even less well informed with regard to its development than about the history of the Mycenae palace. But, whenever it took place, the re-modelling of the palace of Tiryns seems to have been a radical one (Müller, 1930, 206; Alin, 1962, 27.) The Lower Citadel was subjected to closer examination during the 1960s than ever before. Two features revealed in the course of these

excavations offer further points of resemblance to Mycenae.
First, two passages under the north-west section of the
wall were found to lead to a spring: they resemble the
'secret cistern' at Mycenae and, like it, they were lined
with stone walls (Grossmann and Schäfer, 1971, 44.)   Second, the discovery of four small buildings within the
walls (perhaps store-rooms or humble dwellings) recalls
the similar practice at Mycenae (Grossmann and Schäfer,
1971, 48-75.)

Outside the citadel, the town of Tiryns consisted (as at
Mycenae) of houses and graves.   The best-preserved of the
houses near the citadel proved to be a large megaron-type
structure with rectangular hearth (House W), which was
built early in the twelfth century BC, and a smaller house
(M) to the east of this, dating from the thirteenth century
(Gercke and Hiesel, 1971, 11-17.)   The closest Late Helladic parallel to House W is provided by House L at Korakou, whose large megaron with squarish hearth is likewise
equipped with vestibule and portico (Blegen, 1921, 80-3.)
The neighbourhood of Tiryns has not so far produced graves
as numerous as the chamber tombs of Mycenae, nor any comparable to the great tholoi there in size or elaboration.
On the eastern slope of Prophitis Elias (a hill situated
about a mile from the citadel of Tiryns), the German excavators found tholoi and some fifty chamber tombs: even
now, only a small number of these have been published
(Dragendorff, 1913, 347-54; Rudolph, 1973.)   The finds
from these tombs, meagre as they are, show that the cemetery was in use from late in Late Helladic I until well
into the Late Helladic IIIc period.

Although it is possible at Tiryns, as it was at Mycenae,
to distinguish phases of building in the citadel, we are
equally far from establishing a datable sequence of building and destruction.   The chief difficulty is the same at
both places: the rarity of stratified deposits anywhere
and their complete absence in the immediate environs of the
palace itself.   Mycenae, at least, yields good stratification of Late Helladic IIIb pottery within its walls; but
at Tiryns only one stratified deposit has so far come to
light.   This was found at the base of the massive wall
which curves round to protect the West Staircase (Verdelis
and French, 1965.)   The deposit is stratified on four
levels, each of which contains Late Helladic IIIb pottery
and fresco-fragments:
1: burnt
2: unburnt
3: burnt
4: unburnt
Bedrock

Alin, 1962, 27 associates Level 3 with the disaster which
caused the burning not only of the wooden doorway in the
south-east corner but also of Complex XLVI (at the extreme
west side of the palatial building);   Level 1 he equates
with a later fire which affected the western part of the
palace.   These suggestions are plausible and are supported
by good arguments, which show that the sequence discovered
by Verdelis is valuable so far as it goes.   But it cannot,
as Grossmann and Schäfer, 1971, 43-4 suppose, establish a
chronology for the burning of the citadel;   for, as is well
known, the citadel underwent not two but three (or even
more) destructions by fire within Late Helladic III.   It
is plain that the third fire, which destroyed the megaron
itself and the neighbouring rooms, cannot be accommodated
within Verdelis' sequence;   that, in short, the last catastrophe at the Tirynthian citadel is no more susceptible of
accurate dating, in ceramic terms, than the destruction of
Mycenae.   So far as our present information goes, Tiryns
(like Mycenae) may equally well have met its end very late
in the IIIb period (c. 1200 BC) or early in IIIc.

   A number of smaller sites clustered about Tiryns and Mycenae.   To the east of Mycenae lie the extensive cemetery
of Prosymna, which yielded great quantities of Late Helladic IIIb pottery, and a smaller number of tombs at Berbati;
these last probably constitute the burial-places for the
inhabitants of a small walled settlement close by (Alin,
1962, 40.)   Between Mycenae and Tiryns are the tombs of
Dendra, which had already passed their prime by the beginning of Late Helladic IIIb;   but here too is found a
neighbouring citadel at Palaiokastro, whose size and importance are emphasized by Hope Simpson, 1965, 15.   South
of Tiryns, at the coastal site of Nauplion, a number of
chamber tombs have been excavated.   Farther east along the
coast, Asine presents the classic Mycenaean configuration
of walled citadel on a rocky hill, lower town, and cemetery
of chamber tombs.   The houses of the settlement are especially well preserved;   and one of them provides important evidence for cult later in the Mycenaean period.

   The Argive Plain in Mycenaean times therefore presented
a chain of strongly fortified citadels from Mycenae in the
north to Tiryns in the south, with the walled settlements
of Palaiokastro and Asine lying to the east of this line.
Most of the sites are of great antiquity, being equipped
with their massive circuit-walls only late in the fourteenth century BC and, in the case of Tiryns and Mycenae,
with buildings arranged around a megaron-complex.   In
theory, the disposition of Mycenaean sites in the Argolid
could be explained in one of two ways: either these sites
formed a network of defensive positions, which guarded the

plain in concert against some external enemy, or each was
fortified so as to protect its inhabitants from hostile
neighbours.   This, however, is a 'political' question,
which can be answered best (if it can be answered at all)
after we have looked at other Mycenaean sites.

A considerable body of evidence is now available for
the existence of settlements and cemeteries in the central
parts of the Peloponnese (Waterhouse and Hope Simpson, 1960
and 1961):   the sites of Ayios Stephanos and the Menelaion
at Sparta are especially noteworthy.   But the area of outstanding importance in the Mycenaean age, after the Argolid, lay in Messenia.   A picture completely different from
the Argolid situation emerges here.   There is no question
of a number of venerable settlements progressing in power
and size until they form fortified palaces, as at Mycenae
and Tiryns.   On the contrary, there are clusters of small
sites, often provided with elaborate tholoi in Late Helladic I and II.   The wealth of offerings in the tholoi is
exemplified by the deposits at Routsi and Peristeria (Chapters 3 and 4.)   These clusters are particularly dense in
the Kyparissia and Pamisos valleys and in an area near the
west coast, stretching roughly from the modern town of
Pylos to the palace at Ano Englianos, eight miles due
north.   Hereafter, the name 'Pylos' will be applied only
to this palace, since the Linear B tablets found there
certify that this was the name of the site in Mycenaean
times.   More, probably, is now known about Messenia than
about any other part of Mycenaean Greece, thanks to the
investigations of Blegen and others at Pylos, to the
excavation of numerous sites (especially those with tholoi)
by Marinatos, and to the correlation of archaeological and
other data by McDonald and Rapp, 1972.

As we have seen, the numerous small sites of the Messenian plain reached their acme in Late Helladic I and II.
Early in Late Helladic III, the hill at Ano Englianos was
occupied by some buildings and a wall, of which scanty but
distinct traces still remain (Blegen, 1973, 3.)   But in
Late Helladic IIIb all this was cleared so as to make room
for the large palace, which flourished in the thirteenth
century and was destroyed by fire when the Late Helladic
IIIb ceramic style was giving way to IIIc (Blegen, 1966,
421.)   Reluctant though I am to make inferences of a political nature from purely archaeological evidence, I think
that only one plausible explanation accounts for the foregoing developments;   namely, that a large number of petty
states were superseded (whether willingly or through coercion) by a unified kingdom, which had its seat at the
palace of Pylos.   This observation is powerfully confirmed
by some of the Pylos Linear B tablets (notably the Ma ser-

ies, Cn 608, Jn 829, Ng 319, Ng 332, and Vn 20.)   Taken
together, these documents speak of sixteen places in which
the palace officials took a close administrative interest.
These places can be divided into two 'provinces', one lying
closer to the palace, the other farther from it.   Some recent writers on the subject have identified (at least to
their own satisfaction) the names on the tablets with those
of actual places.   Whatever the merits of the individual
identifications, the important point which concerns us here
is that the scribes in the Pylian palace had dealings with
places in various parts of Messenia and regarded them not
as equals but as tributaries.
     The construction of a palace to a unified plan within a
comparatively short span of time, together with the complete lack of fortification, obviously sets Pylos apart
from Tiryns and Mycenae.   But, no less certainly, we see
here a product of the same traditions of design and execution which are evident in the Argolid palaces.   The rich
finds of fresco-fragments, which belong at least in part to
the standard mainland school of fresco-painting, have been
mentioned already.   Like Mycenae and Tiryns, Pylos has a
central unit formed by the megaron (with large circular
hearth), vestibule, and portico, which lead in from a
courtyard.   Like them also, it is equipped with administrative rooms (such as the 'archive rooms' where the
Linear B tablets were found);   store-rooms (for example the
'wine magazine', a separate building just north of the main
palace area);   and a square room with round hearth (known,
for quite insufficient reasons, as the Queen's Hall), which
recalls the small megaron at Tiryns.   A meticulous description of the whole palace is given by Blegen, 1966 (cf.
my Figure 12.)   Not very much of the Mycenaean town of
Pylos has been uncovered by the excavations conducted so
far (Blegen, 1973, 3-68);   two large tholoi, built before
the construction of the palace, remained in use in the palatial period;   in addition to the usual chamber tombs, a
group of graves resembling those at Kleidi (Chapter 3) was
found south of the palace (Blegen, 1973, 71-215.)
     Outside the Peloponnese, Attica is the most intensively
explored part of Greece and, probably for that very reason,
it has proved the richest in Mycenaean remains.   The important tholoi at Thorikos and Marathon were, apparently,
built in Late Helladic II;   but the Menidi tholos tomb,
which was excavated as long ago as the 1870s, is more
likely to date from Late Helladic IIIb.   Cemeteries of
chamber tombs have been found, for example, at Aliki, Vourvatsi, Brauron, Spata, and Eleusis;   at Eleusis, an associated settlement of long standing is well attested.   Athens
does not appear to have reached a dominant position until

the IIIb period.   Little remains of the Mycenaean structures on the Acropolis, because of the successive stages of
building there after the end of the Bronze Age; but a pa-
tient re-examination of the terrain has enabled Iakovidis
to conclude that there were few Mycenaean buildings there
before the fourteenth century BC, while the Cyclopean walls
(which can still be seen here and there) were not constructed before the beginning of Late Helladic IIIb (Iakovidis,
1962, 106-78.)   To this stage of building belong the bastion protecting the West Gate, which is similar in conception to the later gateway at Tiryns (Iakovidis, 1962, 106-
8; Welter, 1939, 2-9) and also a Postern Gate in the north-
east (Iakovidis, 1962, 124-5.)   Another feature which recalls the arrangements at Mycenae and Tiryns is the passage
leading to a spring on the north side of the Acropolis (Iakovidis, 1962, 128-31; Broneer, 1939.)   In fact, there
are so many points of resemblance between what we know of
the Athenian Acropolis and the citadels of the Argolid as
to lend colour to the suggestion that the walls of Athens
and Tiryns were laid out not merely by the same school of
building but by the same builders (Iakovidis, 1962, 228.)
Again like Mycenae and Tiryns, Athens had a lower city outside the citadel, even though little is known about it (Iakovidis, 1962, 179-89.)   Finally, the cemetery of chamber
tombs, which forms a prominent feature of other large Mycenaean settlements, is found at Athens as well.   Over forty
chamber tombs, ranging from large graves with rich burial-
offerings to very modest structures, have been excavated
in the region of the classical Agora; and it seems very
likely that more are yet to be found (Immerwahr, 1971, 96-
266.)
      Boeotian Thebes was evidently a site of the greatest im-
portance in the Mycenaean age.   The imposition of later
buildings on the Mycenaean settlement has made excavation
difficult; and only parts of what were undoubtedly palatial structures stand revealed.   Until very recent times,
it was thought that two successive Mycenaean palaces were
built close to each other (so Symeonoglou, 1973.)   But
more extensive research shows it to be more likely that all
the buildings so far uncovered belong to one and the same
palace, which was constructed at the beginning of Late Helladic IIIb and destroyed at the very end of that period
(Spyropoulos and Chadwick, 1975, 69-71.)   From the ruins
of this palace come the following groups of artefacts.   The
first comprises a large number of inscribed jars, which are
almost certainly imports from eastern Crete and so support
the suggestion, made above on the strength of the Tanagra
evidence, that this part of Greece enjoyed especially close
ties with the Minoans (cf. Symeonoglou, 1973, 26, 33, 74.)

Second, some fresco-fragments enable us to place the Theban
artists in a school of wall-painting familiar at Tiryns and
Mycenae: the researches of Reusch, 1956 on the frieze of
women are of particular importance in this connexion. No
less impressive, though for different reasons, are the discoveries made in the course of excavations which are still
in progress. Different rooms have yielded, in addition to
the usual pottery, a series of Linear B tablets, a hoard of
fine ivory plaques, and a number of cylinder-seals, mostly
of Cypriot or eastern provenience (Chapter 6.) Even
though the ground-plan of the palace cannot be discerned in
its entirety, it certainly included an administrative centre as well as luxurious residential quarters and workshops
producing artefacts of the highest quality. Although
Thebes was not a highly fortified citadel of the same type
as those at Tiryns, Mycenae, or Athens, it did possess
powerful circuit-walls, which have left some scanty remains
(Keramopoullos, 1917, 7-12.) The expected cemeteries of
chamber tombs were found just outside the walls (Keramopoullos, 1917, 99-209); but the single chamber tomb with
fresco-decoration, already mentioned (p. 86), was surely
intended for an extraordinary burial, and its lavish ap-
pointments are quite consistent with our picture of a large
and wealthy palace-complex at the time of its greatest prosperity.
     The Thebans of the Mycenaean age would probably have had
their main access to the Gulf of Corinth at the harbour-
town of Livadostro. About half-way between Livadostro and
Thebes, the route was guarded by the ancient citadel of Eutresis, which had been a flourishing settlement in both
Early and Middle Helladic and was now, in the full Mycenaean period, equipped with massive Cyclopean walls.
     Farther to the north-west, in the heart of Boeotia, lies
Lake Kopais, now drained, which measures some eleven miles
across at its broadest point. Its southern end was protected by a citadel at Haliartos. Near its north-western
extremity stands Orchomenos, which is shown by its Cyclopean walls, large buildings containing fresco-paintings,
and impressive tholos with side-chamber to have been one of
the major palatial sites of Mycenaean Greece. It is not
clear whether or not there was a great catastrophe here at
the end of the Late Helladic IIIb period. North-east of
Lake Kopais, the low hill of Gla is enclosed by an immensely long circuit of Cyclopean walls (c. 3,300 yards.)
Four gates are set in the wall, the two on the south side
being protected by bastions. The ground-plan of a large
building has been uncovered on the northern part of the
hill (Orlandos, 1960a, figs 53-4.) Its lay-out is quite
different from that of the Peloponnesian palaces, the 'me-

garon' illustrated by Orlandos, 1960a, figs 55-6 having little resemblance to the rooms called by that name in southern Greece.   It is true, again, that the finds of pottery
(Orlandos, 1955, 34-5) and fresco-painting (Orlandos,
1961a, fig 49) seem very meagre for a palatial site.   But
it would be wrong to exclude the possibility that a palace
was situated here.   Hope Simpson, 1965, 116-7 argues that
the building was a military barracks, citing the smallness
of the rooms and the total absence of water on the hill.
He overlooks the fact that a water-supply would have been
no less necessary for a 'barracks' than for a palace.   It
should be remembered also that Gla has received only superficial exploration when compared with the intensive excavation at, say, Tiryns or Mycenae;   and, when we bear in mind
the fact that 'secret springs' were not discovered at those
sites for many years, we cannot exclude the possibility
that something similar will yet be found at Gla.   It will
be astonishing if such an enormous fortified area does not
yield some tombs as well.   Whatever the purpose of this
great fortified citadel, it was destroyed by fire in Late
Helladic IIIb and was not re-occupied.

   Not only Gla but also other hills jutting out into the
northern side of Lake Kopais were equipped with Cyclopean
walls: an arrangement which ensured the protection, by a
chain of powerful fortresses, both of the lake and of the
route leading from Orchomenos to the sea.   Kambanis, 1892
and 1893 described Cyclopean embankments in the lake which
were designed to carry off excess water to outlets at the
north and west.   The construction of these dykes he assigned to the 'Minyans' or, as we would now say, to the Mycenaeans.   After a minute examination of the whole region,
Kenny, 1935 accepted this attribution in general, although
he was able to correct some of Kambanis' details.   Indeed,
there is no good reason to deny that the Mycenaeans were
responsible for building the dykes.   The only scholar seriously to impugn their participation in this work is Kahrstedt, 1937;   but his most powerful arguments are that it
is unnecessary to bring the dykes into connexion with the
fortified citadels and that the ancient authors do not attribute the building of the dykes to the Minyans.   The second point is well taken, for Pausanias 9. 38. 6-7 (often
cited in support of a Mycenaean construction of the dykes)
speaks merely of an inundation of the plain;   but, as to
Kahrstedt's first point, it is completely unreasonable to
dissociate the Cyclopean masonry of the embankments inside
the lake from the Cyclopean walls of the citadels adjoining
it.   And, it may be asked, at what other period of history
or prehistory is such a dense settlement of the area around
the lake attested?

This interconnected system, as we should regard it, is certainly the most impressive example we have of the ability of the Mycenaeans to control their environment by the planning and execution of engineering works on a large scale. But, if it is the most impressive example, it is far from being the only one.   What Wace, 1949, 116 well called 'the adapting of the site to the plan rather than the plan to the site' we have seen exemplified in the design of the palace at Mycenae.   A little to the south of Mycenae, the Bronze Age inhabitants of Tiryns, in an attempt to irrigate part of the Argive Plain, erected a large dam carried on Cyclopean walls (Balcer, 1974.)   In fact, we might say that the construction of each of the citadels (often on rocky foundations of varying contours), together with the solution of the related problems, like the provision of water-supplies, irrigation of dry areas, and adequate protection of the populace, constituted a successful application of both administrative and practical skills.   It is hardly necessary to emphasize how prominent these skills were in the building of the largest and most carefully designed tholoi, such as those at Mycenae and Orchomenos. But in no sphere is the engineering ability of the Mycenaeans seen to greater advantage than in road-building.   It may seem presumptuous to speak of a system of roads connecting the major Mycenaean centres, when after all we have only a few traces here and there; nor, of course, is it easy to prove conclusively that a given stretch of road was, in fact, built by Mycenaeans.   But, as with the dykes in the Kopais basin, it is a matter of eliminating the periods at which it is unlikely, or inconceivable, that such works were constructed.   For example, it would be idle to deny to the Mycenaeans well-made stretches of highway in the neighbourhood of Mycenae itself, especially where they are supported on embankments or bridges of Cyclopean construction and where they follow routes for which no one, since Mycenaean times, would have had much need. McDonald, 1964 has assembled the evidence for a Mycenaean system of roads, with special reference to Messenia; roads in the Argolid, particularly those near Mycenae, are discussed by Mylonas, 1966a, 86-7 and Wace, 1949, 109; Oldfather, 1916, 41-2 and Heurtley, 1923, 38-40 trace Mycenaean roads in Boeotia; and Kase, 1973 roads in Phocis.   I cannot understand why Wace and Mylonas, as well as other authors, insist that the Mycenaeans drove chariots along their roads: the ruts found at some points certainly prove the use of wheeled vehicles of some sort, but the stiff, formal depictions of chariots in the palace frescoes do not suffice to demonstrate their common employment for transport or warfare.   Naturally, those who find their history in Homer

are encouraged in the belief that Mycenaeans habitually
drove chariots when they read of Telemachus' journey by
chariot from Messenia to Laconia ('Odyssey' 3. 481-96);
but the two elements, namely the existence of a road between these parts of Greece and the practice of riding in
chariots, did not necessarily come into the epic at the
same time or from the same place (Chapter 1.)

So far as our information goes at present, the Mycenaean
civilization was only an intruder in the far north-west and
far north-east of Greece, that is, in Epirus and Macedonia
(cf. Wardle, 1975.)   Except at Parga in Epirus, which has
yielded a Mycenaean tholos, the culture of neither area was
appreciably influenced by the Mycenaean.   Small amounts of
Late Helladic III pottery and bronze swords of Mycenaean
type have been found at a few sites, appearing sometimes
alongside native wares.   In Thessaly the situation is
quite different.   Here too, in the first place, the Mycenaean culture was introduced from outside, its earliest
manifestations being the tholoi at Volos and Yeoryikon (pp.
64-5.)   During the Late Helladic III period, however, a
number of important Mycenaean settlements were established.
Volos took on a palatial character, passing through five
phases of building, from Late Helladic IIIa to IIIc (Orlandos, 1961b, 53.)   High hills with extensive deposits of
Late Helladic III pottery, sometimes associated with tholoi
or chamber tombs, speak of flourishing Mycenaean settlements at Gritsa, a coastal site south of Volos, at Ktouri
and Chasambli to the north, and even at Gremnos, on the
farther side of the River Peneios.   The most enigmatic
remains uncovered by the German excavators in the 1950s
were at Petra, on the west bank of Lake Karla, between
Volos and the Peneios.   A wall which enclosed a very large
area was attributed to Mycenaeans by Milojcić, 1955b, 222-
9.   The claim is strengthened by the presence of abundant
Mycenaean sherds in the vicinity and also by the difficulty
of suggesting another people who could be associated, with
much plausibility, with the building of circuit-walls in
such a region and on such a scale.

So much for the material culture of the mature Mycenaean
age.   What we may loosely call the 'political' conditions
of the Mycenaean world will be examined after we have
looked at the relations between the Greek mainland and
other parts of the Mediterranean.

NOTES

Pottery.   The evolution of shapes and decorative styles is
treated in the indispensable works of reference Furumark,

1972a and 1972b.   For the fabric of Mycenaean (and Minoan)
pottery, see Catling, Richards, and Blin-Stoyle, 1963.   A
useful description of Mycenaean pottery, though now out of
date in some respects, is given by Mackeprang, 1938.   Individual groups of Mycenaean vases are discussed by: Stubbings, 1947; Elizabeth French, 1963; 1964; 1965; 1966;
1967; 1969a; Wardle, 1969 and 1973; Slenczka, 1974.   On
figured vases: Akerström, 1953 and 1968; Charitonidis,
1953; Catling and Millett, 1965b; Catling, 1970a.   (Like
Furumark, Akerström, 1953, 27 insists that, while there was
a general dependence of potters on fresco-painting, they
did not take over whole scenes as they stood.)
    Fresco-painting.   Mycenae: Rodenwaldt, 1921; Lamb,
1921, 249-55; Taylour, 1969 and 1970; Kritseli-Providi,
1973.   Orchomenos: Bulle, 1907, 71-83.   Pylos: Lang,
1969.   Thebes: Keramopoullos, 1909, 90-5; Spyropoulos,
1971a.   Tiryns: Rodenwaldt, 1912b; Demangel, 1944.
    Painted larnakes.   Vermeule, 1965; Orlandos, 1969;
1970; 1971a; 1973; Lorandou-Papantoniou, 1973.
    Tombs.   Wace, 1921, 338-402; 1932; Vermeule, 1964,
index, under 'burials' and 'tholos tombs'; Mylonas, 1966a,
index, under 'graves'.   The whole subject is in need of a
comprehensive treatment, similar to the work done for Minoan tombs by Pini, 1968.
    Fortifications.   Scoufopoulos, 1971.
    Mycenaean houses and palaces.   General: Graham, 1960;
Schott, 1960; Sinos, 1971, 90-106; Lawrence, 1973, 65-82.
Representation of buildings in Aegean art: Press, 1967.
Development of the megaron: V.K. Müller, 1944; Schweitzer, 1951.   Construction of the megaron-roof: Holland,
1920; Akerström, 1941; Smith, 1942; Dinsmoor, 1942;
Blegen, 1945 and 1966, 82.   Homeric evidence: Bassett,
1919; Lorimer, 1950, 406-51; Gray, 1955; Hiller, 1970,
24-7; Knox, 1973.
    Clay figurines.   Laviosa, 1963 and 1968a (on the ori-
gin.)   Furumark, 1972b, 86-9 (on the typology.)   Elizabeth French, 1971 (largely superseding previous studies.)
Orlandos, 1969, 7.   Tamvaki, 1973.
    Weapons.   Lorimer, 1950, 132-328 presents a remarkably
full account, especially from the Homeric view-point, of
the evidence available to her.   Snodgrass, 1967, 14-34
brings matters up to date.   Koustourou, 1972 on offensive
weapons is too superficial.   On swords the authoritative
accounts are Sandars, 1961 and (especially for the mature
Mycenaean age) 1963.   On arrow-heads: Buchholz, 1962. On
slings: Buchholz, 1965.   On helmets: Borchhardt, 1972,
15-44.   On bronze armour: Yalouris, 1960.   On war-
chariots: Catling, 1968a; Wiesner, 1968, 32-76; Littauer,
1972.   On the description and depiction of weapons in the

Linear B texts and their relevance to the archaeological
material: Snodgrass, 1965; Picard-Schmitter, 1968.   The
depiction of weapons in Mycenaean art: Cassola Guida,
1974.   The Cretan material: Hood and de Jong, 1952,
255-61.
General survey of the Aegean scripts: Buchholz, 1969.
Transcriptions of the Linear B texts.   Inscribed vases
from Crete and the mainland: Raison, 1968.   Knossos
tablets: Chadwick, Killen, and Olivier, 1971.   Mycenae
tablets: Olivier, 1969.   Thebes tablets: Chadwick,
1969b;   Spyropoulos and Chadwick, 1975, 85-107.   Pylos
tablets: Bennett and Olivier, 1973.   Tiryns tablets:
Godart and Olivier, 1976.
Ivory.   General: Kantor, 1956 and 1960;   Blázquez,
1972.   Ivory mirror-handles: Schäfer, 1958.   Hoards of
Mycenaean ivories: Gallet de Santerre and Tréheux, 1947,
154-206 (Delos);   Wace, 1954c (Mycenae);   Symeonoglou,
1973, 44-62 (Thebes.)   Derivation of the griffin-motif:
Frankfort, 1936;   Dessenne, 1957;   Bisi, 1965, 167-95;
Delplace, 1967.
Jewellery: Higgins, 1961, 68-89;   Haevernick, 1963.
Seals and rings.   General: Sakellariou, 1964;   1966;
1974b;   Tamvaki, 1974.   Individual: Sakellariou, 1972.
Place-names on the Pylos tablets and the topography of
the Pylian kingdom: Wyatt, 1962;   Hiller, 1972b;   Le-
jeune, 1972, 113-33;   Chadwick, 1972;   1973a;   1973b;
Shelmerdine, 1973.

6 The Mycenaean expansion overseas

INTRODUCTION

I have suggested in previous chapters that the inhabitants
of the Greek mainland established trading contacts with
other areas as early as the Middle Helladic period and that
these became more extensive in the era of the Shaft Graves
(First Phase of Minoan Influence.)   In the Second Phase,
the initiative to move outwards from the Aegean was taken
mainly by Cretans; but relations between Crete and the
mainland were so close at this juncture that Mycenaeans
were, to some extent, involved in the settlements and trading ventures of the Minoans.   Now, in the Third Phase,
after the fall of Knossos and the end of the Cretan expansion (though not, by any means, the end, of all Cretan
trade with other areas), comes what I call the Mycenaean
expansion: a term which is meant to embrace settlement as
well as trade.   The archaeological evidence for that expansion is copious, but its examination will not detain us
long, since the material remains are described in standard
publications; in consequence, the greater part of this
chapter will be concerned with the difficult problems involved in a consideration of other classes of evidence and
with an assessment of the political nature of the Mycenaean
world.

ARCHAEOLOGICAL EVIDENCE FOR FOREIGN CONNEXIONS

1 The Greek Mainland

It is a surprising fact that, although Mycenaean exports
have been discovered in great quantities abroad, especially in the eastern Mediterranean, objects of foreign provenience appear extremely rarely at sites on the mainland

of Greece.   These objects fall into four groups.   1 Two
metal figurines, one of bronze from Tiryns and one of silver from Thessaly, have been identified as Hittite work.
2 A type of tall amphora with rounded bottom (the so-
called 'Canaanite Jar') was introduced from Palestine into
Egypt and also, in very small numbers, into Greece, where
it is found at Mycenae and Menidi.   3 A collection of
seals has come from the modern excavations at Thebes.   It
is a heterogeneous lot, comprising Mycenaean objects, a
number of Babylonian seals (most of them belonging to the
fourteenth century BC, but a few to earlier periods), a
Syro-Hittite example, and one seal from Mitanni in Mesopotamia.   Fourteen of the Babylonian seals bear cuneiform
inscriptions.   I reject the extravagant deductions which
have been made from the presence of these objects.   They
do not at all suggest that there were direct relations between Thebes and the east; on the contrary, the miscella-
neous character of the items and the fact that they were
all found together make it right to call them a 'collection': perhaps the acquisition of a single traveller and,
therefore, not representative of the imports current at
the time.   Some of the eastern seals are, however, interesting from a different point of view.   It will be seen
in Chapter 8 that some of the drawings they bear are parallel to cult-scenes from the Aegean: for example, a line
of ministrants bringing offerings to a seated figure.   4
Stray seals from other sites (notably the Hittite 'bulla'
from Chamber Tomb 523 at Mycenae, CMS, no 156) have an
eastern origin.

2 The Central Mediterranean

In this area, the most important deposits of Mycenaean
pottery have been found in the Aeolian Islands, attesting
contact with the Aegean from the Middle Bronze Age until
the end of the Mycenaean period; in Sicily, where local
decorative styles and funerary practices show signs of Mycenaean influence; and above all at Scoglio del Tonno,
near Taranto, which has yielded Mycenaean figurines and
several hundred sherds of Late Helladic IIIa and IIIb pottery.   Among the Mycenaean vessels of Greek fabrication
were found some which had been made in Rhodes and Cyprus.

3 Crete

Before the recent excavations at Kydonia, in the west of
Crete, there was little to show that any part of the

island was brought within the Mycenaean ambit during the
great expansion of the fourteenth and thirteenth centuries.
Knossos had ceased to exist as a palatial site; but settlers continued to inhabit the ruins of the palace.   Other
sites in central and eastern Crete were also re-occupied.
The Minoans still had some trading connexions with oversea
areas, including Cyprus and the Greek mainland.   Until recent years, little Late Helladic IIIb pottery was known
from Crete, and none of the other distinctive marks of Mycenaean culture was apparent, during the Late Minoan IIIb
period.   On the contrary, the bulk of the pottery in Crete
was locally made and of native antecedents, while the use
of cult-rooms of purely Minoan type persisted into the
thirteenth century BC.   In this state of the evidence,
there was little enough reason, so far as Crete was concerned, to speak in terms of a 'Mycenaean overlordship' or of
'Crete as part of the Mycenaean world' (Schachermeyr, 1964,
285-93.)   Nor has any discovery been made at Knossos or in
the east of the island which suggests that in those areas
the Mycenaeans made any considerable impact after the fall
of the Cretan palaces.   But at Kydonia the sequence of
events is different.   There, no serious break occurred
when Knossos was destroyed.   Unlike Knossos, again, this
site has yielded Late Helladic IIIa-b pottery, together
with the ground-plan of a megaron, possibly of mainland
type.   Excavation continues; but, if the foregoing observations are confirmed, it will be necessary to reckon
with the existence of a Mycenaean enclave at Kydonia.

The Cyclades

There cannot be much doubt that some at least of the Cycladic islands became virtually part of Mycenaean Greece by
the Late Helladic IIIb period.   The pottery imported into
Amorgos, Delos, Kythera, Melos, and Naxos is almost entirely Mycenaean, while the construction of a megaron of
Mycenaean type at Phylakopi in Melos points to a degree of
actual Mycenaean settlement.

The Dodecanese

Some eighty chamber tombs have been excavated in Rhodes,
chiefly in coastal areas.   The earliest Mycenaean tomb is
situated near Ialysos, in the north of the island, and contains Late Helladic IIb pottery.   Subsequently, Late Helladic III pottery becomes extremely plentiful, some of it
imported from mainland Greece, some made locally but never

deviating far from the standard Mycenaean style.   The
presence in Rhodes of great quantities of Mycenaean pottery (equivalent to several thousand whole vessels), together with the overwhelmingly Mycenaean character of the
tombs, indicates that Mycenaean settlements must have
flourished there in the Late Bronze Age.   It seems, in
fact, that Rhodes became the most important centre of
Mycenaean civilization outside the Greek mainland.   The
islands of Kos and Karpathos show a sequence similar to
that which Furumark established for Rhodes: the earliest
pottery is Cretan, of a transitional Middle-Late Minoan
type, and this is gradually superseded by Mycenaean.   Kos,
like Rhodes, contained a large cemetery of chamber tombs;
as in Rhodes, also, the tombs continued in use into Late
Helladic IIIc.   The Mycenaean chamber tombs in Karpathos
yielded some bronze weapons as well as abundant pottery.

Cyprus

Tombs and settlements in Cyprus have produced enormous
amounts of Late Helladic IIIa2 and IIIb pottery.   Most of
the usual shapes of decorated Mycenaean ware are found,
except stemmed goblets;   in addition, pictorial ware forms
an impressive series at some sites, notably Enkomi and
Kouklia.   Nor do direct imports from the Aegean account
for all the ware of Mycenaean appearance.   Towards the
end of Late Helladic IIIb, pottery of the so-called 'Rude
.Style' began to be manufactured locally in imitation of
Mycenaean prototypes.   The reason for this local manufacture is obscure.   We might suppose either that Mycenaean pottery was so highly prized in Cyprus that in time
imports failed to meet the demand, or that Mycenaeans had
settled in the island in sufficient numbers to make their
own pottery, or that direct communication with the Greek
mainland had been disrupted.

Whatever the true explanation may be, a long line of
scholars (for instance Gjerstad, Sjöqvist, and Catling)
have argued that, despite the great influx of Mycenaean
pottery, especially in Late Helladic IIIb, Cyprus was not
settled by Mycenaeans as early as their settlement of the
Dodecanese.   Long before the first appearance of Mycenaean pottery, it is argued, Cyprus possessed a vigorous
culture of its own, shown by its architectural techniques
(which find their expression in large buildings at Enkomi
and Idalion), by tombs different in kind from those of the
Greek mainland and Rhodes, and by several classes of
native pottery (of which the 'White Slip' and 'Base-Ring'
wares are the most distinctive.)   This indigenous culture,

so far from being submerged by the Mycenaean, lives on in
full vigour during Late Helladic IIIb.   Native Cypriot
pottery is exported in considerable quantities to Egypt and
to the Levant coast.   Above all, there is little trace in
Cyprus of any of the typical marks of Mycenaean culture, except pottery;   while the absence of tombs of Mycenaean type
argues against the probability that Mycenaean 'colonies'
had been established.

The nature of the Mycenaean presence in Cyprus is deba-
ted afresh in MEM.   Most of the contributors to this symposium, except K. Nicolau, agree with Catling that the actual settlement of Cyprus by Mycenaeans must be placed
after the end of Late Helladic IIIb, because it is only in
the twelfth century BC that such unambiguous marks of Mycenaean settlement as architecture, tombs, and metal-work
are seen (Chapter 7.)   By 'settlement' these scholars appear to mean colonization, in the sense that colonies were
planted by the classical Greeks.   The term colonization
implies a conscious political act, which I agree is difficult to associate with Bronze Age Cyprus.   We have little
information about the political circumstances of Cyprus in
the Bronze Age, except the fact that it was sometimes claimed by the Hittite kings as part of their empire (if
'Alasiya' in Hittite texts is indeed to be equated with
Cyprus;   but that equation is not so certain as is often
assumed.)   At the same time I, like Nicolau, am convinced
that it is wrong to deny the probability of some Mycenaean
settlement in Cyprus at the time of the great expansion in
the eastern Mediterranean;   and in my terminology the word
'settlement' carries with it no political implications
whatever.   To my mind, Aegean trade on the immense scale
attested in Cyprus (for a recent estimate of the volume of
pottery, see Aström, 1973) necessarily involves the more
or less permanent presence of Mycenaeans, if only to super-
vise the trading arrangements at their eastern end.   While
there is, admittedly, no weakening of the native Cypriot
culture in our period, it does appear that Mycenaean artefacts penetrated more deeply than was once thought.   Until
a few years ago, virtually all the Mycenaean pottery known
in Cyprus came from sites at or near the southern or eastern coasts, such as Kourion, Hala Sultan Tekké, Kition,
and Enkomi.   This pattern of distribution gave colour to
the idea that Mycenaean pottery was the product of a somewhat superficial, coastal trade.   The deduction is shown
to be faulty by Karageorghis' report of tombs at Akhera,
deep in the interior of the island, which contained an
abundance of Mycenaean pottery, belonging to Late Helladic
IIIa2 as well as to IIIb.

Anatolia

The commerce between the Greek mainland and Troy, which
had probably begun in the Middle Helladic period (Chapter
2), was kept up in the Late Bronze Age, leaving many Late
Helladic IIIa and IIIb sherds in Troy VI and Troy VIIa.
Mycenaean pottery has been found at other sites in western
Anatolia, from the Troad in the north to Lycia in the
south; but, with the exception of a stretch of seaboard
in what was later known as Caria, the Mycenaean pottery
indicates no more than trading contact.   It is true that
a tholos tomb has been excavated at Kolophon; but its
contents have not yet been published fully.   The three
sites which give good evidence of actual Mycenaean occupation are (from north to south) Miletus, Iasus, and Müsgebi.
Miletus, as we have seen, was a Minoan foundation, which
came within the Mycenaean sphere during the fifteenth century BC.   It was of considerable size and importance in
Late Helladic IIIb, when it was protected by a powerful
fortification-wall.   The earliest Aegean pottery at Iasus
is, likewise, Minoan: Late Minoan II pottery being followed directly by Late Helladic IIIa.   Iasus, like Miletus, was protected by a wall of apparently Mycenaean construction.   No Mycenaean settlement has yet been found at
Müsgebi, but the chamber tombs with Mycenaean pottery (the
earliest dated to Late Helladic IIIa2) strongly suggest
the presence of a settlement nearby.

Egypt and the Levant

The only really substantial deposit of Mycenaean pottery in
Egypt was found at Tell el Amarna and is datable, for the
most part, to Late Helladic IIIa2.   The advent of this
ceramic phase marks the effective beginning of Mycenaean
expansion on a large scale, not only in Egypt but also in
other parts of the eastern Mediterranean (Elizabeth
French, 1965, 159.)   A number of New Kingdom tombs, for
example those at Sakkara, Gurob, and as far inland as Abydos and Balabish (about 450 miles from the Nile Delta),
have produced individual examples of Mycenaean pottery,
especially stirrup-jars and pilgrim flasks: these seem to
have been prized articles (presumably filled with oil) for
depositing in tombs.   Apart from the sudden and unique
appearance of Mycenaean artefacts at Amarna, contacts between Greece and Egypt seem to have been constant but not
particularly extensive during the period of Mycenaean expansion.

The situation is different in Syria and Palestine. In
this area, Late Helladic IIIa pottery reached some twenty-
five sites, but rarely in such quantities as to suggest the
presence of Mycenaean settlers. Instead of falling away
in Late Helladic IIIb (as in Egypt), Mycenaean ceramic imports to the Levant actually increase during that period,
being found at some sixty sites from Alalakh in the north
to Ashdod in the south. At most places where Mycenaean
pottery is found, it is associated with Cypriot ware. The
Mycenaean pottery at these sites points to nothing more
than a lively Aegean trade with the Levant, presumably by
way of coastal sites such as Tell Abu Hawam and Byblos and
inland entrepôts like Hazor, north of the Sea of Galilee.
The question of actual Mycenaean settlement in the Levant
hardly arises, except at Ugarit (modern Ras Shamra) and,
possibly, at Tell Abu Hawam and Tell Sukas. These three
places have yielded a few Mycenaean figurines: objects
for which (unlike pottery) it is hard to imagine that anyone except Mycenaeans ever had a use (Elizabeth French,
1971, 175.) But, in other respects as well, Ugarit is
quite exceptional. This great palatial settlement, with
its harbour of Minet el Beida, stands on the Syrian coast
opposite the eastern extremity of Cyprus; and it has some
affinities with the Cypriot culture of the Late Bronze Age.
Long ago, Schaeffer deduced from the mass of Aegean pottery
at Ugarit (which has not, even now, been fully published)
that at some point within the Late Helladic period Mycenaeans had actually settled there, and by doing so had established an important link between the Aegean and the Semitic world. Subsequent excavations at Ugarit have in-
creased the amount of Mycenaean pottery known from that
site, some of it in types poorly represented elsewhere.
The beginning of a significant sequence of Mycenaean pottery comes here, as it does in Egypt, during the Amarna
period (Late Helladic IIIa2.) So far as other evidence
from Ugarit is concerned, the vaulted tombs ought not to
be regarded as necessarily those of Mycenaean settlers,
since any Aegean features discernible in their construction result from Minoan survival rather than from Mycenaean influence (Schaeffer, 1937, 147-56.)
   This purely archaeological treatment of Mycenaean remains in Syria, and particularly at Ugarit, must now be
supplemented by a more thorough-going enquiry into the
nature of the relationship between the peoples of the
Levant and the Mycenaean world.

MYCENAEANS AND SEMITES

The presence of Semitic loan-words in the Linear B texts
of the Aegean Bronze Age (c. 1400-1200 BC) was noted in
Chapter 2. At the very least, five such words can be
identified beyond reasonable doubt:

Mycenaean	ki-to	'tunic'	Ugaritic ktn
	ku-mi-no	'cummin'	kmn
	ku-pa-ro	'galingale'	kpr
	ku-ru-so	'gold'	hrs
	sa-sa-ma	'sesame'	ssmn

The occurrence of these Semitic loans is fully consistent with the archaeological evidence; for the pattern of
Mycenaean contacts along the coasts of Syria and Palestine
and, above all, the Mycenaean enclave (if that is what it
was) at Ugarit in northern Syria imply that there was a
lively trade in commodities westwards from the Semitic
area into the Aegean. So far as our information goes,
Ugarit occupied a unique place in the Mediterranean world
of the fourteenth and thirteenth centuries BC. It ful-
filled something like the function of a modern 'free port',
providing an entrepôt for trade among Cypriots, Aegeans,
Egyptians, and Anatolians. But the clay documents found
in the palace of Ugarit show that it was much more than a
mere trading-centre. Such documents, especially those
dealing with legal and diplomatic matters, are written in
Akkadian, the lingua franca of the whole of the eastern
Mediterranean. Most of the literary and religious texts,
on the other hand, find expression in the Ugaritic alphabet. As well as these, texts are found in Hieroglyphic
Hittite, in Hurrian (a non-Indo-European language origin-
ating in Mesopotamia and used for certain ritual and religious inscriptions), in Egyptian Hieroglyphs, and in the
Cypro-Minoan script. Ugarit was thus a meeting-place of
all the major cultures of the Mediterranean and Anatolia.
Although the Aegean contribution was not great in comparison with that of Babylonia, Mycenaean settlers (and, before
them, Minoans) were undoubtedly present; and therefore the
commonly accepted picture of Ugarit as a kind of bridge
between the Semitic and the Mycenaean world is likely to
be correct. It would be strange if, in such a milieu,
nothing was ever exchanged except objects of trade; and,
indeed, Ugarit is sometimes seen as the vital means of
communication whereby Semites exercised a profound influence upon the culture, and especially upon the literature,
of the Mycenaeans.

Even before the discovery of the texts from Ugarit, it was recognized that certain affinities (both thematic and stylistic) existed between the Old Testament and early Greek literature, especially the poems of Homer and Hesiod. It was not clear, however, whether the points of agreement arose from actual contact between Greeks and Hebrews or from mediation by a third people.   In the eyes of some writers, above all C.H. Gordon, it is Ugaritic literature which provides the background of both the Greek and the Hebrew tradition.   Gordon, 1962 cites numerous parallels between Ugaritic literature and early Greek poetry.   The most important of these by far is the similarity in theme between the legend of Krt and the plot of the 'Iliad'.   The resemblance of the Gilgamesh epic to the 'Odyssey' and correspondences between Hurrian succession myths and Hesiod's 'Theogony' are offered by Gordon as vaguely 'eastern' ingredients in the Greek tradition.   (Neither 'Gilgamesh' nor the Hurrian myths are attested directly at Ugarit.)

To deal in sufficient detail with these and the other topics mentioned in Gordon's book would need another book; and even then the discussion would be more relevant to the study of early Greek poetry than to the elucidation of the Late Bronze Age.   Nevertheless, the subject is necessarily of interest to the prehistorian, since there seem at first sight to be available at Ugarit materials from which more can be gained than from the artefacts which provide the bulk of his data.   Although I do not share Gordon's belief that so much was absorbed into the Greek poetic tradition at this time or in this place, it would be idle to deny the possibility of a degree of literary intercourse at Ugarit, answering to the commercial relationship which undoubtedly existed.

Naturally, Gordon presents the comparative material in a light which is as favourable to his case as possible.   Even so, I can detect only shadowy parallels between the theme of the 'Iliad' and that of the epic of Krt (whose name should be so written: Gordon's transcription Kret is unwarranted and, furthermore, implies a completely spurious connexion with the Aegean.)   Unlike the 'Iliad', the Krt epic is not concerned with the abduction of a king's wife, but with the desolation of his family: a god advises him to perform rites, raise a great army, march to a fortified city, and lay siege to it until the king of the city yields up his daughter for Krt to marry.   Thus, the only two elements which the two poems have in common are the siege and the demand for a woman who is inside the besieged city. If the presence of these common elements proves anything, it proves no more than that there was once a point of contact between the two poetic traditions.

The Gilgamesh epic is known in Old Babylonian and Assyrian versions: the oldest of these reach back to the first half of the second millennium BC and depend on still earlier Sumerian narratives. Fragments of the epic are also extant in Hittite and Hurrian recensions. No version of it has yet turned up at Ugarit, but recently fragments have been discovered at Megiddo (a site about 200 miles south of Ugarit, which has yielded Mycenaean pottery.) This great epic is conceived on a cosmic scale and is, in spirit and outlook, as different as it could well be from the 'Odyssey'. It is true that in both epics a hero wanders far, undergoes a series of adventures, and eventually returns home. But the motive for the wandering is different in each case. Gilgamesh travels because of his restless curiosity, Odysseus because of the unrelenting hatred of a god. Individual scenes sometimes have a vague resemblance to each other, especially those which concern the underworld; but, once again, there is not enough evidence to suggest that the Gilgamesh epic had any direct influence on the tradition represented by our 'Odyssey'.

The Hurrian myth of Kumarbi and Ullikummi, on the other hand, provides parallels so close to the succession of gods described in Hesiod's 'Theogony' as to give it far greater evidential value for our purpose than either of the epics just mentioned. In both the Greek and the Hurrian accounts the details of the early history of the gods are close enough to make it certain that they descend from a common ancestor. A comparison of the principal incidents brings out the similarity:

Alalu, king of the gods, is
overthrown by Anu

Anu is overthrown and castrated by Kumarbi	Uranos, king of the gods, is overthrown and castrated by Kronos
Kumarbi is (presumably) overthrown by Teshub (the Hurrian weather-god), who defeats the monster Ullikummi	Kronos is overthrown by Zeus (the Greek weather-god), who defeats the monster Typhoeus

(Although Ugarit has not yet revealed a version of the Kumarbi myth, it knows of a genealogy of gods, in which El corresponds to the Hurrian Kumarbi and Baal to the Hurrian Teshub.)

However high we estimate the probability of contact between eastern and Mycenaean literature at Ugarit, actual evidence of such contact proves, on investigation, hard to come by. Even where the presence of an eastern element is certain, as with Kumarbi, we have no guarantee that it entered the Greek poetic tradition at Bronze Age Ugarit or, for that matter, within the Bronze Age at all. Although both Homer and Hesiod preserve many Bronze Age features, we are completely without knowledge of the nature of Mycenaean literature at the time of the commerce with Ugarit. Of course, the theories of Gordon and his school presuppose that the Mycenaean contacts in the Near East afforded the only opportunity for the absorption of Semitic and Anatolian motifs into Greek poetry. That would be a sound inference, were the Late Bronze Age the only period at which eastern elements might have entered the Greek tradition. But who can say with certainty whether these elements were taken over in the Greek mainland during the Bronze Age or (what is no less likely) in Anatolia itself when it was settled by Greeks after the end of the Mycenaean period? In the light of excavation at Miletus and Smyrna, the earliest Greek colonization of western Anatolia must now be put back into the tenth or even the eleventh century BC. I do not know whether it is correct to regard this movement as the beginning of the Ionian migration; but about the fact of Greek settlement in the area there can be no doubt. Since it is in this very area (to judge from their prevailing dialect) that the Homeric poems were put into their final form, it seems reasonable to suppose that the eastern motifs entered the Greek tradition by way of the neo-Hittite kingdoms which lay inland from the Greek settlements on the Anatolian coast. The 'Theogony' of Hesiod, whose composition must be assigned to mainland Greece and not to Ionia, presents a difficult problem. But in Hesiod's poetry too, despite its mainland provenience, the Ionic dialect is present in sufficient strength to persuade us of the likelihood that, along with the epic dialect, epic themes (including themes picked up from the east) were brought to the Greek mainland.

   So much for the question of oriental motifs in early Greek poetry; though, I repeat, it is a subject which deserves fuller treatment than can be given here.   M.C. Astour is another scholar who has considered the relationship between the Mycenaean and the Semitic world at the time of the great expansion. He finds evidence in place-names, in religion, and in myth sufficient to prove, in his eyes, a penetration of the Mycenaean area by Semites. 'Not only', he concludes, 'was Phoenician spoken in several parts of Mycenaean Greece, but the entire Mycenaean civilization was essentially a peripheral culture of the Ancient East, its westernmost extension' (Astour, 1967, 357-8.)

This is a truly breath-taking conclusion, which is not
remotely justified by the evidence (bulky though it is)
assembled in the earlier parts of Astour's book. While
the probability remains that the impact of Semites on the
Mycenaean world was greater than historians supposed at the
beginning of our century, yet the essential independence of
the Mycenaean culture manifests itself in every conceivable
aspect (Chapter 5.)   Further, it is between c. 1350 and
1250 BC, precisely when we are invited to believe that they
became part of a Near Eastern cultural community, that the
Mycenaeans most vigorously asserted their independent character.   Previously, it is true, they had owed much to
Crete;   afterwards, under threat or compulsion, they turned
increasingly to Cyprus and the east.   Not so in this era,
when the Helladic culture of mainland Greece reaches its
climax.   Only very powerful arguments could prevail
against the obvious inference from the material features
displayed by the Mycenaean world in the phase of its greatest expansion.   But it is what I may call 'non-material'
features, such as cycles of legend and place-names, which
form the major part of Astour's testimony: these, as has
been shown in earlier chapters, call for the exercise of
very stringent methods - more stringent, certainly, than
are apparent in Astour's discussion.   He is very far from
having proved that there was a Phoenician settlement at
Thebes or shown that there was the slightest connexion between the Danuna of Cilicia and the Danaoi of the Peloponnese.   He has little to say about the material aspects of
the respective civilizations he is comparing (understand-
ably so, since the artefacts of the Mycenaean world betray only small traces of Semitic influence);   but his
remarks in this field also (for example his deduction from
the absence of references to Aegeans in Ugaritic documents
that there can have been no Aegean settlement at Ugarit or
his supposition that the wealth of Mycenaean pottery was
taken to Ugarit not by Mycenaeans but by Phoenicians) show
that the prima facie case for the independence of the Mycenaean culture has not been seriously contested.

THE MYCENAEANS AND THE HITTITES

The cuneiform documents from the Hittite capital (near the
modern Boghazköy in central Anatolia) could be read by the
1920s: that is to say, before the systematic excavation
of Mycenaean sites in Anatolia.   The texts are very numerous and of diverse kinds.   One important class relates
to the foreign affairs of the Hittite kings and comprises
annals, letters, treaties, and the like.   These texts,

some of which (like the Annals of Mursili II in the fourteenth century BC) are immensely detailed, enable us to reconstruct in broad outline the course of Hittite history
during the 'Empire period' (c. 1460-1190 BC.)   The aim of
the Hittite kings, above all, was to secure the frontiers
to the west and south of their empire and, sometimes, to
the east as well.   To this end, they used (besides force)
diplomatic methods, especially by creating vassal-states.
In the west, the Hittites found rebellious vassals very
troublesome;   and it is very doubtful if the Hittite kings
exercised full control, for any long periods, as far as the
western coast of Anatolia.   Alongside these activities on
the frontiers, the Hittite kings engaged in international
diplomacy, especially with Egypt, Assyria, and Babylonia.
For the most part, all these kingdoms managed to live together without resorting to outright war;   but, early in
the thirteenth century, the Hittites pursued an aggressive
policy in the south and marched into Syria.   Such action
threatened Egyptian interests in the area, and at Kadesh
on the Orontes a great battle was fought c. 1285 BC between
the forces of the Hittite king Muwatalli and those of
Ramesses II.   The accounts of the battle in Egyptian inscriptions speak of a conflict between Ramesses (with his
Sherden mercenaries) and a coalition of enemies, the Hittites 'having gathered together all countries from the
ends of the sea to the land of Hatti':

Hittites and vassal-states	Syrian allies
Hatti (Hittites)	Karchemish
Mesa	Ekereth (Ugarit)
Kelekesh	Kode
Lyka (Lycia?)	Nuges
	Kadesh
	Mesheneth (?)

Despite the clear implication of the Egyptian text, the
battle was in fact inconclusive, and Ramesses was not able
to dislodge the Hittites from Syria.   A few years later,
an elaborate treaty (extant in both Egyptian and Hittite
versions) was drawn up, formally recognizing the Hittites
as overlords of Syria and northern Phoenicia.   It has
been suggested that Hittites and Egyptians alike were eager
to settle their differences because the so-called Peoples
of the Sea were already making inroads into their kingdoms
(cf. Chapter 7.)
   The question now arises whether the Mycenaeans took any
part in the boundary-disputes or the international negoti-
ations which exercised several generations of Hittite

kings.   E.O. Forrer was the first to claim that the Hittite documents present conclusive evidence of such activity
on the part of the Mycenaeans.   He discerned a number of
words which, in his view, represented the Hittite spelling
of Greek proper names: above all Ahhiyawa, which he identified as Achaia (originally Achaiwa.)   Ahhiyawa he took
to denote the Mycenaean Greek empire of the fourteenth and
thirteenth centuries BC, with its capital at Mycenae and
its eastern outpost in the south of Anatolia.   The observations made in his papers from 1924 onwards were incorporated into a coherent account of the geography and foreign
relations of the Hittite kingdom and published as Forrer,
1926 and 1929.   Other scholars saw further evidence of
Greek names in the Hittite records: for example, the name
Milawata (which the Hittites also spelt Millawanda) was
identified with the Mycenaean settlement at Miletus, while
Alaksandu the king of Wilusa was taken to reflect Alexand-
ros (Homer's alternative name for Paris) of Wilios (later
Ilios = Troy.)

All these suggestions, and indeed the very notion that
the Mycenaeans were mentioned in the Hittite texts at all,
met with the determined opposition of F. Sommer.   In Sommer, 1932 all the relevant Hittite texts were collected
and translated, with exhaustive historical and linguistic
commentary.   In this important work, and in two later
ones of smaller scope, Sommer brought powerful arguments
against the validity of all the equations proposed, which
he thought were purely coincidental.   Ahhiyawa he regarded as an Anatolian state, having nothing to do with Achaia
or with the Mycenaeans.

The last twenty years or so have witnessed a recrudes-
cence of the 'Ahhiyawa' question.   Although they found
their researches on Sommer's work (as we all must), most
modern writers on the subject have rejected his principal
conclusion.   Whether or not they believe that the strict
equation Ahhiyawa=Achaiwa can be justified on linguistic
grounds, they identify Ahhiyawa either with the Mycenaean
'empire' as a whole or with a part of it.   Among those
who opt for the latter view, Cyprus, Rhodes, and Crete have
all, from time to time, found favour.   Before we can hope
to evaluate these suggestions and consider what light they
throw on the oversea connexions of the Mycenaeans, we must
examine the Hittite texts themselves.   There follows an
outline of all those which are relevant.   I have not considered it worth while to record inscriptions which give
the bare name 'Ahhiyawa' without any context or those in
which the word 'Ahhiyawa' has been restored by the conjec-
ture of modern editors.

No 1 (Sommer, chap. 1)(the 'Tawagalawa Letter')

A Hittite king (second half of the fourteenth century BC?)
complains to the king of Ahhiyawa (whom he addresses as
'my brother') that a certain Piyamaradu, a Hittite vassal
but evidently at present under the protection of Ahhiyawa,
has been raiding Hittite territory. The Hittite king says
that he went into Millawanda to seize Piyamaradu but that
Piyamaradu escaped by sea; he accordingly asks that Piyamaradu should either be sent into the land of Hatti or be
settled in the land of Ahhiyawa. It is emphasized that
the envoy who brings the message is known of old to the
brother of the king of Ahhiyawa as well as to the king of
Hatti. The tone of the letter is by turns reproachful
and conciliatory; there are conflicts of interest between
Hatti and Ahhiyawa, but the Hittite king hopes (or pro-
fesses to hope) that these will be settled amicably. The
reference to the high-born messenger (Column II, lines 58-
61 of the inscription) implies a previous period of close
friendship between the royal houses of Hatti and Ahhiyawa.
The letter contains no clue to the location of Ahhiyawa.
Despite a common assumption, nothing in the letter suggests
that the place Millawanda (as distinct from the person Piyamaradu) is under the protection of Ahhiyawa: precisely
the opposite, since the Hittite king says that he went in
person to Millawanda, in the hope of laying hands on Piyamaradu.

No 2 (Sommer, chap. 2)

A fragment of a letter from a Hittite king refers to Ahhiyawa, Piyamaradu, and ships.

No 3 (Sommer, chap. 3)(the 'Milawata Letter')

In a much damaged letter, a Hittite king writes to a recipient whom he addressas as 'my son', in order to regulate
the frontier between Hatti and Milawata. The letter does
nothing to solve the Ahhiyawa problem: it concerns a
boundary-dispute between two Anatolian rulers.

No 4 (Sommer, chap. 4)

A Hittite king writes an evasive letter, in which he de-
clines to bind himself to share with the recipient (as re-
quested) gifts sent to Hatti by the king of Ahhiyawa. The

content of the letter suggests that good relations obtained
between the two kings at the time of writing.

No 5 (Sommer, chap. 5)

Small fragments of a letter (?) to the king of Ahhiyawa (?)
from a Hittite king (?)   'It is of interest only in so far
as the same text mentions the land of Ahhiyawa (recto, line
1) and the land of Mira (verso, line 8)' (Sommer, 1932,
252.)

No 6 (Sommer, chap. 9)

The land of Ahhiyawa is mentioned in lines 1 and 12 of a
fragmentary letter (probably from a Hittite king), which
in lines 7 and 14 refers to the king of Assuwa (thirteenth
century BC.)

No 7 (Sommer, chap. 10)

A divination text concerned with the illness of the Hittite
king Mursili II (c. 1350-1320 BC.)   Among many other re-
plies, irrelevant for the present purpose, the oracle
states that the god (i.e. the cult-idol) of Ahhiyawa, the
god of Lazpa, and his own personal god have been brought
to heal the king (Column II, lines 57 and 60.)   It explains, further, the ritual to be followed in respect of
the foreign gods.   There is no indication where either
Ahhiyawa or Lazpa is situated; but it is obvious that they
were both regarded, at the time, as friendly states.

No 8 (Sommer, chap. 12)

A small fragment appears to associate the land of Karkiya
(?) with the land of Ahhiyawa (line 15.)

No 9 (Sommer, chap. 13)

A damaged tablet from the reign of Mursili II makes, on
the reverse side (lines 4-6), an obscure reference to the
banishment of the king's mother 'into the land of Ahhiyawa'.

No 10 (Sommer, chap. 14 = Goetze, 1933, 36-7)

A passage from the Annals of Mursili II (soon after 1340
BC) brings the king of Ahhiuwa (sic) into connexion with
the land of Millawanda (line 24);   subsequent lines refer
to attacks by soldiers and horses and the capture of pri-
soners.   The damaged condition of the tablet precludes
any certainty about the nature of the relationship between
Millawanda, Hatti, and Ahhiuwa.

No 11 (Sommer, chap. 15 = Goetze, 1933, 66-7)

Small fragments of the Annals of Mursili II give 'king of
the land of Ahhiyawa' at the end of Column III, line 3 and
'by ship I sent' at the end of line 4.   No historical deductions are permissible, especially since IT.TI, the pre-
position before 'king of the land of Ahhiyawa', can mean
either 'to' or 'with' or 'against'.

No 12 (Friedrich, 1930, 50-3)

A treaty between the Hittite king Muwatalli (floruit 1300
BC) and Alaksandu of Wilusa confirms the long-standing
friendship between the two states and summons Alaksandu to
send him information about any impending rebellion in the
land of the Seha River or in Arzawa (regions which therefore seem to be close to Wilusa) and to render military
assistance to the Hittites if they are involved in war with
any of the great powers (Egyptians, Babylonians, Hurrians,
and Assyrians.)   (Ahhiyawa is not mentioned;   the text is
included here because it forms the most important piece of
evidence for Alaksandu and Wilusa.)

No 13 (Sommer, chap. 16)

Fragments from the Annals of Tudhaliya IV (c. 1265-1215 BC)
record a successful campaign by the king.   It appears
from the beginning of our text that the people who live in
the land of the Seha River (cf. No 12) have rebelled and
have boasted that 'the grandfather of My Sun' ('My Sun' =
the reigning Hittite king) failed to conquer them.   After
a mention of 'war', line 5 states that 'the king of Ahhiyawa withdrew '(?);   line 6 that 'I, the Great King, advanced'.   Two, and only two, deductions can properly be made
from this text, but they are both of great importance: (i)
the king of Ahhiyawa was present in person in Anatolia;
(ii) he lent aid to a rebel against the Hittite king.

No 14 (Sommer, chap. 17)

The extant parts of a solemn treaty between Tudhaliya IV
and the king of Amurru (a state on the coast of Syria,
south of Ugarit) contain a mention of the king of Ahhiyawa,
which, for some reason, has been erased. Column IV reads
as follows:
 1: and the kings who are equal to Myself:
 2: the king of Egypt, the king of Babylonia,
 3: the king of Assyria, ~~the king of Ahhiyawa~~:
 4: if the king of Egypt is a friend of My Sun,
 5: let him be your friend also;
 6: if he is an enemy of My Sun,
 7: let him be your enemy also;
 8: if the king of Babylonia
 9: is a friend of My Sun, let him also be your
10: friend; if of My Sun he
11: is an enemy, let him be your enemy also;
12: as the king of Assyria is an enemy of My Sun,
13: so let him be your enemy also...

No 15 (Sommer, chap. 18)

A very fragmentary list of states (date unknown) mentions
the city of Dattassa (line 4), the land of Mira (line 5),
and the land of Ahhiyawa (line 6.)   (For the association
of Mira with Ahhiyawa, cf. No 5.)

No 16 (Sommer, chap. 19 = Goetze, 1928)(the Madduwatta text)

This text was originally dated (for instance by Goetze,
1928, 158-9) to the reign of Arnuwanda III, shortly before
1200 BC; but reasons have been given for preferring a
higher date, c. 1390 BC.   The re-dating and its implications are discussed below.   According to the text, Madduwatta has been expelled from his country by Attarissiya,
'a man of Ahhiya (sic)', who was intent on his destruction.
After fleeing to 'the father of My Sun', Madduwatta was
accorded refuge by the Hittite king (recto, lines 1-5) and
settled by him in the hill-country of Zippalsa (line 15.)
Subsequently, Attarissiya made another attack on Madduwatta
and, when the Hittite king heard of it, he sent a force
against Attarissiya and restored Madduwatta to his dominion (lines 61-5.)   The writer of the text goes on to speak
of other matters connected with Madduwatta: these are irrelevant here, except that the Hittite king lays claim to
Alasiya and contrasts the vassal-status of Madduwatta with
the independent position of Attarissiya (verso, lines 88-9.)

No 17 (Güterbock, 1936, 321)

A fragmentary text of unknown date gives a list of gar-
ments, fabrics, and utensils; one of which is specified as
'of Ahhiyawa type' (or, possibly, 'from Ahhiyawa'.)

No 18 (Güterbock, 1936, 323-6)

Fragments of a letter (?) from or to a Hittite king relate
the help given in war by a king of Ahhiyawa to the Hittite
king Urhi-Teshub (c. 1290-80 BC.)

According to the 'traditional' system of dating, we have
here a series of references to a land called Ahhiya(wa),
or to the activities of its king, from about the middle of
the fourteenth century until near the end of the thirteenth
century BC.   No 16 was previously thought to reflect the
disturbed conditions which prevailed at a time shortly before the collapse of the Hittite empire.   But it has long
been recognized that this text contains a number of archaic
features, both scribal and linguistic, which belong to a
much earlier period.   The presence of these features used
to be attributed to the archaizing tendency of the school
of writing to which the scribe of our text belonged.   More
recently, the suggestion has been made that these archaic
features can be accounted for more satisfactorily if the
date of No 16 is moved back to a time early, instead of
late, in the history of the Hittite empire; and, it is
said, the state of affairs described in the text (namely
Attarissiya's successful defiance of the Great King over a
long period) is no less appropriate to the time of the establishment of the empire than to that of its disintegration.   The proposal to place the Madduwatta text in a
much earlier period has met with opposition, partly on
linguistic grounds and partly because it throws the accepted Hittite king-list into disarray.   The matter is not
yet settled; but, should some clinching argument ever appear for the earlier date, it will put out of court the
equation Ahhiya(wa)=Achaiwa, since no one (I suppose) is
going to claim that a Mycenaean 'empire' was already in
existence early in the fourteenth century.
    As I see it, the Ahhiyawa question will never be ans-
wered simply by examining the proposed equations Ahhiyawa=
Achaiwa, Alaksandu=Alexandros, and the rest.   As for the
central equation, Ahhiyawa=Achaiwa, on the validity of
which the others to some extent depend, this is neither so
obvious that it can be accepted without question nor so

far-fetched as to be excluded from the discussion altogether.   If a criticism of Sommer's treatment is permissible, it is that he devoted proportionately too much space
to the linguistic problems raised by the equation;   and
even then he was able to demonstrate only that the equation
was inexplicable, not that it was impossible.   It is, indeed, notoriously difficult to control the degree of dis-
tortion which may take place when words, and especially
proper names, are taken over from one language into another;   yet it remains true that a convincing analysis of
the word Ahhiyawa has not been arrived at.   The problem is
complicated further if account is taken of the variants
Ahhiuwa and Ahhiya, especially the latter.   There seems no
obvious way of accounting for this in conformity with the
sound-changes of the Hittite language itself;   nor can
Ahhiyawa and Ahhiya represent the Hittite rendering of two
separate stages in the history of the Greek word, since it
is known that in Greek the -w- sound between vowels was not
lost until after the end of the Bronze Age.

An objection (but not necessarily a fatal objection) to
the identification of Ahhiyawa with Achaiwa is that there
is no evidence for the existence in the Bronze Age of a
Greek word Achaiwa meaning 'the whole extent of Mycenaean
power'.   Homer, indeed, who never applies the term 'Hellenes' to the Greek contingents at Troy, often calls them
Achaioi;   their country, however, he calls not Achaia but
Achaiis - and this, from the way it is used ('Iliad' 3. 75,
etc.), plainly means a part of the Peloponnese, not Greece
as a whole.   When the name 'Achaia' at last appears in
extant Greek literature (Thucydides 1. 115. 1), it still
means no more than Homer meant by his 'Achaiis', namely
one of the states in the Peloponnese.

From a linguistic point of view, then, the equation
Ahhiyawa=Achaiwa is seen to be theoretically possible, but
lacking positive confirmation either on the Greek or on the
Hittite side.   Bearing in mind this theoretical possibility, we next ask what information is provided about Ahhiyawa by the Hittite texts.

The relationship between Hatti and Ahhiyawa was evidently a changing one;   and there is no wonder in that,
since we have to do with an intercourse which lasted for
about a century and a half.   Although Ahhiyawa is sometimes friendly with Hatti (Nos 4, 7, 9, 18), sometimes opposed to it (Nos 13, 16), and sometimes in an equivocal
role (No 1), there can be no doubt about its status in the
eyes of the Hittite court: it is an independent state (No
16), and its king is addressed as 'my brother' (No 1.)   We
must not, however, follow Forrer and Schachermeyr and their
disciples, who deduce from No 14 that Tudhaliya really re-

garded the king of Ahhiyawa as one of the 'Great Kings'
along with those of Egypt, Assyria, and Babylonia.   The
fact that the reference to the king of Ahhiyawa has been
erased absolutely forbids us to draw any such conclusion
(Sommer, 1932, 322; Ranoszek, 1950, 242.)   The reason
for writing this entry in the first place can only be sur-
mised: it might be suggested, for instance, that the
scribe had just written a tablet which did contain the
entry 'king of Ahhiyawa' (though not in such exalted com-
pany) and wrote it again here by an oversight (cf. Carratelli, 1960, 322.)   About the reason for the erasure, on
the other hand, there can be no dispute at all: the 'king
of Ahhiyawa' was erased because he was not, and could not
be thought to be, a mighty sovereign of the same rank as
that of the other kings mentioned.

No fact so far adduced suggests that the Hittite kings,
in dealing with Ahhiyawa, thought they were dealing with a
great empire comparable to their own.   Nor have we any
reason to suppose that they placed Ahhiyawa overseas at
all.   The location of Ahhiyawa anywhere outside Anatolia
is founded on no single statement in the Hittite texts
themselves.   To put Ahhiyawa overseas is to forsake reason for emotion: the same emotion which led writers like
Forrer and Schachermeyr to construct a quite illusory account, in which great empires were seen coming to grips
with each other.   What, after all, are the grounds for
believing that Ahhiyawa was situated outside Anatolia?

No 1 is held to imply that the king of Ahhiyawa exercised only a remote and uncertain control over the activities of Piyamaradu and must therefore have had his seat at
some considerable distance from Millawanda; and that may
well be true, but the location of Ahhiyawa at some other
point on the long coast-line of Anatolia is not thereby
excluded.   A similar consideration applies to No 9.   If
this text really speaks of the banishment of Mursili's
mother into the land of Ahhiyawa, the only inference we
can properly make is the same as before, namely that Ahhiyawa was situated a long way from the Hittite capital, not
that it was outside Anatolia altogether.   It is utterly
mistaken to conclude from Nos 2 and 11 that Ahhiyawa must
have lain overseas because it was necessary to take ship
to get there; only by making extensive and tendentious
'restorations' in the fragmentary texts (and the restorers,
of course, assume the very fact they are seeking to prove,
namely the oversea location of Ahhiyawa) can such a meaning
be extracted from them.   It is clear that no worth-while
historical conclusions can be reached by employing methods
such as these.   On the contrary, the few hints given by
the Hittite documents suggest that Ahhiyawa was situated

in Anatolia.   Not very much can be made of the appearance
in the same text of Ahhiyawa and Mira (No 5) or of Ahhiyawa, Mira, and Dattassa (No 15)(even though Mira, at any
rate, was certainly in Anatolia):   again, our inscriptions
are too fragmentary to let us discern the relative positions of all the places mentioned in them.   But what are
we to make of Nos 13 and 16?   No 13 states distinctly that
the king of Ahhiyawa was present on the Anatolian mainland;
in the absence of the slightest indication that he had arrived in Anatolia from elsewhere, what right have we to
assume that he had not been in Anatolia all along?   So
with No 16.   Here again there is no hint that Attarissiya
has come into Anatolia from outside;   it would be difficult
to imagine that he had done so, in view of his attack on
Zippalsa: a region of Anatolia usually identified with
the classical Mount Dindymus, which is 160 miles from the
sea and separated from it by Arsuwa, Assuwa, Lukka, and
Wilusa (some of which, at least, were friendly to the kings
of Hatti.)   Again, the assumption of an oversea location
for Ahhiyawa is simply not consistent with the testimony
of our texts, unsatisfactory as these are in many ways.
     The identification of Ahhiyawa with the Mycenaean world
or with a part of it outside Anatolia must accordingly be
abandoned.   Is it possible, however, that Ahhiyawa denoted
a Mycenaean state in Anatolia itself?   As we have already
seen, the interior of Anatolia has produced very little in
the way of Mycenaean imports.   Only on the west coast is
it possible to find evidence of actual Mycenaean settlement: even there, Miletus alone is credible as the seat
of a king of Ahhiyawa.   It does not seem to me possible
to take the argument any farther at present.   An interpretation of Hittite geography which would involve the location of Ahhiyawa in the north-west (that is, in the area
of the Troad) has much to recommend it, and I would not
regard with any great dismay the loss of the Wilusa=Wilios
equation;   but, as with all the other suggestions for the
situation of Ahhiyawa, positive identification is lacking.
The most we can say, setting side by side the archaeological evidence of Mycenaean remains and reasonable inferences from the Hittite documents, is that the Mycenaeans
made very little, if any, incursion into the interior of
Asia Minor and that, whatever trade may have existed be-
them and the Hittites, the relationship was commercial
only and not political or diplomatic.   To the wider question, whether there was a Mycenaean empire of the same
character as the Hittite, we must now turn.

CONCLUSIONS

In this and the preceding chapters, we have observed the
rise in mainland Greece of a distinctive Mycenaean culture
and its gradual expansion over much of Greece itself and
subsequently its extension into other areas. The extension overseas, at least to the east and south, did not represent any new and independent ventures on the part of the
Mycenaeans, since for the most part they simply moved into
the gaps left by the contraction of Minoan influence. That
is clearly the pattern of Mycenaean settlement in Rhodes,
in the Cyclades, and at Miletus and Iasus; while Egypt,
Cyprus, and Syria had all been partners in Minoan trade
long before they were reached by Mycenaeans. At some of
the sites in question (for example Phylakopi, Miletus, and
Ialysos) an epoch intervenes between the period of full
Minoan and that of full Mycenaean dominance, in which mainland and Minoan artefacts are found together: a fact which
fairly certainly suggests a gradual supersession of Minoan
by Mycenaean influence; this, in its turn, points to the
conclusion that (at least in its early stages) the Mycenaean expansion, though unquestionably a very vigorous
movement, was essentially a peaceful one, consisting of
the establishment of centres of trade and the opening up
of trade-routes along much the same lines as those followed
by the Minoans in the Late Palace Period.
    Inferences of this limited nature seem to flow quite
naturally from the material evidence. We now have to
consider a wider and much more difficult question: does
the mass of material evidence, together with any other
data that come to hand, enable us to understand the political character of the Mycenaean world at the time of the
great expansion?
    So far as archaeological evidence goes, the external
features of the Mycenaean world can be seen in clear outlines. It is evident that a culture of a highly uniform
kind spread over much of Greece, the Cyclades, and Rhodes,
having walled outposts at Miletus and Iasus and very extensive trading connexions (if they were no more than that)
with Cyprus and the Syrian coast. An examination of the
decorative motifs of exported Mycenaean pottery and also,
so far as it has gone, spectroscopic analysis of its fabric show that the mass of this pottery was not made locally
in the places where it was found but had been produced in
the Greek mainland and sent from there to Mycenaean settlements and trading-posts abroad.
    In default of evidence to the contrary, we might deduce
from the great masses of Mycenaean pottery in the east and
from the very meagre quantities of eastern imports in

Greece that Mycenaean pottery was carried to foreign ports
in Mycenaean bottoms (so, for instance, Immerwahr, 1960,
6.)   The discovery and examination of a Syrian merchant
ship, which was wrecked off Cape Gelidoniya in southern
Anatolia c. 1200 BC, have led to a reconsideration of the
nature of Mycenaean commerce.   The ship carried a cargo
of Cypriot copper ingots, weighing in all about a ton. The
following conclusions have been drawn from the contents of
the wreck by its principal excavator:

> Phoenician merchant ships, including that at Gelidoniya,
> would not have returned with empty holds to Cyprus and
> the near east, and it is reasonable to assume that their
> cargoes consisted largely of Mycenaean pottery which
> often contained perishable goods.   But what had the
> ships originally carried westward on their out-bound
> voyage?... It was metal, above all, that arrived in
> Greece on ships such as that which sank at Gelidoniya
> while carrying its cargo toward the Aegean.   (Bass,
> 1967, 165.)

But the reasoning is faulty.   It is a mere possibility, no
more, that the ship wrecked at Gelidoniya was on its way to
the Aegean;   naturally, the possibility is remoter still
that it was destined for a port in Mycenaean Greece.   Even
if that was its destination, we are not thereby entitled to
conjure up a whole merchant fleet, making in the same
direction and carrying similar cargoes.   Such a far-
reaching deduction from this one particular case seems to
arise from the notion that imports from the east must have
entered Mycenaean Greece as an approximate counter-balance
to the Mycenaean exports.   But to account for all these
ceramic exports by speculating about what the Mycenaeans
imported in exchange is to make a series of unsupported
and unwarranted assumptions: for example, that there was
a discrete Mycenaean 'state' and that the 'economy' of
this state was based on a system of 'balance of payments'.
We may, indeed, be sure that metals (especially copper and
tin) and also spices and ivory formed part of the commerce
in the opposite direction;   and, if we wished to press the
point, we might insist that all the fine Mycenaean ware in
Cyprus was, in origin, 'payment' for Cypriot metal or that
in the Levant for Syrian ivory.   But the explanation
breaks down when we consider the situation in Rhodes: an
island which received a larger amount of Mycenaean pottery
than any other part of the Mediterranean but which (so far
as we can tell) produced nothing on such a scale as concei-
vably to counter-balance these extensive imports.   But the
Mycenaean pottery should not always be regarded as payment
for goods received;   since, given Mycenaean settlements on
the scale attested, what is more natural than that the

Mycenaeans abroad should insist on having artefacts of a
kind to which they were accustomed and, for that reason,
kept whole factories busy in the Greek homeland producing
objects to satisfy their needs?   If we ask, why did the
Mycenaean settlers in the east not use the local wares,
the answer must lie in the admittedly high quality of the
Mycenaean ware, mass-produced though it was.

When we try to go beyond the most obvious conclusions
which may be drawn from the archaeological evidence, we
face the following question: does the homogeneity of Mycenaean artefacts, considered together with their diffusion
from the Greek mainland, impose a belief in the existence
of a recognizable 'empire', having a political centre at
Mycenae, which was able to impose its will at any point
within that empire?   By many writers to-day this question
is answered in the affirmative, not only because of the
strictly archaeological evidence but for these two further
reasons: (i) the mention of Ahhiyawa in contemporary Hittite documents shows that the Hittites were dealing with
an Achaean (Mycenaean) empire; and (ii) such an empire is
consistent with the picture of Greece presented in the
'Iliad'.

Of the three facts adduced in support of the existence
of a Mycenaean 'empire', namely homogeneity of culture,
consistency with the Homeric account, and the witness of
the Hittite documents, the last can be dismissed immediately.   The unified character of the material culture and
its diffusion from the Greek mainland form more substantial
arguments in favour of the hypothesis.   Yet here too we
must be on our guard against drawing conclusions of one
kind from evidence of another.   Although, of course, cultural uniformity is consistent with political unity, its
presence does not by itself necessarily imply that there
was unified political control.   Even without looking beyond the Aegean Bronze Age, we can see in Middle Minoan
Crete (Early Palace Period) the participation in a unified
material culture of at least three separate, and to all
appearance quite independent, palatial centres.   To this
situation that of continental Greece at the time of the
Mycenaean expansion closely corresponds.   Greece, like
Crete in the earlier period, contains not one great centre
and then other sites which are merely its dependencies but
important palaces in different areas (at least five in
number), each of which is surrounded by smaller settlements.   The citadel at Mycenae is equalled, if not sur-
passed, in the strength of its fortifications by that of
Tiryns; while in size and extent of bureaucratic organization the Pylian palace is a close rival.   A fourth administrative centre was situated at Thebes.

The presumption that at the time of the great expansion
Mycenaean Greece consisted of a number of independent kingdoms, without any central over-riding authority, could be
seriously disturbed only by the discovery of documents
similar to those from the capital cities of contemporary
empires.   But, until the king of Mycenae is said by contemporaries to act, or himself claims to act, in order to
uphold his authority not merely in Greece but also in Greek
settlements abroad, I see no reason not to draw the obvious
conclusion from the evidence and to think in terms of independent kings who shared a common material culture and who
might, indeed, sometimes form confederations but who might
equally well engage in mutual hostilities (cf. Thomas,
1970b; Sarkady, 1973.)   Hostile relations between two
states would satisfactorily explain the progressive strengthening of two sites so close to each other as Mycenae and
Tiryns and also, as will be seen in the next chapter, the
disintegration of Mycenaean Greece.

The problem raised by the closeness of the two great
citadels of Tiryns and Mycenae is especially relevant to
these 'political' questions and so calls for closer examination.   When Page took the problem into consideration,
he lucidly stated the three possibilities: either Mycenae
and Tiryns were governed by independent rulers, or they
were built and ruled by the same royal house, or their
rulers were different but not independent (Page, 1959,
130-1.)   They cannot have been the seats of independent
rulers, according to Page, because they would not have left
each other in peace for long enough to accomplish the work
of building the massive fortifications; furthermore, the
custom of inhabiting settlements outside the walls would
never have arisen, if those who dwelt there were liable to
sudden attack.   Neither argument seems very impressive to
me.   There is no reason to assume that relations between
Mycenae and Tiryns remained constant during the whole time
of the building of the fortifications; and, in any case,
we are not dealing here (as Page seems to think) with the
erection of walls in places which formerly did not possess
them, but with the extension and reinforcement of existing
walls, which would have been adequate protection for the
masons engaged in the work.   As for the vulnerability of
the people outside the walls, I fear that this has been
common to such populations throughout the ages; that they
were indeed vulnerable is strikingly proved by the destructions at Mycenae, which affected houses alike within and
outside the citadel.   Page brings obvious, but still
weighty, objections to the idea that both citadels were
built by the same royal house.   Since the first two answers have been rejected, 'a single possibility remains, -

that one place was subordinate to the other;   and that is
what the Catalogue asserts, and the Iliad confirms.   Tiryns
was not directly under the rule of Agamemnon;   it was a
fortress in the realm of Diomedes, and Diomedes, like the
other Greek commanders, acknowledges the divine right of
Agamemnon as overlord' (Page, 1959, 131.)

Even someone who, on the whole, agrees with Page that
the Catalogue of Ships and other parts of the 'Iliad' preserve some surprisingly accurate memories of the Greek
Bronze Age may be excused for demurring at Page's uncritical use of Homeric poetry as evidence for political relations between one chieftain and another.   When Page says
that Diomedes 'acknowledges the divine right of Agamemnon
as overlord', he is presumably thinking of such a passage
as 'Iliad' 9. 38, where Diomedes says to Agamemnon: 'with
the sceptre [Zeus] has granted that you be honoured above
all men'.   But the very same speech proves that Diomedes
is not dependent upon Agamemnon after all, for he goes on
to say that Agamemnon may go back to Greece if he wishes
but that Diomedes and the other chieftains will remain
until they have sacked Troy ('Iliad' 9. 42-9.)   Strange
talk from a vassal to his divinely appointed overlord, we
might think;   but even that is not the end of the matter.
If Diomedes is not dependent on Agamemnon in the Troad, he
is no more so at home.   Although the Catalogue of Ships
does not say explicitly that Agamemnon has no political
rights over Diomedes, it depicts the two chieftains as
ruling over completely separate and independent kingdoms
('Iliad' 2. 559-80;   cf. Hope Simpson and Lazenby, 1970b,
70-1.)

I do not regard the Homeric evidence as affording conclusive proof of any particular interpretation of the political character of the Mycenaean world, partly because
there is no reason to think that in such matters Homer is
a reliable witness, partly because the 'Iliad' is concerned primarily with the conflicts between individual heroes,
not with political organization.   Nevertheless, for what
it is worth, the Homeric account harmonizes quite well with
the testimony of archaeology.   The poet of the 'Iliad'
assumes not a centralized empire with Agamemnon at its head
but a large number of independent kingdoms, some of them
petty, but others so powerful that their rulers (such as
Menelaus, Diomedes, Odysseus, and Nestor) influence the
course of events almost as much as Agamemnon himself does.
Achilles is not even a sovereign in his own right and has
only a small band of retainers;   yet his personal prowess
raises him to the rank of the greatest kings.   The chiefs
who accompany Agamemnon are not his vassals who were bound
to follow him to Troy.   They act on occasion as fully in-

dependent sovereigns, even if for the most part they ac-
knowledge the primacy of Agamemnon, as the king with the
greatest possessions and the largest number of subjects
(e.g. 'Iliad' 1. 281.)　The actual extent of Agamemnon's
domain cannot be discovered by reference to the 'Iliad'
since, as is well known, different accounts of it are
given in different parts of the poem.　But in the Catalogue of Ships, as we have seen, it is said specifically
not to extend over the whole of the Peloponnese, still
less over the whole of Greece.　Both negatively and
positively, then, the situation envisaged in the 'Iliad'
corresponds with the picture constructed from the monuments:　negatively, because the poet knows nothing of a
great Mycenaean empire with a supreme head;　positively,
in that the primus inter pares is said to rule over only
part of the Peloponnese and to achieve his ends (when he
does achieve them) by persuasion and conciliation, not
by coercion.

NOTES

Archaeological evidence for foreign connexions

General.　Pecorella, 1962;　Sulimirski, 1971;　Buchholz
and Karageorghis, 1974;　Stubbings, 1975, 165-87.
　　Greece.　Hittite figurines: Canby, 1969.　Canaanite
jars: Grace, 1956;　Wace, 1955, 179;　Wardle, 1973, 331;
Akerström, 1975.　Oriental seals at Thebes: Platon and
Touloupa, 1964.　The Hittite 'bulla': Boardman, 1966.
　　Central Mediterranean.　Bernabò Brea, 1953;　Taylour,
1958;　Cavalier, 1960;　Biancofiore, 1967;　Bisi, 1968;
De Miro, 1968;　Macnamara, 1970;　Vagnetti, 1970.
　　Crete.　The LM III period in general: Hooker, 1969.
LM IIIb pottery: Popham, 1964.　Relations with Cyprus:
Catling and Karageorghis, 1960, 121-2;　Benson, 1961a, 41;
Tzedakis, 1972.　Inscribed stirrup-jars: Raison, 1968,
193-221;　Heubeck, 1969;　Palmer, 1972b.　The term
ke-re-si-jo we-ke in Pylos tablets: Palmer, 1957, 77;
Bader, 1965, 164-7.　Kydonia: Tzedakis, 1969.
　　Cyclades.　Melos: Edgar and Evans, 1904;　Dawkins
and Droop, 1910;　Scholes, 1956, 39-40;　Coldstream and
Huxley, 1972, 304-5;　Barber, 1974.
　　Dodecanese.　General: Hope Simpson and Lazenby, 1962,
159-75;　1970a;　1973.　Rhodes: Maiuri, 1923;　Monaco,
1941;　Stubbings, 1951a, 5-20;　Furumark, 1950, 262.
Karpathos: Charitonidis, 1961.　Kos: Orlandos, 1959b;
Morricone, 1965 and 1972.

Cyprus.   Excavation reports: Gjerstad, 1934/1937;
Schaeffer, 1952;   Furumark, 1965b;   Karageorghis, 1965;
1967;   1973b;   1974;   P. Aström, 1966;   Dikaios, 1971.
Pottery: Stubbings, 1951a, 25-44;   Karageorghis, 1965,
231-59 (Rude Style);   Furumark, 1972a, 431-59;   P. Aström,
1973.   General: Gjerstad, 1926;   Sjöqvist, 1940;   Cat-
ling, 1964 and 1975a;   Merrillees, 1965 and 1973;   Lena
Aström, 1967;   P. Aström, 1972a and 1972b.   Exports of
Cypriot pottery: Sjöqvist, 1940, 168-80;   Merrillees,
1968 and 1974, 5-11;   Cadogan, 1972, 5-7.   The Alasiya-
Cyprus equation: Merrillees, 1972b;   Muhly, 1972; Masson,
1973.
Anatolia.   General: Bittel, 1967, 17-23;   Mellaart,
1968, 187-200;   D.H. French, 1969, 73.   Troy: reports of
Mycenaean pottery in Blegen, 1953 and 1958.   Kolophon:
Holland, 1944;   Bridges, 1974.   Miletus: Kleiner, 1969.
Iasus: Levi, 1961;   1965;   1967;   1969;   1973;   Laviosa,
1974.   Müsgebi: Gültekin and Baran, 1964;   Boysal, 1967.
Egypt: Pendlebury, 1930;   Stubbings, 1951a, 90-101;
Hankey, 1973.
Levant.   General: Stubbings, 1951a, 59-87;   Hankey,
1966;   1967;   1972;   1974.   Ugarit: Schaeffer, 1932, 12;
1936a, 111;   1949, 136-301;   1963, 127.   Mycenaean pottery at Ugarit: Liliane Courtois, 1969, 135;   J.-C. Courtois, 1973;   Contenson, Courtois, Lagarce, and Stucky,
1974, 10-2.

Mycenaeans and Semites

Affinities between Hebrew and Greek literature: Dornseiff,
1959, 72-95, 203-329.   Cultural affinity between Ugarit
and Greece: Segert, 1958.   Points of resemblance between
Greek and eastern literature: Dirlmeier, 1955;   Lesky,
1955;   Considine, 1969;   Walcot, 1969;   1970;   1972. Criticism of the resemblances: Durante, 1971, 147-50.   The
Krt epic: Gray, 1964b.   I find much to agree with in the
acute paper Muhly, 1970.
Mesopotamian myth in general: Lambert, 1974.   Hurrian
succession-myths and the 'Theogony':   Güterbock, 1946,
100-15;   Erbse, 1964;   West, 1966, 18-22.   Transmission
of the eastern elements: Heubeck, 1955.   Explanation of
Ionic in Hesiod: Edwards, 1971, 201-3.   Ionian migrations: Snodgrass, 1971, 373-8;   Desborough, 1972, 179-84.
Possibility of Luwian mediation: Houwink ten Cate, 1961,
206-15.

Mycenaeans and Hittites

The Hittite empire in general: Goetze, 1957, 90-109; Cornelius, 1973, 120-281.   Relations with Egypt: Helck, 1971.
Critical examination of the Ahhiyawa question: Steiner, 1964; Borukhovich, 1964; Houwink ten Cate, 1973; Muhly, 1974.   Identification of Ahhiyawa with a Mycenaean empire: Forrer, 1924; Schachermeyr, 1935 and 1958; Andrews, 1955; Garstang and Gurney, 1959; Huxley, 1960. Criticism of the Forrer-Schachermeyr approach: (apart from Sommer's works) Friedrich, 1927; Goetze, 1934.   Identification of Ahhiyawa with Crete: Cavaignac, 1946; with Cyprus: Kretschmer, 1954; with Rhodes: Hrozný, 1929; Page, 1959, 1-40; Sacconi, 1969, 18-9.   Re-dating of the Maduwatta text: Otten, 1969; Carruba, 1969b; 1971a; 1971b; Houwink ten Cate, 1970.   Objections to the re-dating: Kammenhuber, 1969a and 1970.   The linguistic equations Ahhiyawa =Achaiwa, Alaksandu=Alexandros, etc.: Kretschmer, 1924; 1930; 1936b; Sommer, 1934 and 1937, 187-224; Szemerényi, 1957, 173; Cornelius, 1962; Harmatta, 1968a and 1968b. Carruba, 1964, 277 proposes the fantastic derivation of Aiolees from a hypothetical *Ahhiyawales.   Mycenaean Achaiwa: Aitchison, 1964.   Situation of Ahhiyawa in north-eastern Anatolia: Goetze, 1957, 183; Macqueen, 1968.

Conclusions

Mycenaean trade in general: Wace and Blegen, 1939;   Immerwahr, 1960; Cadogan, 1973.   Mycenaean shipping: Marinatos, 1933b; Guglielmi, 1971; Dorothea Gray, 1974, 17-57.   Analysis of the fabric of Mycenaean pottery: Catling, Richards, and Blin-Stoyle, 1963.   Agamemnon's kingdom: Allen, 1921, 63-75; Page, 1959, 127-32; Hope Simpson and Lazenby, 1970b, 65-73.

INTRODUCTION

The latter part of the thirteenth century and the beginning
of the twelfth saw the fragmentation of the unified culture
whose nature and outward expansion have been described in
Chapters 5 and 6. The break-up of the Mycenaean culture,
previously so homogeneous, was attendant upon, and no
doubt the immediate result of, the destruction of palatial
centres. Before the manner, effects, and causes of the
destructions are examined, two observations of a general
character should be made. In the first place we witness,
at this period, the end of a system in which (to judge
from the Linear B tablets) the palaces seem to have exercised a rigorous control, and maintained a detailed oversight, over their subjects. The 'end' of the Mycenaean
culture as such is not in question, for indeed it never
came to an end but changed, more or less gradually, into
something else, the civilization of the Geometric age of
Greece. Second, we have to repudiate the notion (tempting
though it has sometimes proved) that the Mycenaean age can
be seen in biological terms; namely, that it passed
through the stages of growth, brilliant maturity, and in-
evitable decay. The metaphor is seductive, but it must
be resisted. As a matter of fact, we have been able to
discern the first two stages, but the assumption of the
third finds no warrant in the material record. The great
centres of the Mycenaean world did not slowly decline on
reaching their peak; on the contrary, they were destroyed
at the very acme of their prosperity. The disasters
which overtook them may have been feared and even guarded
against, but they were hardly expected (Mylonas, 1966a,
224; Tegyey, 1970, 7.) The An tablets from Pylos are
supposed (for instance by Palmer, 1969a, 147-63 and by
Ventris and Chadwick, 1973, 427-30) to relate to military

arrangements for the defence of Pylos; but it is very dangerous to draw such a conclusion from these texts, since the military dispositions which they record may well reflect the regular practice and not extraordinary measures to meet a sudden emergency.

The material upon which a study of the period must be based is lacunose and, often, ill-defined; and, in my own opinion, it will prove impossible to arrive at one simple answer to the complex questions which arise. In this period, as in the much earlier one discussed in Chapter 2, the evidence comes from several different sources, not all of them equally valuable when it comes to the construction of a historical account. The right course is to consider first the archaeological facts, not only in Greece but also in other areas of the Mediterranean; for parts of Mycenaean Greece were still in contact with Cyprus, Rhodes, Syria, Palestine, and Crete, while (at least according to some theories) the disturbances which afflicted Greece were connected with the destruction of sites in Syria and Anatolia and with events on the borders of Egypt.

THE FRAGMENTATION OF THE MYCENAEAN CULTURE

The fragmentation of the Mycenaean culture is, or may be, attested in three ways: 1 by the disappearance of some well-established classes of Mycenaean artefacts; 2 by the disintegration of the homogeneous Mycenaean style into a number of local types; 3 by the introduction of new customs.

1 The passing of the great palaces, at least in southern Greece, meant that there was now much less need for monumental construction in stone. Only at Volos, in Thessaly, were the palatial buildings actually extended in the twelfth century. With the exception of the enlargement of the Cyclopean fortifications at Mycenae to protect the water-supply (if, indeed, this did take place as late as the twelfth century), massive walls were no longer built. There is little evidence even of the construction of stone houses, except at Asine and Tiryns; but it must be admitted that the substantial structures at those two sites do point to a flourishing period of re-occupation. The series of great tholos tombs at Mycenae seems to come to an end well before the close of the Late Helladic IIIb period, and certainly none is known to have been built in IIIc. Elsewhere in Greece, with very rare exceptions, the tholoi fell into disuse (Desborough, 1965, 216.) Chamber tombs, however, remained in use into IIIc; some new cemeteries being laid out in that period.

Whether the art of writing was preserved, or was needed,
at Mycenaean sites after the end of Late Helladic IIIb is
not known for certain. The mere fact that the Linear B
script is not attested after about 1200 BC does not settle
the matter, since it is known that in Crete the script was
in limited use long after the end of the palatial period
at Knossos, while in Cyprus the Cypro-Minoan writing-system
outlived the Bronze Age and had its successors in the classical period.

2 The most vivid witness of the fragmentation is provided by the pottery; and, when that has been discussed, the
figurines may be allowed to add their testimony. The high
degree of uniformity apparent in Late Helladic IIIb pottery
is lost in the next period; and during the twelfth century
a number of different IIIc styles are developed locally
from the homogeneous school of IIIb. Not only that, but
it was possible for two widely divergent styles to flourish
in one and the same place: a state of affairs surely inconceivable in the mature phases of IIIb (Furumark, 1972a,
568.) Late Helladic IIIc pottery was divided into an
earlier (IIIc1) and a later (IIIc2) stage in the monumental
discussions, Furumark, 1944 and 1972a. This terminology I
shall adopt when it is relevant, without following Furumark in his further sub-division of the IIIc1 and IIIc2
phases themselves. Nor do I make the Late Helladic IIIc1
pottery phase of the mainland contemporary with Late Minoan
IIIb2 in Crete: a chronological equation which has produced much confusion. It is more probable that both the
Late Helladic IIIc and the Late Minoan IIIc style came
into use at about the same time, c. 1200 BC (rather later
than Furumark's date for the transition from Late Helladic
IIIb to IIIc.)

No clear break is discernible between Late Helladic
IIIb and the early IIIc1 styles which develop out of it.
But, as the twelfth century advances, IIIc pottery evolves
in two different and contrasting directions. These are
represented contemporaneously at Mycenae by the Granary
Style (which marks the ultimate stage in stylization towards which Mycenaean pottery had been tending even during
IIIb) and the Close Style, well called 'baroque' in contrast to the 'classicism' of IIIb (Furumark, 1972a, 572.)
The vase-painters of the Close Style crowded together geometric and animal motifs such as birds and sea-creatures
on the surface of their vessels, which they divided into
horizontal panels: the whole representing a strong reaction against the decorative tendencies of the Late Helladic IIIb potters. The Granary Style artists, on the
other hand, made use of a few abstract patterns, of which
the commonest comprises horizontal wavy lines (Figure 3.)

The so-called Warrior Vase, which Schliemann found at
Mycenae in a house near Grave Circle A, exhibits the characteristics neither of the Close Style nor of the Granary
Style;   and, for that reason, it calls for special mention
(Figure 3.)   The painter has depicted a column of marching
spearmen and, behind them, a woman in the typical attitude
of mourning, with hands on head, which we saw on the Tanagra larnakes (Chapter 5.)   I therefore agree with Vermeule,
1964, 209 that the scene is best interpreted as an excerpt
from a funeral: an interpretation corroborated by the Warrior Stela (if I may so call it) from Mycenae, which is
roughly contemporary with the Warrior Vase and which shows
a row of marching spearmen of very similar appearance
(Tsountas, 1896.)   The warriors on our vase, each carrying a spear and a rounded (though not circular) shield with
fringes and wearing a plumed helmet and leather greaves,
were described by Schliemann, 1878, 154-8 in his inimitable
manner.   He rightly pointed to the fact that every detail
of their equipment finds a close parallel in the armature
of the Homeric heroes.   That there are very close links
between the vase and the world inhabited by the heroes
(imaginary though that world is in some other respects) is
undeniable.   It is less easy to fit the vase into the sequence of pottery otherwise recognizable at Mycenae.   Becatti, 1965, 43 shows that both Warrior Vase and Warrior
Stela display a monumental and narrative quality different
from the abstract and ornamental styles which prevailed in
the last Mycenaean age.   Becatti himself attributes this
singularity to the re-emergence of a Helladic component
which, in the heyday of the Mycenaean culture, had been
assimilated with Minoan elements.   While this is a perfectly tenable point of view, I wonder if it takes sufficient account of the sporadic appearance of a 'narrative'
style during the Late Helladic IIIb period and the possibility that both vase and stela continued a style which
had long been present, though not always conspicuous, on
the mainland in IIIb: in this connexion, I think again of
the Tanagra larnakes and, from an earlier period, of the
Daemon Ring from Tiryns, all of which depict rows of
figures of the same size.   It should be noted, further,
that the Warrior Vase and Stela are no longer so isolated
as they once were.   A sherd from the palace at Volos is
published by Orlandos, 1960b, 60:   this, small as it is,
plainly shows part of a row of spearmen and appears to
issue from a school very similar to the one which created
the Warrior Vase at Mycenae. (Mingazzini, 1967, 327-35.)
Broadly speaking, the later history of Late Helladic
IIIc pottery sees the gradual fading-away of the Close
Style and the coming to supremacy of the Granary Style,

the latter giving way (at least in Attica) to a pottery-
type known as sub-Mycenaean. Well-stratified deposits of
pottery, allowing the transition from IIIb to IIIc and the
developments within IIIc to be followed in detail, were not
available from the Argolid when Furumark wrote; but the
post-war excavations at Mycenae have yielded such stratification, from which ultimately a comprehensive picture will
emerge; meanwhile, a preliminary examination of the ini-
tial stages of IIIc in the Argolid has been conducted by
Elizabeth French, 1969b. Each of the other areas where
Late Helladic IIIc pottery is well represented follows a
development peculiar to itself, though not always in complete isolation. For example the IIIc ware of Rhodes
shows, at some stages of its evolution, considerable influences from the Argolid (Furumark, 1944, 219.) Again, the
pottery recovered from tombs in Achaea shows rather different trends from those discernible in the Argolid, even
though here too a Granary type and a Close type are in
simultaneous use (Vermeule, 1960, 17-8.) Among recently
excavated sites, the IIIc pottery of Lefkandi has similarities on the one hand with ware from Volos and on the other
with pottery from the Perati cemetery in Attica (Popham and
Milburn, 1971, 348-9.)
    Like the pottery, the Mycenaean female figurines show
changes both in shape and in distribution at about 1200 BC.
The Φ and T types, mentioned in Chapter 5, hardly survive
the end of the thirteenth century; but the Ψ type develops
into a late form, which, besides occurring on the mainland
of Greece, is found in plentiful quantities in the Dodecanese and appears even in southern Crete. This distribution is considerably wider than that of figurines in the
Late Helladic IIIb period and, taken together with the
ceramic and other evidence, it argues for some movement of
Mycenaeans out of Greece in IIIc (Elizabeth French, 1971,
139.)
    3 Under this head will be considered the chief cultural
innovations of the Mycenaean world in the twelfth and eleventh centuries BC: (a) classes of material objects which
modern writers have associated, at one time or another,
with the disturbances of the Late Helladic IIIb-c period,
namely fibulae, swords of Naue's Type II, new kinds of
spear-heads, and intrusive pottery-types; (b) burial-
customs and the introduction of iron; (c) changes in
building-habits.
    (a) Of the material objects mentioned, the fibula (a
more or less ornate safety-pin) should not necessarily be
connected with any area outside the Mycenaean world. It
is found in two main types, which are referred to by the
shape of the curved component: the 'violin-bow' and the

'arched' types.   Although it is unreasonable to expect to
date precisely the first appearance of objects such as
these, the 'violin-bow' fibula was almost certainly in use
in Late Helladic IIIb, to judge from its occurrence with
IIIb pottery at Metaxata (Marinatos, 1933a, 92-3.) Refine-
ments of the violin-bow type become much commoner in IIIc,
having a wide distribution from Macedonia southward into
Crete.   So far as we can tell, the arched type of fibula
made its appearance later than the violin-bow and, in time,
superseded it.   The Mycenaean fibulae have been treated by
Blinkenberg, 1926, 41-78 and by Desborough, 1964, 54-8 and
1972, 300-3: I am not at all convinced by Desborough's
argument in favour of a northern origin for the violin-bow
type (cf. Deshayes, 1966, 208.)   Reduced to its essentials
this argument amounts to little more than the suggestion
that fibulae are more credibly associated with the thick
clothes of northern climates than with the dress of Mycenaean women as it is depicted on the palace frescoes. Even
if it could be shown conclusively that fibulae were introduced from the north (and excavations in northern Greece
may yet establish such a source as the most likely one),
they can have had little or no connexion with the great
disasters, which befell only after the fibulae had come
into use among the Mycenaeans.

The Naue Type II sword is a flange-hilted, cut-and-
thrust weapon, which often has blood-channels or ridges
running along its blade (Figure 4.)   Since its antecedents lie in Europe and not in the Aegean area, it must
have had its origins in regions to the north of Greece
(Cowen, 1955 and 1966; Müller-Karpe, 1962, 259-69; Foltiny, 1964.)   The Naue II sword made its first appearance
in the Mediterranean in the thirteenth century, while
swords of purely Mycenaean ancestry were still current. In
time the Naue II sword ousted weapons of Mycenaean type,
and eventually it was made in iron by Greek craftsmen. In
a series of papers H.W. Catling has examined the distribution and chronology of Naue II swords, basing his classification on the shape of the hilt (Catling, 1956; 1961;
1968b, 101-4; Cypriot swords have been treated by Catling
and also by Lagarce, 1969 and Bouzek, 1971.)   Of the fifty
or so Naue II swords known from the Mediterranean, few are
securely dated.   Examples of Catling's Group I (probably
the earliest) come from Mycenae, Crete, Naxos, Kos, and
Cyprus.   Of these, the Kos sword is firmly associated with
Late Helladic IIIb pottery (Morricone, 1965, 137-9), while
other swords of the type are, just as certainly, found in
IIIc contexts.   Like the violin-bow fibula, the Naue II
sword thus appears in the Mediterranean before 1200 BC;
like the fibula also, it comes into widespread use only

after that date. It is noteworthy that the earlier groups
isolated by Catling are very poorly represented, or not represented at all, in north-western Greece;   so that when
Naue II swords first appear in the Mediterranean they are
found predominantly in the Peloponnese and Crete and in
regions to the east.   Naue II swords so far found in Epirus are later than these (Catling, 1968b, 101-3; but see
Hammond, 1971, 235-41.)

It has long been recognized that a few spear-heads with
undivided sockets found in Greece and the islands at the
same time as the Naue II swords are, like them, of northern
provenience (Childe, 1948, 185.)   To the study of these
objects also Catling has brought much-needed precision,
distinguishing a 'Mouliana' from a 'Kephallenia' type (Catling, 1968b, 105-7.)   The distribution of the two types is
different.   The 'Kephallenia' type (represented by about
ten known examples) is practically confined to Epirus and
the Ionian Islands: the two spear-heads at Metaxata are
certainly of IIIc date, but those from Parga and Kalbaki in
Epirus may go back to IIIb.   The 'Mouliana' type, on the
other hand, while unknown in north-western Greece, has been
found, in very small numbers, at Mycenae and in Crete, Kos,
and Cyprus.   The earliest spear-heads of this type ante-
date the end of Late Helladic IIIb.   In the same tomb in
Kos which yielded the Naue II sword was found a 'Mouliana'
spear-head: this therefore belongs to the IIIb period. An
example from Enkomi in Cyprus is likewise dated late in
the thirteenth century (Catling, 1964, 121, no 1.)   Another, from the Epano Phournos tholos at Mycenae, may go
back even earlier (M.S.F. Hood in Wace, 1953a, 78-9, no
21.)   The well-known head from Mouliana itself (in eastern
Crete) dates from Late Minoan IIIc.

It seems clear that the three classes of objects so far
mentioned were already known, and used, in the Mycenaean
world before the end of the thirteenth century;   and not
only in its northern confines but (at least with regard to
Naue II swords and 'northern' spear-heads) in the far east
of the Mediterranean as well.   Only one type of 'northern'
object appears for the first time in the Mycenaean world
in Late Helladic IIIc: the non-Mycenaean pottery cited
from Korakou by Rutter, 1975a. There is no reason to
doubt Rutter's conclusion that this pottery was made locally by intruders from northern areas who, at the time of
the great disturbances, came to settle in venerable centres
of Mycenaean culture.   At the same time, the amounts of
pottery which can be identified positively as intrusive
even in this period are very small and are not at all consistent with large-scale immigration from the north into
the Mycenaean area.

(b) Three changes, more momentous than these, affected the Mycenaean way of life in the period after c. 1200 BC. These changes did not occur suddenly or simultaneously: they are best seen as a complex series of developments embracing the whole Late Helladic IIIc period and owing their origins to various causes. Within this period three tendencies become apparent: the tendency towards the replacement of bronze by iron as a useful metal; the tendency to cremate, rather than inhume, the dead; and the tendency to bury corpses singly in 'cists' of Middle Helladic type (small box-like graves dug out of the ground and roughly lined), as distinct from the practice of multiple burials in chamber tombs, which had prevailed in Late Helladic IIIa and IIIb. The relevant evidence is scattered and, in places, unsatisfactory; but three regions of mainland Greece allow a rough sequence of changes to be established: these are western Attica (represented by the large cemetery in the Kerameikos, north-west of the Agora in Athens, which remained in use from the twelfth century BC into the classical period); eastern Attica (represented by the Late Helladic IIIc cemetery at Perati); and the Argolid. The cultural changes which concern us here are indicated in Table 9. This scheme, which I hope is not so highly simplified as to be misleading, reveals some very important aspects of the changes. Since the introduction of iron (presumably from the eastern Mediterranean), the appearance of cists, and the adoption of cremation are never, even approximately, contemporaneous at any given site, it is impossible to believe that these three cultural features are connected with one another; further, the continued use of Mycenaean chamber tombs in the Argolid and the construction of new ones at Perati and the persistence of inhumation in these two areas after cremation had come into fashion in the Kerameikos show that there is no question of a fundamental change in burial-customs affecting the whole of Greece.

(c) At a few mainland sites, clear evidence of a change in the pattern of life of the inhabitants is provided by pits, houses, and tombs. The material has been arranged by Desborough in his usual systematic fashion. For example the area of habitation at both Argos and Athens was different in Late Helladic IIIc from that in use in IIIb; more significant still is the fact that at Asine, Mycenae, and Tiryns IIIc cists overlie the Mycenaean settlements of previous epochs (Desborough, 1965, 214-8.) The IIIc population of those places, then, seems to have had little memory of, or little regard for, the customs of earlier times: a fact consistent with the observation made in Chapter 5 that at Mycenae and Tiryns, the two palatial sites which were re-occupied in IIIc, there was a movement away from the palaces into houses near the citadels.

Perhaps this is a convenient place to mention the courses of Cyclopean masonry excavated by Broneer at the Isthmus of Corinth. The courses proved to be the remnants of a Late Mycenaean wall, dated by the fill of Late Helladic IIIb and IIIc1 sherds between the two faces. Broneer himself believes that the wall was built right across the Isthmus, roughly from east to west, in order to check incursions into the Peloponnese from northern Greece (Broneer, 1966 and 1968.) That is certainly a possible explanation; but it is disquieting to read the opinion of another archaeologist who has worked in the same area and who thinks that the courses represent the retaining wall for a road and not a defensive work at all (Kardara, 1971.) At this stage of the debate, it does not seem safe to draw any conclusions of a historical nature from the existence of the Isthmian wall.

THE GREAT DESTRUCTIONS AND THEIR EFFECTS

The details of the cultural changes on the Greek mainland and at Mycenaean sites overseas are only now taking on sharp definition. But it has been recognized for a long time that at about the end of the Late Helladic IIIb period a series of destructions affected the Greek mainland but not the Mycenaean settlements in Rhodes and the Cyclades. At the risk of repeating some of the information already presented in Chapter 5, it will be well to express in tabular form the extent of the evidence available. Naturally, account is taken only of settlements, since the contents of tombs rarely give precise indication of the nature or date of a disaster, though they may point to cultural changes or movements in population.

If we begin with the palatial settlements of Mycenaean Greece, the picture is as follows:

1. Pylos.   Destroyed by fire at the transition between Late Helladic IIIb and IIIc (just after 1200 BC.)   No reoccupation in IIIc.

2. Mycenae.   At least three destructions within the relevant period:
   (i) outside the citadel (end of Late Helladic IIIb1);
   (ii) both outside and inside the citadel (end of IIIb2);
   (iii) inside the citadel (Late Helladic IIIc.)
Palace destroyed by fire, but unknown whether its destruction is to be associated with destruction (ii)(as Alin),

with destruction (iii)(as Wace), or with another destruction altogether.   Long period of re-occupation in IIIc.

3. Tiryns.   At least three destructions in the relevant period.   Palace destroyed by fire, but unknown whether in the second or the third of these or in another (otherwise unattested) destruction.   Plentiful signs of re-occupation in IIIc, with new buildings constructed.

4. Athens.   No detectable destruction in IIIb or IIIc.

5. Thebes.   Destruction of 'Kadmeion' at end of IIIb; clear evidence of re-occupation.

6. Orchomenos.   The latest pottery is IIIb;   destruction attested, but at an unknown date.

7. Gla.   The latest pottery seems to be IIIb (but very little has been published);   destruction attested, but at an unknown date.

8. Volos.   No destruction in IIIb;   continuous occupation into IIIc, when a destruction occurred.

When the evidence from the major sites is presented in this stark and, admittedly, over-simplified form, it is seen to afford very slight support for the statement, almost universally expressed in works on the Aegean Bronze Age, that the Mycenaean world as such came to a violent end with the close of the Late Helladic IIIb ceramic period.   Two palatial sites, and two only, are positively known to conform to that pattern: Pylos and Thebes. With regard to others, either we simply do not know when the end of the palace came (as at Orchomenos and, to be candid, at Mycenae and Tiryns as well) or we can be quite certain that it was not contemporary with the close of IIIb (Volos, Athens.)   Where a site like Gla produces a few IIIb sherds and nothing later, what right have we to assign these to the end rather than to an earlier stage of IIIb (unless, indeed, we are intent on fitting facts into the framework of our own pre-conceptions)?   It would be more scientific to try to equate the IIIb pottery at these destroyed sites with either the earlier or the later phase of this style which appears at Mycenae; or, failing that, to admit that the presence of burnt IIIb pottery does no more than date the destruction of a site within a period of more than a hundred years.   Meanwhile, an examination of the foregoing major sites shows how partial an exposition is contained in a familiar summary:

In the past few years it has come to be recognized that
the end of the ceramic period of Mycenaean III was
marked almost everywhere on the Greek mainland by a
trail of calamity and disaster. At Mycenae itself the
palace and buildings in the citadel were destroyed by
fire, following which there was only a feeble reoccupation during the period of the ceramic style III C. Tiryns suffered a like fate at the same time: the palace
was burned and wrecked and was later reconstructed only
on a modest scale, if at all. The Palace of Nestor at
ancient Pylos perished at the same time in a tremendous
conflagration that laid waste the whole complex of
structures, no doubt after they had been thoroughly
looted. It was never again rebuilt and re-occupied.
The House of Kadmos at Thebes came to its end in a similar disaster, almost surely to be dated to the same
fateful juncture. (Blegen, 1967, 27.)
I hope that enough has been said above to indicate how
defective an account that is of events in Greece during the
thirteenth and twelfth centuries BC: it makes no allowance
for the enormous exceptions of Athens and Volos and it assumes that there are good grounds for dating exactly the
destruction of the palaces at Tiryns and Mycenae. For
another reason also we shall find it necessary to revise
Blegen's account in a radical manner; for, though there
was indeed a 'trail of calamity and disaster' in the Peloponnese, we must add that in other parts of Greece (above
all in Attica) the Mycenaean civilization was not seriously
disrupted and even went on to enjoy a modest prosperity in
Late Helladic IIIc.
Nor do the lesser Mycenaean sites (those few, at least,
which have been carefully excavated and which have yielded
good stratification) afford evidence of an almost total
disaster at the end of Late Helladic IIIc. It is true
that the Mycenaean 'mansion' at the Menelaion was burnt at
that time; but the rest of the evidence is far from being
decisive. Korakou, for example, was not destroyed or
abandoned at the end of IIIb, but remained in occupation
into the IIIc period. The same is true of Lefkandi in
Euboea, Ayios Kosmas in Attica, Asine in Argolis, Nichoria
in Messenia, and Gremnos in Thessaly. Zygouries, Berbati,
Prosymna, Eutresis, and Ayios Stephanos give no evidence
of occupation into IIIc but, on the other hand, there is
nothing to show that they were destroyed at the end of
IIIb: the most we can say of these places (as of Gla and
Orchomenos) is that they seem to have been abandoned at
some point when IIIb pottery was still in use. In Messenia (the one area of Mycenaean Greece where research has
been carried out in a quantitative manner), there is no

sign that a single disaster overtook the whole region at the same time. The destruction of the palace at Pylos was accompanied by the desertion of neighbouring sites, some of which were later re-occupied, but by a far smaller number of inhabitants than had lived there in IIIb (McDonald and Hope Simpson, 1972, 143.)

Such, in very broad outline, is the nature of the horizon of destructions. The archaeological facts suggest a protracted period (lasting considerably longer than a century) of unstable conditions, repeated disasters afflicting different sites at different times, and movements of populations. It is that situation, and not a single almost universal calamity, which we must try to explain. But, before doing so, we have to examine the effects of the destructions upon the Greek mainland and upon other areas.

The effects of the series of destructions which befell Mycenaean sites, especially in the Peloponnese, are seen most vividly in the cemeteries which came into use for the first time in Late Helladic IIIc. Two of these were excavated by Marinatos at Lakkithra and Metaxata in Kephellenia, one of the Ionian Islands off the north-west coast of Greece. Abundant quantities of IIIc pottery were certainly found at these and at some other Kephallenian sites, but it is questionable whether the archaeological evidence quite suffices to support the contention that 'the users of the necklaces and other ornaments of Mycenaean type could have arrived in Kephallenia as refugees from the Mainland as a result of disasters at the end of the LH. III B period' (Desborough, 1964, 107.) The truth is that Late Helladic IIIb pottery also is plentiful in Kephallenia, and so it must remain doubtful whether the discoveries of IIIc ceramic material there necessarily represent a completely new pattern of population in Greece (Benton and Waterhouse, 1973, 23.)

The material from the tombs of northern Achaea is, for the most part, undistinguished in character and of Late Helladic IIIc type. There seems no reason to reject the usual view that these tombs correspond to isolated Mycenaean settlements of only moderate prosperity which were planted in the area after the catastrophes in other parts of the Peloponnese (Vermeule, 1960; Desborough, 1964, 98.) But an important exception is seen in the citadel of Teichos Dymaion, situated near the coast: this settlement flourished in the Late Helladic IIIb period and, after a destruction c. 1200 BC, it was re-occupied in IIIc (pottery: Mastrokostas, 1964, 64-5 and 1965, 132-3; Cyclopean walls: Mastrokostas, 1965, 121.) Perhaps the existence of such a well-fortified place helped to make this part of Greece a magnet for refugees.

The clearest evidence for the state of Mycenaean civilization in Late Helladic IIIc is found in the cemetery of Perati in eastern Attica (Iakovidis, 1969.) This cemetery spans the IIIc period and, according to its excavator, it falls into three chronological phases. The graves number 219, of which 192 are chamber tombs; inhumation is the general rule, but eighteen bodies were cremated. Although no settlement has yet been discovered at Perati, the contents of the tombs are of great historical interest. Two important conclusions may be drawn from this material. The first is that the Late Helladic IIIc civilization, at least in this part of Greece, flourished at a high level of material culture for a long period: a state of affairs which would clearly have been impossible, had the disturbances at the beginning of the period not given way to an era of comparative tranquillity. Some eight hundred clay vessels come from the tombs, and these include fine vases decorated in the local variant of the Close Style. Other objects of purely Mycenaean antecedents are seven Ψ figurines, more than three hundred beads, two gold rings, and some seals. The tombs yielded, in addition, eight fibulae, four of the 'violin-bow' and four of the 'arched' type. The second observation is that unlike Achaea Perati was no isolated enclave of refugees. Table 10 shows the impressive list of imports found in the Perati graves: imports from areas with which the Mycenaeans had long been in contact. The imported material includes, besides Cycladic and Cretan pottery, seals from Syria and Cyprus, scarabs and fragments of a glass vase from Egypt, an amber bead from the Baltic, and an iron knife from Syria. The existence of a two-way traffic is indicated by the presence of two ceramic imports from Perati in Kos and one in Naxos (Iakovidis, 1969, 415.)

EVIDENCE FROM OVERSEAS

The Late Helladic IIIc cemeteries in Greece are plausibly connected by Desborough with a movement of population consequent upon the great destructions: a movement which led to the establishment of an area of reasonably unified Mycenaean culture embracing the Dodecanese, the Cyclades, and eastern Attica. The Cyclades and Dodecanese, indeed, follow a different pattern of events from that observable in most other parts of the Mediterranean. The islands in these groups show no trace of destruction at the end of Late Helladic IIIb; while at Ialysos in Rhodes there is actually evidence for the construction of new chamber tombs during IIIc. The IIIb Mycenaean settlement at Emporio in Chios persisted without interruption into the IIIc period.

In no region are there clearer signs of an influx of Mycenaean settlers than in Cyprus; and this island accordingly calls for close investigation. In Chapter 6 I accepted, with some reservations, the usual view that the large amounts of Late Helladic IIIa and IIIb pottery in Cyprus are to be explained as objects of trade, not as evidence for actual settlement by Mycenaeans: the chief reason being that there are no remains of typical Mycenaean buildings, in the form either of houses or of tombs. But a different situation obtains in the twelfth century. At about the end of the previous century Cyprus, like so many other parts of the eastern Mediterranean, was convulsed by a series of disasters. A number of places were abandoned and the important sites of Enkomi and Sinda (in the east) and Kition (in the south-east) were destroyed at a time when imported IIIb pottery was still in use. At Enkomi, the twelfth century sees the introduction of an early (though not the earliest) phase of IIIc pottery and, what is of greater significance, the erection of monumental buildings of Mycenaean type and the employment, for the first time in Cyprus, of the square-hewn ('ashlar') blocks used by masons on the Greek mainland (Schaeffer, 1952, 343-50; Dikaios, 1971, 514.) There is thus good reason to think that this stage of occupation at Enkomi coincided with a Mycenaean settlement, especially in view of the fine artefacts in ivory and metal which now make their appearance (Catling, 1964, 301; Karageorghis, 1973a, 81.) At the same time, the evidence must not be pressed too far, and I confess that I cannot see there are grounds for more than part of the following assertion: 'Now the immigrants introduced their Greek language, religion, institutions, art and customs' (Aström, 1972b, 776.) It is wrong, for example, to suppose that the Greek language was introduced at this time; for, on the one hand, the Cypro-Minoan script has not yet been deciphered and, on the other, we cannot but suppose that knowledge of Greek was of very long standing in Cyprus. Moreover, the sacral precincts at Cypriot sites in this period, impressive as some of them are, show marked differences from the customs of Mycenaean Greece (Aström, 1972a, 1-11.)

No good evidence for burials has been found at the sites mentioned so far; but excavations at Kouklia, in south-west Cyprus, have uncovered a tomb (TK I) which contained a pure deposit of Late Helladic IIIc1 pottery (Maier, 1972, 101.) This discovery suggests that there may have been an even larger influx of Mycenaeans than had been supposed and that the settlements of the newcomers were even more widely dispersed.

The first phase of Mycenaean settlement in Cyprus was disrupted by a further set of disasters, as a result of which Enkomi, Kition, Sinda, and some other sites were destroyed (c. 1190 BC, according to Dikaios.)   At Enkomi and Kition there ensued a period of modest re-occupation, in which the architectural achievements were at a much humbler level than in the first phase.   Enkomi has yielded closed deposits of Close Style and Granary Style pottery.   In Room 10 at Enkomi was found the bronze statuette of a figure wearing a horned cap, often known as the 'horned god'; in the same room and in adjoining rooms were traces of cult, for example rhyta and the remains of burnt animals (Dikaios 1971, 524.)   I cannot accept the identification of the horned figure with a Mycenaean god (so most recently Hadjioannou, 1971):   if it contains any Mycenaean elements at all, it must represent the fusion of a Mycenaean with a native Cypriot type.   The second phase of Mycenaean settlement at Enkomi comes to an end with yet another destruction, dated c. 1100 BC by Dikaios, 1971, 530.   Thereafter the site continues to be inhabited for another generation (who still use Granary Style pottery), until its final abandonment in 1075 BC (Dikaios, 1971, 534.)

Evidence of Mycenaean incursion into Crete is clear but is confined to a very small number of sites.   As was seen in Chapter 6, Crete never partook in the unified Mycenaean culture of the fourteenth and thirteenth centuries BC.   Although there were undoubtedly contacts between Crete and the mainland, the Minoan civilization developed along independent lines.   A number of the great Cretan sites had been re-occupied at some point after the destructions in Late Minoan I and II.   Of these, Phaistos and Ayia Triada do not present a sufficiently clear picture for any useful conclusions to be drawn.   But the settlements of Gournia, Knossos, Mallia, and Palaikastro were deserted at or near the end of Late Minoan IIIb, at least part of Mallia being burnt.   A little Mycenaean pottery appears among the latest deposits of Late Minoan IIIb ware at Gournia, Knossos, and Palaikastro (Popham, 1965, 333.)

Our present information suggests that there was a break between the abandonment of these sites and a further era of occupation which ensued in the Late Minoan IIIc period. At Palaikastro, a new settlement (Kastri) is inhabited early in the period;   and both there and at Knossos the pottery reveals Mycenaean features both in shape and in decoration (Popham, 1965, 335.)   It is no doubt of great importance that the settlement at Kastri was established on top of a rocky hill, which would have been easy to defend: a natural place of refuge, if the new people who introduced Mycenaean elements into the pottery were indeed

refugees from the Greek mainland.   The assumption that
they were is strengthened by observations at Karphi in eastern Crete, which was settled for the first time after the
beginning of the Late Minoan IIIc period.   Karphi is a
remote and inaccessible site: therefore, like the hill of
Kastri, a likely place for refugees to choose.   A picture
of great interest may be drawn from three classes of finds.
In the first place, the bell-shaped clay idols with raised
arms belong to a specifically Cretan type, which is especially well represented in Late Minoan III (Alexiou, 1958.)
In the second, the presence of a building of megaron-type
suggests the presence of mainlanders, since such buildings
are not of Minoan ancestry and are scarce (if not entirely
absent) in Crete before 1200 BC (Pendlebury and Money-
Coutts, 1937, 137-8.)   In the third, the pottery shows a
blending of Minoan and Mycenaean types: the so-called
Fringed Style being the Cretan variant of the Close Style
which, as we have seen, appears in a number of local versions in the Argolid, Attica, Achaea, Rhodes, and the Cyclades (Seiradaki, 1960, 31-7.)   (Two other sites in the
east of Crete, Vrokastro and Mouliana, produced tombs with
important Late Minoan IIIc material, including objects of
iron and traces of cremation; but they contained also
burial-gifts dating from earlier periods, and so they cannot be used as evidence for the establishment of new settlements in IIIc.)

No less than the parts of the Mediterranean already discussed, Egypt and most of the major sites of Palestine,
Syria, and Anatolia were beset by a series of troubles late
in the thirteenth century and early in the twelfth.   The
capital of the Hittite empire was destroyed in a great fire
shortly after 1200 BC, and with its destruction the empire
itself came to an end.   In the north-west of Anatolia,
Troy VIIa, with its imported Late Helladic IIIb pottery and
local ware made in imitation of it, was burnt before IIIc
pottery came into use.   In Cilicia, intrusive pottery of
an early Late Helladic IIIc type was found above a burnt
level at Tarsus; since there is no evidence of previous
contact between Tarsus and the Mycenaean world, this pottery perhaps represents an incursion by Mycenaeans as a
consequence of the destructions in their homeland.   On the
west coast of Anatolia, the Mycenaean settlement at Miletus
was not destroyed until the use of Late Helladic IIIc pottery was firmly established.

At nearly all the destroyed sites in Syria and Palestine
the latest imported pottery was Late Helladic IIIb.   In the
north of Syria, Alalakh and Ugarit were violently destroyed
at about 1200 BC: the discovery of a cartouche of the
Egyptian king Merenptah in the ruins of Ugarit dates the

destruction of that site to the last quarter of the thirteenth century.   Like Alalakh and Ugarit, most other Levantine sites were destroyed while imported Late Helladic
IIIb pottery (together with Cypriot ware) was still in use;
but a little early IIIc pottery also was found in the destruction levels of Tell Sukas, a coastal site south of
Ugarit, and Beth Shan, in the Jordan valley.   Megiddo
forms the great exception to the general pattern of destruction, in that it was not devastated at the end of the
thirteenth century.
  So far as Egypt is concerned, we possess both documentary and monumental evidence for the course of events.   Towards the end of the thirteenth century and early in the
twelfth, several victorious campaigns were fought by the
Egyptians against coalitions of enemies who threatened
their kingdom, at first from the west and subsequently from
the north-east.   These coalitions are to-day loosely referred to as the 'Sea Peoples' or 'Peoples of the Sea' or
'Land and Sea Raiders'.   Since the activities of the Sea
Peoples are often thought to have a very important bearing
upon the whole course of history in the Mediterranean (not
excluding the Mycenaean area), the conflicts between them
and the Egyptian kings deserve an examination in some detail.   Three campaigns chiefly concern us here.
  The first of these took place in the fifth year of the
reign of Merenptah (c. 1220 BC.)   It is recounted in an
extensive, but much damaged, inscription in the temple at
Karnak.   The king of Libya is said to have advanced
against the western boundaries of Egypt, having formed an
alliance with five other peoples: the Sherden, the Shekelesh, the Ekwesh, the Luka, and the Teresh, who are described as 'northerners coming from all lands.'   The progress of the battle is not immediately relevant; but the
detailed list of enemies slain and taken prisoner is interesting in two respects.   First, the inclusion of women
and children of the king of Libya in the list of dead confirms (what the inscription earlier states) that the Libyan
king led no mere marauding expedition into Egypt but was
driven by hunger to attempt an outright invasion.   Second,
when the Ekwesh are mentioned in the lists, they are specified as coming from the countries of the sea and as having no krnt (probably 'foreskin'.)
  A second battle between the Egyptians and Libyan invaders was triumphantly concluded in the fifth year of Ramesses III (c. 1190 BC.)   In this invasion, according to the
record in the temple at Medinet Habu, the king of Libya
was aided by 'men of northern countries', the Peleset and
the Tjekker.
  The third and most serious of the campaigns to be dis-

cussed here was undertaken in year eight of Ramesses III
(c. 1187 BC.)   The three sources of information about this
campaign are: an inscription at Medinet Habu; scenes painted on walls of the same temple;   the 'Papyrus Harris',
first published in 1876.   A battle was fought both at sea
and on land at some point in the Levant between Egypt and
northern Syria;the enemy was decisively defeated by Ramesses, some of them being brought captive to Egypt, others
settled in Palestine as Egyptian tributaries. The Medinet
Habu inscription contains the following passage:
     The foreigners...in their islands... No one stood
     against them, from Hatti, Kode, Karchemish, Arzawa, and
     Alasiya... They set up a camp in Amor and desolated its
     people and land as though they had never been.   They
     came toward Egypt, the flame prepared before them.
     Their confederates were the Peleset, the Tjekker, the
     Shekelesh, the Denyen, and the Weshesh, united lands.
     They laid their hands upon the lands as far as the cir-
     cuit of the earth, their hearts trusting.
The utter rout of the enemy, by land and by sea, is next
described in highly figurative language.   For the consequences of the defeat of the northern coalition, we have
to turn to the Papyrus Harris:
     I extended all the boundaries of Egypt; I overthrew
     those who invaded them from their lands.   I slew the
     island-dwelling Denyen, and the Tjekker and Peleset were
     made into ashes.   The Sherden and the Weshesh of the
     sea were made like people who do not exist, captured
     together and brought captive to Egypt, as numerous as
     the sands of the shore.   I settled them in strongholds·
     bound in my name...
The various stages of preparation, march to Syria, land-
battle, sea-battle, and presentation of captives to the
king are depicted in a series of detailed reliefs at Medinet Habu.   In one (illustrated for example by Smith, 1965,
fig. 221), Ramesses is shown in his chariot, with bow
drawn, charging the enemy, many of whom wear the high fea-
thered head-dress associated on another relief with the
Peleset.   The fighting has penetrated as far as the women
with their ox-carts: their presence on the battle-field
surely indicates that, at least in the Egyptians' eyes, the
Peleset and their allies were taking part in a migratory
movement from north to south.
     Such, and such only, is the evidence for the activities
of the Sea Peoples.   But these have been seized upon by a
succession of scholars, who make them responsible for all
the troubles of the Near East: that is, they accept as
literally true the statement at Medinet Habu that the Sea
Peoples had destroyed Hatti (the Hittite empire), Arzawa

(a state in western Anatolia), Karchemish (a city on the
Euphrates), and Alasiya (on the assumption that this is to
be equated with Cyprus), before ever they made their incursion into Syria. When these statements are taken so literally, no allowance is made for the bombast traditional,
and perhaps by this time obligatory, in such inscriptions:
bombast which would naturally magnify the number and importance of the states previously subdued by the enemy, so as
to make the Egyptian achievement appear all the more impressive. In other words, we have here something which is
as much an instrument of propaganda as a sober historical
record. But we can go farther. The Egyptian records of
the battle of Kadesh (mentioned in Chapter 6) tell us that
well before the date of the Medinet Habu inscription 'lists
of peoples' had become a recurrent theme in pharaonic epi-
graphy, while another official theme is that of Egyptian
victories over coalitions of enemies (Table 11.)

With this in mind, we might suggest a very different
picture of the 'Sea Peoples' (who, it should be pointed
out, are never called by that name in the records of Ramesses III) from the one often drawn to-day. It is possible
that these bands of migrants, moving by land and sea
through the coastal regions of Syria, were in truth thought
by the Egyptians to pose a serious threat to themselves;
just as likely, however, that the occasion of their defeat
was seized upon to glorify still further the reign of Ramesses III. In any case, it does not appear from the record how it was that the Egyptians could easily rout and
enslave an enemy so formidable that he had vanquished the
Hittite empire together with its vassal-states. Again,
if the northern migrants were really looking for a place
to settle and if they had really subdued the countries
with which they are credited in the Egyptian records, why
did they not, in fact, settle in one of these countries?
If their first conquest was really that of Hatti, as the
account states, where was the need for them to travel farther? Because I find questions of this kind unanswerable,
I find it necessary to reject the picture of the Sea Peoples as a powerful army, moving irresistibly and of set
purpose, until their final defeat at the hands of the Egyptians. That is precisely the picture which the Egyptian
scribes wished to convey; and they have proved all too
successful.

In essay after essay, the Sea Peoples appear as the destroyers of all the Late Bronze Age states of the Near
East, with the sole exception of Egypt. Recently published texts from Boghazköy and Ugarit have formed the
basis of impressive historical reconstructions: for example
by Astour, 1965 and by Lehmann, 1970. Neither of these

authors has the slightest doubt that the Sea Peoples are to
be blamed for all the disasters of the times.   But it is
far from certain that the texts themselves, though unquestionably reflecting a troubled period in the eastern Mediterranean, refer to activities of the Sea Peoples. For instance, a text from Boghazköy (emanating from the chancery
of the last Hittite king, Suppiluliuma II) speaks of war
between Hatti and Alasiya; but, in so far as there was any
decisive outcome, the Hittite king was victorious: 'Now the
ships of the land Alasiya three times met me in the sea for
battle, and I destroyed them; the ships I took and in the
midst of the sea I burnt them; but when I arrived, there
came against me enemies from the land Alasiya in great numbers, for battle' (Keilschrifttexte aus Boghazköi XII 38,
Column III.)   At first sight, the reference to 'enemies
from Alasiya' appears perplexing, because in texts from
Ugarit shortly to be considered Alasiya is the ally of Ugarit (and consequently of the Hittites as well.)   But the
description 'enemies' is explicable if account is taken of
Column I of the same Hittite text: this relates the conquest of Alasiya and the imposition of tribute upon it.   I
take it that Column III describes a situation common in the
course of Hittite history: the revolt, perhaps short-lived,
of a vassal and its suppression by the central power.   It
is, therefore, quite unnecessary to see (as some have done)
the 'enemies' as the Sea Peoples.

Among many new texts from Ugarit published by Virolleaud, 1965 and Nougayrol, 1968, two in particular have
been connected with the Sea Peoples' invasion.   In the
first, the king of Ugarit writes to the king of Alasiya:
'Ships of the enemy have come; they have burnt my cities
by fire and have done terrible things to the land...all my
troops are on duty in the land of Hatti, and all my ships
in the land of Lukka...they have not returned to me and so
the country is abandoned to the enemy...now there are
seven ships of the enemy which have come against me' (R.S.
20. 238, lines 12-29.)   The king of Ugarit admits to a
faulty disposition of his forces; and no doubt seven ships
would suffice to discomfit him, if all his were elsewhere.
But, we may ask, how is it that the enemy (if they are indeed the 'Sea Peoples') have only seven vessels at their
disposal?   'We are in the presence of the first stage of
the Sea Peoples' invasion', answers Astour, 1965, 255,
'the main forces of the enemy are still in the Aegean, but
their intentions are known, and the king of Ugarit, instead
of passively waiting for their arrival, attempts to oppose
their offensive at its very start.'   There is no warrant
in our text, or in any other extant record, for a single
one of these statements.   Lehmann, for his part, is per-

plexed by the small number of ships deployed by the 'Sea
Peoples' and is driven to seek an analogy in the scanty
forces of the Vikings (Lehmann, 1970, 57); and yet I should
be surprised to learn that the Vikings accomplished their
whole work of depredation and invasion with a flotilla of
seven ships.   But we have no need of these desperate explanations.   Another letter from Ugarit (R.S. 18. 148) is
addressed to the king by one of his officers, who urges him
to equip 150 ships (line A4.)   Admittedly, then, the people of Ugarit were menaced from some quarter; but we have
no information which enables us to give definite shape to
that menace; and when we read that they disposed of 150
ships (presumably in addition to the fleet already opera-
tive), we may find it hard to imagine that an enemy with
only seven could have posed any lasting threat.

It is heartening that in recent years a powerful voice
has at last spoken out against the folly of ascribing all
the disasters in the Near East to the Sea Peoples: that of
Schaeffer. He argues that no trace of the Sea Peoples has
been found at Boghazköy, that if they came from coastal
regions (as they did, according to the Egyptian documents)
the Sea Peoples could not have penetrated into the heart of
Anatolia, and that in any case the Hittite empire is shown
by epigraphic evidence to have been beset by famine and so
to hold little attraction for an invader;   as for the destruction of Ugarit, this is better seen as the effect of
an earthquake than as the result of devastation by the Sea
Peoples (Schaeffer, 1968, 754-68.)   If I have any criticism of these arguments, it is that they are not taken far
enough;   since, after all, no other ruined site of the Near
East shows any more trace of the Sea Peoples than Boghazköy
does.   I wish that we could rid our minds altogether of
the over-seductive notion of a migratory movement, vast in
its scope and destructive in its effects, which swept
across Anatolia and the Levant: much better to see the disasters of the time as a reaction to the disintegration of
the great Hittite empire, which had crumbled under its own
weight, the pressure of economic necessity, and the desertion or rebellion of vassals.

To return to the Egyptian documents. All the names of
the tribes which participated in coalitions against Egypt
have been attached to known peoples of the Mediterranean:
for example, the Shekelesh have been seen as Sicilians, the
Teresh as Tyrrhenians, the Denyen as Danaans, and so forth.
Such identifications are matters of faith, as they can be
neither proved nor disproved;   but it would be agreeable
to have heard the last of the ludicrous equation of the
circumcised Ekwesh with Achaiwoi: an equation which at-
tracted the pungent, and fully justified, rebukes of Sommer,

1934, 71-2 and Page, 1959, 21-2.   But one name must detain
us longer: Peleset.   It has never been seriously questioned
that the Peleset are identical with the Philistines of southern Palestine, portrayed in the Old Testament as hated
enemies of the Israelites, by whom they were finally conquered in the reign of David (early tenth century BC.) This
identification is consistent with four facts.   First, we
have the formal similarity between the Egyptian word (however it is to be vocalized) and the Semitic name of Philistia (e.g. Hebrew P^{e}leset.)   Second, the Philistines are
known actually to have inhabited a region in which the Sea
Peoples' coalition was active.   Third, the Philistine
settlements (sometimes fortified) flourished for over a
century after the defeat of the Sea Peoples by Ramesses
III: a circumstance which is in harmony with Ramesses'
statement that he had settled them in strongholds.   Fourth,
the type of head-dress worn by the Peleset (among others)
on the Medinet Habu reliefs is closely similar to that seen
on anthropoid clay coffins at Beth Shan.   This type of
coffin is often thought to be a mark of the Philistine culture; but, since the earliest coffins at Deir el-Balah are
dated to the fourteenth century BC (Trude Dothan, 1973, 138
and 146), we must assume either that the Philistines had
arrived at this site long before Ramesses' battle against
the Sea Peoples or that, on their arrival, the Philistines
took over a custom already well established there.
    Of especial interest from the Aegean point of view is
the highly distinctive type of pottery known as 'Philistine' which has been found at many sites in Philistia (Figure 3.)   Whether or not this ware is peculiar to the
Philistines (Saussey, 1924), it has been clear since the
beginning of our century that it has some connexions with
Mycenaean pottery, and especially Mycenaean pottery of the
Close Style.   The shapes of the bowls and stirrup-jars are
typically Mycenaean.   The vase-painters have a strong tendency to dispose their patterns in panels, separated from
one another by vertical bands.   Virtually all the decorative elements are borrowed from the Mycenaean scheme, for
instance spirals, semi-circles, and above all stylized
birds.   Just as certainly, native Palestinian features are
also present, the most striking of these being the use of
two colours (Heurtley, 1936, 108; Benson, 1961b, 81;
Artzy, Asaro, and Perlman, 1973.)   Although (as Heurtley,
1936 clearly showed) the Philistine style is essentially
eclectic, incorporating elements from more than one regional school of Late Helladic IIIc pottery, it now appears
that the closest resemblance to it is displayed by pottery
from the third period at Sinda in eastern Cyprus (Furumark,
1965b.)   In view of this eclecticism, the Philistine ware

cannot directly reflect a dispersal of Mycenaeans from the homeland.   It results, rather, from a fusion of several different styles: a fusion which, because of the presence of native features, can have taken place nowhere but in Palestine itself.   Direct evidence of the presence of Mycenaeans in southern Palestine in the twelfth century is at present confined to two sites: Ashdod and Tell el-Fara. At Ashdod Late Helladic IIIc1 pottery was found together with Philistine ware.   The Mycenaean ware, like the Philistine, is of local manufacture and therefore suggests that a small Mycenaean enclave had been established here after the great destructions in the Peloponnese.   The cemetery at Tell el-Fara contained, among others, five graves (ranging in date from c. 1150 BC to the eleventh century) which, as their dromoi and rock-cut chambers show, probably descend from Mycenaean prototypes.

   Our examination of the relevant evidence from parts of the Mediterranean other than the Greek mainland allows us to draw some conclusions with reasonable confidence.   Virtually the whole of the Aegean and eastern Mediterranean (except the Cyclades and Dodecanese, which still maintained contact with sites in continental Greece) suffered destruction or disturbance of some sort at the end of the thirteenth century.   In Crete, the disturbance took the form of abandonment of traditional sites and the founding of new ones, with evidence of Mycenaean participation in some of these.   In Anatolia, the collapse of the Hittite empire and the burning of its capital led to the formation of a number of smaller states.   Most of the Levantine sites were destroyed, the most important of them, Ugarit, never being re-occupied.   The rise of Philistine culture in the south was accompanied in two places by the incursion of Mycenaeans.   Cyprus suffered two major destructions, after the first of which there are clear signs of Mycenaean settlement.   The records from Egypt relate that that country was hard pressed by coalitions of invaders both on her western and on her eastern border.   These invaders were defeated and, at least in the case of the Peleset, were settled in Palestine as Egyptian vassals.

   After this survey of the material remains, we must take into account the written records of the Greeks themselves, together with the relevant linguistic evidence.

THE EVIDENCE OF LEGEND HISTORY AND LANGUAGE

The writers of classical Greece were keenly aware that the
'Hellenes' did not comprise a single ethnic group. On the
contrary, they were known to contain several races which
were differentiated from one another by their dialect, by
their geographical distribution, and sometimes by their political system. The clearest line of demarcation could be
drawn between the West Greeks and the East Greeks. The West
Greeks (more loosely, 'Dorians') inhabited the greater part
of north-western Greece, much of the Peloponnese, Crete,
and Dorian colonies abroad, for example in Rhodes and Sicily. In political terms, the chief Dorian city was
Sparta (also known as Lacedaemon) in Laconia. The East
Greeks comprised (to the north) the Aeolians of Boeotia,
Thessaly, and Lesbos and (to the south) the inhabitants of
Attica and of the Ionian settlements in Anatolia. The Greek
philologists of the Hellenistic period generally distinguished four dialect-groups: Attic, Ionic, Aeolic, and
Doric (Hainsworth, 1967.) The epigraphical evidence avai-
lable in modern times has enabled a more scientific class-
ification to be made, as follows. East Greek dialects:
(i) Attic-Ionic, spoken in Attica, Ionia, and the Cyclades;
(ii) Aeolic, spoken in Thessaly, Boeotia, and Lesbos; (iii)
Arcado-Cypriot, spoken in Cyprus and Arcadia. West Greek
dialects: (i) Doric, spoken in the coastal states of the
Peloponnese (Laconia, Messenia, Argolis, etc.) and in the
Dorian colonies; (ii) North-west Greek, spoken in Phocis,
Locris, and Elis.

The 'Mycenaean' dialect represented in the Linear B documents of the Late Bronze Age ante-dates by several centuries the grouping shown above, but it already displays
some of the innovations associated with the East Greek
dialects; it is closest to the Arcado-Cypriot group, but
it has some Aeolic features as well. In general, West
Greek dialects present a more conservative appearance than
those of East Greek; in other words, they tend to preserve
a larger number of features originally inherited by Greek
from Indo-European. It is plain, therefore, that ancestors of the West Greek dialects must have been spoken in
some parts of Greece during the time that Linear B documents were written in the Mycenaean dialect. The peculiar
distribution of the Arcado-Cypriot group affords a clue to
the historical process which gave rise to this situation.
Arcadian forms a kind of dialectal 'island', having much
more in common with the speech of Cyprus than with the
dialects which surround it in the Doric-speaking parts of
the Peloponnese. At first sight, there seems to be only
one reasonably likely explanation for this state of af-

fairs: namely, that in the Bronze Age, at the time of the
great Mycenaean expansion, a dialect of a high degree of
uniformity was spoken both in Cyprus and in the Peloponnese
but that at some subsequent epoch the speakers of West
Greek intruded upon the Peloponnese and occupied the coastal states, but made no significant inroads into Arcadia.

The dialect-situation observable in the Peloponnese in
classical times is consistent with, and to some extent explained by, the accounts told by the Greeks themselves
about their own past. Running through the welter of history, legend, and saga (a fragmentary, discontinuous, and
sometimes self-contradictory corpus) are at least a few
clear strands which will help us in our reconstruction.
For example, the Greek accounts recognize three separate
epochs: the time of the Trojan War, the dynastic struggles
in Greece and elsewhere which preceded it, and the migrations which followed it. Before the Trojan War, famous
dynasties were founded at Thebes by Kadmos and at Athens by
Cecrops. In southern Greece, Pelops came from Anatolia
and established a royal house, thereby giving his name to
the whole peninsula. A later king in the Peloponnese,
Eurystheus, in some way gained a hold over Heracles, the
greatest of the pan-Hellenic heroes who was, in historical
times, regarded by the Dorians as their particular champion. After Heracles' death and apotheosis, his sons (the
Heraclids) were expelled from the Peloponnese by Eurystheus
and it was thereafter the principal ambition of Heracles'
descendants to return to the Peloponnese and to assume the
kingdoms from which they had been dispossessed. There are
several allusions in our sources to attempts by the Heraclids to return: attempts which began even before the Trojan War but which were frustrated, in one way or another,
until, two generations after the capture of Troy, they finally conquered the Peloponnese and established new dynasties there. This conquest was usually called by the
Greeks the Return of the Heraclids; by modern authors it
is often known as the Dorian Invasion. Some time after
the Return of the Heraclids, our sources speak of two colonizing movements from Greece to the coasts of Anatolia:
first the Aeolian migration and then the Ionian migration.

Since the accounts of the Dorian Invasion and matters
connected with it are contained in many widely scattered
sources, I have thought it worth-while to bring together
the most important of them in Appendix 1. There follows a
brief analysis of the course of events which may be reconstructed from the documents. The Dorians are mentioned
only once by Homer (1b), where their division into three
tribes is already alluded to (cf. 3c.)   The first attempts by the Heraclids to return to the Peloponnese are

made before the Trojan War (5e, 9, 11, 12a, 12h.)   The
date of the capture of Troy is variously given as the early
thirteenth century BC (5b), 1218 BC (8), and 1183 BC (13a.)
The Greek world is said to have been in a state of upheaval
after the Trojan War (6a);   and there are hints of internecine conflict, for instance between Athens and Mycenae
(1a.)   Further attempts by the Heraclids are recorded (11,
14.)   Their final conquest of the Peloponnese (11, 12b)
is placed definitely later than the Trojan War, but by
varying intervals (cf. 6a, 9, 12e, 13a.)   Plato has an
account of the Return which differs from that of the other
sources: he regards the new dynasty which seized power in
the Peloponnese not as newcomers but as warriors who had
fought at Troy, had been expelled from their cities when
they returned home, and had then banded together to recover
their lost kingdoms (7.)   The route followed by the Heraclids is given by 5a and in greater detail by 11 and 12i;
in several accounts Oxylos is named as the guide of the
Heraclids (10b, 11, 12f.)   One stopping-place in the migration was Doris in central Greece (3a, 5a), an area later
regarded as the motherland of the entire Dorian race (5d,
6b.)   The final invasion was achieved not through the Isthmus of Corinth but across the sea (10c, 11, 12f, 12i,
14.)   In later times the Lacedaemonians, and in particular
the kings of Lacedaemon, traced their ancestry back to the
Heraclids (3b, 4a, 5c, 12c.)   The earliest allusion to a
division of Greeks into Dorians and non-Dorians is perhaps
that of the Hesiodic Catalogue (2a and 2b);   later, this
division is made more explicit (10a.)   The classification
of the Greek dialects as Ionic, Attic, Aeolic, and Doric
(taught by Alexandrian scholars) is reflected in 10a and
13b.   The Aeolian migration is placed considerably earlier
than the Ionian by a source used by Strabo (10d.)   Sometimes Orestes is said to have led the migrants himself
(4b), but more often one of his descendants appears as the
leader of the Aeolians (10d, 12d, 15.)   The outlines of
the Ionian migration are less clear;   but it is agreed that
a number of Greek tribes participated and subsequently occupied different parts of the Anatolian littoral (12g) the
foundation of Ionia being dated 1077 BC by the Parian
Marble (8.)

THE CAUSES OF THE GREAT DESTRUCTIONS

Even now that all the sources have been assembled, we cannot proceed directly to a synthesis.   The credentials of
the legendary and linguistic evidence must first be scrutinized, in conformity with the principle that these kinds
of evidence have to be accommodated within the archaeological framework.

To begin with the Trojan War and its aftermath.   If by
the 'Trojan War' we mean a complex series of events involving the protracted siege of an identifiable site in north-
west Anatolia by a confederation of Mycenaean states under
the overlordship of the king of Mycenae and the eventual
capture and destruction of that site, we have to state that
the archaeological evidence, so far from confirming the
traditional account, actually tells against it.

As we saw above, the final Mycenaean pottery in the destroyed level of Troy VIIa is of the Late Helladic IIIb
phase, that is to say the same type which is found in the
ruins of Pylos, Mycenae, and Tiryns as well as at sites in
the Levant such as Ugarit, Alalakh, and Tell Abu Hawam.
Prima facie, then, the destruction of Troy VIIa forms part
of the belt of catastrophes which involved the Levant and
Anatolia, as well as Mycenaean Greece, late in the thirteenth century BC.   Since it is hardly conceivable that
the states of Mycenaean Greece could have equipped an ar-
mada and set on foot a successful expedition against Anatolia at a time when they themselves were under such severe
stress, the truth of the Homeric account can be saved only
by recourse to one of two hypotheses: either (with Blegen,
1963, 163) we raise the date of the destruction of Troy
VIIa to c. 1260 BC, so as to place it in a time of Mycenaean prosperity and strength;   or (with Nylander, 1963) we
suppose that when Homer speaks of the siege and fall of
Troy he means Settlement VI, not Settlement VIIa at all.
It is not difficult to see that both hypotheses must be rejected.   That of Blegen is absolutely inadmissible, involving as it does the manipulation of the archaeological evidence in the most blatant manner;   such manipulation is
never justified, least of all when it is practised merely
to preserve the historicity of a legend.   In the absence
of any indication to the contrary, the destruction of Troy
VIIa must be made roughly contemporary with that of other
sites containing Late Helladic IIIb pottery.   We would
be relieved of that necessity only if it were possible to
differentiate IIIb1 from IIIb2 wares at Troy;   but the
Trojan material is hardly of such a nature as to permit
finer classification than has been applied to it so far.
So far as research has gone, or probably can go, a date of

c. 1200 BC for the destruction of Troy VIIa remains the
only tolerable one (so Mylonas, 1964, 366.)   Even if Homer
is left out of the reckoning altogether, the high dating of
the destruction of Troy VIIa now advocated by Blegen is objectionable for the following purely archaeological reason.
It seems to be well established that the earliest Mycenaean
pottery from the re-occupation deposits of Troy VIIb is of
a Granary Style belonging to an advanced stage of Late Helladic IIIc1 (Blegen, 1958, 145.)   That being so, if Troy
VIIa had been destroyed c. 1260 BC, a gap of some three
generations would be left without any imported Mycenaean
pottery at all.   While a gap of that length is not, perhaps, out of the question, it is at least unparalleled in
the history of Troy in the Late Bronze Age and ought not to
be foisted upon the archaeological record without some compelling reason.   Nylander's theory avoids these objections
only to fall foul of another, hardly less fatal: namely,
that Troy VI did not suffer a severe destruction by fire
such as befell VIIa but was destroyed by an earthquake
which left no trace of burning (Blegen, 1953, 14.)

For these reasons I believe that Homer's account of the
Trojan War cannot be regarded as a historical destruction,
in the sense that a confederacy of Mycenaeans actually besieged and destroyed the principal city of north-west Anatolia during the thirteenth century BC.   But it would be
equally wrong to deny all reality to Homer's description
of Troy.   As Blegen, 1958, 11 points out, it cannot be by
mere chance that a large fortified citadel, and no other,
has been discovered in precisely the region which is indicated by the descriptions in the Homeric poems.   I deduce,
accordingly, that the Greeks of the archaic and classical
periods preserved memories of an eastern site which had
been of great importance in the Bronze Age and that this
site, like the seats of the Mycenaean heroes in Greece itself, became a background against which the events imagined
by the epic poets were played out: a conclusion similar to
that reached by Mülder, 1910.   Given the artificial and
composite nature of Homer's poetry and his occasional juxtaposition of manifestly incongruous elements, I find it
uncritical in the highest degree to lump together all the
features of the poems and to argue that, because some of
them are verifiable in the archaeological record, all the
rest must also reflect reality.   The probability that the
epic poets of the Homeric tradition peopled real places
with imaginary heroes seems to me so self-evident that it
is hardly necessary to appeal for parallels to other poetic
traditions;   but the parallels are there, and they have
been ably treated by Finley, 1964, whose view of the genesis of Homer's account of the Trojan War I share in the

main.   This imperative necessity, as I regard it, to dissociate the topographical background from the events narrated means that I am out of sympathy with the approach of
J.M. Cook, who writes:

From at least the eighth century the Greeks of the eastern Aegean understood that during what they regarded as
the age of the heroes a fortified settlement was besieged and captured by Achaeans in the area that we now call
the Plain of Troy.   Incorporated in the epic tradition
as known to us are names belonging to the general geographical setting (Hellespont, Scamander, Ida, Tenedos.)
The geographical situation was therefore not in doubt,
and we have in the Homeric epos an assemblage of stories
of exploits of Achaeans in a particular region that was
located outside the Achaean dominions.   If anyone were
to make a serious attempt to impugn the historicity of
the Achaean attack on the region indicated, he would
need to take up a position on the topographical issue.
He could argue that names such as those here mentioned
already existed in the stories from which our 'Iliad'
was formed and that Greeks of the eighth century and
earlier assigned these names to geographical features of
a particular region of the north-east Aegean in order to
establish a topographical setting for the epos.   Or al-
ternatively he could argue that the names already existed on the ground in the region under review and that
the stories were remodelled to fit into the geographical
framework to which the names belong.   The objections to
either view seem very grave.   (Cook, 1973, 92.)

I wish that Cook had formulated his 'grave objections',
since either of the two positions he attacks seems perfectly tenable to me.   It is only the physical site of
Troy whose knowledge must go back to the 'time of the
heroes' in the Bronze Age: there is no necessary basis in
history for the scale of the epic contest which took place
there or even for the existence of such a contest.   When
the Greek chronographers produce a date for the fall of
Troy between the early thirteenth and the early twelfth
century, the date merely shows that in some respects their
time-scale for prehistoric periods was approximately correct;   it does nothing to confer historicity on the Homeric
details of the siege or sack of Troy.

When we consider the Greek accounts of the great migrations which are said to have followed the Trojan War, the
invasion of the Peloponnese by the Heraclids and the movements of Aeolians and Ionians from the Greek mainland to
the coast of Anatolia, we can say at once that they appear
to receive some support, in a general way, from the archaeological evidence.   The Ionian and Aeolian migrations

are not our main concern here, but it is worth mentioning
that movements of Greeks into Aeolis and Ionia are now confirmed by the Protogeometric pottery which has been found
in both regions.   Since this pottery cannot have been taken
to Asia much later than 1000 BC (Cook, 1958, 10-1), it gives
some support to the date given by the Parian Marble for the
Ionian colonization.

When they speak of movements within Greece itself, the
accounts of the Return of the Heraclids are also consistent
with the picture which we have been able to construct from
the material evidence.   There is no reason to deny that
the Return of the Heraclids represents, however dimly, the
troubled and unstable period which succeeded the Mycenaean
expansion.   It would therefore be wrong to take up the extreme position of rejecting all historical basis for the
Return: a position adopted by Beloch, 1895 and 1913, 76-
96.   When Beloch wrote, the sequence now established for
the Late Bronze Age in Greece (namely formation of a Mycenaean culture, Mycenaean expansion, fragmentation of the
Mycenaean culture into various local styles, and movements
of peoples) was not clearly apprehended, with the result
that it was possible for him to ascribe the legends about
the Return entirely to the work of Dorian apologists.

While Beloch certainly went too far in denying all historicity to the Greek accounts of the Return, it is equally
certain that those accounts cannot be accepted just as they
stand.   When we ask of these narratives the question cui
bono, we see immediately why the record they enshrine has
been shaped in just the way that it has.   The reason is,
first and foremost, to legitimate the dual kingship of the
Spartans and, second, to provide some explanation of the
evident fact that Greece was constituted in a different
way, both ethnically and linguistically, from the situation
which had obtained in the time of the heroes.   Let us examine those reasons in turn.

We have already seen that Beloch found it easy to explain the rise of legends about the Dorian Invasion.   An
earlier and hardly less critical historian, after lucidly
re-telling the legends, thus summed up the motive for their
origin: 'Above all, this legend makes out in favour of the
Dorians and their kings a mythical title to their Peloponnesian establishments; Argos, Sparta, and Messene are presented as rightfully belonging, and restored by just retri-
bution, to the children of Herakles' (Grote, 1851, 7-8.)
No fault is to be found in Grote's reasoning, which betrays
a firm grasp of the principles to be adopted when examining
legendary material.   So far, then, we may say that the
central core of the tradition, namely that movements of
populations accompanied and followed the end of the unified

Mycenaean world, corresponds so well to the events which
have been deduced from the archaeological record that it
should be accepted as a genuine reminiscence from some prehistoric epoch.   But (as we shall see below) details of
the migrations, such as routes followed, places conquered,
and even peoples involved receive no direct confirmation
from the monuments.

I have suggested that the second conceivable motive for
the rise of the legend was the attempt to explain the world
as it appeared to the Greeks of the archaic period and its
differences from the heroic world.   To the Greeks, as to
many writers in modern times, the hypothesis of an invasion
of the Peloponnese by Dorians seemed to explain, simply and
adequately, the linguistic situation to be observed there.

Scholars in ancient as in modern times found the 'model'
of an invasion to provide the answers to their linguistic
questions.   But we must ask, as we asked about that other
'model' of invasion at the beginning of the Middle Helladic
period, whether this simple explanation is necessarily the
correct one.   When dealing with those far-off events, we
found that the introduction of a new language to a given
area could be effected by means other than that of invasion.   Where the archaeological record was silent or am-
biguous, we had the right to consider the alternative of
peaceful and gradual diffusion.   Naturally, the same consideration applies to changes in dialect-grouping.   Whether
or not the archaeological data speak in favour of a Dorian
Invasion, in precisely the form of an intrusion into the
Peloponnese from regions to the north of the Gulf of Corinth, we must ponder in a moment;   for the present, I
deal with the purely linguistic evidence in purely linguistic terms.

The modern classification of the Greek dialects set out
above is accurate only in a descriptive sense.   It shows
what kind of dialect was spoken in a given part of the
Greek world in classical times, but it is too crude in formulation for historical conclusions, other than those of a
very limited nature, to be drawn from it.   Worst of all,
it conveys the impression of a number of discrete dialectal
blocks, which did not communicate with one another;   in
other words, the opposition between dialects is over-
emphasized, at the risk of losing sight of the many similarities which bind the dialects together.   When it is
realized that a dialect, so far from being a monolithic
entity, is a bundle of identifiable phonological and mor-
phological features, many of which recur in other (apparently unrelated) Greek dialects, we are able to make some
observations important for the present purpose.   A great
deal of study has been expended upon features shared by

more than one dialect ('isoglosses'.)   Among Greek dialects there is one especially interesting set of isoglosses.
Despite the general opposition between East and West Greek,
some individual West Greek dialects share with some individual East Greek dialects a large enough number of isoglosses to make it certain that at some point there was close
contact between them (cf. Coleman, 1963, 122-3 and Wyatt,
1970b.)   In recent years, these contacts between east and
west have been dated to the era of the Dorian Invasion and
the break-up of a unified 'Achaean' dialect (Ruipérez,
1953, 262; Risch, 1955, 71.)   At this epoch, it is said,
West Greek and East Greek were in touch for long enough to
permit the sharing of certain linguistic features.   This
explanation, whose inherent merit is not great, suffers
from the capital defect that it tries to account for linguistic phenomena in non-linguistic terms, for there is nothing about the observed isoglosses between east and west
which would place their origin at c. 1200 BC rather than in
another period: nothing, indeed, to suggest that they all
originated at the same time at all.

If the Dorians are regarded (and they are often so regarded) as a collection of rather barbaric tribes who set
out from remote fastnesses in their eagerness to destroy
the Mycenaean world, the resulting picture is a vivid one;
but, whatever other objection may be made to it, a grave
linguistic difficulty presents itself straight away.   The
differences between West Greek and East Greek were never so
great as to inhibit easy communication between the two
areas: a remarkable circumstance, if the Dorians had
really lived in isolation from the Mycenaean world for the
best part of a millennium.   Risch, 1955, 76 notes the cu-
rious fact but draws no conclusion from it.   But is there
not an obvious conclusion to be drawn: one to which our
observation of the east-west isoglosses also leads?   Namely, that the tribes known in historical times as 'Dorian'
were not only in contact with the Mycenaean world long before its collapse but actually formed part of that world.
Such a diagnosis may be at variance with our received no-
tions, but it accords much better with the linguistic evidence;   and yet it is only tentatively and with great re-
luctance that explanations of this kind are at last being
advanced (for example by Bartonek, 1973, 310.)   But, it
may be objected, 'the Linear B tablets from Pylos and Mycenae show that Dorians were not yet present in Greece,
and above all not present in the Peloponnese, in Mycenaean
times' (Schachermeyr, 1967b, 145.)   The Linear B tablets
show no such thing: they show merely that, out of hundreds
of Mycenaean sites in mainland Greece, these two used, for
bureaucratic purposes, an East Greek dialect.   When we

recall that the dialect of the mainland tablets is virtually the same as that of the Knossos documents, written
nearly two hundred years earlier, we can be excused for
suspecting the presence of an ossified official jargon
which gives a poor enough guide to the vernaculars actually
spoken at the places where the tablets were produced: still
less does it form a basis for the supposition that the presence of Dorians can be absolutely excluded.

The linguistic evidence, in short, gives us no reason to
deny that Doric dialects were already spoken in southern
Greece before 1200 BC and provides a few indications that
they probably were.   And this assumption, so far from conflicting with the accounts of the Greek writers, is actually
in accord with them.   The Heraclids, according to our sources, are no semi-barbarians who have entered from Greece
from the outside;   on the contrary, they have their origin
in the heart-land of the Mycenaean culture, the Argolid itself.   Even in Plato's eccentric version (7 in Appendix 1)
the invaders of the Peloponnese are no more 'foreign' than
in the usual accounts, since he regards them as the very
Mycenaean kings who had led the armies at Troy.   Neither
Plato nor any other source (except Herodotus) traces the
route of the Heraclids farther back than Naupaktos.   As for
Doris, it was the mere similarity of name which led to the
association of people with place: 'no conclusion can be
less certain than one drawn from correspondence or similarity between place-names' (Beloch, 1895, 565.)   It is amu-
sing to notice that Plato does not mention the place Doris
but derives the name 'Dorians' from an eponymous Dorieus:
so long as some similar name could be found or invented,
that was sufficient to corroborate a legend.   Herodotus,
for his part, reports that the tribes were not even called
Dorians until their arrival in the Peloponnese (5a in Appendix 1.)   His account is the only one which places the
starting-point of the migration so far to the north as
Thessaly;   the movements across wide areas of Greece at an
unspecified time, mentioned in this account, and the lack
of any allusion to a 'Return' are impossible to reconcile
with the precise details given elsewhere by Herodotus himself (5e), and we are not justified in supposing that, in
origin, 5a and 5e referred to the same migration at all.

To conclude this discussion of the linguistic and legendary aspects of the Dorian Invasion, I would like to suggest that the historical reality underlying the traditional
accounts is rather different from what is commonly supposed.   I begin with four premises: first, there are reasons, both negative and positive, for thinking that speakers of Doric were present in the Mycenaean world when our
Linear B tablets were written;   second, the 'official' dia-

lect of the tablets (or, in other words, the dialect used by the administrative or ruling classes) is of an East Greek, non-Doric complexion; third, in historical times, after the great upheavals we have been considering, the dialects of those parts of the Peloponnese which had produced the Linear B documents were Doric; fourth, in the course of time a body of legends grew up which told of the ousting of the Mycenaean kings by newcomers. There seems to me only one plausible way in which these observations may be reconciled and explained; and I do not pretend that the explanation is either original or other than purely speculative: I say merely that it is the one which best fits the facts as they are known at present. If Doric and non-Doric dialects co-existed in the Peloponnese and if the language of the palatial administrators was non-Doric, is it not likely that the lower classes (the subjects of the palaces) spoke Doric? The 'Dorian Invasion', which, according to the legends, finally achieved its purpose, would then represent, not an incursion into the Peloponnese from outside, but the successful uprising of the Doric-speaking population against the palatial centres.

But what of archaeology? What correlation is possible between the legends and the sequence of events which may be deduced from excavation? In the days before it was possible to suggest relative dates for the cultural changes discussed in the first part of this chapter, it seemed obvious that the widespread destruction of Mycenaean sites was intimately connected with the Dorian Invasion: that, in plain terms, 'the political world of the Mycenaean era, together with its culture, was brought to an end by this migration' (Meyer, 1928, 573.) Lenschau, 1916, 162 actually declared that, if such a movement as the Dorian Invasion had not been recorded in the traditions, it would be necessary to deduce it from other evidene. He meant, of course, that the change from Mycenaean to Archaic Greece was so profound that only a serious disruption, accompanied by the intrusion of a new people, could account for it. That this explanation is still put forward in many quarters to-day argues much more for the persistence of ingrained habits of thought than for any sagacity on the part of those who hold such views. Whatever truth may reside in the traditions (and I think that some truth does), it is impossible to equate the Dorian invaders with the destroyers of the Mycenaean civilization. The absurdity of the equation may be demonstrated by referring briefly to four matters which have been discussed in this and in preceding chapters:

1 It is true that, in the period we are considering, new objects and new customs make their presence felt in the

Mycenaean world. But, as was seen above, new practices like the use of iron instead of bronze and the cremation of the dead never make their first appearance together at any one site. Where and why cremation came into use is utterly unknown: nothing, in any case, connects it with invaders from the north. Iron was introduced probably from the east, by way of Cyprus, and so has nothing to do with northern intruders. Indeed, the coming of iron cannot be connected with the great destructions at all, since only long after they had taken place are iron objects found, in any significant quantities, at mainland sites. As for the objects of admittedly northern provenience: either these are so sparsely represented in the Mycenaean world as to attest no more than sporadic contacts with the north at the time of great disturbance (for instance, lanceolate spearheads and alien pottery); or, like the Naue II swords, they are found in the eastern Mediterranean in contexts dated earlier than 1200 BC - a fact which shows that they are likely to have been present in mainland Greece at an epoch before the horizon of destruction. Even if the objects and practices mentioned could be brought into closer connexion with the disasters than has been possible to date, they would still fall far short of proving the forcible disruption of the Mycenaean world by hostile invaders. As Snodgrass, 1973, 213 rightly holds, the Mycenaean culture was too highly organized and had commercial contacts of too long standing for a hypothesis of foreign immigration to be based on the appearance of new metal types.

2 The objects of northern provenience are, in any event, incompatible with the traditional accounts of the Dorian Invasion, since that was exclusively a movement of Greeks within Greek territory, in which no one from outside Greece participated.

3 The archaeological record provides abundant evidence of destructions; but it shows also that, after the destructions, the Mycenaean civilization was not submerged beneath an alien culture. It becomes less assertive certainly, but it remains the same culture that it had been before the era of destruction. Such a continuous development of culture is inconsistent with the literary traditions, which speak not merely of invasion but of settlement and expropriation.

4 Finally, in purely practical terms, how are we expected to visualize the successful invasion by Dorian intruders? I confess that my own powers of imagination are not equal to the concept of an invading force so elusive as to leave not the slightest trace in the material record and yet so potent and relentless that it was able to make its

way through the Peloponnese and destroy the fortresses of
that region.   The manner in which these could have been
destroyed is also obscure to me;   for we are surely not
expected to believe that the citadels of Mycenae and Tiryns
(to speak of no others) were ever taken by assault?

For one or more of these reasons, the simple identification of the Dorian invaders as the destroyers of Mycenaean
civilization must be rejected.   Equally excluded, by reason
of objection 1, are those vast movements conjured up by Milojcić, 1948 and Kimmig, 1964, which are said to have
brought the new objects of metal to Greece from central Europe.   To the extent that the Mycenaean culture changed,
as it did change at about the end of the twelfth century
BC, the change was an organic one: what emerged after the
change was no 'European' culture but something which was as
much a growth from the soil of Greece as its Mycenaean pre-
decessor.   The new objects of metal (swords, spear-heads,
and the rest), which bulk so large in the accounts of Kimmig and Milojcić, can have had no part in transforming the
Mycenaean culture, since their use on any wide scale hardly
survived the end of Late Helladic IIIc (cf. Catling, 1961,
118 on the chronology of the Naue II sword.)

Among modern scholars who have pondered the causes of
the great destructions, Hammond and Desborough are pre-
eminent because of their attempt to avoid some at least of
the objectionable features of earlier theories.   In a long
series of publications, Hammond has expressed his belief
that the destructions arose as the result of civil war (of
which, indeed, some hint is found in the Greek sources) and
that, while Greece was still in an enfeebled state, it was
over-run by large bodies of intruders who had been forced
out of Epirus by pressure applied to them from Macedonia
and Albania (e.g. Hammond, 1931 and 1973, 36-46.)   But we
look in vain for a single fact which positively establishes
a connexion between events in Epirus and those in the Mycenaean centres.   In his earliest paper on the subject,
Hammond gives two reasons for looking to Epirus for the beginnings of the Dorian Invasion.   The first is that the
name of the Dorian tribe called Dymanes contains an ending
-anes which is common in Epirus (but also, as he admits, in
Kephallenia, Macedonia, and other parts of northern
Greece);   the second is that invaders, whom Thucydides
brings into Boeotia sixty years after the fall of Troy (6a
in Appendix 1), are said by Herodotus to have come from
Thesprotia (an area which, for him, includes Epirus)(Hammond, 1931, 151-6.)   It is safe to say that upon such insubstantial grounds as these no one would ever have advanced the theory of a movement from Epirus to the Peloponnese, were it not for a cultural feature of Greece in the

twelfth century to which attention has already been drawn.
The feature in question is the preference for burial in individual cists rather than in the chamber tombs which had
previously represented the prevalent practice of the Mycenaean age.   If only we could find some connexion between
the Attic and Peloponnesian cists on the one hand and those
of Epirus on the other, would we not have discovered a possible area from which invaders came into Greece?   As is
well known, the cists form an important part of Desborough's
reconstruction, to which I now turn.

Desborough identifies three stages in the period we are
considering.   In the first stage, there is an attack on
Mycenae itself.   Next, at the end of Late Helladic IIIb,
comes a serious invasion, whose effects are attested by the
destruction and desertion of sites and by the movement of
population.   It is impossible that the attack was organized
from within Mycenaean territory; local revolts of the kind
described by Thucydides must be ruled out as well, because
these would have been aimed at the palaces and could not
have caused the abandonment and depopulation which actually
ensued.   The attackers, therefore, came from outside the
Mycenaean world; and there is only one easily conceivable
route by which they could have entered the Peloponnese,
namely through Boeotia, across the Isthmus, and into Argolis, Laconia, and Messenia.   Being probably of a lower
cultural level than the Mycenaeans, these invaders left no
positive trace of their presence but, after completing
their work of destruction, they departed and did not settle
in the districts they had devastated.   This pattern is
exemplified in the Argolid, which sees no fundamental
change in the Mycenaean way of life after the great destructions.   Desborough's third stage ends with the devastation of the Granary at Mycenae.   A sign that the Mycenaean culture has come to an end is seen in the replacement
of family burials by cist-tombs.   The cist-using newcomers
who were responsible for bringing the Mycenaean civilization to a close had earlier made their way into western
Attica.   Since cists have been found in Epirus and Thessaly, it is likely that the invaders came overland from
north-western Greece (Desborough, 1964, 221-32;1965,221-3.)

In the presence of such a deeply-considered treatment as
this, it may seem impertinent to suggest that the author
has all too often based his conclusions on hopelessly insufficient evidence.   But, if there are any intermediate
arguments which might help to bridge the gap, at least
these are not presented to the reader.   For example, it is
unjustifiable to regard the destruction of the houses outside the citadel at Mycenae as the result of an attack
without mentioning the other possible causes of the de-

struction.   Again, pace Desborough, it is far from impossible that the palaces were destroyed by local rebels; except that I would prefer to see the destructions in less simple terms, in which warfare between cities also played a part - but I imagine that Desborough's concept of a unified Mycenaean 'empire' forbids him to think of internecine conflicts of this nature (cf. Andronikos, 1954.) Desborough's objections to the theory of destruction by rebels are not cogent.   If we apprehend rightly the nature of the palatial administration in Mycenaean Greece, we can see that, should the palaces be destroyed or even merely cut off from surrounding areas, serious results would quickly ensue for the population in general.   The Linear B tablets teach us that this was a society in which the palace officials kept a very close eye on the doings of the inhabitants and played a large part in the co-ordination of their activities. It is evident that such a society, once its centre was gone, would be liable to political and economic disintegration, which might very well manifest itself in the abandonment of sites and movements of population we deduce from the material record (so, rightly, Hutchinson, 1975.)   I would by no means exclude the possibility that natural disaster, in the form of famine consequent on a severe drought, played its part in disrupting the economic fabric of Mycenaean life.   The case for such a pattern of events at the end of Late Helladic IIIb has been argued with great eloquence by Carpenter, 1966; and, while I am not able to assess the probability of his case, I note that it has recently been found to be quite consistent with the archaeological evidence (Bryson, Lamb, and Donley, 1974.) However, one observation made at the very beginning of this chapter seems to cast doubt on the correctness of Carpenter's theory, though I do not claim that it invalidates the theory altogether.   As we then saw, the tablets from Pylos reflect an era of prosperity and make none of the allusions to famine which are present in the last inscriptions of the Hittite empire.   The only way of saving Carpenter's hypothesis in this situation is to suppose that famine and other economic calamities affected parts of Greece other than Messenia but that, with the disintegration of the other palatial communities, Pylos was caught up in the general disorder and succumbed to attacks from within the kingdom and also, perhaps, from outside.

    To return to the examination of Desborough's account. Having seen that his objections to a theory of internecine conflict are not insuperable, I suggest that his own suggestions for the causes of his 'second stage' of destruction are open to serious doubt.   Here too a gap in the reasoning is manifest.   We are by no means compelled to

attribute each and every destruction to external attack;
the extraordinary difficulties attending such an explanation have already been mentioned. The great Mycenaean
citadels could never have been taken except by way of famine, disease, or treachery: all of them disasters which
leave open the possibility of local conflict or sedition
but which exclude the theory of destructive invaders. Had
a good case for the presence of invaders been made out, we
might sympathize with Desborough's inability to suggest who
they were, whence they had come, where they returned to,
and why they did not stay to exploit their spectacular victories; but even then there would remain the inexplicable
circumstance that a flourishing and powerful civilization
was dealt a shattering blow by a people whose culture 'was
probably primitive, and anyway far inferior to that of the
Mycenaeans' (Desborough, 1964, 224.)   I observe that Buck,
1969, 284-5 (who equates the Dorian invaders with warlike
tribesmen from north-western Greece) tries to overcome the
difficulty by pointing to the swords and spears which have
been recovered from Epirus; but he does not explain how a
whole armoury of such weapons would have prevailed against
the walls, bastions, and towers of the Mycenaean citadels.

What of Desborough's suggestion that two waves of cist-
using invaders entered the Mycenaean world in Late Helladic
IIIc, the first making its way to western Attica and the
second to Argolis?   Desborough holds that the north-
western provenience of these invaders is shown by three
facts: first, cists are extremely rare in Mycenaean Greece
in the fourteenth and thirteenth centuries; second, the
Late Helladic IIIb Epirot cist-grave described by Dakaris,
1956, 115 is of an appropriate date, since the theory re-
quires the presence of cists in north-west Greece before
they are found in the south and east (it may be added that
the Mycenaean sword does not date the tomb with sufficient
exactness, but it is in any case clear from the treatment
by Vokotopoulou, 1969 that cist-tombs were used elsewhere
in Epirus in the late phases of Late Helladic IIIb); last,
the presence of the cist-grave in Thessaly confirms the
assumption that this type is especially at home in the northern and north-western areas of Greece.

Despite the fact that Desborough's theory enjoys great
prestige and has proved very influential, I have to agree
with Snodgrass, 1971, 177-87, 314-7 that not much can be
said in favour of it. The method of burial in cists is
not the characteristic mark of any particular culture, as,
for example, the use of tholoi is characteristic of the
Mycenaean.   It is a form of interment of the utmost simplicity, which is found just where we would expect to find
it, namely in contexts of relatively impoverished and pro-

vincial cultures: thus, it is common in Greece proper in
Middle Helladic, less common (though still much more so
than Desborough allows) in the Mycenaean age, and normal in
an area like Epirus in Late Helladic IIIb-c. That being
so, there is no reason to associate its re-appearance in
Attica and Argolis with the invasion of newcomers. At
least in Salamis and at Athens, there are no traces of destruction and no marks of an invasion: the pottery, at any
rate, shows a striking continuity of development throughout
Late Helladic IIIc (cf. Desborough, 1965, 219.)

   If, as seems likely on the evidence, burial in cists was
the method which came naturally to the inhabitants of the
Greek mainland when centres of high culture were absent or
inoperative, it is no wonder that cists tended to supersede
chamber tombs in some areas of Greece in Late Helladic
IIIc: the wonder is that they did not supersede them in
all. When Snodgrass, following Deshayes, attributes the
use of cist-tombs to the pre-Mycenaean substratum, upon
which the Mycenaean civilization had been imposed from the
top (1971, 186), his conclusion is not only in accord with
the archaeological evidence but confirms, from another
point of view, my own suggestion made above. I there sur-
mised that the Doric-speaking subjects had been responsible
for the overthrow of the palatial system (and perhaps for
the destruction of the palaces themselves) and that it is
these insurrectionists who are commemorated in the traditions about the Return of the Heraclids. I now suggest
that these 'Dorians' (as we may already call them) were
the very people upon whom Mycenaean civilization had been
'imposed from the top.' I believe, further, that the subject people, in destroying the palaces, brought to an end
the Mycenaean cultural and political system of which they
had formed part. In other words, I embrace the explanation mentioned by Desborough, 1965, 221, only to be rejected by him: 'a take-over of power by a previously down-
trodden, probably servile, population.' After the long
period of disturbance which followed the destructions, I
think that the former subjects of the palatial order established a new order of their own, in which Helladic traits
such as cist-burials, very simple styles of decorated pottery, and habitation in unfortified settlements of modest
size re-asserted themselves. When we observe that the
inhabitants of Greece now sometimes built their houses and
tombs with a different orientation from that of their Mycenaean predecessors, we should ascribe the change not to
the advent of newcomers who had not known the Mycenaeans,
but to a deliberate rejection of former practice by those
who had known them all too well.

As we sum up the events described and the conclusions
reached in the present chapter, we see that the changes
which affected the Greek mainland between about 1200 and
1050 BC are so diverse in character and are felt at such
widely differing times that no one origin can be postulated
for all of them.   Nor are we justified in saying that all
the destroyed sites met their end at the same time.   The
destructions were not, in any event, the work of invaders
who had come from outside the Mycenaean world.   No conceivable body of invaders could have visited the Mycenaean citadels with the havoc that is attested;   and it is equally
hard to believe that the invaders would simply have melted
away after working their havoc.   The Peoples of the Sea
were not responsible, since these formed a heterogeneous
collection of allies from Anatolian and Levantine lands who
have never been proved to have anything to do with the Aegean world and whose importance and potential destructive-
ness have been greatly exaggerated by the Egyptians and,
after them, by some modern historians.   Nor were Dorian
invaders responsible, since in all likelihood the Dorians
were already present in the Mycenaean world.   I suspect
that the real explanation of the disasters and their aftermath is much more complex than a simple hypothesis of invasion.   There are at least three different causes, all
or any of which may, in theory, have operated at different
places: 1 there was open warfare between one centre and
another, perhaps in Argolis and Boeotia (as we have seen,
the literary traditions preserve some memory of such conflicts); 2 local risings either accompanied the internecine warfare or took advantage of the enfeebled state of
the palaces after their devastation (such events also are
mentioned briefly in the tradition); 3 natural disasters
may have contributed to the general picture of destruction,
although it is unlikely that they were the sole cause of
the troubles.
    In discussing events at the end of the Mycenaean age, I
have been even more aware than in previous chapters how
precarious must be any conclusions which rest on the evidence available to-day.   A single discovery could seriously affect our view of the whole period (especially its
chronology); but, for the present, I prefer to interpret
the history of the period along the lines indicated above.

NOTES

General

Biancofiore, 1965;   Buck, 1969;   Bouzek, 1975;   Desborough, 1975.

Evidence from Overseas

Cyclades.   Delos: Gallet de Santerre, 1958, 105-12.
Melos: Furumark, 1972b, 77 (pottery.)   Naxos: Kontoleon,
1951 (successive settlements.)
Dodecanese.   Kalymnos: Furumark, 1972b, 77.   Kos:
Morricone, 1965, 304.   Rhodes: Furumark, 1944, 196-222.
Chios: Hood, 1965.
Cyprus: Dikaios, 1971;   Aström, 1972b, 775-81.
Crete.   Gournia: Boyd Hawes, 1908.   Karphi: Pendle-
bury and Money-Coutts, 1937;   Seiradaki, 1960.   Kephala
Chondrou: Orlandos, 1959c.   Knossos: Popham, 1964, 9.
Mallia: A. Dessenne in Deshayes and Dessenne, 1959, 154.
Mouliana: Xanthoudidis, 1904, 21-50.   Palaikastro: Sac-
kett and Popham, 1965.   Vrokastro: Hall, 1914.   Late
Minoan III pottery: Popham, 1965.
Anatolia.   Miletus: Kleiner, 1969.   Tarsus: Gold-
man, 1956, 205-9;   Elizabeth French, 1969b, 136;   1975.
Troy: Blegen, 1958, 9, 187.
Levant.   Destruction of Alalakh: Woolley, 1955, 398.
Cartouche of Merenptah at Ugarit: Schaeffer, 1955.   Tell
Abu Hawam: Hamilton, 1934, 77 (temporary abandonment
after fire);   Anati, 1963 (last Bronze Age settlement des-
troyed in thirteenth century BC.)
Late Helladic IIIc1 pottery at Beth Shan: Hankey,
1966;   at Tell Sukas: Riis, 1973, 205.
Campaigns against the Sea Peoples.   Egyptian texts:
Breasted, 1906a and 1906b;   Edgerton and Wilson, 1936.
Names in the texts: Helck, 1971, 224-34.   Historical in-
terpretation:Mertens,1960;Stadelmann,1969;Nibbi,1976.   The
texts as propaganda: Donadoni, 1965.   Peoples depicted
in the Medinet Habu reliefs: Wainwright, 1961 and 1965
(their head-dress is discussed by Galling, 1969 and by
Schachermeyr, 1969.)
On the Hittite text KBo XII 38 (the 'Alasiya text'):
Steiner, 1962;   Otten, 1963;   Güterbock, 1967;   Forrer,
1969.
On the two texts from Ugarit: R.S. 20. 238 is published
by Nougayrol, 1968, 87-9;   R.S. 18. 148 by Virolleaud,
1965, 88-9.
The Philistines.   Origin and history: Riemschneider,
1956;   Wainwright, 1959;   Hestrin, 1970;   Barnett, 1975,

371-8.   Philistine pottery and the historical conclusions
to be drawn from its presence in Palestine: Welch, 1900;
Thiersch, 1908, 378-84;   Saussey, 1924;   Heurtley, 1936;
Trude Dothan, 1957;   Benson, 1961b;   Desborough, 1964,
209-14;   Pritchard, 1968, 108-9;   Furumark, 1972b, 118-22.
Anthropoid clay coffins: Albright, 1932;   T. Dothan,
1972 and 1973.

Ashdod.   Late Helladic IIIc1 pottery: Asaro, Perlman,
and Dothan, 1971.   Earliest Philistine pottery: M.
Dothan, 1971, 25-7, 156-62 (the 'Ashdoda' figurine is
similar to Philistine pottery in that it incorporates both
native and Mycenaean elements: Dothan, 1971, 129, 133.)

Tell el-Fara.   The Mycenaean antecedents of the chamber
tombs have been discussed by Waldbaum, 1966:   her arguments are not refuted by Stiebing, 1970.

Date and historicity of the Trojan War: Huxley, 1957;
JHS, 84, 1964, 1-20;   Weigel, 1965;   Geiss, 1975.

8   The Mycenaean civilization

Whatever the Greeks of the Dark Ages and the poets of the
Homeric tradition preserved of the Mycenaean culture, they
know nothing of the complex economic system, and little of
the political structure, which obtained in a Mycenaean
state. It has been truly said that in such matters there
is a wide gulf between the actual world of the Mycenaeans,
with its complex orders of functionaries and highly differentiated economy, and the simple and largely unstruc-
tured society depicted by Homer (Finley, 1957; Papazoglu,
1961, 31.) Even now, we can say nothing for certain about
the political system of the Mycenaean world before the mature palatial epoch of the thirteenth century BC and nothing for certain about any Mycenaean state except Pylos;
although the similarities between the three great Peloponnesian palaces in other respects suggest that the political
and economic structure of Mycenae or Tiryns was not very
different from that of Pylos.
   There follows an examination of the facts that can be
ascertained about the system at Pylos: an examination
based on the only evidence which is admissible at present,
that of the Linear B archives from the Pylian palace. The
texts will yield little meaning indeed unless a certain
degree of interpretation is allowed: the best that can be
done is to present a selection of the most important texts
and let them speak for themselves so far as possible. We
shall soon find that they allow no clear dividing-line to
be drawn between the 'political' and the 'economic' sphere
or, for that matter, between the 'religious' and the 'secular'.
   We would infer from the Pylos Linear B tablets that a
person's status is measured by amounts of grain. For
instance, we read in a text of fundamental importance:

183

```
Er 312.1   wa-na-ka-te-ro te-me-no
     .2   to-so-jo pe-ma WHEAT 30
     .3   ra-wa-ke-si-jo te-me-no WHEAT 10
     .4
     .5   te-re-ta-o[     ]to-so pe-ma WHEAT 30
     .6   to-so-de te-re-ta MAN 3
     .7   wo-ro-ki-jo-ne-jo e-re-mo
     .8      to-so-jo pe-ma WHEAT 6+
     .9
```

The persons mentioned in this text are identifiable because of the similarity of their names to classical Greek
words: thus, wa-na-ka-te-ro (line 1) is the adjective formed from wanax ('lord') and ra-wa-ke-si-jo the adjective of
lawagetas (literally 'leader of the people'); te-re-ta,
which appears in the genitive case in line 5 and in the
nominative in line 6, corresponds formally to Greek telestas 'official', 'one who performs a service'. (The obscure entry in line 7 is not discussed here.) The wanax
is said to have a temenos ('precinct') worth thirty measures of wheat and the lawagetas a precinct one-third as
valuable. The wanax and lawagetas are usually taken to be
the king and his second-in-command respectively; but there
is no need to attribute to either of them divine status because of their ownership of a temenos. It is true that in
later Greek temenos refers to a precinct sacred to a god,
but this reference is not inherent in the word itself,
which means simply 'share', and so 'demesne' (Yampolski,
1958; Manessy-Guitton, 1966; Effenterre, 1967.) There
is equally little warrant in our texts for the assumption
that Mycenaean lawagetas already bears its later meaning
'leader of the war-host' (Palmer, 1969a, 84.) On the contrary, the associations of the lawagetas are rather with
cult. In Un 718 are mentioned offerings of grain, wine,
cheese, honey, and sacrificial animals which are to be made
to Poseidon by: (i) a man called E-ke-ra$_2$-wo (possibly,
but not certainly, the name of the wanax himself); (ii)
the damos ('community'); (iii) the lawagetas; (iv) the
ka-ma (perhaps a cult-organization of some kind.) Un 219,
however, comprises a list of offerings to divine and human
recipients, among whom are found the wanax (line 7, probably) and the lawagetas (line 10.)
    Despite the flood of speculation which has all but sub-
merged this question, little more can usefully be said
about the Mycenaean wanax and lawagetas. Their functions
in the Pylian state, essential as these probably were, remain completely obscure: even the whereabouts of their
temene, as recorded in Er 312, are unknown to us. But we
are in better case with the damos and the telestai. The
word damos I translate (more or less arbitrarily) as 'com-

munity': that seems to be a meaning which well suits the contexts in which damos is found.   The damos is a corporate entity which is regarded by the Linear B scribes as equivalent to a person.   The legal personality of the damos is most clearly evident in Ep 704, which speaks of a dispute about a title to land between the damos and a priestess named E-ri-ta.   We have seen in Un 718 a reference to an offering by the damos.   But it is above all in the land-registers of the E-series that we are given a hint of the importance of the damos in the Pylian kingdom, or at least in that part of it called Pakijana.   Within the E-series two sets of tablets refer to two different kinds of tenure: (i) the Ep tablets (which represent a later recension of the Eb set) dealing with land 'leased' from the damos;   (ii) the En tablets (later versions of the Eo set) with land 'leased' from telestai.

The En tablets (609, 74, 659, 467) speak of the occupation of forty parcels of land at Pakijana by fourteen telestai: these are, therefore, considerable landowners - a status compatible with the important place they have on Er 312 (above), where each telestas is credited with a holding equivalent to that of the lawagetas himself.   In the En tablets the size of the plot held by each telestas is expressed, as usual, in terms of amounts of grain.   The plot is specified as ko-to-na ki-ti-me-na ('settled land', according to Palmer's interpretation, which I follow): from each telestas a number of named persons have an o-na-to, a word which is conventionally translated 'lease' but which it would be wrong to identify exactly with a lease as known in modern land law.   On occasion, a telestas may himself hold a 'lease' from the damos: five telestai are recorded by Ep 301 as holding such 'leases'. This tablet also specifies seven occupiers of land as ko-to-no-o-ko, which ought to mean simply 'plot-holders'; but, since this term is not applied universally to those who hold plots of land, it must denote a tenure of some special kind.

Five of the Ep tablets (212, 301, 539, 704, 705) record a long list of named persons as holding 'leases' pa-ro da-mo (probably, 'from the damos'.)   This formulation clearly points to a difference in title between 'damos-land' and land in the possession of individual telestai; and the difference is emphasized by the fact that the two modes of tenure are expressed by different formulae: whereas a plot 'leased' from a telestas is specified as ko-to-na ki-ti-me-na, that held from the damos is ke-ke-me-na ko-to-na ('share-land', in Palmer's terminology.)

Can anything more be said about the telestai and their
relationship to other dignitaries of the state?   While
Palmer was right to reject the interpretation of telestai
as 'initiation-priests', I find his own suggestion equally
incredible.   He writes as follows: 'Who is the granter of
ki-ti-me-na land corresponding to the damos for the ke-ke-
me-na land?   A clue is given by the designation wa-na-ka-
te-ro, which occurs a number of times among the holders of
this type of land.   It is applied to a fuller (En 74. 3),
an e-te-do-mo (En 609. 5), a potter (Eo 371.)   The lands
in question are at pa-ki-ja-ne(s), where there was a shrine
of po-ti-ni-ja, and the predominance of religious personnel among the holders was apparent from the beginning.
Furthermore, we have evidence for a close connexion between
the wanax and Potnia.   All this suggests that in the En
set we have records relating to the estate of the wanax at
pa-ki-ja-ne(s), and that the wa-na-ka-te-ro personnel owe
service to him' (Palmer, 1969a, 191-2.)   The argument is
unsound.   It is based on a false premise, namely that
someone must, in the first place, have granted lands to the
telestai just as the damos has granted lands to its 'lease-
holders'.   But I am not aware of the existence of any fact
which would lead us to this belief.   Why should the telestai not be, for instance, independent yeomen, holding their
estates by an immemorial tenure roughly equivalent to our
fee-simple?   The description of one of them as a shepherd
(Eo 278) is quite consistent with the assumption of such a
status.   Further, although it is indeed true that the
three 'lease-holders' mentioned by Palmer are specified as
'royal', that is no very impressive number when it is set
against the twenty-nine 'lease-holders' in the En and Eo
series who are not so specified.   If there were really
royal estates at Pakijana and if the telestai held their
lands from the wanax, we would expect firmer evidence than
this.   As for the alleged connexion between wanax and potnia, this will have to be examined further when we come to
discuss the religion of the Mycenaeans; but it is worth
remarking here that, in contexts where it is very hard to
be certain whether the word wanax designates a god or a
human king or a human king under his sacral aspect, we have
no right to select one of these meanings to suit our convenience.   If Palmer's argument falls to the ground, as I
think it must, there is no room for any theory which would
see the operation of a 'feudal' system in Mycenaean Greece.
   Rich in implications for the Pylian economy as the E-
tablets are, only one further observation must suffice
here.   In both the Ep/Eb and the En/Eo sets, many of the
named 'lease-holders' are called te-o-jo do-e-ro (or do-e-
ra): words which can mean nothing else than 'slave of the

god'.   Whatever this designation may have meant originally
it had perhaps degenerated to the level of a mere honorific
title by the time that our tablets were written.   The fact
that all the 'slaves' are given names and are not differentiated in any obvious way from the other 'lease-holders'
forbids us to suppose that they were really of servile status (so Polyakova, 1968.)
     A similar description, i-je-re-ja do-e-ra ('slaves of
the priestess'), occurs on Ae 303;   but here it is more
likely to refer to actual slaves, since the women (more
than fourteen in number) are not named and are connected
with 'sacred gold'.   Other tablets in the A-series (all of
which record men or women in various occupations) do not
describe so exactly the nature of the work engaged in, but
they can be shown to give valuable hints about the organization of labour at Pylos and at other places in the kingdom.   By way of example, we may bring together three A-
tablets which show the disposition of one class of women:

Aa 85   a-ke-ti-ri-ja WOMAN 12 ko-wa 16 ko-wo 8 DA 1 TA 1
          akestriai: 12 women;   16 girls;   8 boys; 1 DA; 1 TA

Aa 717   ro-u-so a-ke-ti-ri-ja WOMAN 32 ko-wa 18 ko-wo 8
                                                    DA 1; TA 1
          Lousos: akestriai: 32 women;   18 girls;   8 boys;
                                                    1 DA;   1 TA

Ad 666   pu-ro a-ke-ti-ra$_2$-o ko-wo MAN 20 ko-wo 7+
          Pylos: 20 sons of akestriai;   7+ boys

It is clear, at least, that akestriai, in the feminine plu-
ral, is an occupation-word of some kind.   Further, the
sons and daughters of the women are recorded as part of
the same 'work-unit'.   In the second and third texts, the
presence of akestriai or of the children of akestriai is
shown at the place Lousos or at the place Pylos.   The
forty-nine texts of the Aa series refer in all to some 650
women.
     I agree with those who argue that the groups of women
assigned by these tablets to Pylos and other places are
slaves: a status suggested not only by the absence of
personal names but, even more insistently, by the fact
that we are confronted here not by women in families or
even by women and their husbands but, invariably, by women
and their children concentrated into 'work-units'(Lencman,
1966, 160.)   The correctness of this deduction is confirmed, to some extent, by the evidence of the Ab set.   This,
like the Aa set, records groups of women;   but, in addition, there are details of 'rations' of figs and grain

which are provided for each detachment.   It has been observed that when DA or TA is present the ration is increa-
sed by a regular amount.   The most likely explanation is
that DA and TA are persons, in all probability the super-
visors of their respective groups of female slaves (so
Palmer, 1969a, 116-8; though I cannot accept his diagnosis
of an 'emergency situation.)   The difficult and unique
text An 607 speaks of the parentage of groups of slave-
women: these are the offspring of parents both of whom
were slaves but who occupied different positions within
the servile class (Deger-Jalkotzy, 1972.)

It is hardly necessary to emphasize the importance of
the information which the A-tablets give us about the economy and, to some extent, about the political and social
structure of the Pylian state.   Despite the obscurity of
many details, three fairly certain facts can be elicited
from this series of tablets alone: manual occupations of
great diversity were followed by well-defined and specialized groups; in all likelihood, these groups consisted of
slaves; their work came under the purview of palace officials, whether it was carried on at Pylos itself or elsewhere.   The high degree of specialization and the minute
care with which the work of artisans was controlled (or at
least recorded) are seen again in the Jn series.   These
tablets are concerned with two different operations involving bronze: its levying and its distribution.   On the
one hand, Jn 829 records the quantities of ka-ko na-wi-jo
(presumably, 'temple bronze') to be contributed by officials at sixteen named places: in each place the ko-re-te
is to give so much bronze (an amount which varies from
place to place), while the po-ro-ko-re-te is to give a
smaller, fixed amount.   The introductory paragraph
states that the bronze is to be used in the manufacture of
arrow-heads and spear-heads.   The other tablets of the Jn
set speak of amounts of bronze allotted to smiths.   Many
problems are encountered in the interpretation of these
texts; but it may be worth while to bring together the
salient points.   The aggregate of bronze involved here is
very large.   The decisive role of the palace as interme-
diary in the economic process is plainly brought out.
Since it is out of the question that such large amounts of
metal were produced locally, they must have been imported
(in ways which, unfortunately, our texts do nothing to
clarify) and then sent out to specified places, and even
to specified smiths within those places, by the central
authority.   No fewer than five classes of personnel are
differentiated in the Jn series: (i) named smiths who have
ta-ra-si-ja; (ii) named smiths who are without ta-ra-
si-ja; (iii) unnamed slaves attached to their respective

smiths;   (iv) named smiths who are specified as po-ti-ni-
ja-we-wo, presumably 'in the service of Potnia' (Ruijgh,
1967b;   Lejeune, 1971, 359-64);   (v) qa-si-re-u, a word
which is formally equivalent to the later Greek basileus
('king') but which seems here to denote little more than an
official (perhaps an overseer) of no very elevated rank.
The meaning of ta-ra-si-ja is not known for certain;   if it
is correctly identified with Greek talansia (cf. talanton),
it means something like 'allocation' (Carratelli, 1963,
246.)   As things are, our interest is naturally aroused
by the connexion of some of the smiths with Potnia, who
may be the goddess whom we shall meet later when discussing
the Mycenaean religion or, perhaps, a queen.   There is no
compelling reason to think (with Palmer, 1969a, 279) that
the Jn tablets speak of a guild of smiths attached to a
cult-place.

The function of the palace as an organ which assessed
and exacted amounts of commodities has been displayed in
Jn 829.   But, for all we know, the metal there listed may
have been required on only one occasion.   Two sets of tablets, the Ma and the Na series, fill out the picture considerably, since their terminology makes it plain that
regular contributions were required, year by year, from
named places and even from specified professions.   The
structure of a Ma tablet is simple.   First the assessment
of a named place is recorded;   then follow details of actual delivery (apudosis) and, sometimes, a statement to
the effect that a certain class (often the bronze-smiths)
o-u-di-do-si, 'do not make their contribution'.   The recurrent character of the exactions is clearly brought out
in Ma 225 by the contrast between za-we-te, 'this year'
and pe-ru-si-nu-wa, 'belonging to last year'.   A detail
added by some of the Na tablets (for example 248, 252, 529)
is e-re-u-te-ro/-ra 'free', the most likely meaning of
which in such a context is 'exempt from payment'.

The last group of Pylos tablets which has an important
bearing on the organization of the kingdom is that known
by the prefix An.   Two different kinds of text are found
within this group.   First we have a tablet like An 1,
which states the number of men from five named places who
are to go to Pleuron as rowers.   In the second place,
there are five tablets (An 657, 519, 654, 656, 661), whose
structure is more complex.   In essence, they record military dispositions.   The tablets, as a set, contain a number of clearly demarcated paragraphs, each of which refers
to an o-ka.   The o-ka (which must be something like 'body
of men', 'detachment') is grouped under a named commander
at a specific place.   All the detachments together are
said to be 'guarding the coastal regions' (An 657. 1.)

After the commander's name in a given paragraph come a number of other names, which might refer to the officers of the detachment in question.   There follows a numeral, presumably applying to the troops.   The paragraph most often ends with a note stating that a named e-qe-ta is present with the detachment.   If the e-qe-ta corresponds to the later Greek hepetās ('follower'), he is probably of high status: an inference in keeping with the occasional attachment of a patronymic to the name of an e-qe-ta.

We can, accordingly, add yet another sphere of activity which was the concern of the palace scribes.   Not only did they record the organization of personnel into work-units, the assessment of contributions due from many different localities, and the details of land held under various tenures, but they kept track of the precise whereabouts of detachments of the Pylian army.   And yet, as I noted at the beginning of Chapter 7, it is impossible to discern in the 'military' tablets, any more than in the other classes, evidence that the resources of the kingdom were being mobilized to meet some imminent threat.   We read in a recent treatise: 'One conclusion from these documents seems inescapable;   that Pylos feared an attack coming by sea, and its subsequent destruction implies that these precautions were in the event in vain' (Ventris and Chadwick, 1973, 430.)   But nothing has been found in these tablets to suggest that they refer to any extraordinary measures; or are we to imagine that the palace of Pylos, unfortified as it was, did not, as a matter of course, set detachments to watch its coasts from year to year?

My treatment of the Pylos tablets, superficial though it has been, suffices to indicate how often we meet references to persons or events with religious connotations. Naturally so, for it is an artificial and arbitrary proceeding to distinguish the 'religious' from the 'secular' in any Bronze Age society.   But, our habits of thought being what they are, it has seemed necessary to set out the facts in this way.   Just as I have tried to give some account of the 'secular' side of Mycenaean society, relying very heavily on the testimony of the Linear B tablets from Pylos, I now consider its 'religious' aspects: an enquiry for which many different types of evidence, as well as the epigraphic, are available.

THE RELIGION OF THE GREEK MAINLAND

Both cult-practices and objects of religious significance are attested for all four centuries of the Mycenaean age, and written documents relating to the end of the period

now add their testimony.   As usual, therefore, we have to
make use of evidence of very diverse kinds;   and, as usual,
the different kinds of evidence must be weighed against one
another to see what information can be extracted from them.
    A point of method must first be clarified.   All too
often, Mycenaean beliefs are not regarded as a proper object of study in their own right, but merely as part of a
larger whole, namely 'Minoan-Mycenaean' or 'prehistoric
Aegean' religion.   This view of the matter, which I am
convinced is erroneous, was formed at a time when it could
well be excused;   for, in the early years of excavation at
Knossos, the whole Aegean civilization of the Bronze Age
was indiscriminately called 'Mycenaean', with the result
that a book like Evans, 1901 (still of value to-day) was
concerned as much with the beliefs of Minoans as with those
of mainlanders.   But, in the ensuing years, the Minoan and
Helladic cultures have been distinguished from each other,
and there is no longer any justification for wilfully con-
fusing the two.   The great impetus to this wrong approach
was given by the most important and most influential treatment of our subject, Nilsson, 1950. Nilsson's book illus-
trates and discusses, often in a very penetrating fashion,
virtually every religious object known to the author from
the Aegean Bronze Age.   And yet it is seriously marred at
the outset by an assumption which makes it impossible for a
systematic exposition of the subject to be undertaken at
all.   Nilsson announces (1950, 6-7) that, since it is in
practice very difficult to dissociate the Helladic element
from the Cretan in what he calls the 'Minoan-Mycenaean'
religion, he will not attempt to do so but, on the supposition that Minoan beliefs were imported wholesale into
the mainland in the sixteenth century BC, will treat every
religious manifestation from the Aegean as one facet of beliefs held in common throughout the whole area.   By this
means, it becomes possible for the would-be interpreter to
evade the first and most serious of his difficulties, the
separation of the Minoan from the mainland elements;   but
such an evasion is illegitimate, since (as will be shown
below) the mainland and the Minoan religions, despite the
profound influence of the second upon the first, retained
some strikingly independent characteristics.   Not content
with regarding the Minoan-Mycenaean religion as a unity (at
least for the purposes of interpretation), Nilsson takes
for the most part a purely synchronic view of the evidence,
with the result that objects not only from different areas
but from very different periods are given equal weight in
the construction of a common 'Aegean' religion: a structure which, in my belief, never really existed at any given
time.   It may not be justifiable to assume that, even

within Crete, the Minoans everywhere practised uniform
cults or worshipped the same gods (so Faure, 1973, 297):
uniformity in such matters is certainly not to be looked
for in the Early Palace Period, and perhaps not even in
the later palaces.

Faulty as Nilsson's method is, he does avoid the most
serious excesses of speculation. These may be seen at
their worst in Persson, 1942b, a book which cites in argument monuments belonging to diverse periods and coming indifferently from Crete or the mainland, so as to establish
the belief of the Aegean peoples in 'the vegetation cycle'
and in 'death and resurrection'. It would be idle to deny
that the Minoans or Mycenaeans may have had settled beliefs
about such matters: equally idle to pretend that we can
elicit knowledge of such beliefs from available sources.

In view of the great influence exerted by treatments
like those of Nilsson and Persson, it is all the more gra-
tifying that two recent books (Dietrich, 1974 and Vermeule,
1974) show a keen awareness of the dangers which arise if
the investigation is conducted according to synchronic
principles.   It is to be hoped that the more scientific
attitude displayed in these works will eventually prevail.
The sources of evidence must be considered class by class;
and the examination of these sources must, as always, be
ordered according to the chronological framework already
established for the Aegean Bronze Age.   The types of evidence are as follows: cult-places; objects of cult; representations of cult-practices, especially in miniature
art but occasionally also in frescoes; tombs and their
appurtenances so far as they are relevant to beliefs about
the after-life; written documents; evidence from Greek
religion of the post-Mycenaean age.

In the Middle Helladic period, there is little religious
manifestation on the Greek mainland to match the contemporary Cretan phenomena.   Nothing so far discovered in
Greece is closely analogous to the cave-sanctuaries of
Crete described by Faure, 1964, 81-197: the only possible
candidate at present is the 'Grotto of Pan' in Attica,
which has produced pottery ranging from Neolithic to Late
Helladic III; but even here little has come to light which
would suggest a religious use (Rutkowski, 1972, 272-4.)
Although it is inconceivable that the Middle Helladic people had no religious beliefs, none of their dwellings has
yielded anything corresponding to the Cretan 'house-
sanctuaries'; while their tombs, though now known in great
numbers, tell us nothing of their beliefs about life and
death.   A welcome reminder that in this period cults were
after all practised comes from the publication of an altar,
associated with burnt sherds and animal-bones, from the

island of Nissakouli off the coast of Messenia (Choremis, 1969.)   At Ayia Irini in the island of Keos (some ten miles east of Cape Sounion), J.L. Caskey has excavated a complex of fortified buildings, including what has come to be called a 'temple'.   The construction of this temple is now placed in the Middle Bronze Age (Caskey, 1966, 369), and it was found to contain an abundance of Minyan and matt-painted wares.   Terracotta statues of human figures were left there from the beginning of the Late Helladic period, perhaps to serve as votive offerings, but their form and size (more than two feet high) are difficult to parallel in the Aegean and appear to preclude any close connexion with the religious observances of the mainland or of Crete (Caskey, 1964, 331.)

Although the Middle Helladic period is poorly documented, so far as religious beliefs and practices are concerned, we might hope to be in better case when we come to the Shaft Grave era; but even here the facts are sometimes disputed and always difficult of interpretation.   The evidence, such as it is, must come from the Grave Circles themselves, since so little is known about the contemporary palace at Mycenae.   Even though the latter contained what was called a 'shrine', with movable altars, there is no clear indication of its date (Wace, 1921, 223-9.)

In view of the nature of previous discussions of the Shaft Graves, it seems necessary to circumscribe within narrow limits the kind of conclusion which it is permissible to draw.   Although isolated clues to the religious beliefs of a people may be afforded by archaeological monuments, the monuments by themselves will never allow us to reconstruct a history of religious and intellectual opinion, as can be done with some other Bronze Age cultures, above all the Egyptian.   Vague generalizations are out of place in such a study as this, and there is little of value in Wace's own approach, which displays far less rigorous argumentation than the subject demands: 'It seems clear from the investigations of Sir Arthur Evans and others that Minoan kings were regarded as semi-divine personages.   The Mycenaeans seem so far as we can tell to have adopted the Minoan religion.   Thus naturally the graves of the kings buried in the Shaft Grave cemetery would have been regarded as sacred.   The kings were the temporary human manifestations of divinities, and to them as such all due rites and offerings were paid' (Wace, 1921, 121.)   Where even the premise is so dubious, no cogent conclusions are likely to follow;   for there is no reason to suppose that Minoan kings were regarded as divine, while to say that the Mycenaeans seem to have adopted the Minoan religion begs the whole question.

The discussion must begin with a negative statement. It is by no means certain that the Shaft Graves betray any overt signs of the Mycenaeans' religious beliefs. Representations of cult-scenes are completely lacking from the gold rings, in contrast to their abundance in contemporary Crete and on the mainland in the subsequent Phase of Minoan Influence (Karo, 1930a, 332.) The superficiality of the Minoan impact on everyday life (as distinct from arts and crafts) is thereby further demonstrated. We might accordingly surmise (but not state as a fact) that Minoan influence on the mainlanders' beliefs was likewise superficial, at least so far as the Shaft Grave period is concerned. Take, for instance, the double axe: one of the central symbols of Minoan cult and at first, probably, something more than a symbol. At first glance, the small double axes in gold foil from Shaft Grave IV look like a direct reflexion of Minoan cult; but there is little reason to think that, among so many other gold trinkets heaped in the same tomb, the double axes were seen by the Mycenaeans as instruments of cult at all. This view is corroborated by a further occurrence of double axes in the Graves. Whenever the double axe is represented in Cretan art, there is no doubt what it is: the basic idea of the object is always conveyed, even though there are many different shapes and stages of elaboration. In particular, the Minoan artist is careful to show the shaft and to associate it clearly with the blade of the axe itself. The shaft has completely disappeared in the drawings of double axes on four vases from Shaft Grave I, while the shape of the blade also has sensibly degenerated (Karo's nos 190-2, 195.) The decoration on these vessels looks like the work of mainlanders to whom the double axe meant nothing as a sacral object.

Again, we have model 'shrines' in gold leaf from Grave IV (Karo's nos 242-4.) These, with their triple division, insertion of a pillar inside 'horns of consecration' of Minoan type, and accompanying birds, would be taken to imply the construction at Mycenae of actual Minoan cult-buildings, if only they had been found in less promiscuous surroundings. The models are so close to the Minoan concept of shrine (of the type depicted on the Miniature Fresco at Knossos, Evans, 1928, 597) and so remote from anything else on the mainland that it is hard to believe they had any religious significance for the Mycenaeans.

On the positive side, however, we can infer with some confidence that the Shaft Grave people had belief in some kind of life after death; for it is beyond all reason that they should have deposited such massive treasures at the time of interment if they thought that nothing of the human

person survived. To say so much is not to imply that the
Mycenaeans possessed a coherent and well-formulated body of
doctrine on the subject (even the Greeks of the classical
period did not possess that): perhaps it was only a vague,
but nevertheless strongly held, superstition which caused
them to act in a given way at death. If we wish to define
more closely the nature of the life after death in whose
existence they believed, we have to take account of two
apparently contradictory facts. On the one hand, the
burial with the corpse in at least some Graves of great
masses of heterogeneous objects forbids us to believe that
the tombs were intended only as temporary shelters for the
body until its decay and that the objects were buried to
serve the dead man on his journey to the lower world. The
probability that the Shaft Graves were recognized as permanent resting-places is immensely strengthened when it is
remembered that long after the construction of Circle A
some levelling of the area took place, stelae were moved,
and a retaining wall was built so as to bring the Grave
Circle within the fortified acropolis. On the other hand,
it is hard to think that the physical remains were held in
any particular respect, at least after the decomposition
of the flesh, because of the habit, attested in Circle B
and at least in Grave II of Circle A, of sweeping aside
the bones of the previous occupant to make room for a new
one (Marinatos, 1953, 65.) Setting these two considerations alongside each other, we can draw the tentative conclusion that the occupants of the tombs were thought to
live on in some sense, unconnected with physical remains,
after burial. (It is not legitimate to go farther and,
in the absence of positive evidence, attribute to the Mycenaeans of the Shaft Grave period or, indeed, to those of
any other era a belief in a discrete 'soul', such as obtained among the Egyptians.) Our conclusion would be
virtually assured if proof could be brought of the existence of a cult of the dead: that is, not simply rites
accompanying the actual burial (for these are amply attested by the presence of burnt offerings) but by continued
rites in honour of the dead. It has often been assumed
that the altar over Grave IV (Schliemann, 1878, 246) and
the cavity between Graves IV and I (Keramopoullos, 1918,
52-7) indicate that a cult of the dead was practised
within the Grave Circle. But the arguments brought by
Mylonas, 1951a against this assumption are powerful ones;
of particular weight is his objection that Schliemann's
altar lay well below the level of the Grave Circle in
later Mycenaean times and so cannot have still been in use.
The alleged examples of a cult of the dead elsewhere in
Greece do not suffice to corroborate its existence here.

The Late Helladic II period sees the culmination of Minoan influence in the depiction of cult as in so many other
respects (Chapter 4.)   It will be of particular interest
to trace the marks of Minoan culture at Mycenaean sites and
to enquire whether, even at this time of close intercourse
between Crete and the mainland, it is possible to separate
Helladic from Minoan beliefs.   But first a word is needed
about the disposal of the dead.   As we have seen, the
Shaft Graves are succeeded at Mycenae by tholoi and chamber tombs, which together form the predominant means of
burial in Late Helladic II and III.   It is, indeed, well
into the Late Helladic III period that the crowning example
of the whole series of tholoi, the Treasury of Atreus, is
to be placed; and yet the earlier and smaller tholoi of
Late Helladic II belong to the same series, and there seems
to be no reason why statements about the religious function
of the later tombs should not hold good for the earlier
ones as well.   Unfortunately, the Mycenae tholoi were de-
spoiled at some unknown period; but we may infer from the
Dendra tomb, which was discovered intact, that corpses
buried in the tholoi, no less than those buried in the
Shaft Graves, were accompanied by rich funerary gifts.   The
tholoi afford even clearer evidence than the Shaft Graves
that the inhabitants of the Peloponnese had some belief in
a life after death.   The interior of the tholos and of the
chamber tomb formed a miniature dwelling-place for the
dead.   It is inconceivable that such mighty structures as
the Treasury of Atreus (still a prominent feature of Mycenae in the time of Pausanias) were mere 'temporary shelters for the trip to the lower world', as Mylonas, 1957,
85 supposes: he is rightly contradicted by Matz, 1958b,
326-7.   It is true that the practice of sweeping aside the
bones of previous occupants is attested in the tholoi and
chamber tombs as well as in the Grave Circles; but dis-
respect for the physical remains does not exclude veneration for an impalpable part of the human personality; and
to some degree of veneration the increasing size and elaboration of the tholoi irresistibly point.   As in the
Shaft Grave period, the Mycenaeans of Late Helladic II and
III continued to make burnt offerings at the time of interment (cf. Mavriyannaki, 1967 and Sakellarakis, 1970.)
    Monumental 'houses of the dead' are alien to the usual
Cretan practice (the Temple Tomb at Knossos forming a rare
exception), and they must therefore be held to represent a
purely Mycenaean development.   But there are certain
manifestations of cult on the mainland in Late Helladic II
which clearly reflect, if they do not at all points coincide with, the Minoan practice.   There is evidence that,
for several centuries before this epoch, the Minoans had

used caves and mountain-tops as cult-places (Nilsson, 1950,
53-76; Faure, 1964; Rutkowski, 1972, 121-88.) The cults
shown on Minoan seals and rings and on some of the frescoes
likewise take place in the open air. Trees and free-
standing pillars, together with rough-hewn altars, appear
frequently. Female adorants are commonly shown: sometimes
these dance ecstatically. A female figure dressed in typical Minoan fashion occupies a prominent place in many of
the extant pictures. Although writers on Minoan religion
from Evans onward have virtually always assumed that this
figure is a goddess, there exists no clinching argument in
favour of the identification; and our ignorance of many of
the conventions of Minoan iconography makes it unlikely
that such an argument can be produced. At the same time,
I am uneasily aware that if the character of a divinity is
denied to the prominent female figure there is little hope
that any definite statement about Minoan religious belief,
as distinct from cult, is possible. Even if she is admitted to be divine, and not a priestess or votaress, it
remains an open question whether our sources show different
facets of one and the same Great Goddess, as Evans believed, or distinct deities (cf. Nilsson, 1950, 392-8; Nock,
1943, 494.) A small (apparently descending) figure is
seen on some Minoan scenes above the 'goddess'. This
figure is often thought to be the young male consort of the
goddess; but, even if he is a god, the divine status of
the female figure is not thereby made out, since he could
still be an adorant. Biesantz, 1954, 85-7 expresses well-
justified scepticism about both the sex and the divinity of
such descending figures.

When we ask how many elements of Minoan cult were taken
over on the mainland, and with what significance, we shall
find the enquiry beset with obstacles; and it is questionable whether at the end any clear picture emerges. The
starting-point must be the so-called Great Goddess Ring
from the Acropolis Treasure at Mycenae, which is to be
dated probably, though not certainly, to a time just after
the end of the Shaft Grave era (Thomas, 1938, 84-6; CMS,
no 17; my Figure 13a.) The ring is usually taken to represent the epiphany of a 'mother goddess', who is seated
under her sacred tree, holding poppy-heads and receiving
the homage of female votaries. The wavy bands below the
schemata of the sun and moon have been variously interpreted, but they are surely the vestiges of a division between
the two registers of a frieze. The surface is very crowded: more so than is usual on Cretan rings and seals.
Moreover, the artist has not been content simply to depict
the adoration of the goddess (if, indeed, that is the meaning of the scene): he has to press home his point that

the whole picture is a cult-scene by inserting religious
symbols.   In the very centre a double axe is clearly represented, but it is not fitted into the picture coher-
ently.   To the right is a tree of a kind found in cult-
scenes from Crete.   I agree with Herkenrath, 1937, 412
that the tree and the axe are mere symbols, not actual
cult-objects: the row of lion-heads along the edge fulfils
a similar function.   Judging from the extant Cretan material, I believe that a Minoan artist who was designing a
work for his own countrymen would simply have shown the act
of homage;   he would not have needed to emphasize so insistently that the scene is a religious one.   The whole may
be interpreted as the attempt by a Mycenaean artist to display a typical facet of the Minoan religion which was now
becoming known on the mainland;   only he has misunderstood
some important particulars.

The Great Goddess Ring must be given careful consideration in any attempt to separate the Helladic from the Cretan elements in the so-called Minoan-Mycenaean religion.   I
have indicated already some traits which look like mainland
features;   and we now consider the small figure to the left
at the top.   At first sight, this appears to be an example
of a descending 'divinity' of the kind well attested in
Cretan cult-scenes.   But a comparison with the gold ring
from Knossos (Evans, 1921, 159-60;   my Figure 13f), which
may be called the locus classicus of the type, discloses
serious differences.   The Knossos ring places the descending figure at the very centre, where we should expect to
find him if he is indeed a god, while to the left stands a
woman with her arms raised in a characteristic gesture of
adoration (Matz, 1958a, 11-2)(compare CMS, no 292 from
Pylos.)   It is evidently after some such model that the
artist of the Mycenae ring has put in his descending figure;   but he has not comprehended its significance.   In
the first place, his figure seems to be female, by analogy
with the very similar representation on a limestone tablet
from Mycenae (Rodenwaldt, 1912a, 134-5.)   Again, it is
hard to think that any artist who equated the descent of
the figure with the epiphany of a divinity would place it
in such an unimportant position, where it is not even regarded by the others, let alone adored by them.   Plainly,
the descending figure (whatever its significance in Minoan
cult) has been transformed into something else: a change
emphasized by the figure-of-eight shield which covers the
whole body.   Now the figure-of-eight shield is derived
from Crete and is frequently represented in Minoan art, especially from the Late Minoan I period onward, sometimes in
a religious context;   but I know of no example from Crete
which shows a descending figure with such a shield.Perhaps,

then, we should regard the figure with shield on the Great
Goddess Ring as the incarnation of a mainland divinity
superimposed upon the quasi-Minoan cult-scene.   As
Schweitzer, 1928, 175 well says, the descending figure is a
'Mycenaean interpolation'; but I am not so sure that he is
correct in assigning to this period the transformation of
the Minoan palace-goddess into a Mycenaean war-goddess. It
is true that, so far as we know, this is the first time
that the goddess was represented in this way; but the people of the Shaft Grave era must have had deities of their
own, of whom a god or goddess of war was surely one.   If
this explanation is right, the figure with shield on our
ring is yet another symbol, but this time a symbol of mainland origin: it is the divine protectress, appropriately
watching over the whole scene - the forerunner of Athena,
or perhaps we should now say Athena herself.

Another cult-scene, corresponding more closely to Minoan
types, is shown on a gold ring from the Vaphio tholos (CMS,
no 219; my Figure 13c.)   It is hard to see just what is
happening.   As with the Great Goddess Ring, the artist has
insisted that some kind of religious ritual is in progress
by representing the double axe, but he has not brought it
into connexion with the rest of the scene;   to the right
below is another religious symbol, called by Evans the
'sacral knot' (cf. Nilsson, 1950, 162-4.)   The woman in
the centre is in violent motion: she is probably dancing,
and the same may be true of the male figure to her right.
The same kind of ecstatic movement is shown on the Vaphio
seal CMS, no 226.   But the most striking illustration of
dancing women appears on a gold ring from Isopata near
Knossos, which is probably a little later than the Vaphio
ring (Evans, 1913, 10; my Figure 13b.)   No altar is re-
resented on the Isopata ring;   but the scene is perhaps to
be interpreted as the epiphany of a god in response to the
entreaties of the dancing votaries (Matz, 1958a, 8-9.)

The sixteenth and fifteenth centuries witness the occurrence of 'daemons' in the art of Crete and the mainland.
Daemons are creatures who partake of some of the characteristics of horses, lions, or donkeys but walk upright, their
backs covered with a loose, scaly skin, a kind of carapace.
The outstanding monument from the mainland depicting daemons is the Daemon Ring from Tiryns (CMS, no 179; my Figure 13d.)   Only an approximate date can be given to this
object on external grounds (Karo, 1930b, 138);   it is assigned to our period solely because of the close similarity
of the daemons to those on two seals from Vaphio (CMS, nos
231 and 232.)   Various views about the origin of the
Minoan daemon are collected in Nilsson, 1950, 376-81;   the
question has been re-opened by Gill, 1964 and 1970;   by

Straten, 1969; and by Crouwel, 1970. For my own part, I
incline to the view, now unfashionable, that the daemons
are stylized versions of human beings wearing animal-skins,
and I believe that this account of their derivation is supported both by the observation that they regularly appear
on monuments as votaries or cult-servants and by the fact
that women and men clad in skins assist at the sacrifice
painted on the Ayia Triada sarcophagus (early Late Minoan
III?)(Nilsson, 1950, 426-34; Long, 1974.) I add that
the painter of the sarcophagus has associated a votaress
(in animal-skin) with the same type of sacral jug which is
carried by daemons in the cult-scenes at Tiryns and Vaphio.
It is not possible to infer with certainty from these representations whether Cretan cults involving daemons were
actually practised in the Peloponnese. The stylized type
of daemon depicted on our monuments, both in Crete and on
the mainland, forms such a striking part of the Minoan gem-
engraver's repertory that its appearance in Greece may
amount to an iconographic rather then a religious borrowing: thus, from an artistic point of view, the four creatures on the Tiryns Daemon Ring recall the Cretan convention seen on the Procession Fresco at Knossos, while the
very type of goddess' chair is derived directly from Cretan
art (Evans, 1935, 387); on the other hand, it is hard to
find a Cretan parallel for a cult-scene set (as this seems
to be) indoors. (Müller, 1927, 1-19 analyses the Daemon
Ring.)
    The very extent of Cretan influence on the material
culture of the mainland in Late Helladic II makes it hard
to draw any certain conclusions from the Mycenaean cult-
representations belonging to this period. The discrepan-
cies with Minoan cult-scenes which have been noted suggest,
indeed, that Cretan beliefs had been modified on their
transference to the mainland; but they might equally well
indicate that the habits of Cretan art had been applied to
the depiction of mainland divinities and their cults. The
latter interpretation is more likely if we make the reasonable assumption that the Mycenaeans already possessed a
pantheon and cults of their own. But the picture is
greatly complicated by two considerations. First, the
notorious difficulty of deciding whether a given work of
miniature art originated on the mainland or in Crete means
that some of the most remarkable cult-scenes found on the
mainland may have been imported solely for their artistic
quality: that could apply to the daemon seals from Vaphio
or to a magnificent lentoid from Routsi (CMS, no 279),
which shows a woman grasping a plant set between horns of
consecration on an altar. Second, even if it is denied
that Minoan cults and religious beliefs were taken whole-

sale to the mainland, the likelihood remains that the
close intercourse between the mainland and Crete led to a
high degree of assimilation, such as came about when the
pantheon of classical Greece became known at Rome.

That some assimilation of Cretan and mainland beliefs
had taken place by the end of the fifteenth century BC is
confirmed, on the Cretan side, by Linear B tablets from
Knossos which record offerings of oil and other substances
to named recipients.   Among many divine names which cannot
now be interpreted with any conviction, three stand out
with remarkable clarity as Greek divinities: these are
Poseidon and Lady Athena (on V 52) and Dictaean Zeus (on Fp
1.)   The last of these shows that the name of an Indo-
European god had already been superimposed upon a venerable
Minoan deity (cf. Willetts, 1962, 207-20.)   We might surmise that syncretism of a similar kind had been applied to
other gods as well.   It has long been observed that the
Minoan goddess represented on rings as the 'mistress of
animals' closely resembles Artemis, while the goddess of
fertility (unless she is the same goddess under a different
aspect) partakes of the character of Demeter (cf. Nilsson,
1967, 307-15.)   Kerényi, 1961, 24 observed that all the
elements of the Greek god Dionysus are present in Minoan
cult-scenes; and, although I do not share the common belief that the name of this god can be read on any extant
Linear B tablet (cf. Gérard-Rousseau, 1968, 74-6), the
possibility remains that the Greek name was attached to a
Minoan god at the time of closest intimacy between the two
areas.

The evidence for Mycenaean religion in Late Helladic III
is greater in bulk and more varied in nature than in preceding epochs.   The use of tholoi and chamber tombs, with
their implications for a belief in the after-life which
have been discussed, persists throughout this period. Comparatively few representations of cult-scenes of Minoan
type are found.   Outstanding among these are three gold
rings from the chamber tombs at Mycenae: the first (CMS,
no 119) shows a man, accompanied by a goat, touching boughs
on an altar; the second (no 126), two women with a man who
grasps a bough set on an altar of distinctly Minoan appearance; the third (no 127), two women antithetically disposed about a religious structure.

In contrast to these representations of cults, which are
plainly of Minoan ancestry even if they do not attest the
actual continuation of Minoan practices on the mainland,
the proliferation of the small clay figurines at Mycenaean
sites marks a purely Helladic habit.   The situation with
regard to cult-places in the Mycenaean world is more complex.   On the one hand, there is the totally non-Cretan

phenomenon of the megaron with its central hearth; on the other, there is the small 'shrine' or cult-room, which is reminiscent of the house-sanctuaries of Minoan Crete.

We have already seen that the great Mycenaean palaces of the Peloponnese contained a megaron, with a large circular hearth fixed at its centre. The question at once arises, what direct evidence have we that the hearths at Pylos, Mycenae, and Tiryns were the focus of a cult. In answering this question, too much is often taken for granted. For Example, Jameson, 1960, 38 writes as follows: 'The masters of the palaces were intimately involved in ritual and ceremony, as can be seen in the arrangements of the throne room at Pylos: a channel for the flow of libations ran by the side of the setting for the royal throne; in frescoes on the wall behind the throne supernatural griffins protected the king; before the throne was the great ceremonial hearth on which offerings and even animal sacrifices were made; near the hearth was a stuccoed offering table on which were found quantities of small cups for libations.' No positive fact supports a single one of the author's deductions. It is undeniable that a channel runs to one side of the megaron, but it is wrong to maintain that it was necessarily used for 'libations': it may have served a much more humble purpose (so also with the 'small cups for libations'.) The notion that the griffins in the fresco are 'supernatural' and that they protected the king is a mere possibility, unconfirmed by any evidence, even from analogies. Nor do I know by what right the 'ashes and charred matter' said by the excavators to cover the hearth (Blegen, 1966, 85) have been transformed into 'offerings and even animal sacrifices'.

But it would be as mistaken to deny that the megaron-complex could have stood at the centre of a cult as it is to assert that it must have done so. The argument, however, must be conducted in a negative, not a positive, way; for, indeed, if the hearth was not intended primarily for a religious use, it is extremely difficult to suggest a plausible explanation for it. At least in the Pylian megaron, the hearth occupies such a large proportion of the total area of the floor that it can never have served as a purely domestic fire-place. That being so, it is not easy to conceive what its function might have been, unless it were that of a cult-centre. The hearths at Mycenae and Tiryns do not take up such a large area; but, since in every other respect the megaron-complex at those two palaces is so similar to the one at Pylos, what holds good at Pylos probably applies there as well. Granted the high probability (though not quite the certainty) that the megaron stood at the centre of a cult, we are very far from having shown that the chief ministrant at the rites in the megaron was the king of the place.   The notion that a sacral kingship was exercised in Mycenaean Greece is totally without foundation.   It is not sufficient to point to Egypt and the Levant (where the institution of sacral kingship undoubtedly existed), as if the mere fact of its existence in those areas means that it was known in the Mycenaean world as well.   It is true that the Linear B scribes seem to apply the term wanax indifferently to divine and to human dignitaries: true also that the Mycenaeans drew no hard and fast line between the religious and the secular;   but the priestly function of the wanax is not thereby made out.   I suspect that, in this as in so many other areas of Mycenaean cult, it is wisest to confess our agnosticism.

At least at Mycenae, cult-rooms of Minoan affinities flourished while the Helladic megaron was still in use, namely in the second half of the thirteenth century BC. Among the complex of buildings to the south-east of Grave Circle A, Tsountas' House has long been recognized as having cult associations because of the remarkable horse-shoe shaped altar and the fresco-fragment with daemons which were found there.   More recently, Mylonas has discovered a large rectangular altar at the entrance to Tsountas' House. The further excavation of the Citadel House (west of Tsountas' House) by Lord William Taylour has revealed a set of cult-rooms without known parallel in Mycenaean Greece. A number of idols, predominantly female in form, were found in two adjoining rooms of this house (Taylour, 1969, pll. XI-XIII and 1970, pll. XXXVIII-XLII.)   These objects, which are between one and two feet high, superficially resemble a Late Minoan type represented at Gazi (Marinatos, 1937); but Taylour has rightly pointed to the considerable differences. Above all (and this is a unique feature in the plastic art of the Aegean Late Bronze Age), each idol has been endowed with an individuality of its own.   But the uniqueness of the idols as artefacts throws no light on their religious significance: it is impossible to say, for example, whether they are intended to be divinities or votaries or to have some fetishistic meaning.   Associated with the idols were coiled snakes finely executed in clay (Taylour, 1969, pl. IX.)   Now 'between the snake-goddess and the other bell-shaped idols there is an indissoluble connexion', wrote Nilsson, 1950, 314.   He was speaking of Crete; and, when we find at a mainland site female idols associated with snakes (even though neither idols nor snakes are of a form directly paralleled in Crete), we can hardly doubt the presence of a cult whose ancestry is Minoan.   The same goes for the remains of a fresco found in another room in

the Citadel House (Taylour, 1969, fig. 2):   a small male
figure with extended arm confronts a woman of much larger
size in a long fringed skirt, while at a lower level a
woman, apparently wearing an animal-skin, carries a sheaf
of corn in each hand.   Here again we have a cult-scene,
many of whose individual elements are found in Minoan art,
even though as a whole it lacks a parallel in Crete. If it
is permissible to set together the fresco, the idol and
snakes, and the altars at Tsountas' House, we may indeed
conclude that the assemblage amounts to a cult-centre. But
when Mylonas, 1972 regards it as the chief cult-centre of
Mycenae, he leaves out of account the importance of the
megaron with its hearth, whose place in the religious life
of the community is not diminished by the new discoveries.
Nor am I certain that the existence of this cult-centre
lends any strong support to the contention of Dietrich,
1974, 149: 'It is important to stress one conclusion,
namely that archaeological evidence for the last years of
the Helladic period does not establish any basic difference
between mainland and Cretan beliefs, despite the presence
of some dissimilar features in both centres.'   The cult-
rooms of the Citadel House cannot be regarded simply as
Cretan house-sanctuaries which have been transplanted to
the mainland.   The evolution and character of the Minoan
house-sanctuary have been studied by Banti, 1941; and, in
contrast to the Cretan norm established in her account, the
rooms at Mycenae betray a number of eccentric features.
These rooms seem to have enshrined a cult which was at a
rather long remove from its ancestors in Crete and which
impinged little upon the main stream of Mycenaean religious observance.   In the field of cult, as in other fields,
the thirteenth century was an epoch which witnessed little
direct communication between Crete and the mainland; although it would be strange if we did not find here and
there (especially in the neighbourhood of great palaces)
continuing traces of Minoan influence.
     A more thoroughgoing kind of syncretism is represented
by the shrine in Room XXXII of House G at Asine.   But it
is to be noted that this shrine is dated by pottery found
in situ to Late Helladic IIIc.   It therefore post-dates
the use of the cult-area at Mycenae already discussed and
belongs to a period of upheaval and movement of population
when, as we saw in the last chapter, there are renewed contacts between Minoans and mainlanders which involve the
actual settlement of Mycenaeans in Crete.   Indeed the
mixture of Helladic and Minoan elements seen at Karphi
finds an analogy, on a small scale, in the artefacts discovered in the Asine shrine.   Upon a ledge, which resembles the ledges in Minoan house-sanctuaries, were dis-

covered a miscellany of clay vessels, some in ritual shapes, Mycenaean female figurines of Ψ-type, and a clay head,
the significance and even the sex of which have been disputed but whose religious character is unquestioned (cf.
Laviosa, 1968b.) The group is described by the excavators
Frödin and Persson, 1938, 298-310 and discussed, in some
very important paragraphs, by Nilsson, 1950, 110-4.
   The Linear B tablets from Pylos add two essential pieces
of information to what may be gleaned from the monuments.
On the one hand, they describe the actual operations of
cult, sometimes at named places; on the other, they give
the names of deities who are the recipients of offerings.
As we would expect in the light of the foregoing discussion, the list of gods which can be compiled from the Pylos
tablets includes members of the Greek 'Olympian' pantheon
(as it was to become) and divinities of much vaguer connotation who, most probably, were taken over by the Mycenaeans at the time of closest connexion with Crete. The most
important single document both from the point of view of
cult and from that of the divine names is Tn 316, the
general sense of which I take to be as follows:
   Obverse.   (In the month of?) Porowitos:
      Pylos.   A sacral ceremony was performed at
               Pakijana; gifts were brought; po-
               re-na were purified.   To the lady:
               one gold cup and one woman.
      To Manasa: one gold bowl and one woman.
      To Posidaia: one gold bowl and one woman.
      To Triseros: one gold cup.
      To Dospotas: one gold cup.
   Reverse.   Pylos.   A sacral ceremony was performed at
               the shrine of Poseidon; the town
               was purified; gifts were brought;
               po-re-na were purified: one gold
               cup and two women...
            Pylos.   A sacral ceremony was performed at
               the shrine of Pe-re-82 and at the
               shrine of Iphemedeia and at the
               shrine of Diwia; gifts were
               brought; po-re-na were purified.
               To Pe-re-82: one gold bowl and one
               woman.   To Iphemedeia: one gold
               bowl.   To Diwia: one gold bowl and
               one woman.   To Hermes Areias: one
               gold bowl and one man.
            Pylos.   A sacral ceremony was performed at
               the shrine of Zeus; gifts were
               brought; po-re-na were purified.
               To Zeus: one gold bowl and one man.

> To Hera: one gold bowl and one
> woman.   To Dirimios the son (?)
> of Zeus: one gold bowl...

Despite the obscurity of many details, the occasion referred to in this tablet is clear enough.   It must have
been the performance of rites (including acts of lustration)
at the shrines of named gods, not only in Pylos itself but
also at the religious centre of Pakijana.   The rites in
question are likely to have been recurrent, if the genitive
in the first line of the obverse is rightly interpreted 'in
the month of'.   Only four 'Olympian' deities certainly
appear in the Pylos tablets, and all of them are mentioned
in our text.   We would judge from the order in which they
are written (Poseidon first, then Hermes, lastly Zeus and
Hera) that their relative standing was different at Pylos
from what the Homeric poems lead us to expect.   It might
even be doubtful if the gods were yet organized in a 'pantheon' at all, were it not for the unmistakable juxtaposition of Zeus and Hera.   These two divinities, at least,
appear to be as closely associated with each other as they
are in later belief. If we are right in thinking that not
only gold vessels but also human beings are 'offered' to
gods, we may have to do here with human sacrifice or, at
the very least, with the dedication of persons to deities;
and the practice of such dedication is easy to reconcile
with the term 'slave of the god',found in the E-series.
In the two Pylos tablets Tn 316 and Un 2, we have to
face the troublesome problem of the meaning of potnia and
wanax.   From her position at the head of the inscription
and from the fact that all the other names on the tablet
seem to refer to gods, it is likely that potnia in Tn 316
is not only a goddess but one of paramount importance.
This cult-title 'Lady' may be seen either as the actual
name of the goddess (in which case she will appear as the
chief Minoan component of mainland religion, namely the
Great Goddess) or as an epithet belonging to one of several
goddesses, for instance Athena, Artemis, or Demeter.   Although we have no means of deciding finally between these
two alternatives, the first explanation seems more satisfactory to me.   In Un 2, both the syntax and even the
meaning of the participle mu-jo-me-no are opaque, and it is
not permissible to think that we can arrive at a convincing
interpretation of this text.   What is plain is that some
ritual act is being performed at Pakijana: an act which
involves the offering of amounts of barley, flour, olives,
figs, and wine, together with an ox, sheep, goats, and
pigs.   The word wanax is present in the dative case preceded by epi.   As usual, the problem is to know whether
wanax is an earthly or a divine 'lord'.

The problem of wanax and potnia confronts us again in the Fr series of Pylian tablets.   These record the disbursement of oil to a number of destinations.   Fr 1224 associates a quantity of oil with the dative case of the god's name Poseidon.   On Fr 1219, two words precede the amount of oil: wa-no-so-i po-se-da-o-ne.   What is the function of wa-no-so-i?   It recurs on cther tablets of this series, in the spelling wa-na-so-i:

Fr 1222   wa-na-so-i to-no-e-ke-te-ri-jo
   1227   wa-na-ka-te wa-na-so-i
   1228   wa-na-so-i e-re-de
1235.1   wa-]na-so-i wa-na-ka-te
     .2   ]wa-na-so-i po-ti-ni-ja

The only meaning which can plausibly be attached to wa-na-so-i in these texts is that of a locative 'at the place Wanaso'.   It is not possible to analyse the word further or worth while to speculate about its relationship with wanax.   I consider it necessary to reject completely the interpretation of Palmer, 1958, which has proved persuasive to many writers.   He regards wa-na-so-i as the dative dual of a word wa-na-sa, 'queen' or 'goddess'; accordingly, wa-na-ka-te wa-na-so-i (1227) means 'to the Lord and to the two Goddesses'.   So far from this interpretation being 'beyond all doubt' (Palmer, 1958, 6), it is made highly improbable by considerations both of morphology (Risch, 1966, 57) and of orthography (Petrusevski, 1970, 127): the interpretation, furthermore, involves the breaking of a rule elsewhere observed in our Mycenaean texts, which would require the two classes of recipients to be joined together by the copula -qe.   On this foundation, frail as it is, Palmer proceeds to build a fantastic edifice.   He finds that the cult-title 'Queen' is widely attested 'in the Orient' (1958, 6): the 'Queen' is sometimes linked with a youthful consort who dies and is resurrected.   But on our tablet, Fr 1227, oil is sent to a 'Lord' (wanax), who is associated with not one but two queens.   According to Palmer, the same association is attested by the ivory group from Mycenae which represents two women and a boy (above, p. 91.)   Since this group was not found in a sacral context and since it lacks a sacral parallel at any Mycenaean site (above all at Pylos), there can be no justification for regarding it as a religious object.   But who is this 'Lord' whom Palmer has identified in the Mycenaean pantheon?   It is Poseidon, 'the Lord of the Earth (Poseidas)', corresponding in name and in function to the Sumerian god EN.KI.

Palmer's treatment has been discussed at far greater length than it really deserves partly because of the remarkable influence it has exerted and partly because it

provides an admirable example of the wrong approach to our
religious texts.   There is nothing to be said in favour of
a method which offends against the usual scribal practices
of Linear B, which involves the simple juxtaposition of
terms from Pylos and from Sumeria without any attempt to
trace the cultural contacts between two areas so remote
from each other, and which brings into the discussion a
work of art whose relevance to the enquiry has never been
demonstrated.   The very equation with which we are presented at the end, namely the identity between wanax and Poseidon, is made suspect by that fact that, within the Fr
series, one and the same scribe sometimes writes wa-na-ka-
te and sometimes po-se-da-o-ne as the recipient of oil.
That he should hesitate between the name and the title of
the god is not impossible, but at least the practice calls
for closer examination.   And his practice is easy to understand if we take wanax in this series of tablets not as
a cult-title but as a word meaning 'lord' in the terres-
trial sphere, most probably (though not quite certainly)
the king of Pylos himself.

Another recipient of oil in the Fr tablets who could
equally well be a human or a divine beneficiary is po-ti-
ni-ja.   As we have seen, this word occurs on Fr 1235 in
parallel with wa-na-ka-te; and, if we are permitted to
interpret this wanax as the king of Pylos, we might suggest that potnia is likely to be his queen.   That being
so, there is nothing in the context of the other occur-
rences of potnia in the Fr series (1206, 1231, 1236) to
show that the term has sacral reference.   Not so with two
other expressions, ma-te-re te-i-ja ('to the divine
mother')(1202) and te-o-i ('to the gods')(1226); but these
are too vague to add anything significant to our knowledge
of the Pylian cult.

The high place occupied by Poseidon in the religious
life of Pylos is confirmed by other tablets. Thirteen tablets in the Es series (645-9, 651-3, 703, 726-9) have a
uniform structure: a list of offerings of grain, of which
the first, that to Poseidon, is by far the largest.   It
would be interesting to know who the other recipients were,
but the spelling leaves their identity quite obscure: it is
not certain that any or all of them are gods.   More complex
is Un 718, which mentions a do-so-mo ('offering') which is
to be made to Poseidon by sa-ra-pe-da (probably the name of
a place.)   Apart from grain, the offering will consist of
wine, cheese, honey, and a bull.   The damos and the lawagetas are to make similar, though smaller, offerings.

CONCLUSIONS

Whereas previously we have been concerned with those achievements of the Mycenaean civilization which are reflected in the material record, the present chapter has had more to say about the organization of Mycenaean society and its religious beliefs.   As in the field of material culture, so in that of religion the Mycenaean age does not form a discrete epoch without clear antecedents or consequences. The Mycenaean indebtedness to Cretan art, great as it was, is matched by the extent to which knowledge of Minoan cults and divinities penetrated the mainland.   We have observed that it is not at all easy to say whether the Minoan cults persisted in any significant manner during the fourteenth and thirteenth centuries BC;   we are hardly justified in concluding that they did so unless a parallel to the Mycenae 'cult-place' is discovered at another mainland site. By itself, the existence of this cult-place cannot be held to attest any extensive inroads by Minoan cult, since there is overwhelmingly strong evidence, both at Mycenae and elsewhere, that distinctively Helladic practices were flourishing at the same time.   So far as the divinities themselves are concerned, however, the position is different.   Whether or not Minoan cults were ever widely practised on the mainland, we cannot but believe that a considerable degree of fusion between Cretan and Helladic religion had taken place during the Late Helladic II period.

The gods whose names and cults survived the end of the Bronze Age were thus Helladic deities, some of whom had received strong Minoan colouring: colouring which is most clearly evident in the case of Zeus himself.   As for the Greek cycles of legend which are connected with Mycenaean centres, these must descend from a Mycenaean tradition of some kind; but it seems to me (as it seemed to Lesky, 1966, 30) that the formation of the concept of a 'heroic age' is most plausibly ascribed to the Dark Ages which separated the Mycenaean from the Geometric period.   It was then, I suppose, that the Greeks began the work of assembling their heroic songs and collating their extensive, though not infallible, memories of the Bronze Age: an assemblage upon which the Homeric tradition was built.

It can be regarded as certain that both the political system and the economic arrangements which had obtained in the palatial centres of Mycenaean Greece were brought to an end during the Dark Ages.   The practice, attested at Pylos, of setting to work highly differentiated groups of skilled artisans under the close supervision of a central authority is utterly different from what later prevailed in Greece.   Neither the Homeric nor any other Greek

tradition preserved the memory of so specialized an economy
as is revealed in the Pylos tablets. That economy has analogies in the Bronze Age states of Anatolia, Mesopotamia,
and the Levant: it belongs firmly in the world of its own
time and has no connexion at all with Archaic or Classical
Greece.

On the one hand, therefore, we have evidence of a complete break, since it does not appear that the classical
Greeks were in any way indebted to, or even aware of, the
political system of the Mycenaeans. But, on the other
hand, the gods of the later Greeks, or at least some of
them, were already known and worshipped during the Bronze
Age. By channels which have not yet been fully elucidated
that knowledge and that worship descended to classical
Greece. It is possible to reconcile these two apparently
contradictory observations if we take the view which was
sketched in Chapter 7. Naturally, if the people who prevailed in southern Greece after the fall of the Mycenaean
palaces (a people whom we may call Dorians) had in fact
been living in that very region during the period of Mycenaean dominance, we would not expect them to have introduced any alien religious beliefs. But they would have
had little reason to remember, still less to celebrate,
the Mycenaean political structure, which (I have suggested)
had been imposed upon them and the end of which they themselves had perhaps compassed.

On the Greek mainland itself, sure evidence of continuity from the Bronze Age to the classical period is hard
to come by except at Athens, Mycenae, Tiryns, and the venerable centres of cult in Amyklai, Eleusis, and Delphi.
The 'settlements of refugees', which (as we saw in the
last chapter) were established in the Cyclades and the
Ionian Islands after the era of the great destructions,
preserved some measure of continuity into the Protogeometric and Geometric ages: of paramount importance are
Delos, Keos, and Naxos in the Cyclades and the cave-
sanctuary at Polis in Ithaca. But it is Athens, above
all, which enters upon the Mycenaean inheritance, which
transforms sub-Mycenaean pottery into Protogeometric, and
which, very early in the first millennium BC, initiates
the migrations to the south-west coasts of Anatolia.

There remains one sphere where we cannot make such
clear-cut definitions as are possible in respect of religion or of political structure: the sphere of art. At a
fairly humdrum level, the evidence for continuity is clear
enough. We have seen how, at least in Attica, the sub-
Mycenaean pottery develops into Protogeometric; and it is
a short step from Protogeometric to the early phases of
Geometric. The difficult problem is posed when the artists

of the Geometric period start to paint scenes and human figures. Since such figures and scenes had been absent from Protogeometric pottery, we might suppose that their appearance in Geometric is due entirely to the importation of oriental motifs; and that is, in fact, a generally held view (see, for example, Carter, 1972.) Yet many of the Geometric motifs find close parallels in Mycenaean art: we may think of the conventional mourning figures, chariot-rides, rows of marching spearmen, stylized shields, and so forth. The presence of such scenes suggests an alternative explanation: namely, that a number of typical Mycenaean motifs were preserved (by means we can only guess at) during the sub-Mycenaean period and the early part of the Dark Ages. That is the explanation urged by Levi, 1968, and by Benson, 1970; and I suspect that it is the correct explanation - otherwise it is difficult to account for the coincidence that so many of the narrative motifs which occur in Geometric art are close to Mycenaean exemplars.

I am not at all unhappy at ending the book with a problem. In dealing with the Mycenaean age, and also with its origins and its aftermath, we have far more often encountered what is problematical than what is certain. Although the acquisition and publication of new material evidence must have pride of place, the precise delineation of the problems and their orderly exposition may also help toward solving them.

NOTES

The economic and political structure of a Mycenaean state

On social conditions in general: Thomson, 1949; M.A. Levi, 1964; Blavatskaya, 1968; Thomas, 1973.

In quoting from the Pylos tablets, I have relied on the transcriptions in Bennett and Olivier, 1973. Works dealing with the interpretation of the Linear B tablets in general are: Stella, 1965; Heubeck, 1966; Wundsam, 1968; Palmer, 1969a; Kerschensteiner, 1970; Ventris and Chadwick, 1973; Chadwick, 1976. On the Mycenaean vocabulary: Landau, 1958; Morpurgo, 1963; Chadwick and Baumbach, 1963; Ruijgh, 1967a; Baumbach, 1971; Lindgren, 1973. On economic vocabulary: Lejeune, 1971, 287-312. On the economic information which can be extracted from the tablets: Finley, 1957.

Special topics. The wanax, lawagetas, etc.: Carratelli, 1959; Walcot, 1967; Adrados, 1968 and 1969; Mylonas, 1969a; Lejeune, 1972, 333-44. The damos: Lejeune, 1972, 137-54. Da-mo-ko-ro: Petrusevski, 1965; Olivier,

1967; Heubeck, 1968; Lindgren, 1968. On te-re-ta: Tyumenev, 1959b; Adrados, 1969. The land-tablets: Bennett,
1956; Brown, 1956; Calderone, 1960; Deroy and Gérard,
1965; Heubeck, 1967. The personnel-tablets, slaves, and
slavery: Tritsch, 1958; Olivier, 1960; Lencman, 1966,
151-202; Polyakova, 1968; Lejeune, 1971, 65-81. Bronze
and bronze-workers: Carratelli, 1963; Lang, 1966b; Morpurgo Davies, 1968; Lejeune, 1971, 169-95; Hiller, 1972a.
The problem of qa-si-re-u: Gschnitzer, 1965; O'Neil, 1970.
The Ma and Na tablets: Lejeune, 1958, 65-91, 127-55; Wyatt
1962; Shelmerdine, 1973. The o-ka tablets and the 'army'
and 'navy' of Pylos: Mühlestein, 1956; Risch, 1958;
Georgiev, 1965; Deroy, 1968; Perpillou, 1968; Schmitt-
Brandt, 1968; Lejeune, 1972, 57-77. On e-qe-ta: Carratelli, 1958; Brock, 1960, 222-5. On the Cn tablets:
Lang, 1966a; Ilievski, 1968.

The religion of the Greek mainland

General: Schweitzer, 1928; Nilsson, 1932; 1950; 1967;
Persson, 1942b; Picard, 1948; Jameson, 1960; Brelich,
1968; Adrados, 1972; Gérard-Rousseau, 1973; Dietrich,
1974; Vermeule, 1974, 27-73; Guthrie, 1975.
    The Minoan background: Evans, 1901; Demargne, 1932;
Marinatos, 1937; Banti, 1941; Alexiou, 1958; Matz,
1958a; Willetts, 1962; Furumark, 1965a; Small, 1966;
Branigan, 1969; Vermeule, 1974, 6-27.
    Cult of the dead: Wiesner, 1938, 139-57; Mylonas,
1951a; Andronikos, 1961, 159-61; Schnaufer, 1970, 15;
Press, 1970, 87.
    Cult-places: Hägg, 1968; Press, 1970; Mylonas, 1972;
Rutkowski, 1972; Dietrich, 1973.
    Cult-scenes: Herkenrath, 1937.
    The Linear B tablets: Carratelli, 1957; Chadwick,
1957 (Potnia); Stella, 1958; Guthrie, 1959; Kerényi,
1961 (Dionysus); Maddoli, 1962 and 1967; Gérard-Rousseau,
1968 and 1971; Hiller, 1969 (wa-na-so-i); Sourvinou, 1970
(Artemis); Petrusevski, 1971 (wa-na-so-i); Christidis,
1972 (Artemis); Gianotti, 1972 (Dionysus.)

The 'Dorian invasion' in Greek sources

No. 1 Homer (floruit c. 700 BC?)

(a) 'Odyssey' 3. 304-8.   Having slain Atreus' son, [Aegis-thus] ruled for seven years over Mycenae rich in gold and subdued the people to himself.   But in the eighth year Orestes of divine descent came back from Athens to work him harm: he slew his father's murderer, the crafty Aegisthus, who had killed his glorious father.

(b) 'Odyssey' 19. 175-7.   [In Crete,] languages are mixed with one another: there dwell Achaioi, great-hearted Eteo-cretans, Kydonians, three-fold (trichaikes) Dorians, and Pelasgians of divine descent.

No. 2 Hesiod (floruit c. 700 BC?)(cited from Merkelbach and West, 1967)

(a) Fragment 9.   And of Hellen the war-loving king were born Doros, Xouthos, and Aiolos who delights in horses.

(b) Fragment 233.   And they are all called three-fold (trichaikes), because they divided into three parts the land far from their country [namely Pelasgians, Achaeans, Dorians].

No. 3 Tyrtaeus (floruit c. 650 BC)(cited from West, 1972)

(a) Fragment 2. 12-5.   For Zeus himself, the son of Kro-nos, the husband of fair-crowned Hera, has given this city [Sparta] to the Heraclids, with whom we left windy Erineos* and came to broad Peloponnese.

* One of the three towns of Doris, between Aetolia and
Phocis, later called the 'motherland' of the Lacedaemonians
(cf. 5d and 6b.)

(b) Fragment 11. 1-2. But, seeing that you are the descendants of the invincible Heracles, have courage!

(c) Fragment 19. 7-8. ...protected by their hollow
shields, the Pamphyloi, Hylleis, and [Dymanes] severally.

No. 4 Pindar (floruit 480 BC)

(a) 'Pythian' 1. 60-5. ...the king of Etna, for whom
Hiero founded that city in god-built freedom, according to
the laws of the rule of Hyllos; and the sons of Pamphylos
and of the Heraclids also, who dwell beneath the heights of
Taygetos, wish to remain for ever under the ordinances of
Aigimios, Dorians.

(b) 'Nemean' 11. 34-5. For [Pisander] came from Amyklai
with Orestes, bringing an army of Aeolians armed with
bronze.

(c) 'Isthmian' 9. 1-4. ...Aegina: founded, under the
gods' dispensation, by the coming of the Dorian host of
Hyllos and Aigimios.

No. 5 Herodotus (earlier fifth century BC)

(a) 1. 56. 3. During the reign of Deucalion, [the
'Hellenic' race] inhabited the land of Phthiotis;* in
the time of Doros, son of Hellen, the region beneath Ossa
and Olympus, known as Histiaiotis;** expelled from Histiaiotis by the Kadmeians, they dwelt in that part of
Pindus called Makednos; from there they moved to
Dryopis;*** and from Dryopis they came to the Peloponnese,
where they were called Dorians.

* South-eastern Thessaly. ** Western Thessaly. *** Cf.
5d and 6b.

(b) 2. 145. 4. Now Dionysus, who was said to be the son
of Semele, the daughter of Kadmos, was about a thousand
years before my time, Heracles the son of Alcmene about
nine hundred years, Pan...later than the Trojan War, that
is, about eight hundred years before me. [I.e. the
Trojan War took place c. 1265 BC.]

(c) 7. 204.   ...Leonidas the son of Anaxandrides the son of Leon the son of Eurykratides the son of Anaxandros the son of Eurykrates the son of Polydoros the son of Alkamenes the son of Teleklos the son of Archelaus the son of Hegesilaus the son of Doryssos the son of Leobotes the son of Echestratos the son of Agis the son of Eurysthenes the son of Aristodemos the son of Aristomachos the son of Kleodaios the son of Hyllos the son of Heracles.

(d) 8. 31.   A narrow tongue of Dorian land stretches in this region, about thirty stades in breadth, between Malis and Phocis, which in ancient times was Dryopis: that place is the motherland of the Dorians of the Peloponnese.

(e) 9. 26. 2-4.   We [Tegeans from Arcadia], of all the allies, have always had the right to hold this post...from the time when, after Eurystheus' death, the Heraclids tried to return to the Peloponnese...When we marched out to the Isthmus along with the Achaeans and Ionians, who then lived in the Peloponnese,...then (the story goes) Hyllos announced that army should not be risked against army but that the man in the Peloponnesian army they judged the bravest should fight with him in single combat, on set terms. The Peloponnesians agreed that this should be done and swore an oath that, if Hyllos defeated the Peloponnesian champion, the Heraclids should return to their ancestral country but that, if he were beaten, the Heraclids should depart to their fatherland and lead their army away and not try to return to the Peloponnese within a hundred years. Then Echemos was chosen...and slew Hyllos in single combat.

No. 6 Thucydides (later fifth century BC)

(a) 1. 12.   Even after the Trojan War, Greece was still involved in migration and settlement, so that it had no period of quiet in which to grow strong. Not only did the belated return of Greeks from Troy cause many changes but civil strife arose generally in the cities, as a result of which people were expelled and took to founding [new] cities.   For example, sixty years after the capture of Troy, the Boeotians (as we now know them), on being expelled from Arne by the Thessalians, settled in the country now called Boeotia, formerly Kadmeis...; further, the Dorians took possession of the Peloponnese in the eightieth year [after the fall of Troy].   When, after a long and troubled period, Greece achieved permanent peace and was no longer disturbed, she sent out colonies: the Athenians colonizing Ionia and most of the islands, the Peloponnesians

colonizing the greater part of Italy and Sicily and also
regions in the rest of Greece. All of these colonies were
established after the Trojan War.

(b) 1. 107. 2. Doris the motherland of the Lacedaemonians.

No. 7 Plato (427-347 BC)

'Laws' 682e-683e. During this ten-year period of the
siege of Troy, the affairs of each of the besiegers suffered greatly because of seditions raised by the younger
generation: these did not receive in an honourable or fitting manner the warriors on their return to their own cities, but in such a way as to bring about many cases of
death, slaughter, and exile.   Those who had been driven
out returned, changing their name from Achaeans to Dorians,
because the man who had mustered the exiles was called
Dorieus...According to the story, they next resolved to
divide their army into three parts and to settle three
cities, Argos, Messene, and Lacedaemon...And Temenos became king of Argos, Kresphontes of Messene, and Procles
and Eurysthenes of Lacedaemon.

No. 8 The Parian Marble (264 BC)(Jacoby, 1929, no 239)

Among the dates given by the Marble, the following are of
immediate interest:

	BC
Cecrops king at Athens	1581
Flood in the time of Deucalion	1528
Kingship of Hellen, son of Deucalion	1520
Arrival of Kadmos at Thebes	1518
Arrival of Danaos in Greece from Egypt	1510
Minos king in Crete	1462
Famine at Athens	1294
Unification of Attica by Theseus	1259
Argive expedition to Thebes	1251
Greek expedition to Troy	1218
Foundation of Ionian cities	1077

No. 9 Diodorus Siculus (floruit 60-30 BC)

4. 57. 2 - 4. 58. 4.   Now after the apotheosis of Hera-
cles his sons settled in Trachis at the court of king Keyx.
But later, when Hyllos and some of the others had grown up,
Eurystheus was afraid that, when they had all reached man-

hood, he would be expelled from his kingdom at Mycenae; he
accordingly resolved to banish the Heraclids from the whole
of Greece.   Therefore he gave notice to king Keyx to expel
the Heraclids...or to submit to war.   The Heraclids and
those with them perceived that they were no match for Eurystheus in war, and decided to flee from Trachis of their
own free will.   Travelling about the most important of
the other cities, they asked to be received as settlers.
None ventured to receive them except the Athenians alone,
who, from an innate sense of fair play, welcomed the Heraclids and settled them...After some time, when all ·the sons
of Heracles had grown up and a spirit of pride had arisen
in the young men by reason of their illustrious descent
from Heracles, Eurystheus looked with suspicion on their
increasing strength and took the field against them with a
considerable force.   But the Heraclids had the assistance
of the Athenians and made Iolaus (the nephew of Heracles)
their leader and, under his generalship and that of Theseus
and Hyllos, they defeated Eurystheus in a pitched battle.
The greater part of Eurystheus' army were slain and Eurystheus himself, his chariot wrecked when he tried to flee,
was cut down by Hyllos the son of Heracles: all of Eurystheus' sons likewise died in the battle.   After this,
now that all the Heraclids had defeated Eurystheus in a
battle which became famous and, because of theur success,
had acquired an abundance of allies, they invaded the Peloponnese with Hyllos in command. After Eurystheus' death,
the kingship at Mycenae had devolved upon Atreus, who,
taking the Tegeans and some others as his allies, went to
meet the Heraclids.   The armies being mustered at the
Isthmus, Hyllos the son of Heracles challenged to single
combat any of the enemy who was willing to meet him, with
the agreement that if Hyllos conquered his opponent the
Heraclids should receive the kingdom of Eurystheus, but
that if Hyllos were defeated the Heraclids would not return
to the Peloponnese within a period of fifty years. Echemos
the king of the Tegeans came out in response to the chal-
lenge; when Hyllos was slain in single combat, the Heraclids desisted from their attempt to return, in accordance
with the agreement, and retired to Tricorythos...When the
period of fifty years had elapsed, they returned to the
Peloponnese.

No. 10 Strabo (c. 64 BC-AD 22)

(a) 8. 1. 2.   Now there have come to be many races in
Greece, but at the remotest epoch there were only so many
as there are Greek dialects which we have ascertained:

there are four of these, but we may say that Ionic is the
same as Old Attic (for the people who then inhabited Attica
were called Ionians, and it is their descendants who colo-
nized Asia and used what is now called the Ionic dialect);
and the Doric is the same as the Aeolic, for all the Greeks
outside the Isthmus (except the Athenians, the Megarians,
and the Dorians who live near Parnassus) are still called
Aeolians.

(b) 8. 3. 33.   Ephoros says that...Oxylos, a descendant of
[Aetolos] and a friend of the Heraclids who accompanied Temenos, showed them the route on their return to the Peloponnese and shared among them the hostile parts of the
country and made other proposals for the conquest of the
territory.

(c) 9. 4. 7.   Naupaktos is so named from the ship-building
which took place there, whether the Heraclids had their ar-
mada built there or (as Ephoros says) the Locrians made
their preparations at an even earlier date.

(d) 13. 1. 3.   The Aeolian migration is said to have occurred earlier than the Ionian; but, having been delayed,
it took a longer time.   Orestes was the instigator of the
expedition but, on his death in Arcadia, his son Penthilos
inherited it and advanced as far as Thrace, sixty years
after the Trojan War, at about the time of the Return of
the Heraclids to the Peloponnese.   Subsequently, his son
Archelaus took the Aeolian expedition to the country near
Daskylion, which is now called Kyzikene.   Archelaus'
youngest son Gras penetrated to the river Granikos and,
having made better preparations, he conveyed the greater
part of the army to Lesbos and seized it.

No. 11 Apollodorus (first or second century AD)

'Library' 2. 8. 1-4.   After the apotheosis of Heracles,
his sons, fleeing from Eurystheus, came to Keyx. Terrified
by Eurystheus' demand for their surrender and threat of
war, they left Trachis and fled through Greece. Being pursued, they came to Athens and were suppliants for aid at
the altar of Mercy.   The Athenians refused to give them
up, undertook war against Eurystheus, and killed his sons
...Eurystheus himself fled in a chariot but was pursued
and slain by Hyllos...After Eurystheus' death, the Heraclids came to the Peloponnese and took all its cities.   A
year after their return, a plague afflicted the whole of
the Peloponnese: this an oracle declared had happened be-

cause the Heraclids had returned before their due time.
They accordingly left the Peloponnese and went to Marathon
and lived there...Hyllos...sought to bring about a return
of the Heraclids.   He went to Delphi and asked how they
were to return.   The god said that they should await the
third harvest before returning.   Hyllos, thinking that the
third harvest meant a period of three years, waited for
that length of time and then returned with his army [lacuna
in the text] of Heracles to the Peloponnese, when Tisamenos
the son of Orestes was ruling in the Peloponnese.   In the
second battle, the Peloponnesians were victorious, while
Aristomachos was slain.   But when the sons of Aristomachos
came to manhood, they asked the oracle about their return
...On hearing the oracle's response, [Temenos] mustered his
army and had ships built in Locris at the place which is
now called Naupaktos from that event...The fleet perished
in shipwreck, the land-army was afflicted by famine, and
the force was disbanded...They made [Oxylos] their guide*
and worsted the enemy on land and at sea and killed Tisamenos the son of Orestes...When they had gained control of
the Peloponnese, they set up three altars to Ancestral
Zeus, sacrificed upon them, and cast lots for the cities:
the first was Argos, the second Lacedaemon, the third Messene.

* Apollodorus does not make explicit the change in the
Heraclids' fortunes.

No. 12 Pausanias (second century AD)

(a) 1. 41. 2.   ...the tomb of Hyllos the son of Heracles,
who fought in single combat with the Arcadian Echemos, the
son of Aëropos...this might rightly be called an expedition
of the Heraclids against the Peloponnese in the time of
Orestes.   [A mistake corrected by Pausanias himself, 12h.]

(b) 2. 18. 6-9.   On the death of Orestes, Tisamenos succeeded to his kingdom...It was in the reign of this Tisamenos that the Heraclids returned to the Peloponnese: they
were Temenos, Kresphontes the son of Aristomachos, and the
sons of Aristodemos who was already dead...They expelled
Tisamenos from Lacedaemon and Argos and the descendants of
Nestor from Messenia...Tisamenos and his sons went with the
army to the country which is now Achaea;   the Neleids...
came to Athens.

(c) 3. 1. 5.   When the Heraclids returned in the reign of
Tisamenos the son of Orestes, Messene fell to Temenos' lot

and Argos to Kresphontes'. In Lacedaemon, since the sons of
Aristodemos were twins, two royal houses came into being.

(d) 3. 2. 1.   Eurysthenes, the elder of Aristodemos' sons,
is said to have had a son Agis; from whom the descendants
of Eurysthenes are called Agids.   In his time, when Patreus the son of Preugenes was founding a city in Achaea
(which even to-day is called Patrai after this Patreus),
the Lacedaemonians assisted in the settlement.   They partook also in a ship-borne expedition to found a colony: an
expedition led by Gras the son of Echelas the son of Penthilos the son of Orestes; it was the destiny of Gras to
occupy the land between Ionia and Mysia, which is called
Aeolis in our own time: earlier still, his ancestor Penthilos had taken the island of Lesbos, which lies opposite
the continent at this point.

(e) 4. 3. 3-6.   Two generations after the conclusion of
the Trojan War and Nestor's death after his return home,
the expedition of the Dorians and the return of the Heraclids expelled the Neleids from Messenia...The ordinary
people of the old Messenian stock were not driven out by
the Dorians but agreed to be ruled by Kresphontes and to
share the land with the Dorians.

(f) 5. 3. 5 - 5. 4. 1.   While Eleios was king in Elis,
there took place an assembly of Dorians with the sons of
Aristodemos, with the object of returning to the Peloponnese...[Oxylos] urged them to return to the Peloponnese in
ships and not to attempt a crossing of the Isthmus with a
land-army.   Such was his advice, and at the same time he
led them on a voyage from Naupaktos to Molykrion...Sus-
pecting that, when the sons of Aristodemos saw what good
land there was in Elis and entirely under cultivation,
they would not want to give it to him, Oxylos led the Dorians through Arcadia and not through Elis.

(g) 7. 2. 1-4.   So it was that Neileus and the other sons
of Codros set out to found a colony, taking with them those
of the Athenians who wished to accompany them;   but the
Ionians formed the bulk of their forces.   This was the
third expedition sent out from Greece under kings who dif-
fered in race from the common people.   The first was that
of the Theban Iolaus, the nephew of Heracles, who led Athenians and Thespians to Sardinia;   then, one generation before the Ionians sailed out from Athens, Lacedaemonians
and Minyans who had been expelled from Lemnos by the Pelasgians were led by the Theban Theras, the son of Autesion,
to the island now called after him but previously named

Kalliste.   Finally, on the third occasion, the sons of
Codros were appointed leaders of the Ionians...Those Greeks
who took part in the Ionian expedition were: Thebans...
Minyans of Orchomenos...all the Phocians except those from
Delphi...When they made land-fall in Asia, different groups
fell upon different cities, the group with Neileus making
for Miletus.

(h) 8. 5. 1.   In the time [of Echemos] the Dorians, who
had made an attack on the Peloponnese under the leadership
of Hyllos the son of Heracles, were defeated in battle by
the Achaeans at the Isthmus of Corinth;   and Echemos slew
Hyllos, who had challenged him to single combat.   This
version seems more likely than the previous one [12a], in
which I wrote that Orestes was king at the time and that it
was during his reign that Hyllos tried to return to the
Peloponnese.

(i) 8. 6. 1.   In the reign of Kypselos, who was king after
his father Aipytos, the Dorian expedition returned to the
Peloponnese, not across the Isthmus of Corinth (as they had
done three generations previously) but in ships to the
place called Rhion.

No. 13 Clement of Alexandria (second century AD)

(a) 'Stromata' 1. 138. 1-3.   Eratosthenes computes the
epochs in the following manner: from the capture of Troy
to the Return of the Heraclids, eighty years;   from then
to the foundation of Ionia, sixty years;   thereafter, to
the stewardship of Lycurgus, 159 years;   to the first year
of the first Olympiad, 108 years;   from this Olympiad to
the crossing by Xerxes, 297 years;   from this to the beginning of the Peloponnesian War, 48 years;   and to its
conclusion and the defeat of the Athenians, 27 years;   and
to the battle of Leuctra, 34 years;   from then to the death
of Philip, 35 years;   from then to the death of Alexander,
twelve years.   [I.e. Troy was captured in 1183 BC.]

(b) 'Stromata' 1. 142. 4.   And the Greeks say that five
dialects are in use among them: Attic, Ionic, Doric, Aeolic, and a fifth which is the 'common' dialect.

No. 14 Eusebius (c. 260-340 AD)

'Preparation of the Gospel' 5. 20. 1-3.   ...the tale of
the Heraclids.   These once, setting out at the Isthmus,

were foiled in their attack on the Peloponnese.   Accordingly Aristomachos the son of Aridaios (after the death of Aridaios in the attack) went to hear from you* concerning the journey...and you said to him: 'The gods show you victory by way of the narrows.'   He, making his attack at the Isthmus, perished in the battle.   His son Temenos, the unlucky son and grandson of unlucky forbears, came and, when you gave him the same testimony you had given his father Aristomachos, he said: 'But he was killed in the attack because he believed you.'   You replied: 'I mean not the narrow neck of land but the broad-bellied sea...'

*   The oracle.

No. 15 Tzetzes (twelfth century AD)

Commentary on Lycophron's 'Alexandra', 1374.   Others relate that Orestes, being told by an oracle to plant a colony, gathered contingents of various races (whom he called Aeolians because they came from diverse places) and went to Lesbos.   He himself died shortly afterward and so was unable to found a city, but after a hundred years his descendant Gras seized Lesbos and founded a city.   Hellanicus of Lesbos describes the colony at Lesbos in Book I of his 'Aeolica'.

Catalogue of Mycenaean sites in Greece

Only the most important or best reported sites are included. For a fuller list see Hope Simpson, 1965 (his site-numbers are given after the entries in this catalogue.) Many of the sites are discussed in detail by: Alin, 1962, 10-147; Desborough, 1964, 73-146; Syriopoulos, 1964 and 1968. The geology of the Peloponnese is treated by Philippson, 1892 and the geographical background of the Aegean Bronze Age by Lehmann, 1932. Philippson, 1950/1959 is the standard work on the geography of Greece.
For special areas of Greece, see the following. Achaea: Vermeule, 1960; Aström, 1965a. Arcadia: Howell, 1970. Argolis: Lehmann, 1937. Boeotia: Heurtley, 1923. Epirus: Hammond, 1967b; Vokotopoulou, 1969. Euboea: Sackett and others, 1966. Ionian Islands: Benton, 1931; AA, 1934, 161-3. Kythera: Coldstream and Huxley, 1972. Laconia: Waterhouse and Hope Simpson, 1960 and 1961. Macedonia: Heurtley, 1939a; Garasanin, 1958; Rodden, 1964; Petsas, 1969; Hammond, 1972. Messenia: McDonald and Hope Simpson, 1961 and 1964; McDonald and Rapp, 1972. Thessaly: Wace and Thompson, 1912; Milojcić, 1959b.

AEGINA (Attica)(392-5): EH-LH IIIc settlements (LH IIIb chamber tombs)
Keramopoullos, 1910, 177-208 (tombs); Harland, 1925, 7-37; Welter, 1938, 7-27.
AETOS (Ithaca)(328): LH IIIc settlement
Heurtley, 1932; Benton, 1953, 267.
AIGION (Achaea)(304): MH and LH III tombs
Yalouris, 1964; Aström, 1965a.
ALIKI (Attica)(355): Chamber tombs with LH IIIa-c pottery
Papadimitriou, 1954a; 1955; 1957.
AMYKLAION (Laconia)(97): EH-LH IIIc settlement
Tsountas, 1892; Fiechter, 1918, 123-36; Buschor and Massow, 1927; Waterhouse and Hope Simpson, 1960, 74-6.

ANALIPSIS (Laconia)(100):   One large and eight smaller
tholoi (LH II-III)
Romaios, 1954.
ARGOS (Argolis)(12):   EH-LH IIIc settlements and cemeteries
(walled citadels on Larisa and Aspis in LH III)(LH II-III
chamber tombs at Deiras)
Larisa: Vollgraff, 1928; Protonariou-Deilaki, 1970.
Aspis: Vollgraff, 1906 and 1907.   Deiras: Vollgraff,
1904;   Deshayes, 1966 and 1969.
ARKINAI (Laconia)(101):   LH III settlement with tholoi
Tsountas, 1889, 132-6;   Waterhouse and Hope Simpson, 1961,
128-30.
ASEA (Arcadia)(91):   EH-LH IIIb settlement
Holmberg, 1944.
ASINE (Argolis)(19):   EH-LH settlement (walled in LH III)
(MH cists and LH II-IIIc chamber tombs)
Frödin and Persson, 1938;   Alin, 1968;   Styrenius and
Vidén, 1971;   Hägg, 1973;   Dietz, 1975;   Styrenius, 1975.
ATHENS (Attica)(348):   EH-LH IIIc2 settlement;   LH IIIb
walled citadel;   cemeteries of chamber tombs and cists
General: Broneer, 1956.   Acropolis: Broneer, 1939;
Iakovidis, 1962.   Agora (chamber tombs):   Vermeule, 1955;
Immerwahr, 1971;   Rutter, 1975b.   Kerameikos cemetery
(LH IIIc cists):   Kraiker and Kübler, 1939, 1-88.
AYIOS IOANNIS (Laconia)(147):   see MONEMVASIA
AYIOS KOSMAS (Attica)(353):   Settlements in EH and in LH
II-IIIc (remains of walls)
Mylonas, 1959.
AYIOS STEPHANOS (Laconia)(120):   EH-LH IIIb walled settle-
ment and tombs
Taylour, 1972.
AYIOS THEODOROS (Thessaly)(497):   LH IIIb tholos
Verdelis, 1951, 150-4;   1952, 181-4.
AYIOS VASILIOS (Laconia)(99):   EH-LH IIIb settlement
Waterhouse and Hope Simpson, 1960, 80-1.
BERBATI (Argolis)(5):   EH-LH IIIb settlement;   late LH II
tholos;   LH II-III chamber tombs
Säflund, 1965.
BRAURON (Attica)(368):   EH-LH IIIc settlement (LH III
chamber tombs)
Stais, 1895, 196-9;   Papadimitriou, 1948;   Theocharis,1950
CHALANDRITSA (Achaea)(293):   LH IIIb-c chamber tombs and
tholoi
Kyparissis, 1928 and 1930.
CHALKIS (Euboea)(553):   20 chamber tombs (LH I-IIIc)
Papavasiliou, 1910, 21-42;   Hankey, 1952.
CHASAMBALI (Thessaly)(506):   MH-LH IIIb settlement
Arvanitopoullos, 1910, 185-6;   Maria Theocharis, 1960b,
53-6.

CORINTH (Corinthia)(56): EH-LH III settlement
Weinberg, 1949, 156-7.
DELPHI (Phocis)(446): MH-LH IIIc settlement
Perdrizet, 1908, 5-21; Lerat, 1935 and 1938.
DENDRA (Argolis)(6): LH II-III chamber tombs; LH IIIa1
tholos
Persson, 1931 and 1942a; Aström, 1967; Verdelis, 1967.
DIAKATA (Kehpallenia)(335): LH IIIc chamber tombs
Kyparissis, 1919, 92-122; Marinatos, 1932, 14-7.
DIMINI (Thessaly)(483): LH II-III tholoi and cists
Lolling, 1884, 99-103; Lolling and Wolters, 1886 and 1887;
Stais, 1901; Tsountas, 1908, 27-68; Wace and Thompson,
1912, 75-85; Theocharis and Chormouziadis, 1969, 224-5.
ELEUSIS (Attica)(386): EH-LH IIIc1 settlement, yielding an
inscribed jar (LH II-IIIc tombs)
Mylonas, 1961.
ELIS (Elis)(277): EH and LH III tombs
Orlandos, 1961d.
EPIDAUROS LIMERA (Laconia)(146): see MONEMVASIA
ERETRIA (Euboea)(562): EH-LH IIIc settlement
Themelis, 1969.
EUTRESIS (Boeotia)(417): EH-LH IIIc settlement (walled
citadel in LH III)
Goldman, 1931.
GALATAKI (Corinthia)(52): LH II-III chamber tombs
Orlandos, 1958b.
GERAKI (Laconia)(105): EH-LH III settlement (MH cists, LH
walls)
Wace and Hasluck, 1904; Wace, 1909; Waterhouse and Hope
Simpson, 1960, 85-6.
GLA (Boeotia)(402): Long walls enclosing LH IIIb settle-
ment
Ridder, 1894; Noack, 1894; Orlandos, 1955; 1956a; 1957a;
1958a; 1959a; 1960a; 1961a.
GOURZOUMISA (Achaea)(299): LH IIIb-c chamber tombs
Kyparissis, 1931 and 1932.
GREMNOS (Thessaly)(515): EH-LH IIIc1 settlement
Milojcić, 1955b, 192-220; 1956; 1959b.
GRITSA (Thessaly)(496): MH-LH IIIc settlement (LH III
tholoi)
Verdelis, 1951, 141-9; 1952, 164-85; 1953, 120-7.
HALIARTOS (Boeotia)(409): EH-LH IIIb settlement (Cyclopean
walls)
Austin, 1931.
IRIA (Argolis)(28): EH-LH IIIc settlement
Döhl, 1973a.
ISTHMIA (Corinthia)(63): EH-LH IIIb settlement (LH IIIb
wall)
Mylonas, 1964; Broneer, 1966 and 1968; Kardara, 1971.

KAKOVATOS (Messenia)(255):   LH I-II tholoi
Dörpfeld, 1908; K. Müller, 1909.
KALAMATA (Messenia)(166):   LH III chamber tombs
Hope Simpson, 1957, 242-3.
KALLITHEA (Achaea)(291):   LH IIIb-c chamber tombs containing bronze military equipment
Yalouris, 1960.
KAMBI (Zakynthos):   LH III pit-graves
Agallopoulou, 1973.
KAMBOS (Messenia)(169):   LH II tholos
Tsountas, 1891b.
KARAOUSI (Laconia)(112):   EH-LH IIIc settlement
Waterhouse and Hope Simpson, 1960, 89-92.
KATARRAKTIS (Achaea)(298):   LH IIIb-c tombs
Orlandos, 1956c.
KATO GOUMENITSA (Achaea)(303):   LH I-III chamber tombs
Kyparissis, 1925.
KIRRHA (Phocis)(449):   EH-LH IIIb settlement
Dor, Jannoray, and Effenterre, 1960; Petrakos, 1973.
KLEIDI (Messenia)(257):   EH-LH IIIb settlement;   MH-LH I tumulus-burials
Yalouris, 1965.
KOKKOLATA (Kephallenia)(337):   LH IIIb tombs
Benton, 1931, 221.
KORAKOU (Corinthia)(60):   EH-LH IIIc settlement
Blegen, 1921.
KORYPHASION (Messenia)(207):   LH I tholos
Blegen, 1954.
KOUKOUNARA (Messenia):   LH II-IIIb tombs
Orlandos, 1974c.
KOUKOURA (Achaea)(289):   LH IIIb-c tombs
Kyparissis, 1937.
KTOURI (Thessaly)(537):   LH IIIb walled citadel
Milojcić, 1955b, 229-31.
LAKKITHRA (Kephallenia)(339):   LH IIIc chamber tombs
Marinatos, 1932, 17-28.
LEFKANDI (Euboea)(554):   EH-LH IIIc settlement
Popham and Sackett, 1968; Popham and Milburn, 1971.
LERNA (Argolis)(13):   EH-LH IIIb settlement (LH tombs)
Caskey, 1954; 1955; 1956; 1957; Gejvall, 1969.
LIVADOSTRO (Boeotia)(422):   EH-LH III walled settlement
Heurtley, 1923, 38-40.
LOMBOKA (Achaea)(300):   LH IIIc chamber tombs
Kyparissis, 1933.
MALTHI (Messenia)(242):   EH-LH IIIb settlement (walled in LH IIIb); lower town; tholoi
Valmin, 1938 and 1953.
MARATHON (Attica)(377):LH II/III tholos with horse-burial.
Sotiriadis, 1932; Marinatos, 1970b.

MARMARIANI (Thessaly)(508):LH IIIa-c settlement with tholoi
Wace and Thompson, 1912, 53-4; Heurtley and Skeat, 1930.
MAVROVOUNION (Laconia)(125): LH IIIb-c chamber tombs
Waterhouse and Hope Simpson, 1961, 114-8.
MELATHRIA (Laconia): LH IIIa-b cemetery
Demacopoulou, 1968a.
MENELAION (Laconia)(95): LH II-IIIb settlement
Wace and Thompson, 1908; Dawkins, 1909; Waterhouse and
Hope Simpson, 1960, 72; Catling, 1975b.
MENIDI (Attica)(382): LH IIIb tholos
Lolling, 1880; Wolters, 1899; cf. Hope Simpson, 1958.
METAXATA (Kephallenia)(340): LH IIIc chamber tombs
Marinatos, 1933a, 73-100; Kalligas, 1974, 187-9.
MISTROS (Euboea): Six tombs with LH IIIb-c pottery
Tsirivakos, 1969.
MONEMVASIA (Laconia)(146, 147): Chamber tombs with LH I-
IIIc pottery
Waterhouse and Hope Simpson, 1961, 136-7; Demacopoulou,
1968b.
MOURIATADA (Messenia)(236): LH IIIb walled settlement
Orlandos, 1960c, 149-52.
MYCENAE (Argolis)(1): EH-LH IIIc2 settlement; walled ci-
tadel with palace (LH III); MH/LH Grave Circles; LH
chamber tombs and tholoi; houses inside and outside the
citadel, some yielding Linear B inscriptions
General: Schliemann, 1878; Wace, 1949; Mylonas, 1957 and
1966a.   Particular: Tsountas, 1887; 1891a; 1895 (houses
and palace.)   Tsountas, 1896 (grave-stela.)   Wace, 1919;
1921; 1953a; 1954a; 1955; 1956a; 1957 (palace, houses,
walls, Grave Circle A.)   Mylonas, 1966b (palace.)   Karo,
1930a (Grave Circle A.)   Karo, 1934a (spring.)   Bennett,
1958b (houses.)   Chadwick, 1963 (houses.)   Orlandos,
1968 and 1974b (LH IIIc destruction levels.) Taylour, 1969
and 1970;   Orlandos, 1971b and 1972; Mylonas, 1972
(houses.)   Tsountas, 1888; Wace, 1932 (chamber tombs.)
Thiersch, 1879; Wace, 1921 (tholoi.)   Marinatos, 1953;
Papadimitriou, 1952; 1953; 1954b; Mylonas, 1973 (Grave
Circle B.)   Elizabeth French, 1963; 1964; 1965; 1966;
1967; 1969a; 1969b; Wardle, 1969 and 1973 (pottery.)
NAUPLION (Argolis)(9): LH IIIa-c chamber tombs
Charitonidis, 1954.
NICHORIA (Messenia)(182): MH-LH IIIc settlement (LH III
tholoi and chamber tombs)
McDonald, 1972.
NIDRI (Leucas)(320): MH settlement
Kalligas, 1968, 320-22.
OIKOPEDA (Kephallenia)(341): LH III tombs
Marinatos, 1932, 10-14.

ORCHOMENOS (Boeotia)(396): EH-LH IIIc1 settlement; LH I
cemetery; LH IIIb palace yielding an inscribed jar; large
LH IIIb tholos
Schliemann, 1881; Ridder, 1895, 177-9; Sotiriadis, 1905,
129-32; Bulle, 1907; Spyropoulos, 1973 and 1974.
PALAIOCHORI (Laconia)(142): EH-LH IIIb settlement (LH II
tholoi)
Waterhouse and Hope Simpson, 1961, 132-5.
PALAIOKASTRO (Arcadia)(92): LH IIIc tombs
Charneux and Ginouvès, 1956, 523-38.
PALAIOKASTRO (Argolis)(7): EH-LH IIIc settlement, walled
in LH III
Persson, 1942a, 3-16.
PARGA (Epirus): LH IIIb tholos
Dakaris, 1960, 123-7.
PARISATA (Kephallenia)(342): LH III tombs
Marinatos, 1951, 185-6.
PERATI (Attica)(367): Large cemetery of LH IIIc chamber
tombs
Stais, 1895, 199-202; Iakovidis, 1969.
PERISTERIA (Messenia)(235): LH I-II tholoi
Marinatos, 1961; 1965a, 204-6; 1966.
PETRA (Thessaly)(499): LH III walled settlement (?)
Milojcić, 1955b, 222-9.
POLIS (Ithaca)(325): Cave-sanctuary with EH-LH IIIb sherds
Benton, 1934, 51-2.
PRIPHTIANI (Argolis)(2): LH III chamber tombs
Charitonidis, 1952.
PROSYMNA (Argolis)(4): EH-LH IIIb settlement (tholos and
chamber tombs)
Waldstein, 1905, 71-101; Blegen, 1937; Protonariou-
Deilaki, 1960.
PYLOS (ANO ENGLIANOS)(Messenia)(197): MH-LH IIIc1 settle-
ment; large LH IIIb palace, yielding Linear B tablets and
sealings; town; tholos; chamber tombs
Blegen, 1966 and 1973; Lang, 1969.
ROUTSI (Messenia)(212): LH II-III tholoi
Marinatos, 1956.
SALAMIS (Attica)(387): LH IIIc cists
Wide, 1910; Styrenius, 1962.
SCHINOCHORI (Argolis)(16): LH IIIa chamber tombs
Renaudin, 1923.
SESKLO (Thessaly)(484): EH-LH III settlement (LH III tho-
loi)
Lolling, 1884, 103-16; Tsountas, 1901 and 1908, 69-114;
Wace and Thompson, 1912, 58-74; Theocharis and Chormou-
ziadis, 1969, 225.
SPATA (Attica)(371): LH IIIb chamber tombs
Milchhöfer, 1877; Haussoullier, 1878.

STAVROS (Ithaca)(324): EH-LH IIIb settlement
Waterhouse, 1952; Benton and Waterhouse, 1973.
SYNORO (Argolis)(27): EH and LH I-II settlement
Döhl, 1973b.
TANAGRA (Boeotia)(429): LH IIIb cemetery with larnax-
burials
Orlandos, 1969; 1970; 1971a; 1973; 1974a.
TEICHOS DYMAION (Achaea)(282): LH IIIb-c walled citadel
Mastrokostas, 1964 and 1965.
THEBES (Boeotia)(416): EH-LH IIIb settlement (walled in
LH III); large palace (Kadmeion), LH II-III, yielding
Linear B tablets and stirrup-jars; cemetery (Kolonaki),
LH I-IIIc; Kastellia tombs, LH III
Kadmeion: Keramopoullos, 1909 and 1930; Symeonoglou and
Touloupa, 1964, 192-7; 1965, 230-40; 1966, 177-94;Symeo-
noglou, 1973; Demacopoulou, 1974; Spyropoulos and Chad-
wick, 1975, 9-81. Kolonaki: Keramopoullos, 1917, 123-
209. Kastellia: Keramopoullos, 1917, 99-111; Spyro-
poulos, 1971b.
THERMON (Aetolia)(313): MH and LH II-III settlement
Sotiriadis, 1900; Romaios, 1915 and 1916.
THISBE (Boeotia)(419): MH-LH IIIb settlement (LH III wal-
led citadel)
Heurtley, 1923, 41; Maier, 1958.
THORIKOS (Attica)(361): MH-LH IIIb settlement (LH I-II
tholoi)
Stais, 1893 and 1895, 221-34; Mussche, 1971, 21-102.
TIRYNS (Argolis)(8): EH-LH IIIc2 settlement; LH III
palace and walled citadel, yielding fragments of Linear B
tablets and jars; tholoi; cemetery of chamber tombs;
houses outside the citadel
Schliemann and Dörpfeld, 1886; Rodenwaldt, 1912b; Dra-
gendorff, 1913; K. Müller, 1930; Karo, 1930b and 1934b;
Verdelis and French, 1965; Gercke and Hiesel, 1971;
Grossmann and Schäfer, 1971; Rudolph, 1971, 88-93 and
1973; Voigtländer, 1973; Gercke and Naumann, 1974;
Slenczka, 1974.
TRAGANA (Messenia)(205): LH II-III tholoi
Kourouniotis, 1914; Marinatos, 1955, 247-54.
TRIKKA (Thessaly)(546): EH-LH III settlement
Maria Theocharis, 1959.
TSASI (Laconia)(115): LH IIIa-b settlement with chamber
tomb
Waterhouse and Hope Simpson, 1960, 92-4.
VALTSA (Kephallenia)(343): LH III settlement
Marinatos, 1932, 5-8.
VAPHIO (Laconia)(98): EH-LH IIIb settlement (LH II tholos)
Tsountas, 1889.

VARKIZA (Attica)(358): LH III chamber tombs
Maria Theocharis, 1960a; Vavritsas, 1968; Themelis, 1974.
VOLIMIDIA (Messenia)(201): MH-LH II graves, including a
shaft
Marinatos, 1965a and 1966; Iakovidis, 1966b.
VOLOS (IOLKOS) (Thessaly)(480-2): EH-LH IIIc2 settlements
(LH II tholos; LH III palace)
Tholos: Wolters, 1889; Kourouniotis, 1906; Arvanito-
poullos, 1912, 229-32.   Settlement: Orlandos, 1956b;
1957b; 1960b; 1961b.   LH IIIa cists at New Ionia: Theo-
charis, 1970.
VOURVATSI (Attica)(359): LH IIIb chamber tombs
Kyparissis, 1927.
YEORYIKON (Thessaly)(545): LH II tholos
Maria Theocharis, 1959, 69.
ZYGOURIES (Corinthia)(48): EH-LH IIIb settlement with
chamber tombs
Blegen, 1928.

Tables

TABLE 1 The Chronology of the Bronze Age

BC	Greece	Crete	Troy	Egypt	Hatti
2000	Early Helladic	Early Minoan	Troy V		
1950					
1900					
1850	Middle Helladic	Middle Minoan — Early Palaces	Troy VI		
1800					
1750					
1700					
1650					
1600	Shaft Graves	Late Palaces		Hyksos	Old Kingdom
1550				XVIII Dynasty	
1500					
1450					
1400	Late Helladic	Late Minoan	Troy VIIa		
1350					
1300		Re-occupation		XIX Dynasty	Empire
1250					
1200	Destructions				
1150			Troy VIIb	XX Dynasty	
1100					
1050					

TABLE 2 Horizons of Destruction in Early and Middle Helladic

	Lerna	Lefkandi	Berbati
Early Helladic II	III		
Early Helladic III	- - - - -* IV (Grey Min- yan)	I II (crude Grey Minyan)	Grey Minyan I
Middle Helladic	V	III (mature Grey Minyan)	Grey Minyan II

Levels of destruction are shown thus: --------

* Destruction of Lerna III, Asine, Ayios Kosmas, Tiryns, Zygouries

** Destruction of Berbati and Eutresis

TABLE 3 Affinities between the Mycenae Grave Circles and
the Peristeria Tombs

Object	Mycenae Grave Circle B	Mycenae Grave Circle A	Peristeria Tombs
	Mylonas, 1973, no:	Karo, 1930a, no:	Marinatos, 1966, pl:
Amber beads	332	100, 101, 513	
Boar's tusks	488, 489	893-6	
Bronze pins with rock-crystal heads	259, 312, 313, 320	102, 103	
Conch		166 (faience)	170γ (gold)
Decorated star in gold leaf	370-3, 438	15-9, 25, 62, 86, 89, 385	
Engraved gems	443, 453 464	116-8	
Full-bellied jug with long spout	48	941, 946, 947, 950, 952	
Gold cup with high-flung handles and bold horizontal rib	357	73, 220, 441, 627, 628, 629	171γ, 172
Gold diadem with pattern of larger and smaller circles	364, 380-3, 404, 410, 411	3, 5, 22, 37, 184, 185, 187, 232-5	171α
Heart-shaped gold leaf		71, 80	168ζ
Ivory pommel on swords	508, 509	490	

Object	Mycenae Grave Circle B Mylonas, 1973, no:	Mycenae Grave Circle A Karo, 1930a, no:	Peristeria Tombs Marinatos, 1966, pl:
Masks	362 (electrum)	253-4, 259, 623-4 (gold)	
Ornaments of spirals of gold wire	413-9, 420-5	56-9, 63-8	
Stylized flowers in gold leaf		373-5	170β
Swords of Type A	250-2, 263-5, 277, 289, 291, 295, 301, 302	399, 401, 402, 404, 414-8, 428, 431-4, 436, 726-8, 730, 731, 750, 751, 766-72, 925	
Swords of Type B	253, 262, 266, 278,	398, 400, 407, 408, 413, 430, 435, 729, 752, 905, 906	

TABLE 4   The Pottery of Grave Circle A at Mycenae (with Karo's Numeration) arranged in Chronological Sequence

Grave	Late Helladic I pottery	Imported Minoan pottery	Middle Helladic pottery	
			Yellow Minyan	Matt-painted
VI	945, 956		942, 955	946*, 947-51, 953
II		221		222
IV			590, 611-5	591
V	856			857, 858**
III	156***			
I	190, 191****, 192****, 194****, 195, 196****, 197, 199			198

* Cf. Kleidi, no 3.

** Cf. Kleidi, no 86.

*** Cf. Kleidi, no 22.

**** Cf. Kleidi, no 34.

TABLE 5 Motifs of Miniature Art in Grave Circle A

Motif	Karo, no:	CMS, no:	Shaft Grave	Cretan parallel
Warrior stabbing lion in mouth	33	9	III	Evans, 1930, 125
Lion on rocks, looking back	34	10	III	Evans, 1935, 546
Animal giving suck	117	13	III	Evans, 1935, 552-4
Combat-scene in glen	241	16	IV	Evans, 1921, 691-2; 1930, 500-1

TABLE 6 The Ancestry of Aigyptos and Danaos

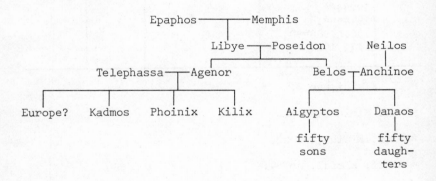

TABLE 7 The Distribution of Linear B Inscriptions on the Mainland

Site	Pots with painted inscriptions (c. 1350-1200 BC)	Clay tablets, labels, and sealings incised with Linear B signs (c. 1250-1200 BC)
Eleusis	one amphora	
Mycenae	c. 12 fragments	c. 60 tablets and 8 sealings from houses inside and outside the citadel
Orchomenos	one stirrup-jar	
Pylos	one fragment	more than 1,000 tablets and some 40 labels and sealings from the palace
Thebes	nearly 70 jars and fragments	c. 40 tablets from the Kadmeion and associated buildings
Tiryns	c. 30 fragments	two or three tablet-fragments from outside the citadel

TABLE 8 Late Bronze Age Destructions at Mycenae

Inside the Citadel		Outside the Citadel
Citadel H. (& Gran.?) built	LH IIIa2 / LH IIIb1	Petsas' H. & 2nd Cyclopean Terrace H. destroyed Houses built:Shields, Lead, W., Sphinxes, Oil Merch.
Lion Gate ???		
	LH IIIb1 / LH IIIb2	Houses destroyed:Shields, Lead, W., Oil Merchant
	NE extension	
Citadel H. destroyed (& Palace - Alin)	LH IIIb2 / LH IIIc1	3rd Cyclopean Terrace H. & Great Poros Wall destroyed
Granary destroyed (& Palace - Wace)		
Final destruction of LH IIIc house adjoining Tsountas' House (c. 1120 BC)		

TABLE 9   Cultural Changes in three Areas of Greece in Late
Helladic IIIc

| BC | W. Attica (Kerameikos) | Inhumation predominant | |
		E. Attica (Perati)	Argolid
C. 1200			
	Inhumation	Phase I	Chamber tombs
		Phase II — Chamber tombs and a few cists — A few iron imports	
	Cremation	Phase III	
C. 1050	iron swords		iron at Tiryns — Cists

(Left margin, vertical: Late Helladic IIIc pottery | Sub-Myc. | Proto-geometric)

TABLE 10   Imports in the Perati Cemetery (Numbers from
Iakovidis, 1969)

Origin	Phase I	Phase II	Phase III
Baltic	Δ197		
Crete	976, Λ6	198, 1088	
Cyclades	866	391	
Cyprus	Λ91, 92	Λ267, M32, 39	
Egypt	Δ11, 132, 142, 196	Δ36-9, 69-75, 88, 128, 129	
Rhodes			961
Syria	Λ1, 309, M206-9	Δ142, Λ106, 208, M53	M85

TABLE 11 Campaigns of Ramesses II, Merenptah,
and Ramesses III

Foreign people	Battle of Kadesh	Libyan coalition against Merenptah	Coalition of 'Sea Peoples' against Ramesses III
Sherden*	Egyptian mercenaries	Libyan allies	
Luka*	Hittite allies	Libyan allies	
Kode	Hittite allies		'subdued by Sea Peoples'
Kárchemish	Hittite allies		'subdued by Sea Peoples'
Shelekesh		Libyan allies	Sea Peoples' allies
Ekwesh		Libyan allies	
Teresh		Libyan allies	
Peleset		Libyan allies	Sea Peoples' allies
Tjekker		Libyan allies	Sea Peoples' allies
Denyen			Sea Peoples' allies
Weshesh			Sea Peoples' allies

* These two peoples are mentioned already in Egyptian texts
of the fourteenth century BC.

Figures

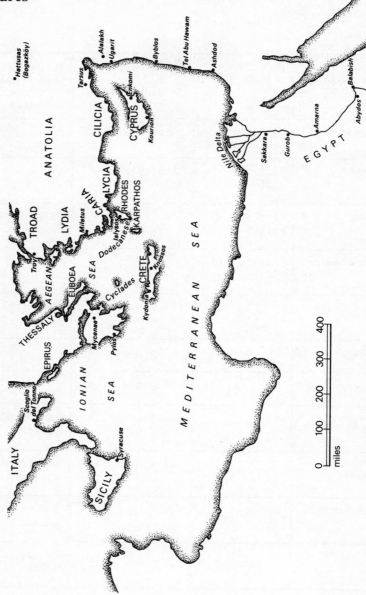

FIGURE 1   Sketch-map of the Central and Eastern
            Mediterranean

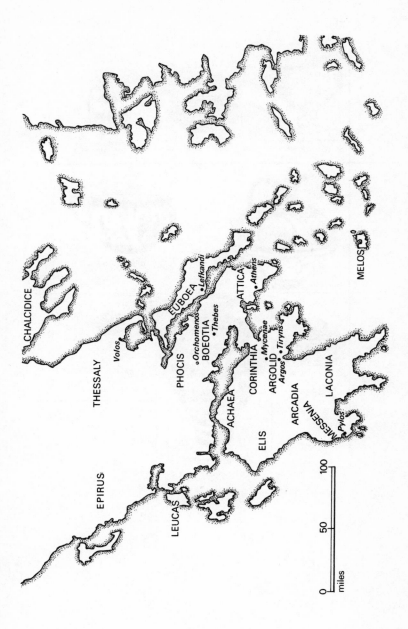

FIGURE 2   Sketch-map of Greece

MH

'Lianokladi' type stemmed
goblet (Grey Minyan)

two-handled cup
(Grey Minyan)

beaked jug
(matt painted)

LH I

Jug

Cup

LH II

alabastron

'Ephyraean' goblet

'Palace Style'
pithoid amphora

Note: All pottery scale about 1:10 except Close Style
bowl from Mycenae which is about 1:4

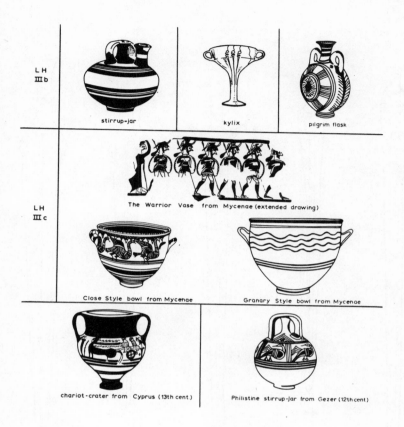

FIGURE 3 Bronze Age pottery

Note: All pottery scale about 1:10 except 'Palace Style'
pithoid amphora which is about 1:20

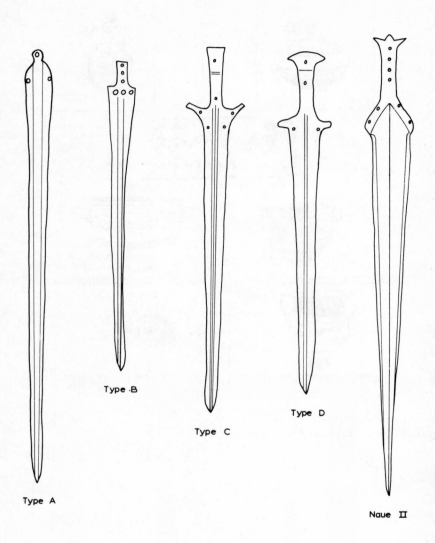

Type A

Type ·B

Type C

Type D

Naue Ⅱ

FIGURE 4 Swords

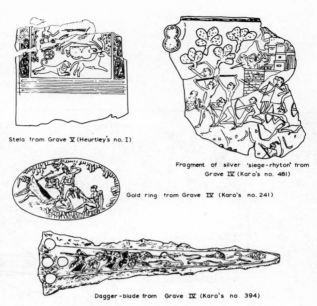

Stela from Grave V (Heurtley's no. I)

Fragment of silver 'siege-rhyton' from Grave IV (Karo's no. 481)

Gold ring from Grave IV (Karo's no. 241)

Dagger-blade from Grave IV (Karo's no. 394)

FIGURE 5 Art in the Shaft Graves

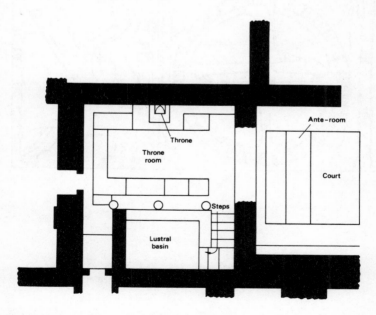

FIGURE 6 The throne-room complex at Knossos

FIGURE 7   Part of the Tiryns chariot-fresco (restored)

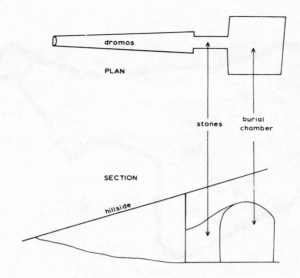

FIGURE 8 Mycenaean chamber tomb

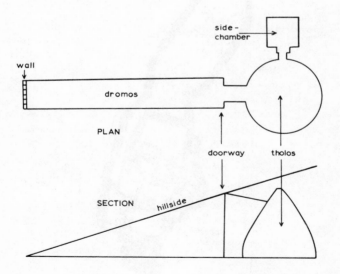

FIGURE 9   The most elaborate form of tholos tomb
(Orchomenos and Treasury of Atreus, Mycenae)

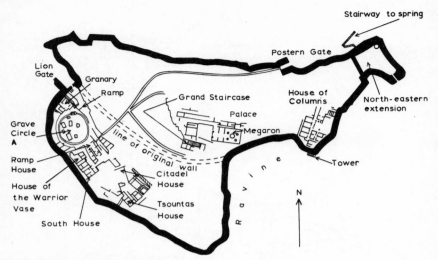

FIGURE 10 The citadel of Mycenae

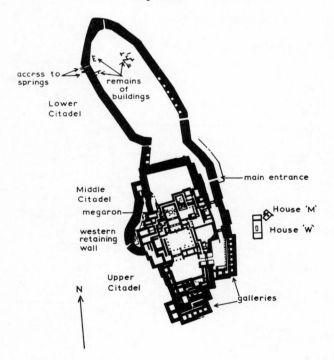

FIGURE 11 The citadel of Tiryns

FIGURE 12   The principal buildings of the palace of Pylos

(a)   Mycenae (CMS, no. 17)

(b)   Isopata

(c)   Vaphio (CMS, no. 219)

(d)   Tiryns (CMS, no. 179)

(e)   Mycenae (CMS, no. 126)

(f)   Knossos

FIGURE 13   Gold rings

Abbreviations

AA	Archäologischer Anzeiger (until 1961 published as part of JDAI; from 1962 published separately)
AAA	Athens Annals of Archaeology
AAA(L)	Annals of Archaeology and Anthropology (Liverpool)
AAS	Annales Archéologiques de Syrie
AB	The Art Bulletin
ABSA	The Annual of the British School at Athens
AC	L'Antiquité Classique
AC(CT)	Acta Classica (Cape Town)
AC(D)	Acta Classica (Debrecen)
ActAnt	Acta Antiqua (Budapest)
ACVT	Acta of the First International Scientific Congress on the Volcano of Thera, Athens, 1971
AD	Ἀρχαιολογικὸν Δελτίον
AE	Ἀρχαιολογικὴ Ἐφημερίς (earlier Ἐφημερὶς Ἀρχαιολογική)
AJA	American Journal of Archaeology
AJP	American Journal of Philology
AK	Antike Kunst
AL	Acta Linguistica
AM	Mitteilungen des Deutschen Archäologischen Instituts (Athenische Abteilung)
AMAT	Atti e Memorie dell'Accademia Toscana di Scienze e Lettere 'La Colombaria'
AMyc	Acta Mycenaea, ed. M.S. Ruipérez, Salamanca, 1972
ANE	The Aegean and the Near East, Studies presented to Hetty Goldman, ed. S.S. Weinberg, New York, 1956
AntAb	Antike und Abendland
AntSurv	Antiquity and Survival

AO	Archiv Orientálni
APA	Acta Praehistorica et Archaeologica
AS	Anatolian Studies
ASA	Australian Studies in Archaeology
ASAA	Annuario della Scuola Archeologica di Atene
AsStud	Asiatische Studien
BAMA	Bronze Age Migrations in the Aegean, ed. R.A. Crossland and Ann Birchall, London, 1973
BCH	Bulletin de Correspondance Hellénique
BICS	Bulletin of the Institute of Classical Studies
BJ	Bursians Jahresbericht über die Fortschritte der Klassischen Altertumswissenschaft
BRGK	Berichte der Römisch-Germanischen Kommission des Deutschen Archäologischen Instituts
BS	Balkan Studies
BVAB	Bulletin van de Vereeniging tot Bevordering der Kennis van de Antieke Beschaving
CAH	The Cambridge Ancient History
CE	Chronique d'Egypte
CJ	The Classical Journal
CMic	Atti e Memorie del 1º Congresso Internazionale di Micenologia, Rome, 1968
CMS	Corpus der Minoischen und Mykenischen Siegel, vol. 1: Die Minoischen und Mykenischen Siegel des Nationalmuseums in Athen, ed. Agnes Sakellariou, Berlin, 1964
CP	Colston Papers (Bristol)
CQ	The Classical Quarterly
EA	Ἐφημερὶς Ἀρχαιολογική (later Ἀρχαιολογικὴ Ἐφημερίς)
EAE	Τὸ Ἔργον τῆς Ἀρχαιολογικῆς Ἑταιρείας
EC	Estudios Clásicos
EHR	The Economic History Review
FF	Forschungen und Fortschritte
GAK	Γέρας Ἀντωνίου Κεραμοπούλλου, Athens, 1953
GR	Greece and Rome
GRBS	Greek Roman and Byzantine Studies
GZ	Geographische Zeitschrift
HT	Historisk Tidskrift
IBK	Innsbrucker Beiträge zur Kulturwissenschaft
IEJ	Israel Exploration Journal
IF	Indogermanische Forschungen
ILN	Illustrated London News
IM	Istanbuler Mitteilungen
JAOS	Journal of the Americal Oriental Society
JDAI	Jahrbuch des Deutschen Archäologischen Instituts
JEA	The Journal of Egyptian Archaeology

JHS	The Journal of Hellenic Studies
JIES	The Journal of Indo-European Studies
JKF	Jahrbuch für Kleinasiatische Forschung
JNES	Journal of Near Eastern Studies
JOAI	Jahreshefte des Österreichischen Archäo- logischen Institutes in Wien
JRGZM	Jahrbuch des Römisch-Germanischen Zentral- museums Mainz
JW	Jahrbuch für Wirtschaftsgeschichte
KBo	Keilschrifttexte aus Boghazköi
KF	Kleinasiatische Forschungen
KS	Κυπριακαὶ Σπουδαί
KX	Κρητικὰ Χρονικά
LF	Listy Filologické
MA	Monumenti Antichi
MDOG	Mitteilungen der Deutschen Orient-Gesellschaft zu Berlin
MEM	Acts of the International Symposium 'The Mycenaeans in the Eastern Mediterranean', Nicosia, 1973
MH	Museum Helveticum
Min	Minoica, Festschrift Johannes Sundwall, ed. E. Grumach, Berlin, 1958
MSS	Münchener Studien zur Sprachwissenschaft
NRS	Nuova Rivista Storica
OA	Opuscula Archaeologica
OAth	Opuscula Atheniensia
PAAH	Πρακτικὰ τῆς ἐν ᾿Αθήναις ᾿Αρχαιολογικῆς ᾿Εταιρείας
PBA	Proceedings of the British Academy
PCPS	Proceedings of the Cambridge Philological Society
PDKS2	Πεπραγμένα τοῦ Β' Διεθνοῦς Κρητολογικοῦ Συνεδρίου, vol. 1, Athens, 1968
PDKS3	Πεπραγμένα τοῦ Γ' Διεθνοῦς Κρητολογικοῦ Συνεδρίου, vol. 1, Athens, 1973
PP	La Parola del Passato
PPDKS	Πρακτικὰ τοῦ Πρώτου Διεθνοῦς Κυπρολογικοῦ Συνεδρίου, vol. 1, Leucosia, 1972
PPS	Proceedings of the Prehistoric Society
PZ	Praehistorische Zeitschrift
QDAP	The Quarterly of the Department of Antiquities in Palestine
QSPEF	Quarterly Statement of the Palestine Explora- tion Fund
RA	Revue Archéologique
RB	Revue Biblique
RDAC	Report of the Department of Antiquities, Cyprus

REG	Revue des Etudes Grecques
RF	Rivista di Filologia
RHA	Revue Hittite et Asianique
RHR	Revue de l'Histoire des Religions
RM	Rheinisches Museum für Philologie
RP	Revue de Philologie
RSA	Rivista Storica dell'Antichità
RSI	Rivista Storica Italiana
SANGSSR	Сообщения Академии Наук Грузинской ССР
SCO	Studi Classici e Orientali
SG	Siculorum Gymnasium
SM	Studia Mycenaea: Proceedings of the Mycenaean Symposium, ed. A. Bartonek, Brno, 1968
SMEA	Studi Micenei ed Egeo-Anatolici
SO	Symbolae Osloenses
TAD	Türk Arkeoloji Dergisi
TAPA	Transactions and Proceedings of the American Philological Association
TPS	Transactions of the Philological Society
UF	Ugarit-Forschungen
VDI	Вестик Древней Истории
VI	Вопросы Истории
VT	Vetus Testamentum
VY	Вопросы Языкознания
WS	Wiener Studien
YCS	Yale Classical Studies
ZA	Ziva Antika
ZDMG	Zeitschrift der Deutschen Morgenländischen Gesellschaft
ZfA	Zeitschrift für Assyriologie (Neue Folge)
ZNM	Зборник Народног Музеја у Београрду
ZRG	Zeitschrift für Religions- und Geistesgeschichte
ZVS	(Kuhns) Zeitschrift für Vergleichende Sprachwissenschaft

Bibliography

ADRADOS, F.R.
(1955), 'Achäisch, Jonisch und Mykenisch', IF, 62, 240-8.
(1961a), 'Más sobre el culto real en Pilos y la distribución de la tierra en época micénica', Emerita, 29, 53-116.
(1961b), 'Micénico -o-i, -a-i = -oι, -αι y la serie Fr de Pilos', Minos, 7, 49-61.
(1968), 'Wa-na-ka y ra-wa-ke-ta', CMic, 2, 559-73.
(1969), 'Te-re-ta wa-na-ka-te-ro y los ἀνακτοτελεσταί', Minos, 10, 138-50.
(1972), 'Les institutions religieuses mycéniennes', AMyc, 1, 170-203.
AGALLOPOULOU, PENELOPE I.
(1973), 'Μυκηναϊκὸν νεκροταφεῖον παρὰ τὸ Καμπὶ Ζακύνθου', AD, 28, A', 198-214.
AITCHISON, JEAN M.
(1964), 'The Achaean homeland: Ἀχαιϝία or Ἀχαιϝίς?', Glotta, 42, 19-28.
AKERSTRÖM, A.
(1941), 'Zur Frage der mykenischen Dacheindeckung', OA, 2, 164-73.
(1953), 'Some pictorial vase representations from the mainland in Late Helladic times', OAth, 1, 9-28.
(1968), 'A Mycenaean potter's factory at Berbati near Mycenae', CMic, 1, 48-53.
(1975), 'More Canaanite jars from Greece', OAth, 11, 185-92.
AKURGAL, E.
(1964), 'Die Kunst der Hethiter', Historia Einzelschrift, 7, 74-118.
ALBRIGHT, W.F.
(1932), 'An anthropoid clay coffin from Sahab in Transjordan', AJA, 36, 295-306.

ALEXIOU, S.
(1952), 'Νέα στοιχεῖα διὰ τὴν ὑστέραν Αἰγαιακὴν χρονο-
λογίαν καὶ ἱστορίαν', ΚΧ, 6, 9-41.
(1958), 'Η Μινωϊκὴ Θεὰ μεθ''Υψωμένων Χειρῶν, Iraklion.
(1964), 'Neue Wagendarstellungen aus Kreta', AA, 785-804.
(1967), 'Υστερομινωϊκοὶ Τάφοι Λιμένος Κνωσοῦ (Κατσαμπᾶ),
Athens.
ALIN, P.
(1962), Das Ende der Mykenischen Fundstätten auf dem
Griechischen Festland, Lund.
(1968), 'Unpublished Mycenaean sherds from Asine', OAth, 8,
87-105.
ALLEN, T.W.
(1921), The Homeric Catalogue of Ships, Oxford.
ANATI, E.
(1963), 'Tell Abu Hawam', IEJ, 13, 142-3.
ANDREOU, E.
(1974), 'Μ.Ε. πρόχους ἐκ Θήρας', ΑΑΑ, 7, 416-22.
ANDREWS, P.B.S.
(1955), 'The Mycenaean name of the land of the Achaians',
RHA, 13, 1-19.
(1965), 'The falls of Troy in Greek tradition', GR, 12,
28-37.
ANDRONIKOS, M.
(1954), ''Η "δωρικὴ εἰσβολὴ" καὶ τὰ ἀρχαιολογικὰ
εὑρήματα', Hellenika, 13, 221-40.
(1961), ''Ελληνικὰ ἐπιτάφια μνημεῖα', AD, 17, Α', ·152-210.
ANGEL, J.L.
(1971), Lerna, 2, Princeton.
ARTZY, M., ASARO, F., & PERLMAN, I.
(1973), 'The origin of the "Palestinian" bichrome ware',
JAOS, 93, 446-61.
ARVANITOPOULLOS, A.S.
(1910), ''Ανασκαφαὶ καὶ ἔρευναι ἐν Θεσσαλίᾳ', PAAH, 168-
264.
(1912), ''Ανασκαφαὶ καὶ ἔρευναι ἐν Θεσσαλίᾳ', PAAH, 154-
246.
ASARO, F. & PERLMAN, I.
(1973), 'Provenience studies of Mycenaean pottery employing neutron activation analysis', MEM, 213-24.
ASARO, F., PERLMAN, I., & DOTHAN, M.
(1971), 'An introductory study of Mycenaean III C 1 ware
from Tel Ashdod', Archaeometry, 13, 169-75.
ASTOUR, M.C.
(1965), 'New evidence on the last days of Ugarit', AJA,
69, 253-8.
(1967), Hellenosemitica, 2nd ed., Leiden.
ASTRÖM, LENA
(1967), Studies on the Arts and Crafts of the Late
Cypriote Bronze Age, Lund.

ASTRÖM, P.
(1965a), 'Mycenaean pottery from the region of Aigion,
with a list of prehistoric sites in Achaia',OAth, 5, 89-110
(1965b), 'Dateringen av Linear B-tavlorna fran Knossos',
HT, 44, 80-92.
(1966), Excavations at Kalopsidha and Ayios Iakovos in
Cyprus, Lund.
(1967), 'Das Panzergrab von Dendra, Bauweise und Keramik',
AM, 82, 54-67.
(1972a), 'The Late Cypriote Bronze Age: architecture and
pottery', The Swedish Cyprus Expedition, 4/1C, Lund.
(1972b), 'The Late Cypriote Bronze Age: relative and absolute chronology, foreign relations, historical conclusions', The Swedish Cyprus Expedition, 4/1D, Lund,675-781.
(1973), 'Comments on the corpus of Mycenaean pottery in
Cyprus', MEM, 122-7.
ASTRÖM, P. & BLOMÉ, B.
(1965), 'A reconstruction of the lion relief at Mycenae',
OAth, 5, 159-91.
AUSTIN, R.P.
(1931), 'Excavations at Haliartos', ABSA, 32, 180-212.
BADER, FRANÇOISE
(1965), Les Composés Grecs du Type de Demiourgos, Paris.
BALCER, J.M.
(1974), 'The Mycenaean dam at Tiryns', AJA, 78, 141-9.
BANTI, LUISA
(1941), 'I culti minoici e greci di Haghia Triada (Creta)',
ASAA, 3/5, 9-74.
(1953), 'Il sentimento della natura nell'arte Minoica e
Micenea', GAK, 119-27.
BARBER, R.
(1974), 'Phylakopi 1911 and the history of the later Cycladic Bronze Age', ABSA, 69, 1-53.
BARNETT, R.D.
(1975), 'The Sea Peoples', CAH, 2/2, 3rd ed., 359-78.
BARTONEK, A.
(1966), 'Mycenaean koine reconsidered', Proceedings of the
Cambridge Colloquium on Mycenaean Studies, ed. L.R. Palmer
and J. Chadwick, Cambridge, 95-103.
(1971), 'Greek dialects in the second millennium BC',
Eirene, 9, 49-67.
(1973), 'The place of the Dorians in the Late Helladic
world', BAMA, 305-11.
BASS, G.F.
(1967), Cape Gelidonya: A Bronze Age Shipwreck, Philadelphia.
BASSETT, S.E.
(1919), 'The palace of Odysseus', AJA, 23, 288-311, 413.

BAUMBACH, LYDIA
(1971), 'The Mycenaean Greek vocabulary II', Glotta, 49,
151-90.
BECATTI, G.
(1965), 'Interrogativi sul Vaso dei Guerrieri di Micene',
Studi in Onore di Luisa Banti, Rome, 33-46.
BECK, C.W., SOUTHARD, GRETCHEN C., & ADAMS, AUDREY B.
(1972), 'Analysis and provenience of Minoan and Mycenaean
amber, IV. Mycenae', GRBS, 13, 359-85.
BELOCH, K.J.
(1890), 'Die dorische Wanderung', RM, 45, 555-98.
(1913), Griechische Geschichte, 1, 2nd ed., Strassburg.
BENNETT, E.L.
(1956), 'The landholders of Pylos', AJA, 60, 103-33.
(1958a), The Olive Oil Tablets of Pylos, Salamanca.
(1958b), The Mycenae Tablets II, Philadelphia (with others)
BENNETT, E.L. & OLIVIER, J.-P.
(1973), The Pylos Tablets Transcribed, 1, Rome.
BENSON, J.L.
(1961a), 'Coarse ware stirrup jars of the Aegean',
Berytus, 14, 37-51.
(1961b), 'A problem in orientalizing Cretan birds: Mycenaean or Philistine prototypes?', JNES, 20, 73-84.
(1970), Horse, Bird and Man, Amherst.
BENTON, SYLVIA
(1931), 'The Ionian islands', ABSA, 32, 213-46.
(1934), 'Excavations in Ithaca, III: the cave at Pólis,
I', ABSA, 35, 45-73.
(1953), 'Further excavations at Aetos', ABSA, 48, 255-361.
BENTON, SYLVIA & WATERHOUSE, HELEN
(1973), 'Excavations in Ithaca: Tris Langadas', ABSA, 68,
1-24.
BERNABO BREA, L.
(1953), 'La Sicilia prehistórica y sus relaciones con
Oriente y con la Península Ibérica', Ampurias, 15/16,
137-235.
BEST, J.G.P. & YADIN, Y.
(1973), The Arrival of the Greeks, Amsterdam.
BETANCOURT, P.P.
(1976), 'The end of the Greek Bronze Age', Antiquity, 50,
40-7.
BIANCOFIORE, F.
(1965), 'Problemi egei alla fine del II millennio', RF,
93, 484-91.
(1967), Civiltà Micenea nell'Italia Meridionale, 2nd ed.,
Rome.

BIESANTZ, H.
(1954), Kretisch-mykenische Siegelbilder, Marburg.
(1958), 'Die minoischen Bildnisgemmen', Marburger
Winckelmann-Programm, 9-25.
BISI, ANNA M.
(1965), Il Grifone, Rome.
(1968), 'Fenici o Micenei in Sicilia nella seconda metà
del II millennio a.c.?', CMic, 3, 1156-68.
BISSING, W. VON
(1923), 'Zur Geschichte der antiken Rhyta', AA, 106-8.
BITTEL, K.
(1956), Review of Blegen, 1953, Gnomon, 28, 241-52.
(1967), 'Karabel', MDOG, 98, 5-23.
BLAVATSKAYA, T.V.
(1966), Ахейская Греция, Moscow.
(1968), 'Über die sozialen Anschauungen in Griechenland im
II. Jahrtausend v.u.Z.', Studien zur Geschichte und Philo-
sophie des Altertums, ed. J. Harmatta, Amsterdam, 9-14.
BLÁZQUEZ, J.M.
(1972), 'Ivoires minoens et mycéniens', AMyc, 2, 398-417.
BLEGEN, C.W.
(1921), Korakou, Boston.
(1928), Zygouries, Cambridge (Mass.)
(1937), Prosymna, Cambridge.
(1945), 'The roof of the Mycenaean megaron', AJA, 49,
35-44.
(1953), Troy, 3, Princeton (with others.)
(1954), 'An early tholos tomb in western Messenia',
Hesperia, 23, 158-62.
(1958), Troy, 4, Princeton (with others.)
(1963), Troy and the Trojans, London.
(1966), The Palace of Nestor, 1, Princeton (with Marion
Rawson.)
(1967), 'The Mycenaean age', Lectures in Memory of Louise
Taft Semple, 1, Princeton, 5-41.
(1973), The Palace of Nestor, 3, Princeton (with others.)
(1975), 'Troy VII', CAH, 2/2, 3rd ed., 161-4.
BLEGEN, C.W. & WACE, A.J.B.
(1930), 'Middle Helladic tombs', SO, 9, 28-37.
BLINKENBERG, C.
(1926), Fibules Grecques et Orientales, Copenhagen.
BOARDMAN, J.
(1963), 'The date of the Knossos tablets', On the Knossos
Tablets, Oxford.
(1966), 'Hittite and related Hieroglyphic seals from
Greece', Kadmos, 5, 47-8.
BORCHHARDT, J.
(1972), Homerische Helme, Mainz.

BORUKHOVICH, V.G.
(1964), 'Ахейцы в Малой Азии', VDI, 89, 91-106.
BOSCH-GIMPERA, P.
(1961), Les Indo-Européens, Paris.
BOUZEK, J.
(1965), 'Mykénské a rane recké vlivy na území stredni Evropy', LF, 88, 241-55.
(1969), Homerisches Griechenland, Prague.
(1971), 'Die Beziehungen zum vorgeschichtlichen Europa der neugefundenen Griffzungenschwerter von Enkomi-Alasia, Zypern', Alasia, 1, Paris, 433-48.
(1972), 'Aegean relations with Europe during the Neolithic and Early Bronze Ages', Acta of the Second International Colloquium on Prehistory, Athens, 138-41.
(1973), 'Bronze Age Greece and the Balkans: problems of migrations', BAMA, 169-77.
(1975), 'Late Helladic III C reconsidered', Actes de la XIIe Conférence Internationale d'Etudes Classiques EIRENE, Bucharest/Amsterdam, 741-3.
BOYD HAWES, HARRIET
(1908), Gournia Vasiliki and other Prehistoric Sites on the Isthmus of Hierapetra Crete, Philadelphia.
BOYSAL, Y.
(1967), 'Vorläufiger Bericht über die Grabungen 1963 in Müskebi', Belleten, 31, 77-83.
BRANDENSTEIN, W.
(1962), 'Das Indogermanenproblem', FF, 36, 45-9.
(1965), 'Die vorgeschichtlichen Völker- und Sprach-bewegungen in der Aegaeis', JKF, 2, new ser., 111-32.
BRANIGAN, K.
(1968), 'A transitional stage in Minoan metallurgy', ABSA, 63, 185-203.
(1969), 'The genesis of the Household Goddess', SMEA, 8, 28-38.
(1970a), The Foundations of Palatial Crete, London.
(1970b), The Tombs of Mesara, London.
(1974), Aegean Metalwork of the Early and Middle Bronze Age, Oxford.
BREASTED, J.H.
(1906a), Ancient Records of Egypt, 3, Chicago.
(1906b), Ancient Records of Egypt, 4, Chicago.
BRELICH, A.
(1968), 'Religione micenea: osservazioni metodologiche', CMic, 2, 919-31.
BRIDGES, R.A.
(1974), 'The Mycenaean tholos tomb at Kolophon', Hesperia, 43, 264-6.
BROCK, NADIA VAN
(1960), 'Notes mycéniennes', RP, 34, 216-31.

BRONEER, O.
(1939), 'A Mycenaean fountain on the Athenian acropolis', Hesperia, 8, 317-433.
(1948), 'The Dorian invasion: what happened at Athens', AJA, 52, 111-4.
(1956), 'Athens in the Late Bronze Age', Antiquity, 30, 9-18.
(1966), 'The Cyclopean wall on the Isthmus of Corinth and its bearing on Late Bronze Age chronology', Hesperia, 35, 346-62.
(1968), 'The Cyclopean wall on the Isthmus of Corinth, addendum', Hesperia, 37, 25-35.
BROWN, W.E.
(1956), 'Land tenure in Mycenaean Pylos', Historia, 5, 385-400.
BRYSON, R.A., LAMB, H.H., & DONLEY, D.L.
(1974), 'Drought and the decline of Mycenae', Antiquity, 48, 46-50.
BUCHHOLZ, H.-G.
(1962), 'Der Pfeilglätter aus dem VI. Schachtgrab von Mykene und die helladischen Pfeilspitzen', JDAI, 77, 1-58.
(1965), 'Die Schleuder als Waffe im ägäischen Kulturkreis', JKF, 2, new ser., 133-59.
(1969), 'Die ägäischen Schriftsysteme und ihre Ausstrahlung in die ostmediterranen Kulturen', Frühe Schriftzeugnisse der Menschheit, Göttingen, 88-150.
(1970), 'Bemerkungen zu bronzezeitlichen Kulturbeziehungen im östlichen Mittelmeer', APA, 1, 137-46.
(1972), 'Das Blei in der mykenischen Kultur und in der bronzezeitlichen Metallurgie Zyperns', JDAI, 87, 1-59.
(1973), 'Grey Trojan ware in Cyprus and northern Syria', BAMA, 179-87.
BUCHHOLZ, H.-G. & KARAGEORGHIS, V.
(1974), 'Ägäische Funde und Kultureinflüsse in den Randgebieten des Mittelmeers', AA, 325-462.
BUCK, R.J.
(1964), 'Middle Helladic mattpainted pottery', Hesperia, 33, 231-313.
(1966), 'The Middle Helladic period', Phoenix, 20, 193-209.
(1969), 'The Mycenaean time of troubles', Historia, 18, 276-98.
BULLE, H.
(1907), Orchomenos, 1, Munich.
BUSCHOR, E. & MASSOW, W. VON
(1927), 'Vom Amyklaion', AM, 52, 1-85.

CADOGAN, G.
(1972), 'Cypriot objects in the Bronze Age Aegean and
their importance', PPDKS, 5-13.
(1973), 'Patterns in the distribution of Mycenaean pottery
in the east Mediterranean', MEM, 166-74.
CADOGAN, G., HARRISON, R.K., & STRONG, G.E.
(1972), 'Volcanic glass shards in Late Minoan I Crete',
Antiquity, 46, 310-3.
CALDERONE, S.
(1960), 'Questioni di terminologia fondiaria micenea', SG,
13, 81-102.
CAMERON, M.A.S.
(1967), 'Unpublished fresco fragments of a chariot composition from Knossos', AA, 330-44.
(1968), 'Unpublished paintings from the "House of the
Frescoes" at Knossos', ABSA, 63, 1-31.
CANBY, JEANNY V.
(1969), 'Some Hittite figurines in the Aegean', Hesperia,
38, 141-9.
CARNOY, A.
(1960), 'Les suffixes toponymiques pré-grecs', AC, 29,
319-36.
CARPENTER, R.
(1966), Discontinuity in Greek Civilization, Cambridge.
CARRATELLI, G. PUGLIESE
(1957), 'L'organizzazione del culto in Pilo micenea', PP,
12, 81-96.
(1958), 'Eqeta', Min, 319-26.
(1959), 'Aspetti e problemi della monarchia micenea', PP,
14, 401-31.
(1960), '"Il re di Ahhijawa" nel trattato di Tudhalijas IV
con Istarmuwa', PP, 15, 321-5.
(1963), 'I bronzieri di Pilo micenea', SCO, 12, 242-53.
CARRUBA, O.
(1964), 'Ahhijawa e altri nomi di popoli e di paesi dell'
Anatolia occidentale', Athenaeum, 42, 269-98.
(1969a), 'Origini e preistoria degli Indoeuropei d'Anatolia', RF, 97, 5-30.
(1969b), 'Die Chronologie der hethitischen Texte und die
hethitische Geschichte der Grossreichzeit', ZDMG Supple-
mentum I, Wiesbaden, 226-49.
(1971a), 'Über historiographische und philologische
Methoden in der Hethitologie', Orientalia, 40, 208-23.
(1971b), 'Über die Sprachstufen des Hethitischen: eine
Widerlegung', ZVS, 85, 226-41.
CARTER, J.M.
(1972), 'The beginnings of narrative art in the Greek
Geometric period', ABSA, 67, 25-58.

CASKEY, J.L.
(1948), 'Notes on Trojan chronology', AJA, 52, 119-22.
(1954), 'Excavations at Lerna, 1952-1953', Hesperia, 23,
3-30.
(1955), 'Excavations at Lerna, 1954', Hesperia, 24, 25-49.
(1956), 'Excavations at Lerna, 1955', Hesperia, 25, 147-73.
(1957), 'Excavations at Lerna, 1956', Hesperia, 26, 142-62.
(1958), 'Excavations at Lerna, 1957', Hesperia, 27, 125-44.
(1960), 'The Early Helladic period in the Argolid',
Hesperia, 29, 285-303.
(1962), 'Excavations in Keos, 1960-1961', Hesperia, 31,
263-83.
(1964a), 'Excavations in Keos, 1963', Hesperia, 33, 314-35.
(1964b), 'Archaeology and the Trojan War', JHS, 84, 9-11.
(1966), 'Excavations in Keos, 1964-1965', Hesperia, 35,
363-76.
(1970), 'Inscriptions and potters' marks from Ayia Irini in
Keos', Kadmos, 9, 107-17.
(1971a), 'Greece, Crete, and the Aegean islands in the
Early Bronze Age', CAH, 1/2, 3rd ed., 771-807.
(1971b), 'Investigations in Keos, part I: excavations and
explorations, 1966-1970', Hesperia, 40, 359-96.
(1972), 'Investigations in Keos, part II: a conspectus of
the pottery', Hesperia, 41, 357-401.
(1973), 'Greece and the Aegean islands in the Middle
Bronze Age', CAH, 2/1, 3rd ed., 117-40.
CASKEY, MIRIAM E.
(1971), 'News letter from Greece', AJA, 75, 295-317.
CASSOLA GUIDA, PAOLA
(1974), Le Armi Difensive dei Micenei nelle Figurazioni,
Rome.
CATLING, H.W.
(1956), 'Bronze cut-and-thrust swords in the eastern
Mediterranean', PPS, 22, 102-25.
(1961), 'A new bronze sword from Cyprus', Antiquity, 35,
115-22.
(1964), Cypriot Bronzework in the Mycenaean World, Oxford.
(1968a), 'A Mycenaean puzzle from Lefkandi in Euboea',
AJA, 72, 41-9.
(1968b), 'Late Minoan vases and bronzes in Oxford', ABSA,
63, 89-131.
(1970a), 'A Mycenaean pictorial fragment from Palae-
paphos', AA, 24-31.
(1970b), 'A bronze plate from a scale-corslet found at
Mycenae', AA, 441-9.
(1975a), 'Cyprus in the Late Bronze Age', CAH, 2/2, 3rd
ed., 188-216.
(1975b), 'Laconia', JHS Archaeological Reports for 1974-
75, 12-15.

265 Bibliography

CATLING, H.W. & KARAGEORGHIS, V.
(1960), 'Minoika in Cyprus', ABSA, 55, 109-27.
CATLING, H.W. & MILLETT, A.
(1965a), 'A study of the inscribed stirrup-jars from Thebes', Archaeometry, 8, 3-85.
(1965b), 'A.study in the composition patterns of Mycenaean pictorial pottery from Cyprus', ABSA, 60, 212-24.
CATLING, H.W., RICHARDS, E.E., & BLIN-STOYLE, A.E.
(1963), 'Correlations between composition and provenance of Mycenaean and Minoan pottery', ABSA, 58, 94-115.
CAUER, P.
(1923), Grundfragen der Homerkritik, 3rd ed., Leipzig.
CAVAIGNAC, E.
(1946), 'La question hittito-achéenne après les dernières publications', BCH, 70, 58-66.
CAVALIER, MADELEINE
(1960), 'Les cultures préhistoriques des îles éoliennes et leur rapport avec le monde égéen', BCH, 84, 319-46.
CHADWICK, J.
(1957), 'Potnia', Minos, 5, 117-29.
(1963), The Mycenae Tablets III, Philadelphia (with others)
(1969a), 'Greek and pre-Greek', TPS, 80-98.
(1969b), 'Linear B tablets from Thebes', Minos, 10, 115-37.
(1970), 'The "Greekness" of Linear B', IF, 75, 97-104.
(1972), 'The Mycenaean documents' in McDonald and Rapp, 1972, 100-16.
(1973a), 'The geography of the Further Province of Pylos', AJA, 77, 276-8.
(1973b), 'ΕΣΤΙ ΠΥΛΟΣ ΠΡΟ ΠΥΛΟΙΟ', Minos, 14, 39-59.
(1975), 'The prehistory of the Greek language', CAH, 2/2, 3rd ed., 805-19.
(1976), The Mycenaean World, Cambridge.
CHADWICK, J. & BAUMBACH, LYDIA
(1963), 'The Mycenaean Greek vocabulary', Glotta, 41, 157-271.
CHADWICK, J., KILLEN, J.T., & OLIVIER, J.-P.
(1971), The Knossos Tablets, 4th ed., Cambridge.
CHARITONIDIS, S.I.
(1952), 'Δύο μυκηναϊκοὶ τάφοι ἐν τῷ χωρίῳ Πρίφτιανι παρὰ τὰς Μυκήνας', AE, parartema, 19-33.
(1953), 'Μυκηναῖος ἀγγειογράφος', AE, Β', 101-6.
(1954), ''Ανασκαφαὶ Ναυπλίας', PAAH, 232-41.
(1961), 'Θαλαμοειδὴς τάφος Καρπάθου', AD, 17, Α', 32-76.
CHARLES, R.-P.
(1965), 'Note sur un scarabée égyptien de Pérati (Attique)', BCH, 89, 10-14.
CHARNEUX, P. & GINOUVÈS, R.
(1956), 'Reconnaissances en Arcadie', BCH, 80, 522-46.

CHILDE, V.G.
(1915), 'On the date and origin of Minyan ware', JHS, 35, 196-207.
(1948), 'The final Bronze Age in the Near East and in temperate Europe', PPS, 14, 177-95.
(1957), The Dawn of European Civilisation, 6th ed., London.
CHOREMIS, A.K.
(1969), 'Μ.Ε. βῶμος εἰς Νησακούλι Μεθώνης', AAA, 2, 10-14.
(1973), 'Μυκηναῖκοῦ καὶ πρωτογεωμετρικοῦ τάφοι εἰς Καρποφόραν Μεσσηνίας', AE, 25-74.
CHRISTIDIS, T.
(1972), 'Further remarks on A-TE-MI-TO and A-TI-MI-TE', Kadmos, 11, 125-8.
COLDSTREAM, J.N. & HUXLEY, G.L.
(1972), Kythera, London.
COLEMAN, R.
(1963), 'The dialect geography of ancient Greece', TPS, 58-126.
CONSIDINE, P.
(1969), 'The theme of divine wrath in ancient east Mediterranean literature', SMEA, 8, 85-159.
CONTENSON, H. DE, COURTOIS, J.-C., LAGARCE, ELISABETH, LAGARCE, J., & STUCKY, R.
(1974), 'La XXXIVe campagne de fouilles à Ras Shamra en 1973, rapport préliminaire', Syria, 51, 1-30.
COOK, J.M.
(1958), 'Old Smyrna, 1948-1951', ABSA, 53/54, 1-34.
(1973), The Troad, Oxford.
COOK, R.M.
(1955), 'Thucydides as archaeologist', ABSA, 50, 266-70.
(1962), 'The Dorian invasion', PCPS, 188, 16-22.
CORNELIUS, F.
(1962), 'Zum Ahhijawaa-Problem', Historia, 11, 112-3.
(1973), Geschichte der Hethiter, Darmstadt.
COURTOIS, J.-C.
(1972), 'Chypre et l'Europe préhistorique à la fin de l' Age du Bronze: données nouvelles sur le monde mycénien finissant', PPDKS, 23-33.
(1973), 'Sur divers groupes de vases mycéniens en Méditerranée orientale', MEM, 137-65.
COURTOIS, LILIANE
(1969), 'Le mobilier funéraire céramique de la tombe 4253 du Bronze Récent (Ville Sud d'Ugarit)', Ugaritica, 6, Paris, 121-37.
COWEN, J.D.
(1955), 'Eine Einführung in die Geschichte der bronzenen Griffzungenschwerter in Süddeutschland und den angrenzenden Gebieten', BRGK, 36, 52-155.

(1966), 'The origins of the flange-hilted sword of bronze in continental Europe', PPS, 32, 262-312.

CROSSLAND, R.A.
(1961), 'The supposed Anatolian origin of the place-name formants in -ss- and -tt', Atti VII Congresso Internazionale di Scienze Onomastiche, 1, Florence, 375-6.
(1971), 'Immigrants from the north', CAH, 1/2, 3rd ed., 824-76.

CROUWEL, J.H.
(1970), 'The Minoan genius in Mycenaean Greece: a review', Talanta, 2, 23-31.

DAKARIS, S.I.
(1956), 'Προϊστορικοὶ τάφοι παρὰ τὸ Καλμπάκι-Ἰωαννίνων', AE, 114-53.
(1958), 'Ἀνασκαφικαὶ ἔρευναι εἰς τὴν ὁμηρικὴν Ἐφύραν καὶ τὸ νεκυομαντεῖον τῆς ἀρχαίας Θεσπρωτίας', PAAH, 107-13.
(1960), 'Ἀνασκαφὴ τοῦ νεκυομαντείου τοῦ Ἀχέροντος καὶ θολωτοῦ τάφου πλησίον τῆς Πάργας', PAAH, 114-27.
(1967a), 'Ἀνασκαφὴ τοῦ ἱεροῦ τῆς Δωδώνης', PAAH, 33-54.
(1967b), 'A Mycenaean IIIB dagger from the Palaeolithic site of Kastritsa in Epirus, Greece', PPS, 33, 30-6.

DANIEL, J.F.
(1941), 'Prolegomena to the Cypro-Minoan script', AJA, 45, 249-82.
(1948), 'The Dorian invasion: the setting', AJA, 52, 107-10.

DAVIS, ELLEN N.
(1974), 'The Vapheio cups: one Minoan and one Mycenaean?', AB, 56, 472-87.

DAWKINS, R.M.
(1909), 'Laconia...the Mycenaean city near the Menelaion', ABSA, 16, 4-11.

DAWKINS, R.M. & DROOP, J.P.
(1910), 'The excavations at Phylakopi in Melos', ABSA, 17, 1-22.

DEGER-JALKOTZY, SIGRID
(1972), 'The women of PY An 607', Minos, 13, 137-60.

DELPLACE, CHRISTIANE
(1967), 'Le griffon créto-mycénien', AC, 36, 49-86.

DEMACOPOULOU, K.
(1968a), 'Ἀνασκαφὴ Μυκηναϊκῶν τάφων Μελαθριᾶς Λακωνίας', AAA, 1, 37-41.
(1968b), 'Μυκηναϊκὰ ἀγγεῖα ἐκ θαλαμοειδῶν τάφων περιοχῆς Ἁγίου Ἰωάννου Μονεμβασίας', AD, 23, Α', 145-94.
(1971), 'A Mycenaean pictorial vase of the fifteenth century BC from Laconia', ABSA, 66, 95-100.
(1974), 'Μυκηναϊκὸν ἀνακτορικὸν ἐργαστήριον εἰς Θήβας', AAA, 7, 162-73.

DEMANGEL, R.
(1944), 'La frise de socle du palais de Tirynthe', BCH, 68/69, 404-10.
DEMARGNE, P.
(1932), 'Culte funéraire et foyer domestique dans la Crète minoenne', BCH, 56, 60-88.
(1947), La Crète Dédalique, Paris.
DE MIRO, E.
(1968), 'Il miceneo nel territorio di Agrigento', CMic, 1, 73-80.
DEROY, L.
(1968), Les Leveurs d'Impôts dans le Royaume Mycénien de Pylos, Rome.
DEROY, L. & GERARD, MONIQUE
(1965), Le Cadastre Mycénien de Pylos, Rome.
DESBOROUGH, V.R.d'A.
(1964), The Last Mycenaeans and their Successors, Oxford.
(1965), 'The Greek mainland, c. 1150 - c. 1000 BC', PPS, 31, 213-28.
(1968), 'History and archaeology in the last century of the Mycenaean age', CMic, 3, 1073-93.
(1972), The Greek Dark Ages, London.
(1973), 'Mycenaeans in Cyprus', MEM, 79-87.
(1975), 'The end of Mycenaean civilization and the Dark Age: (a) the archaeological background', CAH, 2/2, 3rd ed., 658-77.
DESHAYES, J.
(1966), Argos, les Fouilles de la Deiras, Paris.
(1969), 'Les vases Vollgraff de la Deiras', BCH, 93, 574-616.
DESHAYES, J. & DESSENNE, A.
(1959), Mallia, Maisons, 2, Paris.
DESSENNE, A.
(1957), 'Le griffon créto-mycénien: inventaire et remarques', BCH, 81, 203-15.
DEVOTO, G.
(1962), Origini Indeuropee, Florence.
DICKINSON, O.T.P.K.
(1972a), 'The Shaft Graves and Mycenaean origins', BICS, 19, 146-7.
(1972b), 'Late Helladic IIA and IIB: some evidence from Korakou', ABSA, 67, 103-12.
(1974), 'The definition of Late Helladic I', ABSA, 69, 109-20.
DIETRICH, B.C.
(1969), 'Some myth and fact about the Dorians', AC(CT), 12, 47-52.
(1973), 'A religious function of the megaron',RSA, 3,1-12.
(1974), The Origins of Greek Religion, Berlin.

DIETZ, S.
(1975), 'A Bronze Age tumulus cemetery in Asine, Southern
Greece', Archaeology, 28, 157-63.
DIKAIOS, P.
(1963), 'The context of the Enkomi tablets', Kadmos, 2,
39-52.
(1971), Enkomi Excavations 1948-1958, 2, Mainz.
DINSMOOR, W.B.
(1942), 'Notes on megaron roofs', AJA, 46, 370-2.
DIRLMEIER, F.
(1955), 'Homerisches Epos und Orient', RM, 98, 18-37.
DÖHL, H.
(1973a), 'Iria: Die Ergebnisse der Ausgrabungen 1939',
Tiryns, 6, Mainz, 127-94.
(1973b), 'Die prähistorische Besiedlung von Synoro',
Tiryns, 6, Mainz, 195-220.
DONADONI, S.
(1965), 'I testi egiziani sui "popoli del mare"', RSI, 77,
300-14.
DOR, L., JANNORAY, J., EFFENTERRE, H. VAN, & EFFENTERRE,
MICHELINE VAN
(1960), Kirrha, Etude de Préhistoire Phocidienne, Paris.
DORNSEIFF, F.
(1959), Antike und Alter Orient, 2nd ed., Leipzig.
DÖRPFELD, W.
(1908), 'Alt-Pylos: I. Die Kuppelgräber von Kakovatos',
AM, 33, 295-317.
(1927), Alt-Ithaka, 1, Munich.
DOTHAN, M.
(1971), 'Ashdod II-III', 'Atiquot (English Series), 9/10.
(1972), 'Relations between Cyprus and the Philistine coast
in the Late Bronze Age (Tel Mor, Ashdod)', PPDKS, 51-6.
DOTHAN, TRUDE
(1957), 'Archaeological reflections on the Philistine
problem', AntSurv, 2, 151-64.
(1972), 'Anthropoid clay coffins from a Late Bronze Age
cemetery near Deir el-Balah (preliminary report)', IEJ,
22, 65-72.
(1973), 'Anthropoid clay coffins from a Late Bronze Age
cemetery near Deir el-Balah (preliminary report II)', IEJ,
23, 129-46.
DOUMAS, C.
(1974), 'The Minoan eruption of the Santorini volcano',
Antiquity, 48, 110-5.
DRAGENDORFF, H.
(1913), 'Tiryns, Vorbericht über die Grabungen 1913', AM,
38, 329-54.

DRESSLER, W.
(1965), 'Methodische Vorfragen bei der Bestimmung der "Urheimat"', Die Sprache, 11, 25-60.
DURANTE, M.
(1971), Sulla Preistoria della Tradizione Poetica Greca, 1, Rome.
EDEL, E.
(1966), Die Ortsnamenlisten aus dem Totentempel Amenophis III., Bonn.
EDGAR, C.C. & EVANS, A.J.
(1904), Excavations at Phylakopi in Melos (Hellenic Society Supplementary Paper no. 4), London (with others.)
EDGERTON, W.F. & WILSON, J.A.
(1936), Historical Records of Ramses III, Chicago.
EDWARDS, G.P.
(1971), The Language of Hesiod in its Traditional Context, Oxford.
EFFENTERRE, H. VAN
(1967), 'Téménos', REG, 80, 17-26.
EFFENTERRE, H. VAN & MICHELINE VAN
(1974), 'Vers une grammaire de la glyptique crétomycénienne', Die Kretisch-mykenische Glyptik und ihre Gegenwärtigen Probleme, Boppard, 22-9.
(1975), 'Comment croire à l'Helladique Ancien III?', BCH, 99, 35-42.
ERBSE, H.
(1961), 'Zur Geschichtsbetrachtung des Thukydides', AntAb, 10, 19-34.
(1964), 'Orientalisches und Griechisches in Hesiods Theogonie', Philologus, 108, 2-28.
ERLENMEYER, MARIE-LOUISE & H.
(1964), 'Über Philister und Kreter, IV', Orientalia, 33, 199-237.
(1965), 'Kassitische Goldarbeiten aus dem Schachtgrab III in Mykene?', Kadmos, 3, 177-8.
EVANS, A.J.
(1901), The Mycenaean Tree and Pillar Cult, London.
(1905), 'The prehistoric tombs of Knossos', Archaeologia, 59, 391-562.
(1913), 'The "Tomb of the Double Axes" and associated group, and the Pillar Rooms and ritual vessels of the "Little Palace" at Knossos', Archaeologia, 65, 1-94.
(1921), The Palace of Minos at Knossos, 1, London.
(1928), The Palace of Minos at Knossos, 2, London.
(1930), The Palace of Minos at Knossos, 3, London.
(1935), The Palace of Minos at Knossos, 4, London.

FAURE, P.
(1964), Fonctions des Cavernes Crétoises, Paris.
(1966), 'Les minerais de la Crète antique', RA, 45-78.
(1973), La Vie Quotidienne en Crète, Paris.
(1975), La Vie Quotidienne en Grèce au Temps de la Guerre de Troie, Paris.
FIECHTER, E.
(1918), 'Amyklae', JDAI, 33, 107-245.
FINLEY, M.I
(1957), 'The Mycenaean tablets and economic history', EHR, 10, 128-41.
(1964), 'The Trojan War', JHS, 84, 1-9.
(1970), Early Greece: The Bronze and Archaic Ages, London.
FOLTINY, S.
(1964), 'Flange-hilted cutting swords of bronze in central Europe, northeast Italy and Greece', AJA, 68, 247-57.
FORRER, E.O.
(1924), 'Vorhomerische Griechen in den Keilschrifttexten von Boghazköi', MDOG, 63, 1-22.
(1926), Forschungen, 1, Berlin.
(1929), Forschungen, 2, Berlin.
(1969), 'Der Untergang des Hatti-Reiches', Ugaritica, 6, Paris, 207-28.
FORSDYKE, E.J.
(1914), 'The pottery called Minyan ware', JHS, 34, 126-56.
FOSSEY, J.M.
(1973), 'The end of the Bronze Age in the south west Copaic', Euphrosyne, 6, new ser., 7-21.
FRANKFORT, H.
(1936), 'Notes on the Cretan griffin', ABSA, 37, 106-22.
(1939), Cylinder Seals, London.
FRENCH, D.H.
(1966), 'Some problems in Macedonian prehistory', BS, 7, 103-10.
(1967), 'Prehistoric sites in northwest Anatolia, I', AS, 17, 49-96.
(1969), 'Prehistoric sites in northwest Anatolia, II', AS, 19, 41-98.
(1973), 'Migrations and "Minyan" pottery in western Anatolia and the Aegean', BAMA, 51-7.
FRENCH, ELIZABETH
(1963), 'Pottery groups from Mycenae: a summary', ABSA, 58, 44-52.
(1964), 'Late Helladic IIIA 1 pottery from Mycenae', ABSA, 59, 241-61.
(1965), 'Late Helladic IIIA 2 pottery from Mycenae', ABSA, 60, 159-202.
(1966), 'A group of Late Helladic IIIB 1 pottery from Mycenae', ABSA, 61, 216-38.

272 Bibliography

(1967), 'Pottery from Late Helladic IIIB 1 destruction contexts at Mycenae', ABSA, 62, 149-93.
(1969a), 'A group of Late Helladic IIIB 2 pottery from Mycenae', ABSA, 64, 71-93.
(1969b), 'The first phase of LH IIIC', AA, 133-6.
(1971), 'The development of Mycenaean terracotta figurines', ABSA, 66, 101-87.
(1975), 'A reassessment of the Mycenaean pottery at Tarsus', AS, 25, 53-75.
FRIEDRICH, J.
(1927), 'Werden in den hethitischen Keilschrifttexten die Griechen erwähnt?', KF, 1, 87-107.
(1930), Staatsverträge des Hatti-Reiches in Hethitischer Sprache, 2, Leipzig.
FRÖDIN, O. & PERSSON, A.W.
(1938), Asine, Stockholm.
FURNÉE, E.J.
(1972), Die Wichtigsten Konsonantischen Erscheinungen des Vorgriechischen, The Hague/Paris.
FURUMARK, A.
(1944), 'The Mycenaean III C pottery and its relation to Cypriote fabrics', OA, 3, 194-265.
(1946), 'Nestor's cup and the Mycenaean dove goblet', Eranos, 44, 41-53.
(1950), 'The settlement at Ialysos and Aegean history c. 1550-1400 BC', OA, 6, 150-271.
(1965a), 'Gods of ancient Crete', OAth, 6, 85-98.
(1965b), 'The excavations at Sinda: some historical results', OAth, 6, 99-116.
(1972a), The Mycenaean Pottery: Analysis and Classification, 2nd ed., Stockholm.
(1972b), The Chronology of Mycenaean Pottery, 2nd ed., Stockholm.
GALLET DE SANTERRE, H.
(1958), Délos Primitive et Archaique, Paris.
GALLET DE SANTERRE, H. & TRÉHEUX, J.
(1947), 'Rapport sur le dépôt égéen et géométrique de l'Artémision à Délos', BCH, 71/72, 148-254.
GALLING, K.
(1969), 'Die Kopfzier der Philister in den Darstellungen von Medinet Habu', Ugaritica, 6, Paris, 247-65.
GARASANIN, M.V.
(1958), 'Neolithikum und Bronzezeit in Serbien und Makedonien', BRGK, 39, 1-130.
GARDINER, A.H.
(1947), Ancient Egyptian Onomastica, 1, Oxford.
GARSTANG, J. & GURNEY, O.R.
(1959), The Geography of the Hittite Empire, London.

GEISS, H.
(1975), 'Troja - Streit ohne Ende', Klio, 57, 261-7.
GEJVALL, N.-G.
(1969), Lerna, 1, Princeton.
GEORGIEV, V.
(1965), 'Interprétation de la liste pylienne des rameurs absents (PY An 724)', PP, 20, 239-45.
(1973), 'The arrival of the Greeks in Greece: the linguistic evidence', BAMA, 243-57.
GÉRARD-ROUSSEAU, MONIQUE
(1968), Les Mentions Religieuses dans les Tablettes Mycéniennes, Rome.
(1971), 'Les sacrifices à Pylos', SMEA, 13, 139-46.
(1973), 'Connections in religion between the Mycenaean world and Anatolia', BAMA, 163-7.
GERCKE, P. & HIESEL, G.
(1971), 'Grabungen in der Unterstadt von Tiryns von 1884 bis 1929', Tiryns, 5, Mainz, 1-19.
GERCKE, P. & NAUMANN, U.
(1974), 'Tiryns-Stadt 1971/1972', AAA, 7, 15-24.
GIANOTTI, G.F.
(1972), 'Orfeo e Dioniso micenei', RF, 100, 522-33.
GIL, L.
(1968), 'El substrato pregriego: ojeada histórica y panorámica actual', EC, 12, 249-85.
GILL, MARGARET A.V.
(1964), 'The Minoan "genius"', AM, 79, 1-21.
(1970), 'Apropos the Minoan "genius"', AJA, 74, 404-6.
GIMBUTAS, MARIJA
(1970), 'Proto-Indo-European culture: the Kurgan culture during the fifth, fourth, and third millennia BC', Indo-European and Indo-Europeans, ed. G. Cardona, H.M. Hoenigswald, and A. Senn, Philadelphia, 155-97.
(1973), 'The beginning of the Bronze Age in Europe and the Indo-Europeans', JIES, 1, 163-214.
GINDIN, L.A.
(1971), 'К проблеме генетической принадлежности "Пеласгского" догреческого слоя', VY/1, 44-53.
GJERSTAD, E.
(1926), Studies on Prehistoric Cyprus, Uppsala.
(1934/1937), The Swedish Cyprus Expedition, 1-3, Stockholm.
GODART, L. & OLIVIER, J.-P.
(1976), 'Nouveaux textes en linéaire B de Tirynthe', Tiryns, 8, Mainz, 37-53.
GOETZE, A.
(1928), Madduwattas, Leipzig.
(1933), Die Annalen des Mursilis, Leipzig.
(1934), Review of Sommer, 1932, Gnomon, 10, 177-83.
(1940), Kizzuwatna and the Problem of Hittite Geography, Yale.

(1957), Kleinasien, 2nd ed., Munich.
GOLDMAN, HETTY
(1931), Excavations at Eutresis in Boeotia, Cambridge
(Mass.)
(1956), Excavations at Gözlü Kule, Tarsus, Princeton.
GORDON, C.H.
(1962), Before the Bible, London.
GRACE, VIRGINIA R.
(1956), 'The Canaanite jar', ANE, 80-109.
GRAHAM, J.W.
(1960), 'Mycenaean architecture', Archaeology, 13, 46-54.
GRAY, DOROTHEA H.F.
(1955), 'Houses in the "Odyssey"', CQ, 49, 1-12.
(1974), Seewesen, Göttingen.
GRAY, J.
(1964a), The Canaanites, London.
(1964b), The KRT Text in the Literature of Ras Shamra, 2nd
ed., Leiden.
GROSSMANN, P. & SCHÄFER, J.
(1971), 'Tiryns: Unterburg, Grabungen 1965', Tiryns, 5,
Mainz, 41-75.
GROTE, G.
(1851), History of Greece, 2, 3rd ed., London.
GRUMACH, E.
(1969), The Coming of the Greeks, Manchester.
GSCHNITZER, F.
(1965), 'Βασιλεύς, ein terminologischer Beitrag zur Früh-
geschichte des Königtums bei den Griechen', IBK, 11, 99-
112.
GUGLIELMI, M.
(1971), 'Sulla navigazione in età micenea', PP, 26, 418-35.
GÜLTEKIN, H. & BARAN, M.
(1964), 'The Mycenaean grave found at the hill of Aya-
suluk', TAD, 13/2, 125-33.
GÜTERBOCK, H.G.
(1936), 'Neue Ahhijava-Texte', ZfA, 9, 321-7.
(1946), Kumarbi, Zurich/New York.
(1967), 'The Hittite conquest of Cyprus reconsidered',
JNES, 26, 73-81.
GUTHRIE, W.K.C.
(1959), 'Early Greek religion in the light of the decipherment of Linear B', BICS, 6, 35-46.
(1975), 'The religion and mythology of the Greeks: Minoan
and Mycenaean religion', CAH, 2/2, 3rd ed., 856-83.
HADJIOANNOU, K.
(1971), 'On the identification of the horned god of
Engomi-Alasia', Alasia, 1, Paris, 33-42.
HAEVERNICK, THEA E.
(1963), 'Mycenaean glass', Archaeology, 16, 190-3.

HÄGG, INGA & R.
(1973), Excavations in the Barbouna Area at Asine, Uppsala.
HÄGG, R.
(1968), 'Mykenische Kultstätten im archäologischen Material', OAth, 8, 39-60.
(1974), Die Gräber der Argolis in Submykenischer, Proto-geometrischer und Geometrischer Zeit, 1, Uppsala.
HAINSWORTH, J.B.
(1967), 'Greek views of Greek dialectology', TPS, 62-76.
HALBHERR, F.
(1903), 'Resti dell'età micenea scoperti ad Haghia Triada presso Phaestos', MA, 13, 5-74.
HALEY, J.B. & BLEGEN, C.W.
(1928), 'The coming of the Greeks', AJA, 32, 141-54.
HALL, EDITH H.
(1914), Excavations in Eastern Crete: Vrokastro, Phila-delphia.
HALLER, A.
(1954), Die Gräber und Grüfte von Assur, Berlin.
HAMILTON, R.W.
(1934), 'Tall Abū Hawam', QDAP, 3, 74-80.
HAMMOND, N.G.L.
(1931), 'Prehistoric Epirus and the Dorian invasion', ABSA, 32, 131-79.
(1967a), 'Tumulus-burial in Albania, the Grave Circles of Mycenae, and the Indo-Europeans', ABSA, 62, 77-105.
(1967b), Epirus, Oxford.
(1971), 'The dating of some burials in tumuli in south Albania', ABSA, 66, 229-41.
(1972), A History of Macedonia, 1, Oxford.
(1973), Studies in Greek History, Oxford.
(1974), 'The tumulus-burials of Leucas and their connec-tions in the Balkans and northern Greece', ABSA, 69, 129-44
(1975), 'The end of Mycenaean civilization and the Dark Age: (b) the literary tradition for the migrations', CAH, 2/2, 3rd ed., 678-712.
HAMPL, F.
(1960), 'Die Chronologie der Einwanderung der griechischen Stämme und das Problem der Nationalität der Träger der mykenischen Kultur', MH, 17, 57-86.
(1962), 'Die Ilias ist kein Geschichtsbuch', IBK, 7/8, 37-63.
HANCAR, F.
(1955), Das Pferd in Prähistorischer und früher Histor-ischer Zeit, Vienna.
HANKEY, VRONWY
(1952), 'Late Helladic tombs at Khalkis', ABSA, 47, 49-95.
(1966), 'Late Mycenaean pottery at Beth-Shan', AJA, 70, 169-71.

(1967), 'Mycenaean pottery in the Middle East: notes on finds since 1951', ABSA, 62, 107-47.
(1972), 'Aegean finds at Late Bronze Age sites in the south-eastern Mediterranean', BICS, 19, 143-5.
(1973), 'The Aegean deposit at El Amarna', MEM, 128-36.
(1974), 'A Late Bronze Age temple at Amman', Levant, 6, 131-78.
HANKEY, VRONWY & TUFNELL, OLGA
(1973), 'The tomb of Maket and its Mycenaean import', ABSA, 68, 103-11.
HÄNSEL, B.
(1973), 'Eine datierte Rapierklinge mykenischen Typs von der unteren Donau', PZ, 48, 200-6.
HARDING, A. & HUGHES-BROCK, HELEN
(1974), 'Amber in the Mycenaean world', ABSA, 69, 145-72.
HARLAND, J.P.
(1925), Prehistoric Aigina, Paris.
HARMATTA, J.
(1968a), 'Zur Ahhiyawa-Frage', SM, 117-24.
(1968b), 'Ahhiyawa names-Mycenaean names', CMic, 1, 401-9.
HAUSSOULLIER, B.
(1878), 'Catalogue descriptif des objets découverts à Spata', BCH, 2, 185-228.
HAWKES, C.F.C.
(1940), The Prehistoric Foundations of Europe to the Mycenaean Age, London.
(1948), 'From Bronze Age to Iron Age: Middle Europe, Italy, and the north and west', PPS, 14, 196-218.
HEATH, MARTHA C.
(1958), 'Early Helladic clay sealings from the House of the Tiles at Lerna', Hesperia, 27, 81-121.
HÉDERVARI, P.
(1971), 'An attempt to correlate some archaeological and volcanological data regarding the Minoan eruption of Santorin', AD, 26, A', 1-15.
HELCK, W.
(1971), Die Beziehungen Ägyptens zu Vorderasien im 3. und 2. Jahrtausend v. Chr., 2nd ed., Wiesbaden.
HERKENRATH, E.
(1937), 'Mykenische Kultszenen', AJA, 41, 411-23.
HESTER, D.A.
(1957), 'Pre-Greek place names in Greece and Asia Minor', RHA, 15, 107-19.
(1965), '"Pelasgian" - a new Indo-European language?', Lingua, 13, 335-84.
(1968), 'Recent developments in Mediterranean "substrate" studies', Minos, 9, 219-35.
HESTRIN, RUTH
(1970), The Philistines and other Sea Peoples, Jerusalem.

HEUBECK, A.
(1955), 'Mythologische Vorstellungen des Alten Orients im archaischen Griechentum', Gymnasium, 62, 508-25.
(1959), 'Zu mykenischen Namen und Titeln', IF, 64, 119-35.
(1961), Praegraeca, Erlangen.
(1966), Aus der Welt der Frühgriechischen Lineartafeln, Göttingen.
(1967), 'Myk. ke-ke-me-no', ZA, 17, 17-21.
(1968), 'Da-mo-ko-ro', CMic, 2, 611-5.
(1969), 'Zu den Linear B-Texten auf mutterländischen Vasen', Athenaeum, 47, 144-53.
HEURTLEY, W.A.
(1921), 'Excavations at Mycenae: the grave stelai', ABSA, 25, 126-46.
(1923), 'Notes on the harbours of S. Boeotia, and seatrade between Boeotia and Corinth in prehistoric times', ABSA, 26, 38-45.
(1932), 'Excavations in Ithaca, I: LH III-Protogeometric cairns at Aetós', ABSA, 33, 22-65.
(1936), 'The relationship between "Philistine" and Mycenaean pottery', QDAP, 5, 90-110.
(1939a), Prehistoric Macedonia, Cambridge.
(1939b), 'A Palestinian vase-painter of the sixteenth century BC', QDAP, 8, 21-37.
HEURTLEY, W.A. & SKEAT, T.C.
(1930), 'The tholos tombs of Marmáriane', ABSA, 31, 1-55.
HIGGINS, C.G.
(1966), 'Possible disappearance of Mycenaean coastal settlements of the Messenian peninsula', AJA, 70, 23-9.
HIGGINS, R.A.
(1961), Greek and Roman Jewellery, London.
HIGGINS, R.A., HOPE SIMPSON, R., & ELLIS, S.E.
(1968), 'The façade of the Treasury of Atreus at Mycenae', ABSA, 63, 331-6.
HILLER, S.
(1969), 'Wanasoi tonoeketerijo', Minos, 10, 78-92.
(1970), 'Die Aithusa bei Homer', WS, 83, 14-27.
(1972a), 'Allgemeine Bemerkungen zur Jn-Serie', SMEA, 15, 51-72.
(1972b), Studien zur Geographie des Reiches um Pylos nach den Mykenischen und Homerischen Texten, Vienna.
(1975), 'Die Explosion des Vulkans von Thera', Gymnasium, 82, 32-74.
HILLER, S. & PANAGL, O.
(1971), 'Linear B: Fortschritte und Forschungsstand', Saeculum, 22, 123-94.
HOLLAND, L.B.
(1920), 'Primitive Aegean roofs', AJA, 24, 323-41.
(1944), 'Colophon', Hesperia, 13, 91-171.

HOLMBERG, E.J.
(1944), The Swedish Excavations at Asea in Arcadia, Lund.
HOLMES, Y. LYNN
(1976), 'The foreign trade of Cyprus during the Late Bronze Age', The Archaeology of Cyprus, Recent Developments, ed. N. Robertson, Park Ridge, N.J., 90-110.
HOOD, M.S.F.
(1960a), 'Tholos tombs of the Aegean', Antiquity, 34, 166-76
(1960b), 'Schliemann's Mycenae albums', Archaeology, 13, 61-5.
(1961), 'Knossos', AD, 17, B', 294-6.
(1965), 'Excavations at Emporio, Chios, 1952-55', Atti del VI Congresso Internazionale delle Scienze Preistoriche e Protostoriche, 2, Rome, 224-7.
(1967), 'The Tartaria tablets', Antiquity, 41, 99-113.
(1970), 'Lerna and Bubanj', ZNM, 6, 83-90.
(1971a), 'Late Bronze Age destructions at Knossos', ACVT, 377-83.
(1971b), The Minoans, London.
(1973a), 'Mycenaean settlement in Cyprus and the coming of the Greeks', MEM, 40-50.
(1973b), 'Northern penetration of Greece at the end of the Early Helladic period and contemporary Balkan chronology', BAMA, 59-71.
(1973c), 'The eruption of Thera and its effects in Crete in Late Minoan I', PDKS3, 111-8.
HOOD, M.S.F. & DE JONG, P.
(1952), 'Late Minoan warrior-graves from Ayios Ioannis and the New Hospital site at Knossos', ABSA, 47, 243-77.
HOOKER, J.T.
(1967a), 'The Mycenae siege rhyton and the question of Egyptian influence', AJA, 71, 269-81.
(1967b), 'The beginnings of Linear B', Europa, Festschrift E. Grumach, ed. W.C. Brice, Berlin, 132-42.
(1968), 'The context of the Knossos tablets', SMEA, 5, 71-91.
(1969), 'Homer and Late Minoan Crete', JHS, 89, 60-71.
HOPE SIMPSON, R.
(1957), 'Identifying a Mycenaean state', ABSA, 52, 231-59.
(1958), 'Nemesis: a Mycenaean settlement near the Menidi tholos tomb', ABSA, 53/54, 292-4.
(1965), A Gazetteer and Atlas of Mycenaean Sites (BICS Supplement 16), London.
HOPE SIMPSON, R. & LAZENBY, J.F.
(1962), 'Notes from the Dodecanese', ABSA, 57, 154-75.
(1970a), 'Notes from the Dodecanese II', ABSA, 65, 47-77.
(1970b), The Catalogue of the Ships in Homer's Iliad, Oxford
(1973), 'Notes from the Dodecanese III', ABSA, 68, 127-79.
HOUWINK TEN CATE, P.H.J.
(1961), The Luwian Population Groups..., Leiden.

(1970), The Records of the Early Hittite Empire (c. 1450-
1380 BC), Istanbul.
(1973), 'Anatolian evidence for relations with the West in
the Late Bronze Age', BAMA, 141-61.
HOWELL, R.J.
(1970), 'A survey of eastern Arcadia in prehistory', ABSA,
65, 79-127.
(1973), 'The origins of the Middle Helladic culture',
BAMA, 73-106.
HROZNÝ, B.
(1929), 'Hethiter und Griechen', AO, 1, 323-43.
HURST, A.
(1968), 'A propos des forgerons de Pylos', SMEA, 5, 92-6.
HUTCHINSON, J.S.
(1975), 'An analogical approach to the history of Late
Helladic III', BICS, 22, 215-6.
HUTCHINSON, R.W.
(1954), Review of Alexiou, 1952, Antiquity, 28, 183-5.
(1956), 'A tholos tomb on the Kephala', ABSA, 51, 74-80.
(1962), Prehistoric Crete, Harmondsworth.
HUXLEY, G.L.
(1957), 'Thucydides and the date of the Trojan War: a
note', PP, 12, 209-12.
(1960), Achaeans and Hittites, Oxford.
IAKOVIDIS, S.E.
(1962), Ἡ Μυκηναϊκὴ Ἀκρόπολις τῶν Ἀθηνῶν, Athens.
(1966a), 'A Mycenaean mourning custom', AJA, 70, 43-50.
(1966b), 'Περὶ τοῦ σχήματος τῶν λαξευτῶν τάφων εἰς τὰ
Βολιμίδια Μεσσηνίας', Χαριστήριον εἰς Ἀ.Κ. Ὀρλάνδον, 2,
Athens, 98-111.
(1969), Περατή: Τὸ Νεκροταφεῖον, Athens.
(1973), 'Rhodes and Ahhijava', MEM, 189-92.
ILIEVSKI, P.H.
(1968), 'A re-examination of the Pylos Cn tablets', CMic,
2, 616-32.
IMMERWAHR, SARA A.
(1960), 'Mycenaean trade and colonization', Archaeology,
13, 4-13.
(1971), The Athenian Agora, 13, Princeton.
IRIMIA, M.
(1970), 'Das mykenische Bronzeschwert aus Medgidia',
Dacia, 14, 389-95.
ISAAC, D.
(1938), 'Les démons minoens', RHR, 118, 55-91.
JACHMANN, G.
(1958), Der Homerische Schiffskatalog und die Ilias,
Cologne/Opladen.

JACOBY, F.
(1923), Die Fragmente der Griechischen Historiker, 1,
Berlin.
(1929), Die Fragmente der Griechischen Historiker, 2B,
Berlin.
JAMESON, M.
(1960), 'Mycenaean religion', Archaeology, 13, 33-9.
JOHNSTONE, W.
(1971), 'A Late Bronze Age tholos tomb at Enkomi',
Alasia, 1, Paris, 51-122.
KAHRSTEDT, U.
(1937), 'Der Kopaissee im Altertum und die "minyschen"
Kanäle', AA, 1-19.
KALLIGAS, P.G.
(1968), ''Αρχαιότητες καὶ μνημεῖα 'Ιονίων νησῶν', AD, 23,
Β'2, 302-22.
(1974), 'Κεφαλληνιακά Β', AAA, 7, 186-90.
KAMBANIS, M.L.
(1892), 'Le dessèchement du Lac Copais par les anciens',
BCH, 16, 121-37.
(1893), 'Le dessèchement du Lac Copais par les anciens,
2e art.', BCH, 17, 322-42.
KAMMENHUBER, ANNELIES
(1968), 'Die Sprachen des vorhellenistischen Kleinasien in
ihrer Bedeutung für die heutige Indogermanistik', MSS, 24,
55-123.
(1969a), 'Konsequenzen aus neueren Datierungen hethitischer
Texte', Orientalia, 38, 548-52.
(1969b), 'Hethitisch, Palaisch, Luwisch und Hieroglyphen-
luwisch', Altkleinasiatische Sprachen, Leiden, 119-357.
(1970), 'Die Vorgänger Suppiluliumas I', Orientalia, 39,
278-301.
KANTOR, HELENE J.
(1947), 'The Aegean and Orient in the second millennium
BC', AJA, 51, 3-103.
(1956), 'Syro-Palestinian ivories', JNES, 15, 153-74.
(1960), 'Ivory carving in the Mycenaean period', Archaeology, 13, 14-25.
KARAGEORGHIS, JACQUELINE V.
(1958), 'Quelques observations sur l'origine du syllabaire
chypro-minoen', RA, 1-19.
(1961), 'Histoire de l'écriture chypriote', KS, 25, 43-60.
KARAGEORGHIS, V.
(1957), 'The Mycenaean "window-crater" in the British
Museum', JHS, 77, 269-71.
(1958), 'Myth and epic in Mycenaean vase painting', AJA,
62, 383-7.
(1965), Nouveaux Documents pour l'Etude du Bronze Récent à
Chypre, Paris.

(1967), Excavations in the Necropolis of Salamis, Nicosia.
(1973a), 'A Late Cypriote hoard of bronzes from Sinda',
RDAC, 72-82.
(1973b), 'Kition: Mycenaean and Phoenician', PBA, 59.
(1974), Excavations at Kition, 1, Nicosia.
KARDARA, CHRYSOULA P.
(1971), 'The Isthmian wall', AAA, 4, 85-9.
KARO, G.
(1911), 'Minoische Rhyta', JDAI, 26, 249-70.
(1930a), Die Schachtgräber von Mykenai, Munich.
(1930b), 'Schatz von Tiryns', AM, 55, 119-40.
(1934a), 'Die Perseia von Mykenai', AJA, 38, 123-7.
(1934b), Führer durch Tiryns, 2nd ed., Athens.
KASE, E.W.
(1973), 'Mycenaean roads in Phocis', AJA, 77, 74-7.
KAVVADIAS, P.
(1912), 'Περὶ τῶν ἐν Κεφαλληνίᾳ ἀνασκαφῶν', PAAH, 247-68.
KENNA, V.E.G.
(1960), Cretan Seals, Oxford.
KENNY, E.J.A.
(1935), 'The ancient drainage of the Copais', AAA(L), 22,
189-206.
KERAMOPOULLOS, A.D.
(1909), ''Η οἰκία τοῦ Κάδμου', EA, 57-122.
(1910), 'Μυκηναϊκοὶ τάφοι ἐν Αἰγίνῃ καὶ ἐν Θήβαις', AE,
177-252.
(1917), 'Θηβαϊκά', AD, 3.
(1918), 'Περὶ τῶν βασιλικῶν τάφων τῆς ἀκροπόλεως τῶν
Μυκηνῶν', AE, 52-60.
(1930), 'Αἱ βιομηχανίαι καὶ τὸ ἐμπόριον τοῦ Κάδμου', AE,
29-58.
KERÉNYI, K.
(1961), Der Frühe Dionysos, Oslo/Bergen.
KERSCHENSTEINER, JULA
(1970), Die Mykenische Welt in ihren Schriftlichen Zeug-
nissen, Munich.
KIMMIG, W.
(1964), 'Seevölkerbewegung und Urnenfelderkultur', Studien
aus Alteuropa, ed. R. von Uslar and K.J. Narr, 1,
Cologne, 220-83.
KIRK, G.S.
(1960), 'Objective dating criteria in Homer', MH, 17,
189-205.
(1964), 'The Trojan War: the character of the tradition',
JHS, 84, 12-17.
KLEINER, G.
(1969), 'Stand der Erforschung von Alt-Milet', IM, 19/20,
113-23.

KNOX, MARY O.
(1973), 'Megarons and μέγαρα: Homer and archaeology', CQ, 67, 1-21.
KONTOLEON, N.M.
(1951), ''Ανασκαφὴ ἐν Νάξῳ', PAAH, 214-23.
(1965), 'Zwei beschriftete Scherben aus Naxos', Kadmos, 4, 84-5.
KORRES, G.S.
(1968), 'Διπλαῖ θεότητες ἐν Κρήτῃ καὶ Μυκηναϊκῇ 'Ελλάδι', PDKS2, 2, 107-19.
KOUROUNIOTIS, K.
(1906), ''Ανασκαφὴ θολωτοῦ τάφου ἐν Βόλῳ', EA, 211-40.
(1914), 'Πύλου Μεσσηνιακῆς θολωτὸς τάφος', EA, 99-117.
KOUSTOUROU, MAGDA
(1972), 'Μυκηναϊκὰ ἐπιθετικὰ ὅπλα', AAA, 5, 325-37.
KRAHE, H.
(1954), Sprache und Vorzeit, Heidelberg.
(1957), 'Indogermanisch und Alteuropäisch', Saeculum, 8, 1-16.
KRAIKER, W.
(1939), 'Nordische Einwanderungen in Griechenland', Die Antike, 15, 195-230.
KRAIKER, W. & KÜBLER, K.
(1939), Kerameikos: Ergebnisse der Ausgrabungen, 1, Berlin.
KRETSCHMER, P.
(1896), Einleitung in die Geschichte der Griechischen Sprache, Göttingen.
(1909), 'Zur Geschichte der griechischen Dialekte', Glotta, 1, 9-59.
(1924), 'Alaksandus, König von Vilusa', Glotta, 13, 205-13.
(1925), 'Die protindogermanische Schicht', Glotta, 14, 300-19.
(1930), 'Zur Frage der griechischen Namen in den hethitischen Texten', Glotta, 18, 161-70.
(1936a), 'Zum Balkan-Skythischen', Glotta, 24, 1-56.
(1936b), 'Nochmals die Hypachäer und Alaksandus', Glotta, 24, 203-51.
(1940), 'Die vorgriechischen Sprach- und Volksschichten', Glotta, 28, 231-79.
(1943), 'Die vorgriechischen Sprach- und Volksschichten', Glotta, 30, 84-218.
(1954), 'Achäer in Kleinasien zur Hethiterzeit', Glotta, 33, 1-25.
KRITSELI-PROVIDI, IOANNA
(1973), 'Τοιχογραφία ὀκτωσχήμου ἀσπίδος ἐκ Μυκηνῶν', AAA, 6, 176-81.
KRONASSER, H.
(1960), 'Παρνασσός-Λαρνασσός', Indogermanica: Festschrift für W. Krause, Heidelberg, 51-62.

KYPARISSIS, N.
(1919), 'Κεφαλληνιακά', AD, 5, 83-122.
(1925), ''Ανασκαφαὶ ἐν Κάτῳ Γουμενύτσῃ τῶν Καλαβρύτων',
PAAH, 43-7.
(1927), ''Εξ 'Αθηνῶν καὶ 'Αττικῆς', AD, 11, parartema,
44-66.
(1928), ''Ανασκαφὴ Μυκηναϊκοῦ νεκροταφείου ἐν 'Αγίῳ Βασι-
λείῳ Χαλανδρίτσης 'Αχαΐας', PAAH, 110-9.
(1930), ''Ανασκαφαὶ Μυκηναϊκῶν νεκροταφείων τῆς 'Αχαΐας',
PAAH, 81-8.
(1931), ''Ανασκαφαὶ ἐν Γουρζουμίσῃ ἀρχαίας 'Αχαΐας', PAAH,
71-3.
(1932), ''Ανασκαφαὶ λαξευτῶν θαλαμοειδῶν τάφων ἐν Γουρζουμίσῃ ἀρχαίας 'Αχαΐας', PAAH, 57-61.
(1933), ''Ανασκαφὴ Μυκηναϊκῶν νεκροταφείων ἀρχαίας
'Αχαΐας', PAAH, 90-3.
(1937), 'Μυκηναϊκὰ νεκροταφεῖα ἀρχαίας 'Αχαΐας', PAAH, 84-
93.
LABAT, R.
(1962), 'Le rayonnement de la langue et de l'écriture
akkadiennes au deuxième millénaire avant notre ère',
Syria, 39, 1-27.
LAFFINEUR, R.
(1974), 'L'incrustation à l'époque mycénienne', AC, 43,
5-37.
LAGARCE, J.
(1969), 'Quatre épées de bronze provenant d'une cachette
d'armurier à Enkomi-Alasia (Chypre)', Ugaritica, 6, Paris,
349-68.
LAMB, WINIFRED
(1919), 'Excavations at Mycenae: III. Frescoes from the
Ramp House', ABSA, 24, 189-99.
(1921), 'Mycenae: palace frescoes', ABSA, 25, 162-72, 249-
55.
LAMBERT, W.G.
(1974), 'Der Mythos im Alten Mesopotamien, sein Werden und
Vergehen', ZRG, 26, 1-16.
LANDAU, O.
(1958), Mykenisch-griechische Personennamen, Gothenburg.
LANG, MABEL L.
(1966a), 'Cn flocks', Proceedings of the Cambridge Colloquium on Mycenaean Studies, ed. L.R. Palmer and J. Chadwick, Cambridge, 250-9.
(1966b), 'Jn formulas and groups', Hesperia, 35, 397-412.
(1969), The Palace of Nestor, 2, Princeton.

LAROCHE, E.
(1957), 'Notes de toponymie anatolienne', Μνήμης Χάριν,
Gedenkschrift Paul Kretschmer, 2, Vienna, 1-7.
(1958), 'Etudes sur les hiéroglyphes hittites', Syria, 35,
252-83.
(1961), 'Etudes de toponymie anatolienne', RHA, 19, 57-98.
LAVIOSA, CLELIA
(1963), 'Sull'origine degli idoletti fittili micenei',
ASAA, 41/42, 7-24.
(1968a), 'Origini minoiche della plastica micenea', PDKS2,
1, 374-82.
(1968b), 'Il Lord di Asine è una "sfinge"?', CMic, 1, 87-90
(1969), 'La marina micenea', ASAA, 47/48, 7-40.
(1974), 'La campagne de fouilles de 1972 à Iasos', TAD, 21,
103-8.
LAWRENCE, A.W.
(1973), Greek Architecture, 3rd ed., Harmondsworth.
LEHMANN, G.A.
(1970), 'Der Untergang des Hethitischen Grossreiches und
die neuen Texte aus Ugarit', UF, 2, 39-73.
LEHMANN, H.
(1932), 'Die geographischen Grundlagen der kretisch-
mykenischen Kultur', GZ, 38, 334-46.
(1937), Argolis, 1, Athens.
LEJEUNE, M.
(1958), Mémoires de Philologie Mycénienne, 1, Paris.
(1971), Mémoires de Philologie Mycénienne, 2, Rome.
(1972), Mémoires de Philologie Mycénienne, 3, Rome.
LENCMAN, JA.A.
(1966), Die Sklaverei im Mykenischen und Homerischen
Griechenland, Wiesbaden.
LENSCHAU, T.
(1916), 'Bericht über griechische Geschichte (1907-1914)',
BJ, 176, 129-99.
LERAT, L.
(1935), 'Trouvailles mycéniennes à Delphes', BCH, 59,
329-75.
(1938), 'Fouilles de Delphes (1934-1935)', RA, 183-227.
LESKY, A.
(1955), 'Griechischer Mythos und Vorderer Orient',
Saeculum, 6, 35-52.
(1966), 'Der Mythos im Verständnis der Antike I: Von der
Frühzeit bis Sophokles', Gymnasium, 74, 14-44.
LEVI, D.
(1925), 'Le cretule di Haghia Triada', ASAA, 8/9, 71-156.
(1960), 'Per una nuova classificazione della civiltà
minoica', PP, 15, 81-121.
(1961), 'Le due prime campagne di scavo a Iasos (1960-
1961)', ASAA, 39/40, 505-71.

(1962), 'Ricerca scientifica e polemica sull'evoluzione della civiltà minoica', PP, 17, 206-30.
(1965), 'Le campagne 1962-1964 a Iasos', ASAA, 43/44, 401-546.
(1967), 'Gli scavi di Iasos', ASAA, 45/46, 537-90.
(1968), 'Continuità della tradizione micenea nell'arte greca arcaica', CMic, 1, 185-215.
(1969), 'Iasos: le campagne di scavo 1969-70', ASAA, 47/48, 461-532.
LEVI, M.A.
(1964), 'Aspetti della società micenea e dello stato miceneo', NRS, 48, 91-9.
LINDGREN, MARGARETA
(1968), 'Two Linear B problems reconsidered from a methodological point of view', OAth, 8, 61-76.
(1973), The People of Pylos, Uppsala.
LITTAUER, MARY A.
(1972), 'The military use of the chariot in the Aegean in the Late Bronze Age', AJA, 76, 145-57.
LITTAUER, MARY A. & CROUWEL, J.
(1973), 'Evidence for horse bits from Shaft Grave IV at Mycenae?', PZ, 48, 207-13.
LOLLING, H.G.
(1880), Das Kuppelgrab bei Menidi, Athens.
(1884), 'Mittheilungen aus Thessalien', AM, 9, 97-116.
LOLLING, H.G. & WOLTERS, P.
(1886), 'Das Kuppelgrab bei Dimini', AM, 11, 435-43.
(1887), 'Das Kuppelgrab bei Dimini II', AM, 12, 136-8.
LONG, CHARLOTTE R.
(1974), The Ayia Triadha Sarcophagus, Gothenburg.
LOPEZ EIRE, A.
(1967), 'Los topónimos en "-ssos" y "-nthos" y el Indo-europeo', Zephyrus, 18, 129-35.
(1970), 'Las migraciones griegas a la luz de la dialectología', Zephyrus, 21/22, 289-98.
LORANDOU-PAPANTONIOU, P.
(1973), 'Τμῆμα Μυκηναϊκῆς λάρνακος ἐκ τῆς Συλλογῆς Κ. Πολύτου', AAA, 6, 169-76.
LORD, L.E.
(1939), 'Watchtowers and fortresses in Argolis', AJA, 43, 78-84.
LORIMER, HILDA L.
(1950), Homer and the Monuments, London.
LUCE, J.V.
(1969), The End of Atlantis, London.
(1976), 'Thera and the devastation of Minoan Crete: a new interpretation of the evidence', AJA, 80, 9-18.

MCDONALD, W.A.
(1964), 'Overland communications in Greece during LH III, with special reference to southwest Peloponnese', Mycenaean Studies, ed. E.L. Bennett, Madison, 217-40.
(1972), 'Excavations at Nichoria in Messenia: 1969-71', Hesperia, 41, 218-73.
MCDONALD, W.A. & HOPE SIMPSON, R.
(1961), 'Prehistoric habitation in southwestern Peloponnese', AJA, 65, 221-60.
(1964), 'Further exploration in southwestern Peloponnese: 1962-1963', AJA, 68, 229-45.
(1972), 'Archaeological exploration' in McDonald and Rapp, 1972, 117-47.
MCDONALD, W.A. & RAPP, G.R. (EDITORS)
(1972), The Minnesota Messenia Expedition: Reconstructing a Bronze Age Regional Environment, Minneapolis.
MACKEPRANG, M.B.
(1938), 'Late Mycenaean vases', AJA, 42, 537-59.
MACNAMARA, ELLEN
(1970), 'A group of bronzes from Surbo: new evidence for Aegean contacts with Apulia during Mycenaean III B and C', PPS, 36, 241-60.
MCNEAL, R.A.
(1972), 'The Greeks in history and prehistory', Antiquity, 46, 19-28.
(1975), 'Helladic prehistory through the looking-glass', Historia, 24, 385-401.
MACQUEEN, J.G.
(1968), 'Geography and history in western Asia Minor in the second millennium BC', AS, 18, 169-85.
MADDOLI, G.
(1962), 'Studi sul pantheon miceneo', AMAT, 27, 51-130.
(1967), 'Potinija asiwija, Asia e le relazioni micenee con l'Anatolia settentrionale', SMEA, 4, 11-22.
(1970), 'Δᾶμος e βασιλῆες, contributo allo studio delle origini della polis', SMEA, 12, 7-57.
MAIER, F.G.
(1958), 'Die Stadtmauer von Thisbe', AM, 73, 17-25.
(1972), 'Recent discoveries at Kouklia (Old Paphos)', PPDKS, 93-102.
MAIURI, A.
(1923), 'Jalisos, 1: la necropoli micenea', ASAA, 6/7, 86-256.
MALLORY, J.
(1973), 'A short history of the Indo-European problem', JIES, 1, 21-65.
MANESSY-GUITTON, JACQUELINE
(1966), 'Temenos', IF, 71, 14-38.

MARINATOS, S.N.
(1932), 'Αἱ ἀνασκαφαὶ Goekoop ἐν Κεφαλληνίᾳ', AE, 1-47.
(1933a), 'Αἱ ἐν Κεφαλληνίᾳ ἀνασκαφαὶ Goekoop 2', AE, 68-100
(1933b), 'La marine créto-mycénienne', BCH, 57, 170-235.
(1937), 'Αἱ Μινωϊκαὶ θεαὶ τοῦ Γάζι', AE, 278-91.
(1939), 'The volcanic destruction of Minoan Crete',
Antiquity, 13, 425-39.
(1951), ''Ανασκαφαὶ ἐν Κεφαλληνίᾳ', PAAH, 184-6.
(1953), 'Περὶ τοὺς νέους βασιλικοὺς τάφους τῶν Μυκηνῶν',
GAK, 54-88.
(1955), ''Ανασκαφαὶ ἐν Πύλῳ', PAAH, 245-55.
(1956), ''Ανασκαφαὶ ἐν Πύλῳ', PAAH, 202-6.
(1961), ''Ανασκαφαὶ Πύλου', AD, 17, Β', 101-3.
(1965a), ''Ανασκαφαὶ ἐν Πύλῳ (1964)', AD, 20, Β'1, 201-6.
(1965b), ''Ανασκαφαὶ ἐν Πύλῳ', PAAH, 102-20.
(1966), ''Ανασκαφαὶ ἐν Πύλῳ', AD, 21, Β'1, 166-8.
(1968), Excavations at Thera, 1, Athens.
(1969), Excavations at Thera, 2, Athens.
(1970a), Excavations at Thera, 3, Athens.
(1970b), ''Ανασκαφαὶ Μαραθῶνος', PAAH, 5-28.
(1971), Excavations at Thera, 4, Athens.
(1972), Excavations at Thera, 5, Athens.
(1973), Die Ausgrabungen auf Thera und ihre Probleme,
Vienna.
(1974), Excavations at Thera, 6, Athens.
MASSON, EMILIA
(1967), Recherches sur les plus Anciens Emprunts Sémitiques
en Grec, Paris.
(1969), 'La plus ancienne tablette chypro-minoenne (Enkomi,
1955)', Minos, 10, 64-77.
MASSON, O.
(1973), 'A propos de l'île d'Alasia', Kadmos, 12, 98-9.
MASTROKOSTAS, E.I.
(1964), ''Ανασκαφὴ τοῦ τείχους Δυμαίων', PAAH, 60-7.
(1965), ''Ανασκαφὴ τοῦ τείχους Δυμαίων', PAAH, 121-36.
MATZ, F.
(1928), Die Frühkretischen Siegel, Berlin/Leipzig.
(1958a), Göttererscheinung und Kultbild im Minoischen
Kreta, Mainz.
(1958b), Review of Mylonas, 1957, Gnomon, 30, 321-8.
(1973), 'The zenith of Minoan civilization', CAH, 2/1, 3rd
ed., 557-81.
MAVRIYANNAKI, CATERINA
(1967), 'Incinerazioni del Tardo Minoico III nella Creta
occidentale', ASAA, 45/46, 167-79.
(1972), Recherches sur les Larnakes Minoennes de la Crète
Occidentale, Rome.

MEGAS, G.A.
(1933), 'Die Sage von Danaos und den Danaiden', Hermes, 68,
415-28.
MELLAART, J.
(1958), 'The end of the Early Bronze Age in Anatolia and
the Aegean', AJA, 62, 9-33.
(1960), 'Anatolia and the Balkans', Antiquity, 34, 270-8.
(1968), 'Anatolian trade with Europe and Anatolian geography and culture provinces in the Late Bronze Age', AS,
18, 187-202.
(1969), Review of Crossland, 1971, JHS, 89, 172-3.
(1971), 'Anatolia, c. 2300-1750 BC', CAH, 1/2, 3rd ed.,
681-703.
MELLINK, MACHTELD J.
(1956), 'The royal tombs at Alaca Hüyük and the Aegean
world', ANE, 39-58.
MERKELBACH, R. & WEST, M.L.
(1967), Fragmenta Hesiodea, Oxford.
MERRILLEES, R.S.
(1965), 'Reflections on the Late Bronze Age in Cyprus',
OAth, 6, 139-48.
(1968), The Cypriote Bronze Age Pottery found in Egypt, Lund
(1972a), 'Aegean Bronze Age relations with Egypt', AJA,
76, 281-94.
(1972b), 'Alasia', PPDKS, 111-9.
(1973), 'Settlement, sanctuary and cemetery in Bronze Age
Cyprus', ASA, 1, 44-57.
(1974), Trade and Transcendence in the Bronze Age Levant,
Gothenburg.
(1976), 'Problems in Cypriote history', The Archaeology of
Cyprus, Recent Developments, ed. N. Robertson, Park Ridge,
N.J., 15-38.
MERTENS, P.
(1960), 'Les peuples de la mer', CE, 35, 65-88.
MEYER, E.
(1928), Geschichte des Altertums, 2/1, 2nd ed., Stuttgart.
MILCHHÖFER, A.
(1877), 'Altes Grab bei Spata', AM, 2, 82-4.
MILOJCIĆ, V.
(1948), 'Die dorische Wanderung im Lichte der vorgeschichtlichen Funde', AA, 12-36.
(1955a), 'Zur Frage der Schnurkeramik in Griechenland',
Germania, 33, 151-4.
(1955b), 'Vorbericht über die Ausgrabungen auf den Magulen
von Otzaki, Arapi und Gremnos bei Larisa 1955', AA, 182-231.
(1956), 'Bericht über die Ausgrabungen auf der Gremnos-
Magula bei Larisa 1956', AA, 141-83.
(1959a), 'Bericht über Ausgrabungen in Thessalien, 1958',
AA, 36-56.

(1959b), 'Ergebnisse der deutschen Ausgrabungen in Thessalien (1953-1958)', JRGZM, 6, 1-56.
(1974), 'Bericht über die deutschen archäologischen Ausgrabungen in Thessalien 1973', AAA, 7, 43-75.
MILTNER, F.
(1934), 'Die dorische Wanderung', Klio, 27, 54-68.
MINGAZZINI, P.
(1967), 'Spigolature vascolari', ASAA, 45/46, 327-53.
MITTELBERGER, H.
(1966), 'Genetiv und Adjektiv in den altanatolischen Sprachen', Kratylos, 11, 99-106.
MOMIGLIANO, A.D.
(1958), 'The place of Herodotus in the history of historiography', History, 43, 1-13.
MONACO, G.
(1941/1949), 'Scavi nella zona micenea di Jaliso', Clara Rhodos, 10, Rhodes, 45-183.
MONEY, J.
(1973), 'The destruction of Acrotiri', Antiquity,47, 50-3.
MORPURGO DAVIES, ANNA
(1963), Mycenaeae Graecitatis Lexicon, Rome.
(1968), 'Fabbri e schiavi a Pilo', PP, 23, 220-2.
MORRICONE, L.
(1965), 'Eleone e Langada: sepolcreti della tarda età del bronze a Coo', ASAA, 43/44, 5-311.
(1972), 'Coo - scavi e scoperte nel "Serraglio" e in località minori (1935-1943)', ASAA, 50/51, 139-396.
MÜHLESTEIN, H.
(1956), Die oka-Tafeln von Pylos, Basel.
MUHLY, J.D.
(1970), 'Homer and the Phoenicians', Berytus, 19, 19-64.
(1972), 'The land of Alashiya: references to Alashiya in the texts of the second millennium BC and the history of Cyprus in the Late Bronze Age', PPDKS, 201-19.
(1973), Copper and Tin: The Distribution of Mineral Resources and the Nature of the Metals Trade in the Bronze Age, New Haven.
(1974), 'Hittites and Achaeans: Ahhijawa redomitus', Historia, 23, 129-45.
MÜLDER, D.
(1910), Die Ilias und ihre Quellen, Berlin.
MÜLLER, K.
(1909), 'Alt-Pylos II', AM, 34, 269-328.
(1915), 'Frühmykenische Reliefs aus Kreta und vom griechischen Festland', JDAI, 30, 242-336.
(1930), Die Architektur der Burg und des Palastes, Tiryns, 3, Augsburg.

MÜLLER, V.K.
(1918), 'Die Ziernadel aus dem III. mykenischen Schachtgrab', AM, 43, 153-64.
(1927), 'Studien zur kretisch-mykenischen Kunst II',
JDAI, 42, 1-29.
(1944), 'Development of the "megaron" in prehistoric
Greece', AJA, 48, 342-8.
MÜLLER-KARPE, H.
(1962), 'Zur spätbronzezeitlichen Bewaffnung in Mittel-
europa und Griechenland', Germania, 40, 255-87.
MUSSCHE, H.F. (EDITOR)
(1967a), Thorikos 1964, Brussels.
(1967b), Thorikos 1965, Brussels.
(1968), Thorikos 1963, Brussels.
(1969), Thorikos 1966/1967, Brussels.
(1971), Thorikos 1968, Brussels.
(1973), Thorikos 1969, Brussels.
MYLONAS, G.E.
(1951a), 'The cult of the dead in Helladic times', Studies
Presented to D.M. Robinson, 1, St Louis, 64-105.
(1951b), 'The figured Mycenaean stelai', AJA, 55, 134-47.
(1956), 'Seated and multiple Mycenaean figurines in the
National Museum of Athens, Greece', ANE, 110-21.
(1957), Ancient Mycenae, London.
(1958), ''Η ἀκρόπολις τῶν Μυκηνῶν', AE, 153-207.
(1959), Aghios Kosmas, Princeton.
(1961), Eleusis and the Eleusinian Mysteries, Princeton.
(1962), 'The Luvian invasions of Greece', Hesperia, 31,
284-309.
(1964), 'Priam's Troy and the date of its fall', Hesperia,
33, 352-80.
(1966a), Mycenae and the Mycenaean Age, Princeton.
(1966b), 'The east wing of the palace of Mycenae',
Hesperia, 35, 419-26.
(1969a), 'The wanax of the Mycenaean state', Classical
Studies Presented to B.E. Perry, Urbana/Chicago, 66-79.
(1969b), ''Ο πέμπτος λακκοειδής τάφος τοῦ κύκλου A τῶν
Μυκηνῶν', AE, 125-42.
(1972), Τὸ Θρησκευτικὸν Κέντρον τῶν Μυκηνῶν, Athens.
(1973), 'Ο Ταφικὸς Κύκλος B τῶν Μυκηνῶν, Athens.
MYLONAS, G.E. & TRAVLOS, I.
(1952), ''Ανασκαφαὶ ἐν 'Ελευσῖνι', PAAH, 53-72.
NEHRING, A.
(1961), 'Zur "Realität" des Urindogermanischen', Lingua,
10, 357-68.
NIBBI, ALESSANDRA
(1976), The Sea Peoples and Egypt, Park Ridge, N.J.

NICOLAOU, K.
(1973), 'The first Mycenaeans in Cyprus', MEM, 51-61.
NILSSON, M.P.
(1932), The Mycenaean Origin of Greek Mythology, Berkeley/
Los Angeles.
(1950), The Minoan-Mycenaean Religion, 2nd ed., Lund.
(1960), Opuscula Selecta, 3, Lund.
(1967), Geschichte der Griechischen Religion, 1, 3rd ed.,
Munich.
NINKOVICH, D. & HEEZEN, B.C.
(1965), 'Santorini tephra', CP, 17, 413-53.
NOACK, F.
(1894), 'Arne', AM, 19, 405-85.
NOCK, A.D.
(1943), Review of Persson, 1942b, AJA, 47, 492-6.
NOUGAYROL, J.
(1968), 'Textes suméro-accadiens des archives et bibliothèques privées d'Ugarit', Ugaritica, 5, Paris, 1-446.
NYLANDER, C.
(1963), 'The fall of Troy', Antiquity, 37, 6-11.
OELMANN, F.
(1912), 'Ein achäisches Herrenhaus auf Kreta', JDAI, 27,
38-51.
OLDFATHER, W.A.
(1916), 'Studies in the history and topography of Locris
I', AJA, 20, 32-61.
OLIVIER, J.-P.
(1959), 'Etude d'un nom de métier mycénien: di-pte-ra-
po-ro', AC, 28, 165-85.
(1960), A Propos d'une 'Liste' de Desservants de Sanctu-
aire, Brussels.
(1967), 'Le damokoro: un fonctionnaire mycénien', Minos,
8, 118-22.
(1969), The Mycenae Tablets IV, Leiden.
O'NEIL, J.L.
(1970), 'The words Qasireu, Qasirewija and Kerosija', ZA,
20, 11-14.
ORLANDOS, A.K.
(1955), 'Κωπαΐς (Γκλᾶ)', EAE, 34-5.
(1956a), '"Αρνη (Κωπαΐς)', EAE, 32.
(1956b), ''Ιωλκός (Βόλος)', EAE, 43-50.
(1956c), ''Αχαΐα: Φαραί', EAE, 88-90.
(1957a), '"Αρνη Κωπαΐδος (Γκλᾶ)', EAE, 25-30.
(1957b), ''Ιωλκός', EAE, 31-6.
(1958a), 'Κωπαΐς, "Αρνη (Γκλᾶ)', EAE, 42-8.
(1958b), 'Κορινθΐα: Σολύγεια (Γαλατάκι)', EAE, 112-8.
(1959a), 'Κωπαΐς, "Αρνη (Γκλᾶ)', EAE, 20-3.
(1959b), 'Κῶς', EAE, 131-4.
(1959c), 'Κρήτη: Κεφάλα Χόνδρου', EAE, 134-9.

(1960a), 'Κωπαΐς, "Αρνη (Γκλᾶ)', EAE, 37-48.
(1960b), ''Ιωλκός', EAE, 55-61.
(1960c), 'Πύλος', EAE, 145-58.
(1961a), 'Κωπαΐς, "Αρνη-Γλᾶς', EAE, 39-48.
(1961b), ''Ιωλκός', EAE, 51-60.
(1961c), 'Μυκῆναι, ἔξω τῶν τειχῶν', EAE, 156-62.
(1961d), ''Αρχαία "Ηλις', EAE, 177-88.
(1968), 'Μυκῆναι', EAE, 5-12.
(1969), 'Τάναγρα', EAE, 5-11.
(1970), 'Τάναγρα', EAE, 13-22.
(1971a), 'Τάναγρα', EAE, 11-21.
(1971b), 'Μυκῆναι', EAE, 131-43.
(1972), 'Μυκῆναι', EAE, 59-67.
(1973), 'Τάναγρα', EAE, 11-14.
(1974a), 'Τάναγρα', EAE, 10-16.
(1974b), 'Μυκῆναι', EAE, 53-7.
(1974c), 'Μεσσηνία', EAE, 78-82.
OTTEN, H.
(1963), 'Neue Quellen zum Ausklang des hethitischen
Reiches', MDOG, 94, 1-23.
(1969), Sprachliche Stellung und Datierung des Madduwatta-
Textes, Wiesbaden.
PAGE, D.L.
(1959), History and the Homeric Iliad, Berkeley/Los Angeles
(1964), 'Homer and the Trojan War', JHS, 84, 17-20.
(1970), The Santorini Volcano and the Desolation of Minoan
Crete (Hellenic Society Supplementary Paper 12), London.
PALMER, L.R.
(1955), Achaeans and Indo-Europeans, Oxford.
(1957), 'A Mycenaean tomb inventory', Minos, 5, 58-92.
(1958), 'New religious texts from Pylos (1955)', TPS, 1-35.
(1961), 'Linear B texts of economic interest', IBK, 7/8,
1-12.
(1963), 'The find-places of the Knossos tablets', On the
Knossos Tablets, Oxford.
(1965), Mycenaeans and Minoans, 2nd ed., London.
(1969a), The Interpretation of Mycenaean Greek Texts, 2nd
ed., Oxford.
(1969b), The Penultimate Palace of Knossos, Rome.
(1972a), Descriptive and Comparative Linguistics: A
Critical Introduction, London.
(1972b), 'Mycenaean inscribed vases II', Kadmos, 11, 27-46.
PANAGL, O.
(1973), 'Eine Wortstellungsopposition im Mykenischen',
AC(D), 9, 3-14.
PAPADIMITRIOU, I.
(1948), ''Ανασκαφαὶ ἐν Βραυρῶνι τῆς 'Αττικῆς', PAAH, 81-90.
(1952), ''Ανασκαφαὶ ἐν Μυκήναις', PAAH, 427-72.
(1953), ''Ανασκαφαὶ ἐν Μυκήναις', PAAH, 205-37.

(1954a), 'Μυκηναϊκοὶ τάφοι 'Αλυκῆς Γλυφάδας', PAAH, 72-88.
(1954b), ''Ανασκαφαὶ ἐν Μυκήναις', PAAH, 242-69.
(1955), 'Μυκηναϊκοὶ τάφοι 'Αλυκῆς Γλυφάδας', PAAH, 78-99.
(1957), 'Μυκηναϊκοὶ τάφοι 'Αλυκῆς Γλυφάδας', PAAH, 29-34.
PAPAVASILIOU, G.A.
(1910), Περὶ τῶν ἐν Εὐβοίᾳ 'Αρχαίων Τάφων, Athens.
PAPAZOGLU, F.
(1961), 'К вопросу о преемственности общественного строя в микенской и гомеровской Греции', VDI, 75, 23-41.
PARRY, A.M.
(1972), 'Thucydides' historical perspective', YCS, 22, 47-61.
PECORELLA, P.E.
(1962), 'Aspetti e problemi della espansione micenea verso l'oriente', AMAT, 27, 1-50.
PEET, T.E.
(1927), 'The Egyptian writing-board B.M. 5647, bearing Keftiu names', Essays in Aegean Archaeology Presented to Sir Arthur Evans, ed. S. Casson, Oxford, 90-9.
PELON, O.
(1974), 'Sur deux tholoi de Messénie', BCH, 98, 37-50.
PENDLEBURY, J.D.S.
(1930), 'Egypt and the Aegean in the Late Bronze Age', JEA, 16, 75-92.
(1939), The Archaeology of Crete, London.
PENDLEBURY, J.D.S. & MONEY-COUTTS, M.
(1937), 'Karphi: a city of refuge of the early Iron Age in Crete', ABSA, 38, 57-145.
PERDRIZET, P.
(1908), Fouilles de Delphes, ed. T. Homolle, 5, Paris.
PERPILLOU, J.-L.
(1968), 'La tablette PY AN 724 et la flotte pylienne', Minos, 9, 205-18.
PERSSON, A.W.
(1931), The Royal Tombs at Dendra, Lund.
(1942a), New Tombs at Dendra, Lund.
(1942b), The Religion of Greece in Prehistoric Times, Berkeley/Los Angeles.
PETRAKOS, V.
(1973), ''Ανασκαφὴ ἐν Κύρρᾳ κατὰ τὸ 1972', AAA, 6, 70-3.
PETRUSEVSKI, M.D.
(1965), 'Aukewa Damokoro', ZA, 15, 12.
(1970), 'Interprétations de quelques mots grecs mycéniens', SMEA, 12, 121-35.
(1971), 'Zum Gesellschaftsaufbau der Mykener: Die myke-nische Form wa-na-so-i und ihre Bedeutung', JW, 2, 49-53.
PETSAS, Ph.M.
(1969), 'Χρονικὰ ἀρχαιολογικὰ 1966-1967', Makedonika, 9, 101-216.

PHILIPPSON, A.
(1892), Der Peloponnes: Versuch einer Landeskunde auf
Geologischer Grundlage, Berlin.
(1950/1959), Die Griechischen Landschaften, Frankfurt.
PICARD, C.
(1948), Les Religions Préhelléniques, Paris.
PICARD-SCHMITTER, MARIE-THÉRÈSE
(1968), 'Observations sur les "cuirasses" mycéniennes à
propos de l'inscription de Pylos Sh 736', CMic, 1, 134-52.
PIGGOTT, S.
(1965), Ancient Europe, Edinburgh.
PINI, I.
(1968), Beiträge zur Minoischen Gräberkunde, Wiesbaden.
(1974), 'Zur Chronologie der Glyptik in Späthelladisch
III', Die Kretisch-mykenische Glyptik und ihre gegenwärtigen Probleme, Boppard, 96-100.
PISANI, V.
(1959), 'Indogermanisch und Sanskrit', ZVS, 76, 43-51.
(1974), Indogermanisch und Europa, Munich.
PLATON, N.
(1959), 'Συμβολὴ εἰς τὴν σπουδὴν τῆς μινωικῆς τοιχο-
γραφίας', KX, 13, 319-45.
(1963), ''Ανασκαφαὶ Ζάκρου', PAAH, 160-88.
PLATON, N. & TOULOUPA, EVA
(1964), 'Oriental seals from the Palace of Cadmus: unique
discoveries in Boeotian Thebes', ILN, 28 November, 859-61.
POLYAKOVA, G.F.
(1968), 'Teojo doero/ra в системе Пилосского землев-
ладения', VDI, 103, 13-27.
POPHAM, M.R.
(1964), The Last Days of the Palace at Knossos, Lund.
(1965), 'Some Late Minoan III pottery from Crete', ABSA,
60, 316-42.
(1970), The Destruction of the Palace at Knossos, Gothenburg.
(1973), 'The Unexplored Mansion at Knossos', JHS Archaeological Report, 19, 50-61.
(1975), 'Late Minoan II Crete: a note', AJA, 79, 372-4.
POPHAM, M.R. & MILBURN, ELIZABETH
(1971), 'The Late Helladic IIIC pottery of Xeropolis
(Lefkandi), a summary', ABSA, 66, 333-52.
POPHAM, M.R. & SACKETT, L.H.
(1968), Excavations at Lefkandi, Euboea, 1964-66, London.
PORZIG, W.
(1954), 'Sprachgeographische Untersuchungen zu den alt-
griechischen Dialekten', IF, 61, 147-69.

PRESS, LUDWICKA
(1967), Architektura w Ikonografii Przedgreckiej, Wroclaw/
Warsaw/Krakow.
(1970), 'Ägäische Grabstätten und Bestattungsriten', Das
Altertum, 16, 83-8.
PRIGNAUD, J.
(1964), 'Caftorim et Kerétim', RB, 71, 215-29.
PRITCHARD, J.B.
(1968), 'New evidence on the role of the Sea Peoples in
Canaan at the beginning of the Iron Age', The Role of the
Phoenicians in the Interaction of Mediterranean Civili-
zations, Beirut, 99-112.
PROTONARIOU-DEILAKI, EVANGELIA
(1960), ''Ανασκαφὴ λαξευτοῦ Μυκηναϊκοῦ τάφου ἐν 'Ηραίῳ
"Αργους', AE, 123-35.
(1965), 'Περὶ τῆς πύλης τῶν Μυκηνῶν', AE, 7-26.
(1970), 'Δύο μυκηναϊκοὶ τάφοι εἰς Λάρισαν "Αργους', AAA,
3, 301-3.
PULGRAM, E.
(1959), 'Proto-Indo-European reality and reconstruction',
Language, 35, 421-6.
RACHET, G.
(1971), 'Les tombes à tholos dans le monde égéen',
Archeologia (Paris), 42, 64-9.
RAISON, J.
(1963), 'Une controverse sur la chronologie des tablettes
cnossiennes', Minos, 7, 151-70.
(1964), 'Nouvelles discussions sur la stratigraphie
cnossienne', REG, 77, 260-73.
(1966), Review of Catling and Millett, 1965a, RA, 358-9.
(1968), Les Vases à Inscriptions Peintes de l'Age
Mycénien, Rome.
RANOSZEK, R.
(1950), 'A propos de KUB XX III 1', AO, 18/4, 236-42.
RAPP, G. & COOK, S.B.
(1973), 'Thera pumice recovered from LH IIA stratum at
Nichoria', AAA, 6, 136-7.
RENAUDIN, L.
(1923), 'La nécropole "mycénienne" de Skhinokhori-
Lyrkeia (?)', BCH, 47, 190-240.
RENFREW, A.C.
(1972), The Emergence of Civilisation, London.
REUSCH, HELGA
(1953a), 'Vorschlag zur Ordnung der Fragmente von Frauen-
friesen aus Mykenai', AA, 26-56.
(1953b), 'Ein Schildfresko aus Theben (Böotien)', AA, 16-25
(1956), Die Zeichnerische Rekonstruktion des Frauenfrieses
im Böotischen Theben, Berlin.

(1958), 'Zum Wandschmuck des Thronsaales in Knossos', Min,
334-58.
RIDDER, A. DE
(1894), 'Fouilles de Gha', BCH, 18, 271-310.
(1895), 'Fouilles d'Orchomène', BCH, 19, 137-224.
RIEMSCHNEIDER, M.
(1956), 'Die Herkunft der Philister', ActAnt, 4, 17-29.
RIIS, P.J.
(1970), Sūkās, 1, Copenhagen.
(1973), 'The Mycenaean expansion in the light of the
Danish excavations at Hama and Sukas', MEM, 198-206.
RISCH, E.
(1955), 'Die Gliederung der griechischen Dialekte in neuer
Sicht', MH, 12, 61-76.
(1958), 'L'interprétation de la série des tablettes carac-
térisées par le mot o-ka', Athenaeum, 36, 334-59.
(1966), 'Mykenisch seremokaraoi oder seremokaraore?',
SMEA, 1, 53-66.
RODDEN, R.J.
(1964), 'Recent discoveries from prehistoric Macedonia',
BS, 5, 109-24.
RODENWALDT, G.
(1911a), 'Die Wandgemälde von Tiryns', AM, 36, 198-206.
(1911b), 'Fragmente mykenischer Wandgemälde', AM, 36,
221-50.
(1912a), 'Votivpinax aus Mykenai', AM, 37, 129-40.
(1912b), 'Die Fresken des Palastes', Tiryns, 2, Athens.
(1921), Der Fries des Megarons von Mykenai, Halle.
ROMAIOS, K.A.
(1915), ''Εκ τοῦ προϊστορικοῦ Θέρμου', AD, 1, 225-79.
(1916), '"Ερευναι ἐν Θέρμῳ', AD, 2, 179-89.
(1954), ''Ανασκαφικὴ ἔρευνα κατὰ τὴν 'Ανάληψιν', PAAH,
270-86.
ROMILLY, JACQUELINE DE
(1956), Histoire et Raison chez Thucydide, Paris.
RUDOLPH, W.
(1971), 'Tiryns 1968: Mykenische und nachmykenische
Streufunde von der Unterburg', Tiryns, 5, Mainz, 87-103.
(1973), 'Die Nekropole am Prophitis Elias bei Tiryns',
Tiryns, 6, Mainz, 23-126.
RUIJGH, C.J.
(1967a), Etudes sur la Grammaire et le Vocabulaire du Grec
Mycénien, Amsterdam.
(1967b), 'A propos de myc. po-ti-ni-ja-we-jo', SMEA, 4,
40-52.
(1972), 'Quelques hypothèses en marge des tablettes En-Ep/
Eo-Eb de Pylos', SMEA, 15, 91-104.

RUIPÉREZ, M.S.
(1953), 'Sobre la prehistoria de los dialectos griegos',
Emerita, 21, 253-66.
RUTKOWSKI, B.
(1972), Cult Places in the Aegean World, Wroclaw/Warsaw/
Krakow/Gdansk.
RUTTER, J.B.
(1975a), 'Ceramic evidence for northern intruders in
southern Greece at the beginning of the Late Helladic IIIC
period', AJA, 79, 17-32.
(1975b), 'Evidence for a Mycenaean tomb of the Late Helladic IIA period in the Athenian Agora', Hesperia, 44, 375-8.
SACCONI, ANNA
(1969), 'Gli Achei in età micenea ed in Omero', ZA, 19,
13-19.
SACKETT, L.H.
(1966), 'Prehistoric Euboea: contributions toward a
survey', ABSA, 61, 33-112 (with others.)
SACKETT, L.H. & POPHAM, M.R.
(1965), 'Excavations at Palaikastro VI', ABSA, 60, 248-315.
SÄFLUND, G.
(1965), Excavations at Berbati 1936-1937, Stockholm.
SAKELLARAKIS, J.A.
(1970), 'Das Kuppelgrab A von Archanes und das kretisch-
mykenische Tieropferritual', PZ, 45, 135-219.
(1972), 'Μυκηναϊκὸς ταφικὸς περίβολος εἰς Κρήτην', AAA, 5,
399-419.
SAKELLARIOU, AGNES
(1953), 'La représentation du casque en dents de sanglier
(époque minoenne)', BCH, 77, 46-58.
(1962), '"Ενα σφράγισμα ἀπὸ τὴν Πύλο', Festschrift für
Friedrich Matz, Mainz, 19-22.
(1964), Die Mykenische Siegelglyptik, Lund.
(1966), Μυκηναϊκὴ Σφραγιδογλυφία, Athens.
(1971), 'Scène de bataille sur un vase mycénien en
pierre?', RA, 3-14.
(1974a), 'Un cratère d'argent avec scène de bataille provenant de la IVe tombe de l'acropole de Mycènes', AK, 17,
3-20.
(1974b), 'A propos de la chronologie des gemmes mycéniennes', Die Kretisch-mykenische Glyptik und ihre Gegenwärtigen Probleme, Boppard, 133-42.
(1975), 'La scène du "siège" sur le rhyton d'argent de
Mycènes d'après une nouvelle reconstitution', RA, 195-208.
SANDARS, NANCY K.
(1961), 'The first Aegean swords and their ancestry',
AJA, 65, 17-29.
(1963), 'Later Aegean bronze swords', AJA, 67, 117-53.

(1964), 'The last Mycenaeans and the European Late Bronze
Age', Antiquity, 38, 258-62.
(1971), 'From Bronze Age to Iron Age: a sequel to a sequel',
The European Community in Later Prehistory, Studies in
Honour of C.F.C. Hawkes, London, 1-29.
SARKADY, J.
(1973), 'Zur politischen Karte Griechenlands im mykenischen
Zeitalter', AC(D), 9, 15-24.
SAUSSEY, E.
(1924), 'La céramique philistine', Syria, 5, 169-85.
SCHACHERMEYR, F.
(1935), Hethiter und Achäer, Leipzig.
(1949), 'Welche geschichtlichen Ereignisse führten zur
Entstehung der mykenischen Kultur?', AO, 17/2, 331-50.
(1950), Poseidon und die Entstehung des Griechischen
Götterglaubens, Munich.
(1951), 'Streitwagen und Streitwagenbild im Alten Orient
und bei den mykenischen Griechen', Anthropos, 46, 705-53.
(1954), 'Prähistorische Kulturen Griechenlands', Paulys
Realencyclopädie der Classischen Altertumswissenschaft,
22/2, Stuttgart, 1350-548.
(1955), Die Ältesten Kulturen Griechenlands, Stuttgart.
(1958), 'Zur Frage der Lokalisierung von Achiawa', Min,
365-80.
(1962), 'Luwier auf Kreta?', Kadmos, 1, 27-39.
(1964), Die Minoische Kultur des Alten Kreta, Stuttgart.
(1967a), Ägäis und Orient, Vienna.
(1967b), 'Dorische Wanderung', Der Kleine Pauly, 2,
Stuttgart, 145-7.
(1968), 'Zum Problem der griechischen Einwanderung', CMic,
1, 297-317.
(1969), 'Hörnerhelme und Federkronen als Kopfbedeckungen
bei den "Seevölkern" der ägyptischen Reliefs', Ugaritica,
6, Paris, 451-9.
(1971), 'Forschungsbericht über die Ausgrabungen und Neu-
funde zur ägäischen Frühzeit, 1961-1965', AA, 295-419
(with others.)
(1974), 'Forschungsbericht über die Ausgrabungen und Neu-
funde zur ägäischen Frühzeit, 1961-1965', AA, 1-28.
(1976), Die Ägäische Frühzeit, 1, Vienna.
SCHAEFFER, C.F.-A.
(1932), 'Les fouilles de Minet-el-Beida et de Ras Shamra,
3me. campagne', Syria, 13, 1-27.
(1936a), 'Les fouilles de Ras Shamra-Ugarit, 7me. campagne', Syria, 17, 105-49.
(1936b), 'Sur un cratère mycénien de Ras Shamra', ABSA,
37, 212-35.
(1937), 'Die Stellung Ras Shamra-Ugarits zur kretischen
und mykenischen Kultur', JDAI, 52, 139-65.

(1949), Ugaritica, 2, Paris (with others.)
(1952), Enkomi-Alasia, 1, Paris.
(1953), 'La coupe en argent incrustée d'or d'Enkomi-Alasia', Syria, 30, 51-64.
(1955), 'A bronze sword from Ugarit with cartouche of Mineptah', Antiquity, 29, 226-9.
(1963), 'La XXIVe campagne de fouilles à Ras Shamra-Ugarit 1961', AAS, 13, 123-34.
(1968), 'Commentaires sur les lettres et documents trouvés dans les bibliothèques privées d'Ugarit', Ugaritica 5, Paris, 607-768.
SCHÄFER, J.
(1958), 'Elfenbeinspiegelgriffe des zweiten Jahrtausends', AM, 73, 73-87.
SCHERER, A.
(1956), 'Hauptprobleme der indogermanischen Altertumskunde (seit 1940)', Kratylos, 1, 3-21.
(1965), 'Indogermanische Altertumskunde (seit 1956)', Kratylos, 10, 1-24.
(1972), 'L'indeuropeizzazione dell'Europa e la formazione delle famiglie linguistiche indeuropee', Le Lingue dell' Europa, Atti del V Convegno Internazionale di Linguisti, Brescia, 21-36.
SCHLERATH, B.
(1973), Die Indogermanen, Innsbruck.
SCHLIEMANN, H.
(1878), Mykenae, Leipzig.
(1881), Orchomenos, Leipzig.
SCHLIEMANN, H. & DÖRPFELD, W.
(1886), Tiryns, Leipzig.
SCHMITT-BRANDT, R.
(1968), 'Die Oka-Tafeln in neuer Sicht', SMEA, 7, 69-96.
SCHNAUFER, A.
(1970), Frühgriechischer Totenglaube, Hildesheim.
SCHOLES, K.
(1956), 'The Cyclades in the Later Bronze Age: a synopsis', ABSA, 51, 9-40.
SCHOTT, A.
(1960), 'Minoische und mykenische Palasthöfe', JOAI, 45, 68-80.
SCHWEITZER, B.
(1928), Review of 1st ed. of Nilsson, 1950, Gnomon, 4, 169-93.
(1930), 'Hunde auf dem Dach', AM, 55, 107-18.
(1951), 'Megaron und Hofhaus in der Ägäis des 3-2. Jahrtausends v. Chr.', ABSA, 46, 160-7.
SCOUFOPOULOS, NIKI C.
(1971), Mycenaean Citadels, Gothenburg.

SEGERT, S.
(1958), 'Ugarit und Griechenland', Das Altertum, 4, 67-80.
SEIRADAKI, MERCY
(1960), 'Pottery from Karphi', ABSA, 55, 1-37.
SHELMERDINE, CYNTHIA W.
(1973), 'The Pylos Ma tablets reconsidered', AJA, 77, 261-75.
SINOS, S.
(1971), Die Vorklassischen Hausformen in der Ägäis, Mainz.
SJÖQVIST, E.
(1940), Problems of the Late Cypriote Bronze Age,Stockholm.
SLENCZKA, E.
(1974), Figürlich Bemalte Mykenische Keramik aus Tiryns, Tiryns, 7, Mainz.
SMALL, T.E.
(1966), 'A possible "shield-goddess" from Crete', Kadmos, 5, 103-7.
SMITH, E.B.
(1942), 'The megaron and its roof', AJA, 46, 99-118.
SMITH, W. STEVENSON
(1965), Interconnections in the Ancient Near East, Yale.
SNIJDER, G.A.S.
(1936), Kretische Kunst, Berlin.
SNODGRASS, A.M.
(1965), 'The Linear B arms and armour tablets - again', Kadmos, 4, 96-110.
(1967), Arms and Armour of the Greeks, London.
(1971), The Dark Age of Greece, Edinburgh.
(1973), 'Metal-work as evidence for immigration in the Late Bronze Age', BAMA, 209-14.
(1974), 'An historical Homeric society?', JHS, 94, 114-25.
(1975), 'Climatic change and the fall of the Mycenaean civilization', BICS, 22, 213-4.
SOMMER, F.
(1932), Die Ahhijava-Urkunden, Munich.
(1934), Ahhijavafrage und Sprachwissenschaft, Munich.
(1937), 'Ahhijava und kein Ende?', IF, 55, 169-297.
SOTIRIADIS, G.
(1900), ''Ανασκαφαὶ ἐν Θέρμῳ', EA, 161-212.
(1905), 'Untersuchungen in Boiotien und Phokis', AM, 30, 113-40.
(1932), ''Ανασκαφαὶ Μαραθῶνος', PAAH, 28-43.
SOURVINOU-INWOOD, CHRISTIANE
(1970), 'A-TE-MI-TO and A-TI-MI-TE', Kadmos, 9, 42-7.
(1972), 'The Theban stirrup-jars and East Crete', Minos, 13, 130-6.

SPYROPOULOS, T.G.
(1971a), 'Μυκηναϊκὰ τοιχογραφήματα ἐκ Θηβῶν', AD, 26, Α',
104-19.
(1971b), 'Μυκηναϊκὸς βασιλικὸς θαλαμωτὸς τάφος ἐν Θήβαις',
ΑΑΑ, 4, 161-4.
(1973), 'Εἰδήσεις ἐκ Βοιωτίας', ΑΑΑ, 6, 375-95.
(1974), 'Τὸ ἀνάκτορον τοῦ Μινύου εἰς τὸν Βοιωτικὸν
'Ορχομενόν', ΑΑΑ, 7, 313-25.
SPYROPOULOS, T.G. & CHADWICK, J.
(1975), The Thebes Tablets, 2, Salamanca.
STADELMANN, R.
(1969), 'Die Abwehr der Seevölker unter Ramses III',
Saeculum, 19, 156-71.
STAÏS, V.
(1893), ''Ανασκαφαὶ ἐν Θορικῷ', PAAH, 12-17.
(1895), 'Προϊστορικοὶ συνοικισμοὶ ἐν 'Αττικῇ καὶ Αἰγύνῃ,
Θορικός', ΕΑ, 193-264.
(1901), 'Αἱ ἐν Διμύνι (Θεσσαλίας) ἀνασκαφαί', PAAH, 37-40.
STEFANINI, R.
(1969), 'Il genitivo aggettivale nelle lingue anatoliche',
Athenaeum, 47, 290-302.
STEINER, G.
(1962), 'Neue Alasija-Texte', Kadmos, 1, 130-8.
(1964), 'Die Ahhijawa-Frage heute', Saeculum, 15, 365-92.
STELLA, LUIGIA A.
(1958), 'La religione greca nei testi micenei', Numen, 5,
18-57.
(1965), La Civiltà Micenea nei Documenti Contemporanei,
Rome.
STIEBING, W.H.
(1970), 'Another look at the origins of the Philistine
tombs at Tell el-Far'ah (S)', AJA, 74, 139-43.
STRATEN, F.T. VAN
(1969), 'The Minoan "genius" in Mycenaean Greece', BVAB,
44, 110-21.
(1970), 'A reaction upon "The Minoan genius in Mycenaean
Greece: a review"', Talanta, 2, 33-5.
STUBBINGS, F.H.
(1947), 'The Mycenaean pottery of Attica', ABSA, 42, 1-75.
(1951a), Mycenaean Pottery from the Levant, Cambridge.
(1951b), 'Some Mycenaean artists', ABSA, 46, 168-76.
(1973), 'The rise of Mycenaean civilization', CAH, 2/1,
3rd ed., 627-58.
(1975), 'The expansion of Mycenaean civilization; the
recession of Mycenaean civilization', CAH, 2/2, 3rd ed.,
165-87, 338-58.

STYRENIUS, C.-G.
(1962), 'The vases from the Submycenaean cemetery on
Salamis', OAth, 4, 103-23.
(1967), Submycenaean Studies, Lund.
(1975), 'Some notes on the new excavations at Asine',
OAth, 11, 177-83.
STYRENIUS, C.-G. & VIDÉN, A.
(1971), 'New excavations at Asine', AAA, 4, 147-8.
SULIMIRSKI, T.
(1971), 'Aegean trade with eastern Europe and its consequences', Mélanges Offerts à André Varagnac, Paris, 707-28.
SYMEONOGLOU, S.
(1973), Kadmeia, 1, Gothenburg.
SYMEONOGLOU, S. & TOULOUPA, EVA
(1964), ''Αρχαιότητες καὶ μνημεῖα Βοιωτίας', AD, 19, Β'2,
191-203.
(1965), ''Αρχαιότητες καὶ μνημεῖα Βοιωτίας', AD, 20, Β'2,
228-44.
(1966), ''Αρχαιότητες καὶ μνημεῖα Βοιωτίας', AD, 21, Β'1,
176-205.
SYRIOPOULOS, K.T.
(1964), 'Η Προϊστορία τῆς Πελοποννήσου, Athens.
(1968), 'Η Προϊστορια τῆς Στερεᾶς 'Ελλάδος, Athens.
SZEMERÉNYI, O.J.L.
(1957), 'The Greek nouns in -εύς', Μνήμης Χάριν, Gedenkschrift Paul Kretschmer, 2, Vienna, 159-81.
TAMVAKI, ANGELA
(1973), 'Some unusual Mycenaean terracottas from the
Citadel House area 1954-69', ABSA, 68, 207-65.
(1974), 'The seals and sealings from the Citadel House
area: a study in Mycenaean glyptic and iconography',
ABSA, 69, 259-93.
TAYLOUR, W.D.
(1958), Mycenean Pottery in Italy and Adjacent Areas,
Cambridge.
(1964), The Mycenaeans, London.
(1969), 'Mycenae, 1968', Antiquity, 43, 91-7.
(1970), 'New light on Mycenaean religion', Antiquity, 44,
270-80.
(1972), 'Excavations at Ayios Stephanos', ABSA, 67, 205-63.
TEGYEY, I.
(1968), 'The communities of Pylos', SM, 143-6.
(1970), 'Messenia and the catastrophe at the end of Late
Helladic III B', AC(D), 6, 3-7.
THEMELIS, P.G.
(1969), ''Ερετριακά', AE, 143-78.
(1974), 'Μυκηναϊκὸς δακτύλιος ἐκ Βαρκίζης', AAA, 7, 422-33.
THEOCHARIS, D.P.
(1950), ''Εκ τῆς προϊστορικῆς Βραυρῶνος', PAAH, 188-93.

THEOCHARIS, D.P. & MARIA D.
(1970), ''Εκ τοῦ νεκροταφείου τῆς 'Ιωλκοῦ', AAA, 3, 198-203.
THEOCHARIS, D.P. & CHORMOUZIADIS, Ch.
(1969), ''Αρχαιότητες καὶ μνημεῖα Θεσσαλίας', AD, 24, B'2, 221-6.
THEOCHARIS, MARIA D.
(1959), ''Εκ τῆς προϊστορικῆς Τρίκκης', Thessalika, 2, 69-79.
(1960a), 'A Knossian vase from Attica', Antiquity, 34, 266-9.
(1960b), 'Μυκηναϊκὰ ἐκ Λαρίσης', Thessalika, 3, 47-56.
THIEME, P.
(1953), Die Heimat der Indogermanischen Gemeinsprache, Wiesbaden.
THIERSCH, F.
(1879), 'Die Tholos des Atreus zu Mykenae', AM, 4, 177-82.
THIERSCH, H.
(1908), 'Die neueren Ausgrabungen in Palästine (Fortsetzung)', AA, 344-413.
THOMAS, CAROL G.
(1970a), 'The Mycenaean domesday records', PP, 25, 301-11.
(1970b), 'A Mycenaean hegemony? A reconsideration', JHS, 90, 184-92.
(1973), 'Matriarchy in early Greece: the Bronze and Dark Ages', Arethusa, 6, 173-95.
THOMAS, HELEN
(1938), 'The acropolis treasure from Mycenae', ABSA, 39, 65-87.
THOMSON, G.
(1949), Studies in Ancient Greek Society: The Prehistoric Aegean, London.
TOVAR, A.
(1954), 'Linguistics and prehistory', Word, 10, 333-50.
(1970), 'Zur Frage der Urheimat und zum Wort für "Name" als Kriterium für zwei Sprachwelten', IF, 75, 32-43.
TOYNBEE, A.J.
(1969), Some Problems of Greek History, Oxford.
TRITSCH, F.J.
(1958), 'The women of Pylos', Min, 406-45.
TRUBETZKOY, N.S.
(1939), 'Gedanken über das Indogermanenproblem', AL, 1, 81-9.
TSIRIVAKOS, I.
(1969), 'Μυκηναϊκὰ εἰς Μίστρον Εὐβοίας', AAA, 2, 30-1.
TSOUNTAS, K.D.
(1887), ''Αρχαιότητες ἐκ Μυκηνῶν', EA, 155-72.
(1888), ''Ανασκαφαὶ τάφων ἐν Μυκήναις', EA, 119-80.

(1889), '῎Ερευναι ἐν τῇ Λακωνικῇ καὶ ὁ τάφος τοῦ Βαφειοῦ', EA, 129-72.
(1891a), ''Εκ Μυκηνῶν', EA, 1-44.
(1891b), 'Τάφος θολωτὸς ἐν Κάμπῳ', EA, 189-91.
(1892), ''Εκ τοῦ 'Αμυκλαίου', EA, 1-26.
(1895), 'Zu einigen mykenischen Streitfragen', JDAI, 10, 143-51.
(1896), 'Γραπτὴ στήλη ἐκ Μυκηνῶν', EA, 1-22.
(1901), ''Ανασκαφαὶ ἐν Σέσκλῳ', PAAH, 41-2.
(1908), Αἰ Προϊστορικαὶ 'Ακρόπολεις Διμηνίου και Σέσκλου, Athens.
TYUMENEV, A.I.
(1959a), 'Восток и Микены', VI, 12, 58-74.
(1959b), 'Tereta пилосских надписей', VDI, 70, 24-32.
TZEDAKIS, Y.
(1969), ''Αρχαιότητες καὶ μνημεῖα δυτικῆς Κρήτης', AD, 24, Β'2, 428-36.
(1972), 'Κυπριακὴ κεραμεικὴ στὴ δυτικὴ Κρήτη', PPDKS,163-6.
VAGNETTI, LUCIA
(1970), 'I Micenei in Italia: la documentazione archeo-logica', PP, 25, 359-80.
VALMIN, M.N.
(1938), The Swedish Messenia Expedition, Lund.
(1953), 'Malthi-Epilog: Vorläufiger Bericht über die Schwedische Ausgrabungen in Messenien 1952', OAth, 1, 29-46
VAVRITSAS, A.
(1968), ''Ανασκαφὴ τριῶν μυκηναϊκῶν τάφων εἰς Καμίνι Βαρ-κίζης', AAA, 1, 110-2.
VENTRIS, M.G.F.
(1956), 'Mycenaean furniture on the Pylos tablets', Eranos, 53, 109-24.
VENTRIS, M.G.F. & CHADWICK, J.
(1973), Documents in Mycenaean Greek, 2nd ed., Cambridge.
VERCOUTTER, J.
(1954), Egyptiens et Préhellènes, Paris.
(1956), L'Egypte et le Monde Egéen Préhellénique, Paris.
VERDELIS, N.M.
(1951), ''Ανασκαφικαὶ ἔρευναι ἐν θεσσαλίᾳ', PAAH, 129-63.
(1952), ''Ανασκαφικαὶ ἔρευναι ἐν θεσσαλίᾳ', PAAH, 164-204.
(1953), ''Ανασκαφικαὶ ἔρευναι ἐν θεσσαλίᾳ', PAAH, 120-32.
(1958), 'Ο Πρωτογεωμετρικὸς Ρυθμὸς τῆς θεσσαλίας, Athens.
(1967), 'Neue Funde von Dendra', AM, 82, 1-53.
VERDELIS, N.M., FRENCH, ELIZABETH, & FRENCH, D.H.
(1965), 'Τίρυνς: Μυκηναϊκὴ ἐπίχωσις ἔξωθεν τοῦ δυτικοῦ τείχους τῆς ἀκροπόλεως, AD, 20, Α', 137-52.
VERMEULE, EMILY T.
(1955), 'A Mycenaean chamber tomb under the Temple of Ares', Hesperia, 24, 187-219.
(1958), 'Mythology in Mycenaean art', CJ, 54, 97-108.

(1960), 'The Mycenaeans in Achaia', AJA, 64, 1-21.
(1963), 'The fall of Knossos and the Palace style', AJA, 67, 195-9.
(1964), Greece in the Bronze Age, Chicago.
(1965), 'Painted Mycenaean larnakes', JHS, 85, 123-48.
(1967), 'The decline and end of Minoan and Mycenaean culture', A Land Called Crete: A Symposium in Memory of Harriet Boyd Hawes, Northampton (Mass.), 81-98.
(1974), Götterkult, Göttingen.
(1975), The Art of the Shaft Graves of Mycenae, Cincinnati.
VIROLLEAUD, C.
(1965), Le Palais Royal d'Ugarit, 5, Paris.
VITALIANO, C.J. & VITALIANO, DOROTHY B.
(1974), 'Volcanic tephra on Crete', AJA, 78, 19-24.
VLADÁR, J.
(1975), 'Mykenische Einflüsse im Karpatengebiet', Das Altertum, 21, 92-8.
VOIGTLÄNDER, W.
(1973), 'Zur Chronologie der spätmykenischen Burgen in Tiryns', Tiryns, 6, Mainz, 241-66.
VOKOTOPOULOU, IOULIA P.
(1969), 'Νέοι κιβωτιόσχημοι τάφοι τῆς ΥΕ ΙΙΙΒ-Γ περιόδου ἐξ 'Ηπείρου', ΑΕ, 179-207.
VOLLGRAFF, W.
(1904), 'Fouilles d'Argos', BCH, 28, 364-99.
(1906), 'Fouilles d'Argos', BCH, 30, 5-45.
(1907), 'Fouilles d'Argos', BCH, 31, 139-84.
(1928), 'Arx Argorum', Mnemosyne, 56, 315-27.
VRANOPOULOS, E.A.
(1967), 'Τάφοι τῆς Μεσοελλαδικῆς περιόδου καὶ ταφικὰ ἔθιμα αὐτῆς', Χαριστήριον εἰς 'Α.Κ. 'Ορλάνδον, 4, Athens, 280-94.
WACE, A.J.B.
(1909), 'Laconia III, early pottery from Geraki', ABSA, 16, 72-5.
(1919), 'Mycenae', ABSA, 24, 185-209 (with others.)
(1921), 'Excavations at Mycenae', ABSA, 25, 1-434 (with others.)
(1932), 'Chamber tombs at Mycenae', Archaeologia, 82.
(1949), Mycenae, Princeton.
(1953a), 'Mycenae, 1939-1952', ABSA, 48, 1-93 (with others)
(1953b), 'The façade of the Treasury of Atreus', GAK, 310-4.
(1953c), 'The history of Greece in the third and second millenniums BC', Historia, 2, 74-94.
(1954a), 'Mycenae 1939-1953', ABSA, 49, 231-98 (with others.)
(1954b), 'Pausanias and Mycenae', Neue Beiträge zur Klassischen Altertumswissenschaft: Festschrift zum 60. Geburtstag von Bernhard Schweitzer, Stuttgart, 19-26.

(1954c), 'Ivory carvings from Mycenae', Archaeology, 7, 149-55.

(1955), 'Mycenae 1939-1954', ABSA, 50, 175-250 (with others.)

(1956a), 'Mycenae 1939-1955', ABSA, 51, 103-31 (with others.)

(1956b), 'The last days of Mycenae', ANE, 126-35.

(1957), 'Mycenae 1939-1956, 1957', ABSA, 52, 193-223 (with others.)

(1973), Foreword to Ventris and Chadwick, 1973.

WACE, A.J.B. & BLEGEN, C.W.

(1916), 'The pre-Mycenaean pottery of the mainland', ABSA, 22, 175-89.

(1939), 'Pottery as evidence for trade and colonisation in the Aegean Bronze Age', Klio, 32, 131-47.

WACE, A.J.B. & HASLUCK, F.W.

(1904), 'Laconia II, Geraki', ABSA, 11, 91-9.

WACE, A.J.B. & THOMPSON, M.S.

(1908), 'Laconia I, excavations at Sparta, 1909; the Menelaion', ABSA, 15, 108-16.

(1912), Prehistoric Thessaly, Cambridge.

WAINWRIGHT, F.T.

(1962), Archaeology and Place-names and History, London.

WAINWRIGHT, G.A.

(1956), 'Caphtor - Cappadocia', VT, 6, 199-210.

(1959), 'Some early Philistine history', VT, 9, 73-84.

(1961), 'Some Sea-Peoples', JEA, 47, 71-90.

(1965), 'Two groups among the Sea Peoples',JKF,2,new ser., 481-9.

WALCOT, P.

(1967), 'The divinity of the Mycenaean king', SMEA, 2, 53-62.

(1969), 'The comparative study of Ugaritic and Greek literatures', UF, 1, 111-8.

(1970), 'The comparative study of Ugaritic and Greek literatures II', UF, 2, 273-5.

(1972), 'The comparative study of Ugaritic and Greek literatures III', UF, 4, 129-32.

WALDBAUM, JANE C.

(1966), 'Philistine tombs at Tell Fara and their Aegean prototypes', AJA, 70, 331-40.

WALDSTEIN, C.

(1905), The Argive Heraeum, 2, Cambridge (Mass.)

WARDLE, K.A.

(1969), 'A group of Late Helladic IIIB 1 pottery from within the Citadel at Mycenae', ABSA, 64, 261-97.

(1973), 'A group of Late Helladic IIIB 2 pottery from within the Citadel at Mycenae', ABSA, 68, 297-342.

(1975), 'The northern frontier of Mycenaean Greece', BICS, 22, 206-12.

WARREN, P.M.
(1967), 'Minoan stone vases as evidence for Minoan foreign connexions in the Aegean Late Bronze Age', PPS, 33, 37-56.
(1969), Minoan Stone Vases, Cambridge.
WARREN, P.M. & HANKEY, VRONWY
(1974), 'The absolute chronology of the Aegean Late Bronze Age', BICS, 21, 142-52.
WATERHOUSE, HELEN
(1952), 'Excavations at Stavros, Ithaca, in 1937', ABSA, 47, 227-42.
WATERHOUSE, HELEN & HOPE SIMPSON, R.
(1960), 'Prehistoric Laconia, part I', ABSA, 55, 67-107.
(1961), 'Prehistoric Laconia, part II', ABSA, 56, 114-75.
WEBSTER, T.B.L.
(1964), From Mycenae to Homer, 2nd ed., Homer.
WEICKERT, C.
(1959), 'Die Ausgrabung beim Athena-Tempel in Milet 1957', IM, 9/10, 1-96 (with others.)
WEIGEL, HILDEGARD
(1965), Der Trojanische Krieg: Beitrag zur Lösung des Problems, Berlin.
WEINBERG, S.S.
(1949), 'Investigations at Corinth, 1947-1948', Hesperia, 18, 148-57.
WELCH, F.B.
(1900), 'The influence of the Aegean civilisation on south Palestine', QSPEF, 342-50 (reprinted in ABSA, 6, 1899/1900, 117-24.)
WELTER, G.
(1938), Aigina, Berlin.
(1939), 'Vom Nikepyrgos', AA, 1-22.
WERNER, R.
(1967), 'Neue gesehene Zusammenhänge im Ostmittelmeerraum des zweiten vorchristlichen Jahrtausends', AsStud, 21, 82-98.
WEST, M.L.
(1966), Edition of Hesiod's 'Theogony', Oxford.
(1972), Iambi et Elegi Graeci ante Alexandrum Cantati, 2, Oxford.
WIDE, S.
(1910), 'Gräberfunde aus Salamis', AM, 35, 17-36.
WIESNER, J.
(1938), Grab und Jenseits, Berlin.
(1968), Fahren und Reiten, Göttingen.
WILLETTS, R.F.
(1962), Cretan Cults and Festivals, London.
WOLTERS, P.
(1889), 'Mykenische Vasen aus dem nördlichen Griechenland', AM, 14, 262-70.

(1899), 'Vasen aus Menidi II', JDAI, 14, 103-35.
WOOLLEY, L.
(1955), Alalakh: An Account of the Excavations at Tell Atchana, Oxford.
WRIGHT, H.E.
(1968), 'Climatic change in Mycenaean Greece', Antiquity, 42, 123-7.
WUNDSAM, K.
(1968), Die Politische und Soziale Struktur in den Myke- nischen Residenzen nach den Linear B Texten, Vienna.
WYATT, W.F.
(1962), 'The Ma tablets from Pylos', AJA, 66, 21-41.
(1968), 'Greek names in -σσος/-ττος', Glotta, 46, 6-14.
(1970a), 'The Indo-Europeanization of Greece', Indo- European and Indo-Europeans, ed. G. Cardona, H.M. Hoenigs- wald, and A. Senn, Philadelphia, 89-111.
(1970b), 'The prehistory of the Greek dialects', TAPA, 101, 557-632.
(1973), 'The Aeolic substrate in the Peloponnese', AJP, 94, 37-46.
XANTHOUDIDIS, S.A.
(1904), ''Εκ Κρήτης', EA, 1-56.
YALOURIS, N.
(1954), ''Ανασκαφἠ ἐν Αἰγύῳ', PAAH, 287-90.
(1960), 'Mykenische Bronzeschutzwaffen', AM, 75, 42-67.
(1965), 'Μυκηναϊκὸς τύμβος Σαμικοῦ', AD, 20, A', 6-40.
YAMPOLSKI, S.I.
(1958), 'К вопросу о τέμενος', SANGSSR, 21, 509-11.

Index